The International Society for Science & Religion was established in 2002 to promote education through the support of inter-disciplinary learning and research in the fields of science and religion. Our current membership of 140 comes from all major faith traditions and includes non-religious scholars. Inducted by nomination only, they are drawn from leading research institutions and academies worldwide. The Society embraces all perspectives that are supported by excellent scholarship.

In 2007, the Society began the process of creating a unique resource, *The ISSR Library*, a comprehensive reference and teaching tool for scholars, students, and interested lay readers. This collection spans the essential ideas and arguments that frame studies in science, religion, and the human spirit.

The Library has been selected through a rigorous process of peer review. Each constituent volume makes a substantial contribution to the field or stands as an important referent. These books exhibit the highest quality of scholarship and present distinct, influential viewpoints, some of which are controversial. While the many perspectives in these volumes are not individually endorsed by the ISSR, each reflects a facet of the field that is worthy of attention.

Accompanying the Library is *The ISSR Companion to Science and Religion*, a volume containing brief introductory essays on each of the Library's constituents. Users are encouraged to refer to the *Companion* or our website for an overview of the Library.

Pranab K. Das II, Executive Editor

Editorial Board
John Hedley Brooke
Philip Clayton
V. V. Raman
Wesley J. Wildman

Christopher Knight, ISSR Executive Secretary
Ronald Cole-Turner, ISSR Board Liaison

For a complete list of Contributing Editors, please visit
www.issrlibrary.org/contributingeditors

For a complete list of Library Selections please visit
www.issrlibrary.org/selections

SCIENCE AND RELIGIOUS ANTHROPOLOGY

Science and Religious Anthropology explores the convergence of the biological sciences, human sciences, and humanities around a spiritually evocative, naturalistic vision of human life. The disciplinary contributions are at different levels of complexity, from evolution of brains to existential longings, and from embodied sociality to ecosystem habitat. The resulting interpretation of the human condition supports some aspects of traditional theological thinking in the world's religious traditions while seriously challenging other aspects. Wesley Wildman draws out these implications for philosophical and religious anthropology and argues that the modern secular interpretation of humanity is most compatible with a religious form of naturalistic humanism.

This book resists the reduction of meaning and value questions while taking scientific theories about human life with full seriousness. It argues for a religious interpretation of human beings as bodily creatures emerging within a natural environment that permits engagement with the valuational potentials of reality. This engagement promotes socially borne spiritual quests to realize and harmonize values in everything human beings do, from the forging of cultures to the crafting of personal convictions.

Ashgate Science and Religion Series

Series Editors:

Roger Trigg, *University of Warwick, UK*
J. Wentzel van Huyssteen, *Princeton Theological Seminary, USA*

Science and religion have often been thought to be at loggerheads but much contemporary work in this flourishing interdisciplinary field suggests this is far from the case. The *Ashgate Science and Religion Series* presents exciting new work to advance interdisciplinary study, research and debate across key themes in science and religion, exploring the philosophical relations between the physical and social sciences on the one hand and religious belief on the other. Contemporary issues in philosophy and theology are debated, as are prevailing cultural assumptions arising from the 'post-modernist' distaste for many forms of reasoning. The series enables leading international authors from a range of different disciplinary perspectives to apply the insights of the various sciences, theology and philosophy and look at the relations between the different disciplines and the rational connections that can be made between them. These accessible, stimulating new contributions to key topics across science and religion will appeal particularly to individual academics and researchers, graduates, postgraduates and upper-undergraduate students.

Other titles published in this series:

Theology, Psychology and the Plural Self
Léon Turner
9780754665199 (hbk)

Creation: Law and Probability
Edited by Fraser Watts
9780754658900 (pbk)

Christology and Science
F. LeRon Shults
9780754652243 (hbk)
9780754652311 (pbk)

Mind, Brain and the Elusive Soul
Human Systems of Cognitive Science and Religion
Mark Graves
9780754662266 (hbk)

Science and Religious Anthropology

A Spiritually Evocative Naturalist Interpretation of Human Life

WESLEY J. WILDMAN
Boston University, USA

ASHGATE

Published by
Ashgate Publishing Limited
Wey Court East
Union Road
Farnham
Surrey, GU9 7PT
England

Ashgate Publishing Company
Suite 420
101 Cherry Street
Burlington
VT 05401-4405
USA

www.ashgate.com

British Library Cataloguing in Publication Data
Wildman, Wesley J., 1961–
    Science and religious anthropology: a spiritually evocative naturalist interpretation of human life – (Ashgate science and religion series)
    1. Theological anthropology. 2. Philosophical anthropology. 3. Naturalism – Religious aspects. 4. Religion and science.
    I. Title II. Series
    218-dc22

Library of Congress Cataloging-in-Publication Data
Wildman, Wesley J., 1961–
    Science and religious anthropology: a spiritually evocative naturalist interpretation of human life / Wesley J. Wildman.
        p. cm. – (Ashgate science and religion series)
    Includes bibliographical references and index.
    ISBN 978-0-7546-6592-2 (hardcover: alk. paper) – 1. Religion and science. 2. Anthropology of religion. 3. Theological anthropology.
    I. Title.
    BL240.3.W53 2009
    215–dc22

2009011255

ISBN 9780754665922 (hbk)
ISBN 9780754696704 (ebk)

Mixed Sources
Product group from well-managed forests and other controlled sources
www.fsc.org Cert no. SA-COC-1565
© 1996 Forest Stewardship Council
FSC

Printed and bound in Great Britain by
MPG Books Group, UK

For the graduates, students, and faculty of Boston University's doctoral program in Science, Philosophy, and Religion

Contents

List of Figures and Tables

Figures

Tables

Foreword

Philip Clayton

This is the first in what will be a series of books by Wesley Wildman on science, philosophy, comparative religious studies, and theology. It will be joined shortly by *Science and Ultimate Reality* and *Religious Philosophy as Multidisciplinary Comparative Inquiry: Envisioning a Future for the Philosophy of Religion*. Taken together, these books, and what will presumably be successor volumes within the same overarching project, present the most sophisticated and broad-based defense to date of religious naturalism, or what Wildman calls a "spiritually evocative naturalist interpretation of human life."

Wildman is well aware of the conceptual difficulties with—not to mention the social prejudices against—this project. Practitioners in most of the world's religious traditions are happy to engage the methods and results of contemporary science—up to a point. But at some stage, it seems, they are compelled to move beyond the methods and results of the sciences and, at least in that sense, to oppose them. Most theists in the three Abrahamic faiths find it necessary to identify a divine origin and a divine telos, a "before" and an "after" the natural history that science studies, a moment or process of creation and a culmination or perfecting of the process. Most Hindus and Buddhists affirm *karma*, a form of moral causation that appears to be inaccessible to scientific study in the ordinary sense of the term, as well as the doctrines of reincarnation and final liberation (*moksha*). Even great metaphysical philosophers such as Hegel, Whitehead, and Sri Aurobindo reach points where, it seems, they must move from nature to super-nature.

Scientific naturalists are famous for claiming that they never need to leave the methods and the results of the sciences behind. The problem here is different: in most cases their commitments to scientific inquiry eventually cause them to place themselves outside the human religious project altogether. Sometimes they become hostile opponents to all things religious, as one sees in the works of the self-styled "New Atheists" of recent years. Sometimes they retain a deep interest in religion, but only from the standpoint of the outsider. These scholars study religious beliefs and practices, seeking to understand them in terms of natural scientific causes or social scientific theories, but without actually espousing or engaging in them. And sometimes scientific naturalists settle in as "spiritual but not religious," retaining a place for spiritual feelings or experiences that they (and others) sharply distinguish from a religious identity. The wonderful thing about the term "spiritual" is that it can be ratcheted down until it is compatible with virtually any view of what reality ultimately consists of; indeed, it can be made independent of any claims about reality whatsoever. I well remember a meeting in Paris a few years back at which a group of religious people were trying to convince a very well-known atheist scientist that he too could be "spiritual." Bit by bit they removed all religious associations from the term, until it required only that one sometimes felt awe and wonder. "Well," concluded the scientist, somewhat quizzically, "if that's all you mean by being spiritual, then I guess there's no way that I can fail to qualify."

Wildman's project is not outside the sphere of the religious, merely looking in. But nor does it accept the need to affirm a metaphysic, a view of ultimate reality, that diverges from the naturalism that undergirds all scientific inquiry. Religious naturalists, he writes, "universally reject a super-nature," no matter what form it may take. If he is right, the dichotomy presupposed by *both* sides of the debate is mistaken. In this text and its companion volumes he sets out to present the whole range of data and inferences that are required to make good on this claim: genetics, evolutionary theory and history, population biology, ecology, neurology, evolutionary psychology, sociology, comparative anthropology, comparative religious studies—as well as the methodological arguments that are required to turn the various empirical results into a convincing philosophical argument.

In this particular volume Wildman reflects on the specific scientific results that bear on religious belief and practice, subjecting them to close, and sometimes critical, analysis. Even those with little or no personal tendency toward religious affiliation will still find the data on the evolution, neurology, and sociology of religion to be fascinating and provocative. What sets this presentation apart from many other works in the scientific study of religion is that Wildman does not marshal the scientific data to debunk religion as such. But he does think that humanity's deepest religious interests can still be satisfied within the framework of a naturalistic study of the world, without the use of additional metaphysical postulates.

When one consults the relevant scholars, one finds a fairly strong consensus on what it means to engage in scientific studies that cover the whole range of religious phenomena, including the biological and cultural factors that cause and explain them. By contrast, it turns out to be rather more difficult to specify what exactly constitutes religious interest. We have already noted that the bar for "spiritual" is frequently dropped so low that merely being human is enough to constitute one as a vibrantly spiritual person. This is where Wildman's non-reductive use of comparative religious studies is especially powerful. Because he is genuinely and (one senses) existentially interested in the whole range of deep religious responses across the world's traditions, one finds no tendency in these pages to reduce religious phenomena to social scientific causes. The comparative studies reveal the full range of what can constitute "the religious," continually breaking stereotypes and expanding one's imagination in the process.

But religious practices and institutions by themselves would not be enough, for religious persons also hold beliefs, beliefs that are, in many cases, vital to their religious life and practice. Across the world's traditions, religious persons have been some of the primary participants, if not *the* primary ones, in constructing theologies, theories about the nature of ultimate reality. Wildman's method places theological categories and symbols alongside science and comparative religious studies as an indispensable component in the overall task. One may sometimes worry that the parameters of his religious reflection are *too* strongly constrained by science, religious studies, or philosophical pragmatism. Still, it is indisputably Wildman's goal to give a close and sympathetic reading of the theological claims and symbol systems of believers across the world's traditions, rather than to dismiss their actual beliefs as irrelevant or incompatible with scientific study. What is offered here, Wildman writes at one point, is "a theological account of values in nature," although for him it must be one that avoids "falling prey either to supernaturalistic portrayals of souls and miracles or to supranaturalistic portrayals of divine beings."

It is a fascinating and ambitious project. It may just be the most defensible candidate among all the currently available positions that neither exit science on the one hand nor separate themselves from religion on the other. I write this as one who is in many respects the sort of theist whose position Wildman believes is undercut by the data—the sort of theist whom the book seeks to win over. Still, I share Wildman's sense that it is crucial for religious believers and scholars who are *not* naturalists to incorporate and respond to the data summarized in these pages. I echo his call, both to readers on his left and those on his right, to atheists (old or new) and theists alike, to pay close attention to what the sciences and comparative religious studies are revealing, for all credible philosophical and theological discussions today must start here.

As with all bold systematic attempts, readers will challenge this proposal from both sides. Some will fault it for not going far enough in the directions they value, others for going *too* far in directions they abhor. Some scientists will find it puzzling, to say the least, that Wildman listens to religious thought and practice with such a sympathetic ear and is willing (sometimes) to use the term "theology" with a positive connotation. Some religious studies scholars will fault him for giving up the rigor, and perhaps the ultimacy, of social scientific methods, for showing an openness to forms of philosophical reflection and mystical response that are not accessible to social scientific study. And, as already signaled, theologians in many traditions will find themselves uncomfortable with Wildman's clear preference for an apophatic mysticism over kataphatic or "constructive" theology in one or more of its various forms. In the end, he holds tight to the commitment of the apophatic theologians, and with them he posits "that ultimate realities are finally inexpressible, not just for human beings, but for any and all forms of cognitive-emotional engagement anywhere and anytime in reality."

Still, the critical responses will come as no surprise. Anyone who ventures as boldly as Wildman does into so many different fields of contentious inquiry and dispute must be ready to take some hits along the way. Indeed, for years now Wildman has made this pursuit of genuine critical inquiry the cornerstone of his theory of knowledge and his academic practice. In these pages, and in the books to follow, he boldly claims that his own alternative does the best job among all the competitors at doing justice to the full range of competing demands. Only time, and the debate itself, will tell.

Preface

Can there be a spiritually evocative yet thoroughly naturalist interpretation of human life? Can an account of the human condition shed ancient superstitions while remaining religiously potent? Yes. Indeed, the central argument of this book supports a naturalistic interpretation of the human being as *homo religiosus*. That is, religious behaviors, beliefs, and experiences—understood sufficiently broadly— constitute human nature not only historically, culturally, or circumstantially, but also ontologically, essentially, and inescapably. A thoroughgoing and consistent naturalism is inevitably also profoundly spiritual and religious. This remains so even though religious communities with traditional theological outlooks hesitate to embrace religious naturalism, and despite the fact that many naturalists and humanists are leery of all things religious.

This claim that human beings are *homo religiosus* has been articulated before, with various meanings, some rather different than the meaning it has here. The breadth of meaning accorded "religious behaviors, beliefs, and experiences" in this treatment offers a way to grasp the significance of the central claim. Religion here includes not only the characteristic behaviors, beliefs, and experiences of organized institutional religious groups but also existentially potent behaviors, beliefs, and experiences in every domain of life, from wonder at nature to awe in the face of human frailty. Religion in this sense applies even to the fervent prophets of secular humanism who devote themselves to the liberation of human beings from what those prophets take to be the delusions of supernatural religious mythologies and the bondage imposed by groups that promote such delusions. Religion in this generous sense is a matter of people's ultimate existential, spiritual, and social concerns. It pertains to the way we bind ourselves (*religio*) to that which has surpassing meaning for us, and bear this reflexive or elective bondage in every aspect and circumstance of life. Religion *in this sense* suffuses every aspect of human life, and appears to spring from the valuational depth structures and dynamics of nature and culture that are the fecund sources of meaning and life possibilities.

One reason this generous interpretation of religious behaviors, beliefs, and experiences is relatively uncommon is that, while descriptively accurate at its own level, it is semantically strained relative to more common usages. I acknowledge this without hesitation but wish to argue that this usage of religion in "religious anthropology" and "religious naturalism" is appropriate and beneficial.

The diverse meanings of "religion" usually take shape in two ways. On the one hand, "religion" refers to organized social groups of those who supposedly share specific religious beliefs and practices. On the other hand, "religion" refers to the putative objects of religious belief and practice as most commonly understood— namely: supernatural beings from Gods to ghosts, from angels to demons, and from bodhisattvas to ancestors; and supernatural narratives about how to escape the problems of the human condition, whether they refer to heaven and hell, saṃsāra and nirvana, guilt and freedom, or blissful immortality and mindless extinction. Certainly the anthropology of religion, the sociology of religion, the psychology of religion, and the cognitive neuroscience of religion are typically guided by such assumptions about religion. Even theology and philosophy of religion are dominated by theories of ultimate reality that embrace the supernaturalist metaphysics so common within the belief systems of many religious traditions. The considerable virtues of this approach to religious phenomena derive from the statistically appealing fact that this is how *most people* understand religion in practice.

In an essentially philosophical work of synthetic interpretation, however, an approach to inquiry corresponding to this narrower understanding of religion would be flawed by the fact that it registers what is dominant at the cost of not being responsive to exceptions. These exceptions include great thinkers who gave birth to fertile ideas that structure many forms of religious self-understanding, such as Plato and Aristotle, Śaṅkara and Nāgārjuna, Confucius and Laozi. They include many of the great mystics whose reflective experience takes them away from the anthropomorphic limitations of supernaturalism. They include the skeptics of every culture and era who have always intuited that the religious beliefs and practices of their environment were what they were later discovered to be in part: social constructions for regulating human behavior in an uncertain world perpetually on the edge of chaos. They include the anti-religious but profoundly spiritual seekers of the modern world for whom the spell of religion has been broken and the lure of supernaturalism lost, and yet the mystery of human life in an awesome natural environment persists, ever strengthened by increasingly detailed knowledge of its wondrous workings.

Focusing on religion's statistically and historically dominant forms only yields the conclusion that human beings are not *homo religiosus* ontologically, essentially, and inescapably; rather, religiosity is an optional and dispensable aspect of the human condition, and one that we might be better off without. At this level of analysis—that is, using the historically and statistically dominant forms of human religiosity to delimit inquiry—I consider this conclusion deeply compelling because I judge supernaturalist metaphysics to be mistaken and I recognize that some elements of religion have often exercised social control ignorantly and unjustly. Yet I also consider this conclusion profoundly unrealistic with regard to the prospects of human beings managing without religion, historically one-sided through neglecting the wonderful cultural and moral achievements of religion, and shockingly neglectful of the symbolic richness of religion that facilitates authentic human engagement with the material and value-laden world in and through sometimes fanciful mythical worldviews and bizarre practices.

At some fundamental level, I believe that lovers of the truth, whether calling themselves religious or not, would cautiously but definitely choose enlightened awareness over the delusions of fanciful worldviews if they were convinced that the fancies were false and the worldviews wrongheaded. They would so choose even knowing that their choice would mean risking a frightfully complicated social reengineering project with uncertain benefits. That is, they would take Jesus' side over the Grand Inquisitor's side in Dostoyevsky's famous fantasy. This passionate, ascetic truth-bondage, surely, has as much claim on our attention as the statistically and historically dominant supernatural myth-bondage when our task is to understand human religiosity.

Along this and similar paths, then, I am led to conclude that we do not reach to the depths of human religiosity by focusing solely on its statistically dominant forms. Our value commitments, our efforts at meaning construction, and our socially borne explorations of life possibilities reach far beyond the historically most prominent forms of religiosity, and into every nook and cranny of our lives. It is at this axiological level, beneath the most overt beliefs and practices of both religious and non-religious people, that we find *homo religiosus*. From there we can trace the impact of human religiosity *in a properly general sense* on existential awareness, on moral choices, on the social construction of reality, and on vast civilizational projects—and we can do this in such a way as to account for the fabulous variation in religious and spiritual expressions across culture and eras, traditions and individuals.

I am convinced that the theoretical machinery required for such a synthetic analysis of the human being as *homo religiosus* crucially depends on the metaphysical hypothesis of religious naturalism. This is because a properly generous interpretation of human religiosity inclusive of the full variety of spiritual and axiological sensitivities of the human condition—a view of religiosity rich enough to discern that human beings are *homo religiosus* not merely historically, culturally, or circumstantially, but also ontologically, essentially, and inescapably—requires a metaphysically minimalist framework that registers species-wide features of the human condition. For example, if the metaphysical framework guiding theological interpretation were to include a supernatural ultimate religious object of any kind, the proper meaning of religion inevitably contracts. And if metaphysical neutrality is attempted, which is the posture (if not the actual achievement) of many social-science approaches to religion, the philosophical interest in evaluative questions of meaning and purpose is sacrificed and there is no possibility of producing a properly *religious* or *theological* interpretation of the human condition. I have had to adopt a particular strategic approach to the religious-naturalism hypothesis in this book, accordingly. Specifically, it has the status of a *presupposition* for the inquiry, in the sense that it is not evaluated overtly here. But I certainly intend to evaluate religious naturalism indirectly by means of its theoretical fruits, and for that purpose the entire book is the argument. The companion volume to this book, *Science and Ultimate Reality*, takes up the task of justifying religious naturalism in relation to its most serious theological competitors.

One of the preliminary chapters discusses the meaning of religious naturalism. In this prefatory context it suffices to say that religious naturalism rules out both supernaturalism and all views of ultimate reality as an active, focally aware entity, but that it affirms an ultimate reality in the axiological (that is, valuational) depth structures and dynamics of nature. This view of nature and ultimate reality is reflexively appealing to a wide range of modern people—religious, non-religious, and anti-religious—but it also has impressive credentials and ancient standing in all of the world's religious and philosophical traditions. Some of the ways religious naturalism can be elaborated metaphysically and theologically are discussed in the chapter on 'Habitat'. One way of expressing its relationship with the statistically and historically dominant supernatural-determinate-entity portrayals of ultimate reality in the world's religions is to say that it persists on the underside of these traditions. From there it offers an intellectually and morally compelling refuge for those who have always needed to retreat from what they come to see as the garish offense of anthropomorphically excessive forms of religion, and it also profits from the social viability of the obverse, supernatural face of religion. In short, religious naturalism in a variety of forms enjoys a symbiotic relationship with religious supernaturalism. It has always done so, and it will continue to do so at least for some time into the future.

The great social-engineering question concerning religion, when reexpressed in these terms, is whether this symbiosis needs to be permanent, or whether at some point religious naturalism can separate and live on its own, apart from supernaturalism, and possibly fully opposed to the anthropomorphic and credulous excesses of supernatural religion. However this question is finally answered, I think we can affirm with some confidence that the ending of this symbiotic entanglement would *neither* be an exhibition of the human species evolving to some higher plane, *nor* an intrinsically stable cultural arrangement. On the contrary, it would be a matter of creatively constructing a new reality, one that would disintegrate were the human species to lose the stable civilizational conditions for such high-energy ventures in social engineering. Like gender equality, economic justice, scientific inquiry, high-quality health care, and the rejection of ingroup–outgroup discrimination, cultural practices built around religious naturalism and its vision of the divine in the axiological depths of nature would be hard-won social achievements requiring consistent education of human beings against a number of cognitive impulses that tend toward belief in supernaturalism and divine beings. A collapse of civilizational stability would interfere with the necessary conditioning processes and thus inevitably provoke a reversion to default cognitive and emotional modes of world-interpretation.

So much for the central claim of the book—human beings as *homo religiosus*—and its primary presupposition—religious naturalism. Methodologically speaking, this book is an extended argument on behalf of the thesis that the natural and social sciences meaningfully constrain without finally determining religious interpretations of the human condition. Equally, it is an attempt to demonstrate that theological reflection can be conducted not on behalf of any particular religious tradition, but rather with the secular academy as its institutional home and multiple religious and philosophical traditions as its discussion partners. These characterizations can be compressed into one by saying that this is an exhibition of religious philosophy in the sense of multidisciplinary comparative inquiry, with the subject matter for the inquiry being human beings as *homo religiosus*. The methodological considerations most pertinent to assessing the possibility and prospects of this type of intellectual work are laid out in another volume, *Religious Philosophy as Multidisciplinary Comparative Inquiry: Envisioning a Future for the Philosophy of Religion* (Wildman 2009). Apart from some necessary preliminary comments in the first two chapters of this book, I do not revisit those issues here.

A lot of science is surveyed in the chapters of this book, chiefly in evolutionary biology, evolutionary psychology, the cognitive neurosciences, and the human sciences from psychology to sociology. Crystallizing the formidably complex unfolding processes of scientific inquiry in any given discipline is a difficult task—one made easier but also more perilous by not being a specialist. While I have attempted to be thorough and accurate, and also to stay close to consensus territory, the complexity and diversity of scientific opinion will make many of my judgment calls questionable. At the same time, while I am more deeply acquainted with the scientific study of religion and the literary and philosophical study of religions, thanks to my primary training, I can easily see a number of ways in which my presentation and coverage decisions even in these areas could plausibly be challenged. I venture to say, however, that these kinds of weaknesses are inevitable in multidisciplinary comparative inquiry. This is particularly so in these early decades of attempts to generate communities capable of supporting such forms of inquiry against and above the barriers inevitably erected by the social reality of conventional university disciplines. I believe these weaknesses should be risked because of the intrinsic value of multidisciplinary comparative inquiries. In the final analysis, of course, whether the risk is worth taking in the case of the present inquiry depends on the quality of the product. And that is for others to decide.

Wesley J. Wildman
Boston, 2009

Acknowledgments

I am grateful to a number of people who have helped me refine my understanding of the ideas presented in this book. Portions of several chapters were presented at various gatherings of scholars, including the American Academy of Religion, the American Theological Society, the Boston Theological Society, the Highlands Institute for American Religion, Philosophy, and Theology, the New Haven Theological Discussion Group, and the Society for Buddhist-Christian Studies; and in various lecture and discussion settings at Adelaide College of Divinity, Albertus Magnus College, Beijing Normal University, Boston University, Dartmouth College, University of Duisburg, Edith Cowan University, Graduate Theological Union, Harbin College, Harbin Institute of Technology, Harbin Normal University, Heilong Jiang University, Jilin University, Leuven University, Nanjing University, Indian Institute of Science in Bangalore, Oklahoma City University, Providence College, Simmons College, Sydney College of Divinity, Truman State University, Tufts University, Tulane University, Williams College, and Zhe Jiang University. In all cases I profited from the ensuing discussions and penetrating feedback and I am deeply grateful to those who organized these events.

I am particularly pleased to acknowledge memorable conversations about topics from this book with Nathaniel Barrett, Leslie Brothers, Mark Burrows, Catherine Caldwell-Harris, John Darling, Gordon Kaufman, Patrick McNamara, Olga Naidenko, Robert Neville, Paul Santmire, and a number of other people scattered around the world. I am grateful to Roger Trigg and J. Wentzel van Huyssteen, editors of The *Ashgate Science and Religion Series*, for caring about the project, to Sarah Lloyd for shepherding the book through Ashgate's acquisitions process, to Barbara Pretty for overseeing production, and to Sarah Price for her sharp editorial eye. I am grateful to a remarkable high school art teacher, Charlotte Ayers, and her talented student, Sarah Dennis, for the beautiful cover art. Derek Michaud could have a career in indexing, based on his fine work on this book, except that he is a talented theologian with books of his own to write. I am deeply grateful to Philip Clayton for his generosity in agreeing to write a foreword to a book on religious anthropology that operates within a religious naturalist framework, which differs in important ways from his own theological outlook. This double gesture—the invitation and the gracious response—demonstrates our shared commitment to the value of sustained comparative analysis of multiple theological worldviews. I do not present here the philosophical case for religious naturalism over powerful competitor views such as Clayton's, however; that will have to wait until the appearance of the companion volume, *Science and Ultimate Reality*.

I dedicate this book to the graduates and students of Boston University's doctoral program in Science, Philosophy, and Religion, to the half-dozen core faculty colleagues who make this unique educational venture possible, and to the several dozen other faculty members who offer their time and energy to supervise and educate our students in particular specialties. I could not wish for a more inspiring context in which to labor over the numerous relevant literatures that matter for multidisciplinary inquiries of the sort presented in this book, to participate in compelling multidisciplinary conversations, and to train amazingly creative young minds. I count myself fortunate to be employed at a university that understands the importance of multidisciplinary inquiry and seeks to support it through programs such as this one.

Finally, this work draws on some previously published material. The pattern of my multidisciplinary research has been to develop competence in new areas by working with experts or with groups of scholars laboring together on a specific project, and then publishing articles or book chapters with those people. In this way, over several years, I learn more than I can express from other scholars and hopefully offer something to them in return. It is difficult for me to conceive of conducting this kind of research in any other way because the number and complexity of the disciplines involved is daunting. Though few sentences remain unchanged from these older publications, none is incorporated as a whole, and the bulk of the book is entirely new, there is some overlap with the items below. I am glad to acknowledge the original publishers of these items, a few of them from quite some time ago, as follows:

"A Theological Challenge: Coordinating Biological, Social, and Religious Visions of Humanity," *Zygon* 33/4 (December, 1998): 571–97.

(with Leslie A. Brothers) "A Neuropsychological Semiotic Model of Religious Experiences," in Robert John Russell, *et al.*, eds., *Neurosciences and the Human Person: Scientific Perspectives on Divine Action* (Vatican City State: Vatican Observatory and Berkeley: Center for Theology and the Natural Sciences, 1999).

"The Use and Abuse of Biotechnology: A Modified Natural-Law Approach," in *American Journal of Theology and Philosophy* 20/2 (May, 1999): 165-79.

"Consciousness Expanded," in B.V. Sreekantan and Sangeetha Menon, eds., *Consciousness and Genetics: A Discussion* (Bangalore, India: National Institute of Advanced Studies, 2002): 125-41.

"The Significance of the Evolution of Religious Belief and Behavior for Religious Studies and Theology," commentary and analysis essay for Patrick McNamara, ed., *The Evolutionary Psychology of Religion: How Evolution Shaped the Religious Brain*, vol. 1 of *Where God and Science Meet: How Brain and Evolutionary Studies Alter Our Understanding of Religion*, 3 vols. (Westport, CT: Greenwood Press, 2006).

"Radical Embodiment and Theological Anthropology," in *American Journal of Theology and Philosophy* 28/3 (September, 2007): 346–363.

"The Philosophical Import of Contemporary Physical Cosmology," *Theology and Science* 6/2 (May 2008): 197–212.

"Hand in Glove: Evaluating the Fit between Method and Theology in van Huyssteen's Interpretation of Human Uniqueness," *Zygon* 43/2 (June, 2008): 475–491.

"Cognitive Error and Contemplative Practices: The Cultivation of Discernment in Mind and Heart," *Buddhist-Christian Studies* 29 (2009): 59–79.

PART I
Preliminaries

CHAPTER 1

Inquiry

Introduction

Religion is one of the most important and distinctive aspects of human existence. It is virtually universal across cultures, though in such a fabulous parade of diverse forms that it famously defies neat definition. Religion is a vital factor in politics, economics, education, cultural production, and social life. Religion is central to the self-understanding of many people, both now and in the past, who navigate their existential environments by means of its narratives, practices, and communities. Religion has had historic impact in every civilization and every cultural context. Religion has helped to inspire historical and scientific understandings of the human condition. I find it difficult to make generalizations about the human species in relation to the worlds of cultural production and existential meaning because human expressions in these realms are so diverse and intricately textured. Nevertheless, one of the safest generalizations is that the human being is every bit as much *homo religiosus* as *homo rationis* or *homo sapienta*, *homo agens* or *homo communis* or *homo economicus* (the rational or wise, the agential or communal or economic human being).

The question, therefore, is not *whether* the human being is *homo religiosus* but *how* to understand this fact of human life, and how to evaluate it. With regard to understanding, precisely how does human religion work in individuals and in groups? What are its causal conditions and effects? What activities and thoughts of the human being are religious and what do those manifestations of religion imply about the human condition? With regard to evaluation, is religiousness the avenue toward the highest human fulfillment or a recalcitrant species defect to be overcome through education and social engineering? (I shall argue that both responses to human religiousness are appropriate in different respects.) And are human beings *homo religiosus* merely historically, culturally, and circumstantially, or also ontologically, essentially, and inescapably? (I shall argue the latter, but only by enlarging the scope of religious behaviors, beliefs, and experiences to encompass everything relevant to human meaning and value, for on narrower construals the former is very likely to be correct.)

This book presents a religious anthropology, in the sense of an interpretation of the human being as *homo religiosus*. Western scholars and scientists have taken up questions bearing on religious anthropology in a wide variety of ways since the academic study of religion was born in the European Enlightenment. Controversy swirls around these diverse approaches and the assumptions they express about human nature, human religion, and the ultimate environment of human life.

The book's argument is thoroughly entangled in these politically charged controversies. As just one example, consider that even to use the word "anthropology" is potentially problematic, given that I intend a more philosophical conception of the word than the academic discipline of anthropology presupposes. To be sure, this philosophical usage is considerably older than that of the social science called "anthropology," but priority and propriety are not the same. There are many other conceptual and methodological tangles surrounding a work in religious anthropology, some far more perplexing than who gets to use the word "anthropology."

One of the deepest controversies pertains to the fact that the interpretation offered here is an essentially philosophical and theological one that intends to go well beyond description of the human being as *homo religiosus* to explanations and evaluations. This intention will seem deeply problematic to many scientists, particularly since the academic study of religion has diligently tried to root out bias in all its forms. The problem of bias has haunted philosophy and theology ever since scholars—particularly cultural anthropologists—began in the late nineteenth century to point out that the intricacy of human cultural life resists species-wide generalizations of the sort that were routinely, and even cavalierly, offered by philosophers and theologians in the business of constructing interpretations of it. The inevitable conclusion is that any such generalizations are likely to encode the investigator's hidden assumptions about what is important and valuable in human life.

The problem of bias so framed has been nowhere more evident than in religious anthropologies rooted in theological traditions that take for granted their own theological narratives as universally relevant for interpreting the human condition. So, for example, a Christian theological anthropology might interpret the human condition in terms of the narrative framework of Catholic or Orthodox or Calvinist religious doctrines, without taking responsibility for the particularity of the interpretative outlook and its poor fit with certain religious and cultural settings. And the same is true of Buddhist interpretations of the human condition, which often take for granted the universal perfection of the narrative framework suggested by the Four Noble Truths. This kind of generalization is least problematic when the theological interpreter is fully aware of the specificity of the narrative framework in play. It can be refreshing and even bracing to witness a theological anthropology functioning as a kind of experimental declaration that remains open to correction in principle. Such self-awareness has typically been lacking in theologically framed interpretations of the human condition, unfortunately, but the problem of blinkered religious anthropologies is gradually easing. Wider knowledge of the world's numerous religions is increasing sensitivity among religious thinkers to the particularity of their own interpretative frameworks. Even when theologians recognize the particularity of their own interpretative perspectives, however, concrete responsiveness to alternative interpretative frameworks, and even to relevant empirical data from the social and biological sciences, often languishes.

From the outset, therefore, it is important to distinguish this philosophically and theologically voiced religious anthropology from the kinds of theological anthropologies that are most liable to the problems of bias and non-responsiveness to relevant data. Fairness of interpretation and responsibility in relation to data and theories offering corrective insights are priorities in this inquiry. These are some of the virtues of religious philosophy as I have elaborated it elsewhere (see Wildman 2009). I shall not recapitulate here the theory of inquiry presented in that book, nor shall I sketch the associated argument concerning the possibility and prospects of the multidisciplinary comparative form of philosophy of religion employed in the present work. Nevertheless, some methodological preliminaries are important.

The first task of this introductory chapter is to indicate how this book's approach to religious anthropology manages the methodological challenges confronting all attempts to give an interpretation of human beings as *homo religiosus*. In particular, I shall discuss the relation of the present effort in religious anthropology to the "stakeholder disciplines": the scientific study of religion, the academic study of religion, and theology. Each of these stakeholder disciplines is actually a cluster of disciplines offering valuable insights into human nature. A properly accountable religious anthropology should be fully responsive to those insights and should strive to coordinate them in a synthetic interpretation of the human being as *homo religiosus*.

A second task of this chapter is to introduce the themes of religious naturalism and epistemological pragmatism that furnish the interpretative framework and methodological procedures for the theoretical and evaluative phases of the argument. An argument on behalf of these framing presuppositions is implicit in the quality of the interpretations they foster, and rarely made explicit. At one level, these framing assumptions express my view of human nature and the ultimate environment human beings inhabit. At another level, I regard the framing assumptions as optimal in the sense that, properly understood, they prejudge theological issues as little as possible while still allowing important theological questions to arise within the inquiry. That is, these framing assumptions allow relevant theological aspects of religious anthropology to come to the surface alongside insights from the biological and human sciences, where they can all be seen and discussed together without invidious reductionism or oversimplification of the scientific or theological kinds. Theology understood in the broadest cross-traditional sense is a stakeholder in any discussion of religious anthropology, just as the academic study of religion and the scientific study of religion are stakeholders—the latter including what the biological sciences and the social sciences have to offer on the subject. Eliminating any of these stakeholders from the outset expresses an ideological posture for which there is no adequate justification—one that can only impoverish the resulting interpretation of human life. The practical benefit of the framework constituted by religious naturalism and epistemological pragmatism is that it allows all stakeholders to cooperate with one another for the sake of a conceptually rich and highly textured interpretation of the human being as *homo religiosus*.

The practical benefit of the framework constituted by religious naturalism and epistemological pragmatism persists even if someone disagrees with the naturalistic way I interpret the human condition or opposes my rejection of supernaturally authorized sources of information about human nature. For example, if a theologian wants to present a religious anthropology commensurate with his or her beliefs in supernatural personal theism, perhaps as putatively revealed in one or another tradition's sacred scriptures, nothing in the argument of this book directly rules out that possibility. Such an interpretation is here framed as not strictly necessary and thus as a kind of over-belief, to recall the phrase of William James (1902), or a theological elaboration, as I shall refer to it here. The book does imply constraints on such theological elaborations. In particular, any such theistic (or Buddhist or Daoist ...) theological elaboration should be no less responsive to the multidisciplinary and crosscultural insights adduced here than the religious naturalist interpretation I furnish is. I think that many traditional theological anthropologies fail to meet this standard, despite their other virtues. Thus, the constraints the book's argument imposes on theological elaborations are non-trivial ones that demand a transformation in theological approaches to religious anthropology.

Similarly, a multidisciplinary interpretation of the human condition in a naturalistic and pragmatic framework challenges the fallacy of scientific interpretations claiming comprehensiveness as exclusively scientific achievements. Such bluntly ideological deployment of the sciences beyond their proper limitations (sometimes called *scientism*) is rationally unjustifiable from within the sciences themselves, though it can seem politically and morally justified to scientists in the heat of battle with what strikes them as narrow-minded and potentially dangerous theological interpretations of the human condition. The naturalist and pragmatist framework of this inquiry makes such political and moral exertions on the part of social scientists and evolutionary biologists unnecessary in this case. Humanists and scientists can achieve a richer perception of the human condition, while protecting the dignity and freedom of human beings from religious zealotry and secular forms of authoritarianism, by cooperating with one another in a framework defined by religious naturalism and epistemological pragmatism.

Religious Anthropology and Disciplinary Stakeholders

Let us begin with a few key definitions. By *scientific study of religion*, I mean the interdisciplinary study of the cognitive, emotional, psychological, social, and communicative elements of religion using the methods of the natural and human sciences. The scientific study of religion has profound connections to the wider academic study of religion—i.e. *religious studies*, pursued by *religionists*, to use a term that seems to be gaining currency. It is also deeply connected to scholarly reflection on religious beliefs and practices—i.e. *theology*, pursued by *theologians*, who may belong to theistic and non-theistic religious traditions, or may have religiously non-affiliated or secular projects. If religionists and experts in the scientific study of religion typically frame their research as that of objective observers striving for neutrality, theologians tend to be insiders, making a virtue of their existentially lively religious commitment to generate profound insights that outsiders cannot easily grasp or express. Of course, there are exceptions on both sides of this insider–outsider contrast. Typically, it is not the case that a particular thinker simply *is* an insider or outsider by nature; rather, he or she *functions* as an insider or an outsider in a given inquiry. Many intellectuals can work effectively in both modes and move easily between the two.

All three domains—the scientific study of religion, religious studies, and theology—generate valid insights that a properly multidisciplinary and crossculturally alert religious anthropology should synthesize. Thus, all three groups are disciplinary stakeholders in a religious anthropology. But this requires explanation and perhaps justification because some contemporary interpretations of religion in human life neglect one or more of these disciplinary stakeholders. For example, even within the scientific study of religion, social scientists frequently neglect evolutionary theory's contributions to an understanding of the origins of religion, as if evolutionary origins and biological constraints were unimportant in the contemporary analysis of the social functions of religion. Evolutionary biologists and neuroscientists routinely neglect the rich descriptions of religion that cultural anthropologists and psychologists supply, happily but sometimes disastrously oversimplifying religion for the sake of the tractability of scientific research programs. Meanwhile, religionists and theologians usually neglect the scientific study of religion, and religionists and theologians themselves are often at loggerheads over what kinds of theories and interpretations are admissible in the academic study of religion. Investigations pertinent to religious anthropology can be useful without taking account of every disciplinary stakeholder, of course, but religious anthropology understood as it is here is committed to striving for a high degree of inclusiveness and consistency. It is deeply problematic for such a religious anthropology, therefore, that the advisability and even the possibility of cooperation between the disciplinary stakeholders in religious anthropology are not more widely embraced. I shall discuss these questions of advisability and possibility together in what follows.

Cooperation between Disciplinary Stakeholders

Contrary to the balkanization I have just described, I am one of a growing number of scientists, religionists, and theologians who regard a rich multidisciplinary understanding of the origins, functions, and value of religion as a worthy ideal, and a practical albeit challenging goal. This is one of the intellectual commitments of the field of science and religion, certainly as represented by the platform of its leading scholarly organization, the International Society for Science and Religion; though the same commitment arises elsewhere. Clearly, our motivations do not always cohere. We all find religious phenomena intrinsically fascinating. We can certainly all see that religion is often a crucial factor in geopolitics, economics, social change, and culture wars. We probably work in the hope that understanding will bring empathy and self-control, virtues badly needed in the often passionate and sometimes violent sphere of religion. But our ultimate purposes are far from harmonious. Some of us imagine that understanding religion may give us the power we need to eliminate it and to deliver its victims into humanistic enlightenment. Others dream of a form of religion that can remain authentically spiritual while being fully aware of its evolutionary origins, social functions, psychological dynamics, and economic implications. Yet others hope to confirm their personal religious outlook or the doctrinal assumptions of a religious tradition to which they are committed.

Despite these discrepant motivations, cooperation is feasible so long as we can suspend our hidden or not-so-hidden personal and social agendas for the sake of a quest for understanding of the human being as *homo religiosus*, and so long as we can agree on a framework that allows the insights of all disciplinary stakeholders to be registered within the inquiry. This framework can't be merely the "lowest common denominator" territory of biology. The biological sciences produce the most universal and least culturally bound insights into the human condition, but these insights are also existentially relatively inert and cannot register the full power and intricacy of religious behaviors, beliefs, and experiences in human life. To go further, we also need the anthropologist's rich descriptions of religion in its varied cultural settings, the psychologist's intricate tracings of religion in human emotions and behaviors, and the sociologist's group-level analyses of the role of religious beliefs and behaviors in maintaining social order and powering social change. Historical analyses can help knit the different levels of description together, so that connections between groups and individuals become apparent. But even this does not go far enough.

Though the biological and human sciences furnish much of the raw material for any interpretation of the human condition, by themselves and even marshaled by historians they do not allow for an *evaluation* of the role of religion in human life, which is an essential task of a religious anthropology. We cannot simply read off such an evaluation from the descriptive and theoretical material of the natural and human sciences and we should not pretend that the sciences somehow inevitably imply a particular evaluation of religion. Regulating the move from descriptive and theoretical work to full-blown evaluation requires philosophy and, in the broad sense introduced above and employed throughout this book, theology. Does this make theology the king of the castle and the queen of the sciences? Not at all: disciplinary stakeholders do not serve theological interests, they constrain theological and philosophical evaluations. But to omit philosophy and theology altogether is either to forsake the evaluative task—not a possibility for a religious anthropology in the sense of this book—or wrongly to pretend that evaluation is a trivial matter needing no disciplinary guidance and no special expertise.

Painful and often embarrassing experience has taught us that data are theory laden, that so-called "pure" description and "objective" analysis are ideals we can only ever approximate, that theories express cultural and philosophical assumptions in ways we do not always immediately notice, and that evaluations often serve explicit or implicit ideological agendas. All disciplinary workers have sometimes been oblivious to the presence of these problems in their midst, and when consciousness is raised an excruciating self-scrutiny can be the result. This is partly why some scholars are skeptical about evaluative approaches to religion. But banning evaluation only scratches the surface of the bias problem, which also affects theories, analyses, descriptions, and data—in short, interpretation of every type and at all levels of complexity. The optimal solution is neither to give up evaluation nor to sin boldly by producing hasty and opinionated evaluations. Rather, we need to take responsibility for evaluation by tracing out and comparing assumptions, and mounting arguments explicitly for the assumptions we believe, in light of expert training, are best. This is precisely the domain of philosophy and, in relation to religious matters, the domain of theology (again, in the sense that word has in this book). Far from representing the most egregious violations of impartiality, therefore, theology here is the main tool for regulating bias, for striving to achieve objective evaluations, and for making sure that every disciplinary stakeholder counts in the inquiry into religious anthropology. This, along with the importance of its distinctive subject matter, is the basis for theology's place in the secular academy (again, see Wildman 2009).

Theology *in this sense* functions as the host at a party of disciplinary stakeholders, facilitating conversation and ensuring that everyone feels comfortable. Theology *in this sense* hosts for practical reasons: it has the largest house and can be more inclusive. But theologians *in this sense* are typically not merely neutral hosts. Most are ready to make their own evaluations of religion within the human condition, and the associated arguments have to be held to the same standards as evaluative arguments of any other participant in the conversation. My own theological evaluation of the human phenomenon of religion is bivalent—that is, both appreciative and critical in different respects—and expresses assumptions reflecting the ontological framework of religious naturalism and the epistemological framework of pragmatism, as I have said. These assumptions are not congenial to many other theologians, but they are assumptions for which I argue elsewhere and that the argument of this book indirectly supports. The heart of that argument is that the religious naturalist and pragmatist approach to the human being as *homo religiosus* allows for a more comprehensive, inclusive, and persuasive interpretation of the offerings of all disciplinary stakeholders than competitor theological interpretations, whether theistic or atheistic, strongly affirmative or wholly critical. Other argumentative approaches, including formal philosophical evaluation of competing theories of ultimate reality, will have to wait for another volume. As self-appointed host of this particular party, therefore, I do have an evaluative case to make. But the case itself is highly commensurate with the goal of including the perspectives of disciplinary stakeholders. This is what it means to have the largest house and the best party venue. The biologist *as such*, the social scientist *as such*, and even the historian *as such* cannot host this party in the same inclusive way. Now, this book is more like a report on the aftermath of the party than the party itself, as the conversation has already taken place and I write alone. But the important point is that there has been a long series of penetrating conversations and that these conversations continue even as

I pause to state provisional conclusions and arguments. Presumably, the ongoing discussions in which I participate will refine my point of view over time.

The Challenge of Incommensurability

The question about the possibility of cooperation among disciplinary stakeholders has a sharper answer, namely, that the possibility does not exist because the disciplinary stakeholders operate within incommensurable worlds of discourse. The scientific study of religion, religious studies, and theology are quite different discourses, and sometimes shockingly disconnected, it is true. As one who bridges all three, I have concluded that they are not incommensurate but often so differently angled that fitting them together is challenging. This conceptual jigsaw is simplest when religionists and theologians allow the scientist to do his or her work, and then see how that affects their projects. But many more complex interactions are possible. It is in these more complex interactions that the question of incommensurability of disciplinary discourses tends to arise. I shall attempt to explain why this is a tractable difficulty rather than the death of all prospects for multidisciplinary cooperation.

Consider religious studies and the scientific study of religion. Religious studies as a field is deeply committed to registering the complexity and intricacy of religion by means of phenomenological descriptions, historical reconstructions, and sociological models. It is profoundly interdisciplinary, much as political economy is. Because of its encompassing nature, religious studies has the ability to absorb and respond to scientific perspectives on religion without having to abandon its own fundamental methodological commitments. The scientific study of religion has a different set of commitments. Scientists work within methodological limitations that promote the simplification of endlessly complex religious phenomena to the few salient features that prove tractable for scientific investigation. Scientists can be interested in the whole complexity of religion, and do well to know something about it for the sake of avoiding embarrassing caricatures. But their first commitment is to finding something they can work with, so they must argue (or simply hope) that selecting certain limited strands from the interwoven fabric of religion does not invalidate their results.

This contrast between religious studies and the scientific study of religion suggests incommensurability of disciplinary discourses. But closer analysis shows that there is a basis for mutual criticism and thus mutual understanding and adjustment. Consider how these mutual criticisms might be expressed.

On the one hand, religionists would argue that the scientist's oversimplification of religion for the sake of tractability of inquiry is appallingly reductionist. To religionists, the descriptions of religious phenomena that some scientists offer, without any trace of self-consciousness or hint of apology, are comically, or perhaps dangerously, unsophisticated. Religionists will point out that a high conceptual price is being paid for this reductionist strategy even when they do not immediately know how to advise the scientist who would gladly work with a more nuanced interpretation of religion. At the very least, the price of casual reductionism is a social one. Most people in the large world cultures of the contemporary world listen to scientists no matter what they are saying. Their propagation of superficial understandings of religion can have potentially serious social and political consequences, from distorted understandings of religion and deep suspicion of science in the general religious public, to the gradual loss of scientific prestige as reeducation painstakingly corrects careless scientific oversimplifications. The scientist can hear and understand this criticism, and often respond by deploying more sophisticated interpretations of religion. Thus, we don't have incommensurability but merely a clash of disciplinary habits of mind.

On the other hand, despite their invidious oversimplifications, scientists still achieve fascinating results in their study of religious behaviors, beliefs, and experiences. Knowing that religious ideas take certain repeatable forms or that a tendency toward certain religious behaviors is heritable should be useful within the broader framework of religious studies. To capitalize on these benefits, scientists will argue that the religionist must get past an allergic reaction to the reductionist approach, and reverse the trend of religious studies taking too lightly the scientific study of religion. Scientists will rightly say they have been setting a challenging new agenda for religious studies over the last several decades and it is past time that more religionists engage it, if only to test it from their own perspectives. Again, this is not incommensurability but a conflict of disciplinary practices to which there can be constructive responses.

Now consider the relationship between the scientific study of religion and theology. Here again we do not have incommensurable disciplinary discourse but very differently angled disciplinary viewpoints that, in the right context, can prove to be mutually illuminating. Theology typically ventures distinctive claims about the origins and functions of religion, perhaps through an intellectual interpretation of a founding narrative, through a doctrine that purportedly conveys a divinely revealed truth about the purpose of a religious ritual, or through a reflective interpretation of the astonishing experiences that can occur in meditation or corporate worship. Such theological claims usually concern only one part of a single religion, and few traditional theologians ever attempt to coordinate such claims into a theoretical edifice that arches across religious traditions. In fact, most traditional theologians seem uninterested in religion, in the sense of the whole collection of phenomena that religious studies examines—not a good thing, in my view, and not consistent with the view of theology adopted here, but understandable given the way such traditional theologians often work on behalf of particular living religious communities. More importantly, theological claims frequently do not harmonize well with what the scientific study of religion has to say about the evolution of religious beliefs and behaviors, and about the origins and functions of religion. Theologians have usually avoided this conflict problem, just as religionists have, by withdrawing into supportive communities with social identities strong enough to maintain local plausibility structures regardless of wider intellectual currents. From such local havens of acceptance and relevance they need pay no social price for ignoring what scientists say about the evolutionary origins and functions of religion.

By contrast, there are intellectually compelling sub-traditions within most theological traditions that seek to engage what other intellectuals have to say about matters of concern to theology. Such theologians—theologians in the sense of this book and the ones likely to appreciate its approach to religious anthropology— exert great effort to learn what religionists and scientists have discovered about religion and seek to take account of those discoveries in their theological theories. Theological theories on some topics may operate conceptually independently of the scientific study of religion—for instance, the theme of divine creation or the aesthetic and moral ideal of effortless flow of life within the Dao may be compatible with virtually any finding of the natural or human sciences. But many theological theories have conceptual and logical traction with parts of the scientific study of religion. Even some scientists presume such traction when they informally and sometimes publicly pronounce on the theological significance (often negative or critical significance) of the latest scientific discovery about religion. Unfortunately, the discipline of theology is often identified with its most shrill and narrow-minded exponents, as much by cultural luminaries with an anti-religious axe to grind as by conservative religious leaders with a tradition to defend. But the work of imaginative intellectuals seeking to integrate the scientific study of religion and religious studies into a specifically theological theory of religion persists quietly around the margins of religiously driven culture wars and in the interstices of the socially complex world of theological studies. Such theological theories seek not only to theorize the origins and functions of religion but also to evaluate the value of religious practices and the truth of religious claims, and they seek to do this coherently by uniting every relevant perspective into a consistent theory.

It follows that theology can and does learn from the scientific study of religion. For its part, the scientific study of religion can learn from theology that settling deeply controverted questions—say, about the evolutionary origins of religion— does not thereby settle the question of the existential and social value of religion in the present. Evaluations of this sort require the care and expertise of the theologian. Thus, there can be conceptual traction between parts of the disciplinary worlds of science and theology, and there can be mutual learning and adjustment. This should largely overcome incommensurability based concerns about the possibility of cooperation between disciplinary stakeholders in religious anthropology.

Two Levels of Cooperation

Collaborative discussion between scientists, religionists, and theologians in an inquiry into the meaning of human being as *homo religiosus* unfolds—or can unfold—on two levels. First, at the level of conceptual content, there should be two-way traffic between scientific theories and the associated empirical research, on the one hand, and what religionists and theologians say about religious beliefs and practices, on the other. Most obviously, religious studies and theology furnish basic data for the scientific study of religion. The most intellectually well-crafted statements about the beliefs of a religion are typically delivered by expert theologians so scientists studying religion should ensure that they know about such statements rather than confining themselves to the knowledge base of popular religious self-understandings. Similarly, the most sophisticated descriptions of religious practices come from religionists and theologians specializing in ritual studies so scientists ought to take account of these descriptions in deciding on the most salient aspects to study in detail. Doing this would have an immediate effect on the quality of scientific work. Scientists would be far more precise about what they are studying—not religious ritual but a particular religious practice, and not a universal religious belief but an idea found in some parts of some religions and not others—and far more cautious about drawing obviously fallacious conclusions about religion as a whole from whatever part of religion they actually are studying.

In the other direction, religionists and theologians ought to have some response to emerging scientific theories of the origins of religion, to the dawning intelligibility of bizarre religious activities, and to theories of cognition that predict the recurrence of supernatural beliefs. Evolutionary psychology and cognitive neuroscience should influence theological claims about ultimate and proximate realities, salvation and liberation, the meaning and purpose of life, and how so many human beings come to believe in such things. For example, the scientific study of religion forces theologians to ask how well traditional theological assertions about sacred religious communities comport with the emerging evolutionary account of their origins. Can theologians continue to say everything they have formerly said about the theological meaning of church and synagogue, temple and *sangha*? If so, how? If not, what should they say instead?

The second level of collaborative discussion concerns method. On the one hand, results from the scientific study of religion demand an evaluation of the nature and function of theology. Is theology a socially embedded intellectual activity specializing in legitimating identity by nurturing deflective and projective responses of religious groups to an uncertain natural environment? Is it a divinely given responsibility on behalf of a supernaturally established body of sacred revelation? Is it a religiously neutral form of philosophical inquiry? Can it be all of these at once within different sub-communities, or even in a single person? Scientific understandings of religion should impact the theologian's perception of what it means to assert and evaluate religious truth claims both as a representative of the intellectual wing of a religious group, when the theologian works in that mode, and as a representative of the secular academy, when that is the context of theological labors. Similarly, the scientific study of religion raises sharp questions for religionists about the adequacy of the generally humanistic, literary, and historical approaches to the study of religion. Does not the scientific study of religion show that these approaches need to be complemented, and possibly constrained, by the approaches of natural and human scientists?

On the other hand, the insights of religious studies and theology should chasten the scientific study of religion, inhibiting its tendency toward hasty and sometimes hostile reductionism in approaching religious phenomena. Religionists and theologians who accept an evolutionary theory of religion will inevitably assert that the evolution of human social tendencies and higher cognitive capacities provoked and promoted religious behaviors. They will say that this particular product of the evolutionary process opened up a universe of religious depth that would have remained closed otherwise. They will picture the existential coloring and spiritual potency of reality gradually becoming a part of the environment of human life as human beings evolved the abilities to engage it. This viewpoint makes a virtue of the evolutionary account of the origins and functions of religious behaviors and beliefs. Religionists and theologians tend to agree on this much even if theologians then go further to speculate on the meaning of all this whereas religionists typically remain content to analyze its functions and effects. The scientist studying evolution and religion may not be able to speak to the reality of religious phenomena, but it is dangerous for that scientist simply to refuse to consider, or even to note, the role that religious realities may play in conditioning the evolutionary process itself.

This presents a serious methodological conundrum for the scientist. The scientist does not want to leave out factors relevant to an inquiry about the evolutionary origins of religious beliefs and behaviors, yet the scientific method appears unable to make use of the hypothesis of the causal relevance of religious realities (the alleged partial exception of Intelligent Design theory to the contrary notwithstanding). Scientists may be tempted to rule out religious realities *a priori*, rather than remaining neutral to them, because they are intractable within the scientific framework of analysis. In that case, alert religionists and theologians, as well as other scientists, must be ready to call the wayward back to the straight and narrow path of scientific discipline. If science cannot settle metaphysical questions about the reality of religious objects positively, then neither can it settle such questions negatively. Scientists must *bracket* the questions—in the sense of noting their presence but suspending consideration of them—and also remain alert to the fact that such bracketing can limit the validity of their conclusions.

Evidently, the potential interactions among the scientific study of religion, religious studies, and theology are conceptually and methodologically complex, perhaps forbiddingly so. I have sketched these complexities with just enough detail to suggest how this book fits into a wider intellectual venture, with a sizable and growing body of literature. Whether these two levels of collaborative discussion among disciplinary stakeholders in a religious anthropology produce valuable results is an important question. For the body of science–religion literature on religious anthropology to which I am referring, I think the answer is unquestionably in the affirmative.

The Very Idea of *Homo Religiosus*

In introducing the task of religious anthropology as that task is understood in this book—to interpret and evaluate the human being as *homo religiosus*—I described the virtually universal presence of religion in human cultures and emphasized its importance wherever it appears. This near ubiquity is the most basic meaning of *homo religiosus*. It is vital to note in setting out on this inquiry that other less theologically neutral meanings of this phrase exist and indeed are prominent in religious studies. For example, Mircea Eliade used the phrase, but in a quite different sense. His usage took for granted the twin theological claims that (i) the sacred, in the sense of a transcendent other, is real and can break through into human experience as manifestations of power; and (ii) that appreciating, relating to, and orienting oneself by manifestations of this sacred transcendent other, which human beings are definitively suited to do, is the key to human self-understanding and fulfillment (see Eliade 1959). Given that Eliade tried to make sense of these claims with reference to data from cultural anthropology, it is not surprising that a few anthropologists have criticized his use of an essentially theologically loaded conception of *homo religiosus* (for example, see Saliba 1976).

Yet Eliade's theological framework is quite generous and encompassing in most respects. His fondness for transcendence imagery and his connected tendency sometimes to speak of a transcendent other as a determinate entity—that is, to treat the religious object in an only partly naturalized way—seems a superficial habit of discourse. In practice, that tendency is kept in check by his wide appreciation of religious symbolism—symbolism that encompasses time and space, earth and sea and sky, cultural products and physical life necessities. Thus, when interpreted most generously, Eliade's framework is relatively non-prejudicial, theologically speaking, and quite open to a range of ontological and cosmological specifications. As such, it has the great virtue of allowing authentically theological questions to figure in discussions of the roles of religion in human life. If Eliade did not achieve the accuracy that an anthropologist would prefer in handling culturally diverse material, at least his theological framework appears readily generalizable so that nothing about the human encounter with the Sacred would be alien to it. Of course, where Eliade took the Sacred to be the heart and soul of religion and religiousness in all its forms, I can only demur. Religion and religiousness alike are about many things, not just emotionally processing and intellectually theorizing encounters with the Sacred, which is what Eliade and the phenomenological tradition within religious studies tend to stress (see Otto 1923, Van der Leeuw 1986).

In order to appreciate the generosity of Eliade's theological framing for interpreting the human being as *homo relgiosus*, consider that most other theologically oriented approaches are considerably less inclusive. For example, to conceive of human beings in a *saṃsāra-mokṣa* framework is dramatically narrower than Eliade's approach, despite the wealth of spiritual outlooks and religions that this framework supports in practice. Again, to conceive of human beings in a heaven–hell framework dominated by divine judgment, divine mercy, and divine providence is also dramatically to narrow the scope of interpretation relative to Eliade's approach. An even narrower approach is to adopt one or another primacy-of-revelation views, whereby whatever we say about the human condition is subordinate to what is taken to be manifested in an authoritative sacred text or other revelation. Swiss Christian theologian Karl Barth does this when he treats Jesus Christ as the key for interpreting the human condition, thereby rising above what Barth sees as blinkered attachment to empirically derived interpretations that religious studies and the scientific study of religion can produce (Barth 1975: Part IV). An important logical alternative that must be kept in mind, such primacy-of-revelation views make for poor hosts of the sorts of multidisciplinary conversations that I seek to support. Eliade's viewpoint is extremely generous relative to all of these interpretative frameworks, and I think we can do even better than Eliade in this respect.

My working usage of *homo religiosus* is descriptive and presupposes only the importance and near-ubiquity of religion in human life. This demarcates a theologically more neutral and intellectually more welcoming space for inquiry than is possible using Eliade's theologically charged definition of *homo religiosus*, or others that are theologically far less inclusive than his. But using a more descriptive definition settles nothing of significance and merely temporarily deflects the problem of a theological framework for interpreting religion in human life. In order to allow the existentially and morally potent phenomena of religious behaviors, beliefs, and experiences properly to impact the inquiry, it is necessary to deploy a theological framework that is tuned to such phenomena and can register them appropriately as factors to be explained and evaluated. So there is no evading the insight of the phenomenological tradition of religious studies: something is going on in human religiousness that requires theorizing in theological terms.

Were we to borrow a highly specific theological framework for diagnosing such phenomena, we would distort a lot of important information. For example, to speak of the feeling of attachment, entrapment, and weariness that triggers a thirst for enlightenment is to deploy categories that are quite serviceable for making sense of the reported experiences of many religious people in some South Asian cultures and in places to which South Asian religions have traveled. And to speak of the presence of the Holy Spirit guiding and comforting the follower of Jesus the divine Christ and leading the disciple to unity with God Almighty is to deploy categories well tuned to make sense of religious experience and belief in a Trinitarian Christian setting. But these categorial schemes are not obviously compatible with one another, even though representatives of these disparate categorial worlds frequently claim that their conceptual schemas are universally applicable across human individuals and cultures, and thus hold the key to any theologically adequate interpretation of *homo religiosus*. A religious anthropology that rises above the theologically trivial must include within it at least the nub of a solution to the problem of religious and theological pluralism.

The best way forward, I contend, is to adopt a categorial framework that is well positioned in the spectrum between the extremes of inconsequential vagueness and distorting determinateness. For example, we should not speak in narrowly distorting fashion of human beings as fallen because of a divine curse issued after a primordial couple in a mythical garden made an ill-considered decision about what and where to eat, or as doomed to a *saṃsāric* cycle of lives because of karmic dust particles that accumulate through actions, thereby weighing down the soul and preventing its escape to the bliss of nirvana. Nor should we speak in inconsequentially vague style of human beings as indefinable mysteries with unlimited potential whose diversity defeats categorization. Rather, it is best to speak in mid-level categories with a degree of vagueness tuned to the actual self-interpretations that human beings employ, the actual problems they seek to solve, and actual solutions they construct. Thus, we can speak of the human condition with its opportunities and frustrations, of spiritual quests with a variety of goals bearing on fulfillment of longings and the resolution of challenges, of corporate resources in the form of wisdom traditions and spiritual practices—and all of this deployed reflexively in an environment that most human beings are able to perceive as somehow sacred thanks to a capacity for intense aesthetic and spiritual experiences. This middle level of vagueness deploys categories that are determined empirically through actual study of what works with least distortion to describe human religion and religiousness across the world's religions, diverse cultures, and varied personalities. That this is possible, as well as what categories get the job done, was the burden of the Crosscultural Comparative Religious Ideas Project, which was informed by a wealth of work in comparative religions (see Neville 2001a, 2001b, 2001c).

Properly tuned vague categories are too vague to constitute a functional religious outlook. To live vibrantly within a religious faith, most people need more lively imagery and more specific narratives than empirically derived theological categories permit. But properly tuned vague categories do define a basic theological framework relative to which more specific theological outlooks can be considered elaborations. That is, the Trinitarian Christian theologian, the Pure Land Buddhist theologian, and the fervent secular humanist intellectual can use their native categories to extend the analysis of the human condition produced within a religious anthropology that uses properly tuned vague categories—and they can venture such elaborations without introducing violent inconsistencies with the theologically minimal religious anthropology, even if such elaborations are profoundly at odds with one another. This is not to claim that a theologically minimal starting point for subsequent theological elaboration is somehow theologically innocent or neutral; far from it. In fact, many Trinitarian Christian, Pure Land Buddhist, and secular humanist intellectuals would doubtless say that the theological framework for a religious anthropology defined by properly tuned vague categories is incorrect precisely through being vague in a way that does not agree with their singular points of view. But I do claim that a theological framework for a multidisciplinary comparative inquiry in religious anthropology can host serious theological discussions without cutting that inquiry off from the natural and human sciences—can so host, that is, when its leading categories are properly vague rather than overly vague or overly specific.

Conclusion

Once the "properly tuned vagueness" approach is accepted, at least for the sake of argument, the natural question is what kind of theological framework can do for this inquiry what Eliade's framework did for his (and Van der Leeuw's for his, Schleiermacher's for his, Hegel's for his, Otto's for his, Lévi-Strauss's for his, etc.). With so many attempts to choose from, it might appear that we are assaulted by incompatible and equally serviceable alternatives at this point, but it is not so. In fact, the frameworks to which I have alluded, and host of others besides, converge at or around what I and many others call *religious naturalism.*

A religious naturalist approach allows us to speak of religious experiences as genuine events of encounter or engagement without prejudging the nature of that which is encountered or engaged, except to say that it is the Whence of the encounter, the Logical Object of engagement, and rooted somehow in the valuational, meaning-laden depth structures and dynamics of nature. This approach allows us to speak of religious behaviors and beliefs as natural responses to social pressures and psychological needs in a spiritually luminous environment without prejudging the correctness of beliefs or the appropriateness of actions. In other words, it gets as much as possible from the disciplinary stakeholders into the discussion at a level that permits a theologically sophisticated analysis and evaluation of the human being as *homo religiosus.* It is, thus, the ideal framework for my purposes.

An important practical consequence of employing religious naturalist categories for diagnosing the meaning of human religiosity is that the scope of religious behaviors, beliefs, and experiences is widened far beyond participation in recognized religious communities to include every kind of spiritual seeking and value exploration that human beings do, whether or not this would normally be called religious. Even the passionate critiques of religion that seek to deliver human beings from its toxicity are intrinsically religious activities in this generous sense. Most importantly, it is only in this most generous sense that human beings can be said to be *homo religious* not merely historically, culturally, or circumstantially, but also ontologically, essentially, and inescapably.

There are many varieties of religious naturalism, of course, but the categories deployed here are compatible with virtually all of them, so more specific naturalist theories are not eliminated from the outset. With this in mind, I turn in the next introductory chapter to a more detailed discussion of religious naturalism.

CHAPTER 2

Naturalism

Introduction

In the previous preliminary chapter, I argued that religious naturalism can supply properly tuned vague categories that facilitate the development of a religious anthropology without distorting relevant data, without prejudging questions of evaluation, without marginalizing insights from disciplinary stakeholders, and without excluding broadly or subtly religious phenomena that do not fit the narrow conceptions of religion defined by its dominant manifestations. I distinguished this basic framework for hosting a multidisciplinary and cross-traditional inquiry into religious anthropology from theologically more detailed elaborations of the human condition. And I argued that such theological elaborations must be at least as organically consistent with stakeholder insights as is the religious anthropology deriving from the religious naturalist framework.

In this chapter I elaborate the interpretative framework itself in more detail. This involves defining religious naturalism, which supplies to the inquiry properly vague ontological categories about the human condition and the ultimate environment of human life. This task also involves discussing the pragmatic epistemology of inquiry, the role of which is to ensure that the insights of stakeholder disciplines are properly registered and operationalized for the correction and improvement of interpretations of the human being as *homo religiosus*.

Defining Religious Naturalism

Tillich on Religious Naturalism

In the introduction to volume 2 of his *Systematic Theology* (1957), German-American Christian theologian Paul Tillich reflected on some of the recurring challenges he faced in handling responses to volume 1 (1951). One of these challenges was his readers' confusion over precisely what he meant by moving "beyond naturalism and *supra*naturalism" (5–10; italics added to draw attention to the surprising spelling). The result is an intriguing statement of what Tillich rejects and affirms, one that is slightly clearer than what appears in volume 1, and one that holds steady through volume 3 (1963). It is also an excellent starting point for a discussion of the meaning of religious naturalism and some of the problems surrounding this term.

By *supranaturalism*, Tillich meant the idea of God as highest being, separate from but also alongside other beings, who "brought the universe into being ..., governs it according to a plan, directs it toward an end, interferes with its ordinary processes in order to overcome resistance and to fulfill his purpose, and will bring it to consummation in a final catastrophe" (6). His critique of supranaturalism is similar to all critiques of this version of onto-theology: "it transforms the infinity of God into a finiteness which is merely an extension of the categories of finitude" (6). He thus regards the anti-supranaturalist critique that naturalism levels against this view as "valid" and as representing "the true concern of religion" (6). For Tillich, supranaturalism is a kind of idolatrous distortion of ultimate reality, despite its ubiquity in theistic religions.

By *naturalism*, Tillich meant any view that "identifies God with the universe, with its essence or with special powers within it" (6). Tillich does not mean strict pantheism, which he rightly regards as a philosophically absurd viewpoint with no exemplars in the history of myth or philosophy. Rather, he is referring to the religious versions of naturalism, such as those of John Scotus Eriugena and John Duns Scotus that identify God with "*natura naturans*, the creative nature, the creative ground of all natural objects" (6; this appears to be the theological resting place of Gordon Kaufman, the author of a noted religious anthropology [1993]; see Kaufman 2004, 2006). Tillich regarded modern materialism as virtually eliminating these religious dimensions, and he understood why this might have been necessary for the limited purposes of positivist projects. But even where the religious dimensions are retained, he saw a big problem with naturalism. Specifically, "it denies the infinite distance between the whole of finite things and their infinite ground," which eventually makes the term *God* "semantically superfluous" (7).

Tillich's third way agrees with religious naturalism insofar as they both affirm that God is "the creative ground of everything that has being, ... the infinite and unconditional power of being or, in the most radical abstraction, ... being-itself" (7). But Tillich goes beyond what he thought religious forms of naturalism can accommodate when he insisted on the self-transcendent character of the world as confirming divine transcendence: "God as the ground of being infinitely transcends that of which he is the ground" (7). This is an ecstatic idea of God in that it "points to the experience of the holy as transcending ordinary experience without removing it. Ecstasy as a state of mind is the exact correlate to self-transcendence as the state of reality" (8).

Tillich, it appears, is an ecstatic naturalist, or a self-transcendent naturalist, though he did not call himself this, possibly for fear of being tarred with the naturalist brush and then covered with ridiculous and ontologically innocent materialist feathers. He would have been right to worry about this, especially fifty years ago. But the problem here is that the line between Tillich's form of (what I shall continue to call) ecstatic naturalism and other forms of religious naturalism is razor thin, and may actually vanish upon the closest examination. It is not at all clear, despite what Tillich wrote on the subject, that religious naturalism excludes ecstatic or self-transcendent elements. Some forms of naturalism simply bracket such questions, to be sure. And the Whiteheadian process form of naturalism rejects self-transcendence in Tillich's sense because Whitehead rejects the idea of God as the transcendent ground of the creative process, rendering God an actual entity with a special integrative and evaluative role in the cosmic process (see Whitehead 1978). But many forms of religious naturalism do have ecstatic and self-transcendent elements built into them.

We appear to have a semantic quagmire surrounding the word "naturalism." Since Tillich's time, a vast and unwieldy literature has grown around the theme of naturalism, only some of it related to his own position. Many sub-parts of this literature are isolated and the result is rampant terminological confusion. The best treatments clearly thematize concern with the theological limitations of naturalism, even if they know nothing of Tillich's grappling with this issue. Robert Corrington's *Ecstatic Naturalism* (1994; also see Corrington 1992, 1996, 1997, 2000) is one of the best treatments—indeed, from a thinker influenced by Tillich. Corrington distinguishes between (i) descriptive naturalism (Dewey, Santayana, Buchler); (ii) honorific naturalism focusing on spirit (Schelling, Emerson, Heidegger); (iii) honorific naturalism focusing on creativity (Whitehead, Teilhard, Hartshorne, Neville); and (iv) ecstatic naturalism (Peirce, Tillich, Bloch, Jung, Kristeva, and himself). Most importantly, Corrington regards ecstatic naturalism in much the same way that Tillich thinks of his view: as pointing to the self-transcendent elements of the world, and to the ecstatic qualities of experience by which we register the fact of self-transcendence. In effect, Corrington shows that the word "naturalism" is serviceable and indeed practically unavoidable for expressing views that affirm the self-transcending and ecstatic elements of the natural world.

Unlike Tillich, therefore, I have no hesitation in using the phrase "ecstatic naturalism" to describe his viewpoint, or the more encompassing phrase "religious naturalism" to denominate the general class of views to which my own view belongs. Both phrases achieve two overridingly important practical purposes. On the one hand, they establish a beachhead against supranaturalistic metaphysics, including in their most sophisticated and iconoclastic forms, and from there they fight against the anthropomorphic and idolatrous metaphysics of God as a determinate entity. (Note, anthropomorphic *symbols* of God are not necessarily idolatrous, depending on how they are deployed and how their ultimate brokenness is recognized.) On the other hand, the qualifications "ecstatic" or "religious" effectively point out the limitation of the value-averse, spiritually flat, and metaphysically naïve kinds of materialism that sometimes pass under the banner of "naturalism", as much these days as ever (see Nielson 2001). Religious naturalism regards these views as more or less unwelcome interlopers, too empirically underdeveloped to be of any real philosophical or theological interest.

The Circularity of Naturalism

It is important to acknowledge that the conceptual point of speaking of religious naturalism is, in the final analysis, not completely clear. The practical point, which I have just described, is clear enough. But the conceptual point is obscure because, in respect of its practical usage, "naturalism" actually expresses a negation of other views, as I have just described, and thus is parasitic upon them. In relation to *supra*naturalism, which is itself a kind of negation, naturalism actually represents a double negation reaching back to its own semantic content, and thus is an infuriatingly circular term. No matter how *practically* useful it may be to think of naturalism as "anti-supranaturalism", therefore, some *conceptual* work is required to escape the semantic circle entailed in this usage. As with all semantic questions going to the heart of long-running ontological debates, terminological clarity is ephemeral, and negotiated semantic settlements appear arbitrary as soon as we notice the wider network of meanings. Because naturalism is necessarily a radically inclusive term, we can't say what it includes without defining reality, and we can only say what it excludes on the basis of a provisional account of reality that is determinate enough to exclude something at the same level of determinateness.

For example, for naturalism to exclude the discarnate intentional beings of *supernaturalism* (note: this is not supranaturalism, which specifically relates to ultimate reality), naturalism must specify a provisional understanding of embodied intentionality sufficiently precise to stabilize the idea of discarnate intentionality— in ideas of ghosts, angels, demons, ancestors—that is being rejected. Moreover, since naturalism's most urgent concern is to reject not the discarnate intentionality of supernaturalism but to overcome the anthropomorphic conception of ultimate reality as a determinate entity (e.g. a personal deity), a serious question arises as to whether a properly framed naturalism that rejects *supranaturalism*'s conception of ultimate reality as a determinate, focally intentional entity must also reject *supernaturalism*'s discarnate intentionality of other beings. In other words, it ought to be possible for religious naturalism to accept discarnate entities such as ancestors and ghosts, demons and angels *as aspects of nature*, so long as anti-supranaturalism is rigorously maintained by rejecting personal theism and allied forms of determinate-entity accounts of ultimate reality. These considerations show that, strictly speaking, while the word "naturalism" can be construed as rejecting a determinate-entity account of ultimate realities, by itself it says little or nothing about the ontological qualities and possibilities of the nature to which its name refers. Nature is what it is and even very surprising and currently unfashionable ontological components may be included within a naturalist ontology, depending on what our experience of nature suggests is required to describe and explain it.

Despite these ambiguities and complexities, in a given context it is possible to stipulate what is excluded from the ontological inventory of reality as a kind of hypothetical way of theorizing about all of reality. The context stabilizes the meanings of terms enough to permit drawing lines between the ontologically admissible (the putatively natural, for a naturalist) and the ontologically inadmissible (the supernatural and the supranatural, for a naturalist of my sort), without entirely eliminating the circularity and without obliviously falling victim to it either.

The Meaning of Naturalism in This Project

Several ontological lines are crucial for defining the approach to religious anthropology that I am exploring. Tentatively drawing each one is important for making my approach both open to criticism and worthy of it. I present them here in increasing degrees of restrictiveness for the kinds of reasoning that can work in a religious anthropology.

First, *anti-supranaturalism*, in Tillich's sense, is a basic boundary line for my hypothetical naturalistic approach to human nature. I find it important here to be clear about my categories to avoid repeating blunders of the past surrounding the way religions relate to ontology. "Ultimacy" is my preferred general term for the logical object that is of final concern within religions. "Ultimate realities" and "ultimate concerns" are the objective and subjective sides of ultimacy, respectively, and are capable of diverse and inconsistent specification in the way that all vague categories are. Again, this categorial deployment follows a usage argued to be optimally clear and minimally distorting in the Crosscultural Comparative Religious Idea Project (see Neville 2001b, and also 2001a, 2001c), which itself draws on earlier usages in Tillich (1951) and sociologist Max Weber (1951). It is in relation to ultimate realities, not only in relation to theism, that the question of supranaturalism arises. In all such contexts, naturalism resists treating ultimate reality as an ontological object with determinate features that make sense apart from natural reality. That is, all determinate features of ultimate reality derive from and emerge in relation to the world; apart from the world (i.e. *a se*, or in itself) ultimate reality is nothing—not Tillich's ontologically derivative μὴ ὄν (mē on), but the absolute nothing and sheer emptiness that he calls οὐκ ὄν (ouk on). This is the basis for a theoretical rapprochement between theistic "ground of being" models of ultimate reality and South Asian Buddhist *śūnyatā* (emptiness) models of ultimate reality, though this association is far from straightforward even in these terms. Without the naturalist limitation of anti-supranaturalism, however, this synthetic theoretical move is impossible.

Second, *anti-supernaturalism* is an ontologically more aggressive stipulation of naturalism, and also manifests naturalism at its most unattractively circular, as I have noted. Tillich appears simply to have taken for granted that supernaturalism (again, in the sense of discarnate focal awareness, intentionality, and causal powers such as those attributed to ghosts, demons, angels, souls, and ancestors) is mistaken, at least in the common senses of the term. As a result he glosses over the circularity problems. Naturalists—even the smaller group of explicitly religious naturalists—disagree sharply over what kinds of phenomena cross the supernaturalistic line. Some would exclude paranormal phenomena while others would not, for example. Some would locate the line so as to divide what the natural sciences are in principle capable of investigating from everything else. My approach, rather than masking the import of arbitrary stipulations of the natural, directly exposes the relevant criteria to scrutiny. The supernatural is any ontological inventory item or process that (i) implies supranaturalism; (ii) furnishes the basis for the absolute authorization of truth claims (this is akin to what Tillich [1951] meant by "heteronomy"; see below); (iii) affirms disembodied awareness or intentionality; or (iv) proposes disembodied wielders of causal powers. It is *supernaturalism specifically in this sense* that I hypothetically reject in my form of religious naturalism. Notice that this stipulation does not settle many other ontological questions, such as the meanings of materialism, physicalism, matter–energy, consciousness, or values; naturalism in my general sense of the phrase can be rendered consistent with a variety of ontological stances on such issues.

Third, and as a consequence of the first two stipulations, naturalism requires the rejection of self-authorizing means of knowledge about ultimate reality, including direct self-interpreting experiences and special revelation through sacred texts or sacred traditions. All such sources of putative knowledge, to be self-interpreting and self-authorizing, require supernaturalism and possibly also supranaturalism, which naturalism rejects. This does not entail the rejection of the idea of sacred religious classics (see Tracy 1981), nor the idea of revelation understood as the manifestation of the self-transcendent sacred depths of nature (see Hardwick 1996, Ricoeur 1977). But it does rule out any interpretation of such things that implies supernatural authorization or short-circuits (through appeal to supernatural illumination) the complex process of human interpretation.

From this three-fold stipulation of the basic ontological and epistemological commitments of religious naturalism, it follows that every determinate feature of ultimate reality—and thus every characteristic that can be thought, experienced, discovered, or believed—is constituted by the relation between nature and its self-transcendent ground. Ultimacy has no determinate characteristics apart from its expression in the valuational depth structures and self-transcendence of nature; in itself, ultimate reality is empty of determinacy. It is in this sense that philosophical theologian Robert Neville conceives of God as creator *ex nihilo* (see Neville 1968) and also in this sense that the account of God in Whitehead and many subsequent process thinkers is not an account of ultimate reality (as Whitehead himself realized; see the discussion of the "categoreal scheme" in Whitehead 1978, 20–30). It is in this sense, rather than out of mere epistemological modesty, that theologian Friedrich Schleiermacher dreamed of an account of the Christian faith that made no reference to propositions about God but only to propositions about human states of consciousness (see the discussion of the fundamental dogmatic form in Schleiermacher 1928, §30, 125–127). It is in this sense that the apophatic mystical traditions within every religion rightly affirm the unspeakability of ultimate reality *a se* however this ultimacy is spoken of in provisional terms along the various paths toward silence that these traditions articulate. And it is in this sense that the self-appointed postmodern guardians of the unspeakable rightly criticize the onto-theological tradition for presuming to speak of ultimacy as a reality possessing a character apart from the world of our experience (see Marion 1991, Ruf 1989, Westphal 2001, Wrathall 2003).

The anti-supranaturalist theological heritage is ancient, stretching from Plato and Aristotle (almost always, at least) in the West to Śaṅkara and Nāgārjuna in South Asia to Laozi and Confucius in East Asia. They include apophatic mystics in all traditions. Within Christianity, theologians such as Augustine and Thomas Aquinas, Martin Luther and John Calvin, are significantly anti-supranaturalist in respect of their metaphysics of God, even while preserving supranaturalist elements in other phases of their theological work, and retaining supernaturalist worldviews with miracles, angels, and demons. I hold (without argument, here) that these are inconsistent positions, but the inconsistency requires a thoroughly post-medieval worldview to be properly appreciated. In the modern period, Christian theologian Friedrich Schleiermacher is a classic case of an anti-supranaturalist and also one of the earliest modern Christian theologians to overcome what I take to be the inconsistency of his medieval forebears on this issue. In the contemporary era, Christian theologians such as Gordon Kaufman and Robert Neville are both thoroughly anti-supranaturalistic and completely anti-supernaturalistic. Many other Christian theologians have sympathy for this standpoint but do not articulate their metaphysical commitments with enough precision to determine whether they are consistently opposed to supranaturalism and supernaturalism.

Theological traditions affiliated with many other religions also have representatives of anti-supranaturalism and anti-supernaturalism. Typically, such views persist to various degrees on the underside of the main tradition, which continues to articulate supranaturalistic views of ultimate reality and supernaturalistic worldviews. But the locations of such views are not always obvious. One might assume that fundamentally atheistic religious traditions such as Buddhism, Daoism, and Confucianism (if deemed a religion) support theological systems with anti-supranaturalistic and anti-supernaturalistic qualities. But many forms of theological reflection in these traditions are thoroughly supernaturalistic—being replete with Gods and demons, ancestors and discarnate entities, angels and bodhisattvas—despite anti-supranaturalistic resistance to determinate formulations of ultimate reality in itself. Religious naturalism in the context of this book is thoroughgoing and consistent in its rejection of both supranaturalism and supernaturalism.

The Pragmatic Epistemology of Inquiry

The epistemological framework furnished by this account of naturalism affects inquiry into ultimacy and inquiry into religious anthropology in similar ways. The world of naturalism as delimited here admits no disembodied forms of intentionality, no disembodied causal powers, no self-interpreting experiences, no self-authorizing revelations, and no role for absolute authorities in justifying beliefs. These restrictions rule out less than it may appear at first. Most avenues of human inquiry remain completely open, including most that are important in theological work. But the epistemological strategy does shift. It shifts away from unpacking putatively revealed sources of information, and toward first-order inquiries into the natural world. On the pragmatic view of epistemology that accompanies the naturalist view of ontology, it is first-order inquiries into the natural world that uncover everything there is to know about human beings, and about the ultimate realities and ultimate concerns that human beings engage in and through nature. *All theology is, on this view, natural theology*—admittedly not in the traditionally narrow sense of the term, but rightly called "natural theology" just the same. Indeed, the distinction between natural theology and revealed theology utterly collapses, and all theology is also revealed theology, as we can describe the depths of nature equally well as discovered through inquiry and as manifested through encounters with nature.

Several important themes in traditional forms of religious anthropology are worth discussing to clarify the pragmatic epistemology of inquiry employed here.

First, the pragmatic understanding of theological epistemology casts Christian theologian Karl Barth's discussion of the *analogia entis* (analogies between the being of God and the being of the created world), the *vestigia trinitatis* (traces in nature of the essential Trinitarian nature of God), and natural theology into an intriguing light (see numerous places in Barth 1975). Barth deployed arguments against all three in order to ensure that God could never be tamed by knowledge of this world, and in particular by anthropomorphic images of God and reasoning based on nature or human religious experience. He also used his interpretation of these themes to rule out exclusive reliance on naturalistic means of studying human beings, thereby securing the authority of revelation to stipulate the essential content of any adequate religious anthropology. The analogy of being in any literal sense is impossible in the anti-supranaturalistic framework of religious naturalism because ultimate reality is not a being and has no being in itself. Vestiges in nature of the essential character of God, at least when "essential" is understood to refer strictly to the divine nature *a se*, are also not possible in a naturalistic framework because ultimate reality has no essential nature apart from relations to nature. For different reasons than he gave, then, Barth's strictures on human knowledge in these modes are unproblematic for the religious naturalist. Moreover, the religious naturalist finds profound common ground with Barth's intention forcefully to limit the apparently irresistible anthropomorphic urges of human beings in their theological constructions of the *imago dei*. Barth consistently placed around the divine aseity a protective belt of human ignorance: in case his rejections of the *analogia entis*, of the *vestigia trinitatis*, and of natural theology fail to drive home the point, Barth also construed God's self-revelation in Christ as manifesting the divine in important respects as unknown.

The religious naturalist appreciates these moves as ways of achieving a worthy goal, and readily acknowledges that these ways are not available to religious naturalism because any specific feature in ultimate reality is determinate specifically and exhaustively in virtue of its relationship to nature. But paying attention to nature—to nature actually and not merely to idealized anthropocentric images of it—amply and potently disrupts anxious and controlling anthropomorphic images of ultimate reality. Nature, in other words, is a potent resource for iconoclastic religious naturalists. And the religious naturalist approach does not tolerate the more or less unlimited vulnerability to the exercise of absolutized and uncorrectable authority that Barth's strategy allows. In the final analysis, the religious naturalist has a profound account of ultimacy as partly known, but known as passing understanding; and also as good and true and beautiful in some senses, while in other senses expressing aesthetic and moral music utterly unscaled to human cognitive and experiential grasp.

Second, a traditional theme in South Asian theological epistemology with profound bearing on religious anthropology is *pramāṇa* theory, which concerns the epistemologically relevant factors in knowledge, and particularly religious knowledge. Different schools of Indian philosophy expressed their epistemological viewpoints by specifying which *pramāṇa* they accept and which they reject. The broad categories of *pramāṇa* theory exist thanks to an extensive tradition of philosophical debate, which stimulated an extraordinarily rich epistemological tradition. It is possible to specify the pragmatic epistemological standpoint of this book in terms of the categories and distinctions of *pramāṇa* theory as follows.

With all of the Indian schools, pragmatic epistemology accepts knowledge by means of sense perception (*pratyakṣa*), except that pragmatic naturalism rejects some aspects of the Nyāya school's interpretation of extraordinary (*alaukika*) perception, such as supernatural knowledge based on alleged Yogic powers (*yogaja*). Pragmatic naturalism also accepts knowledge by means of logical inference (*anumāna*), with all of the Indian schools, though it joins the Nyāya logicians in being cautious about causal inferences from known effects to unknown antecedents and from known antecedents to unknown effects, caveats that are very important in reasoning about the ultimate spiritual environment of human life. Pragmatic naturalism does not follow the *Advaita Vedānta* and Nyāya schools in accepting analogy and comparison as means of knowledge (*upamāna*) even though it makes extensive use of comparison to assemble information so as to structure sound inference. Comparative approaches are especially valuable for mounting inference-to-best-explanation arguments, as against direct syllogistic arguments (see Wildman 2006a, 2009). Most importantly, pragmatic naturalism rejects knowledge by means of sacred texts (*vaidika śabda* or *agama*), which is very important to *Advaita Vedānta*, and takes a cautious approach to knowledge by ordinary testimony (*laukika śabda*) because of awareness of susceptibility to cognitive error in the human species.

Third, pragmatic naturalism adopts a fallibilist, hypothetical view of knowledge that is quite alien to the foundationalist instincts of Barth's theological epistemology and difficult to express within the epistemological framework of *pramāṇa* theory. The fact that traditional religious anthropologies have typically sought perfectly certain knowledge in regard to the human condition is understandable; there is nothing more important from a practical religious point of view than to understand with confidence the spiritual condition of human beings and to know with certainty how to nurture human virtues and overcome human defects. But pragmatic naturalism takes with great seriousness the failure of foundationalist aspirations to perfect knowledge. In place of the foundationalist goal of certain knowledge, therefore, pragmatic naturalism accepts the fallibilism and thus the hypothetical status of all knowledge claims. Associated with this is the experimental quality of inquiry, which in this framework is a process of generating insightful hypotheses and then searching for corrective resources capable of improving and refining them, and perhaps giving grounds for rejecting them. Inquiry advances both through the generation of hypotheses and through their correction and rejection. This pragmatic approach to inquiry was richly developed in the early American pragmatists Charles Peirce and John Dewey (see Peirce 1940, 1958, and Dewey 1938), and has been elaborated in a variety of ways by subsequent thinkers in the pragmatist philosophical tradition (see Neville 1981, 1989, 1995, Wildman 2009).

With the epistemological and ontological framework of pragmatic religious naturalism in mind, the reader should approach the arguments about religious anthropology that I offer here as something like conceptual experiments. These experimental forays are capable of mutually reinforcing one another to support a compelling account of human beings in all aspects, including their religious behaviors, beliefs, and experiences. It is possible to develop a religious anthropology on some other understanding of the relationship between nature and its self-transcending, ecstatic ground; indeed, such alternative approaches have been extremely common in the history of theology. But this religious naturalist approach has special virtues: (i) it properly registers universal or near-universal features of the human condition, from the cultural to the biological; (ii) it integrates every discipline and level of understanding about the human condition and human nature; (iii) it naturally relates these features of human life to the depths of natural reality in such a way that the determinate character of those ecstatic depths is disclosed; (iv) it renders more conceptually consistent the religious schemas that govern the interpretation of symbols of the human condition that arise within cultural and religious spheres of wisdom; and (v) while it does not appeal to everyone, it is profoundly intellectually illuminating and spiritually rewarding for those drawn to it.

The conceptual experiments in religious anthropology that we might undertake are virtually unlimited. For example, we could focus attention on evolution, groups, justice, brains, language, cognition, emotion, meaning, bodies, sex, food, family, technology, economy, and dozens of other themes. I take up many of these topics in the chapters that follow, but space prevents taking up every possible line of religious-anthropological inquiry. The unifying theme of religious naturalism is reinforced in each chapter, however. The result is a vision of human beings as bio-social explorers in a fascinating and surprising natural environment. The structural features of this environment can be perceived, understood, and manipulated for an endless variety of purposes. The natural environment's valuational features can also be perceived, understood, and manipulated, giving human beings access not only to food and water but also to love and hate, creativity and lassitude, power and receptivity, goodness and evil, truth and lies, beauty and waste. These valuational features in their depths are the actual immediate referents, intended or not, of talk about ultimate religious objects such as Gods and Dao and Emptiness. It is in reaction to this environment, as structured and regulated and transformed by personal inclinations and social interests, that religions take on the varied forms they do. And it is in the combination of existential engagement and social context that human beings emerge as *homo religiosus*.

Conclusion

I have said that religious naturalism has the special virtue of being a generous and inclusive framework for hosting a multidisciplinary comparative inquiry into religious anthropology. I have also said that theologically more intricate interpretations of the human being as *homo religiosus* are possible. I myself have a theologically more elaborated account of religious anthropology that, unlike many alternatives, remains thoroughly consistent with the foundational interpretative posture of religious naturalism. In the name of full disclosure and also to show that a religious naturalist approach to religious anthropology is not theologically limp, I shall say a word about this theological elaboration of religious naturalism, and also ask how theologians who do not accept religious naturalism might respond to the spiritually evocative naturalist interpretation of religious anthropology I offer here.

Religious naturalism in the sense of this book stipulates the answers to some ontological questions, as we have seen, but it merely constrains without settling the theological account of ultimate realities that defines the ultimate existential and ontological environment for human life. I have concluded that the most apt theological account of ultimacy to complement a religious naturalist analysis of the human being as *homo religiosus* is apophatic mystical theology. This phrase refers to a mode of theological reflection with traces in every religious tradition having a complex literary heritage. The central claim of apophatic mystical theology is that ultimacy is essentially beyond human cognitive grasp, so that apophasis, or turning away from language, is intellectually and spiritually necessary in order to remain true to the actual character of ultimacy as we encounter it. The very opposite of anthropomorphic theological postures, apophatic mystical theology makes good *prima facie* sense, given the fact that reality appears to be enormously more complicated than human beings can appreciate at any one stage of their cultural and cognitive development. But the particular virtue of apophatic mystical theology is that it furnishes the core of a solution to the problem of religious pluralism, including the diversity of religious insights into human nature. In conjunction with a rich theory of religious symbolism, the apophatic framework has enormous explanatory power and helps to account for the way that religious traditions generate such diverse patterns of behavior, belief, and experience despite the fact that they all take their rise within the same natural world, a world with the same valuational depth structures and possibilities.

The apophatic mystical approach also boasts endlessly rich spiritual resources for the hardy explorer. It is tough spiritual territory for some, admittedly, because of its systematic resistance to reflexively anthropomorphic modes of human conceptualizing and coping. But the purpose of a framework for inquiry is not to comfort or to save but to bring understanding. In traditional South Asian terms, the landscape of an apophatically framed religious naturalism supports *karma yoga* (the way of good works) and *bhakti yoga* (the way of devotion), but first and foremost *jñāna yoga* (the way of knowledge and spiritual illumination). For the one who feels at home in its endless canyons and plains and oceans, this spiritual territory is fully and truly bracing and incites works of great mercy and courage. But its finest virtues are its sponsorship of great understanding, empathy for the differently minded, and an intellectual vision of harmonious perspectives onto kaleidoscopic axiological depths that defy final comprehension.

What are differently inclined theologians to do with this account of the manifestation of the ultimately incomprehensible depths of nature in human religion and spirituality? This view presumes that human beings are social organisms whose evolutionary heritage bestows on them the ability to engage at least some of the valuational depths of nature—a far cry from the portrayals of traditional religious anthropologies, such as created beings seeking relationship with a divine being or souls trapped in a *saṃsāric* cycle of lives. Religious naturalists embrace the images of ultimacy that result, often as a relief from the endless anthropocentrism and anthropomorphism of supranaturalist religious talk about the human condition. They also appreciate the evolutionary framework and other supports for religious naturalism, welcoming them as invitations to more authentic engagement with ultimacy. Their spiritual inclination and calling is to love not what could be and not what we long to be, but what is.

Interestingly, intelligent fundamentalists of many religions really grasp the threat of this view to their traditional religious outlook and as a consequence furiously fight evolutionary theory and other support points for religious naturalism in an attempt to protect their supranaturalist and supernaturalist religious narratives. This reaction is utterly mistaken, in my view, but at least it intelligently gauges the theological meaning of the evolutionary framework and the threat to supranaturalism of the religious naturalist framework.

Mainstream supranaturalist religious intellectuals, who constitute the majority of theologians, reject fundamentalism's brash deployment of mysteriously absolutized authority but also tend to ignore religious naturalism, or else they play down its close fit with the sciences, hoping to construct a harmonious interpretation of the human condition on their own terms. These supranaturalist theologians are faced with a problem as a result—how can they maintain supranaturalism against both fundamentalists and religious naturalists? This problem is easy to solve but the solution is costly. The easy solution is simply to reject the absolutized authority of the fundamentalists and also to establish a belt of epistemological separation between nature and ultimate reality that blocks the reasoning of the religious naturalist. This works; it has always worked. In particular, it removes the traction that forces awareness of errors in conflicting narratives about human religiousness, which allows the theologian to affirm whatever narrative structures are deemed valuable in a given religious community, safe from evidence-based contradiction either from other religious traditions or from the scientific study of religion.

For example, supranaturalist theologians can frame the personality of their determinate-entity God in such a way that it is separate from the created depth structures of nature, much as the personality of human creators is not necessarily consistent with or relevant to the character of the house they build or the pot they mould or the meal they cook. In this way, theologians block the inferences from nature to its creator that manifest contradictions. It is such contradictions—between the natural suffering of predation and chance accident and human foolishness, on the one hand, and the putative focal awareness of a loving, protective deity, on the other hand—that lead the religious naturalist away from supranaturalism. But the supranaturalist neatly blocks those lines of inference by insisting that God's creation need not match God's personality and values.

This easy solution is bought at a steep price because two kinds of cognitive dissonance just won't go away. On the one hand, this easy solution renders the problem of religious pluralism theoretically intractable. The resources needed to resolve it decisively—including identifying nature's valuational depth structures as the locus of the most reliable knowledge of ultimacy regardless of what particular religious traditions say about it in their sacred texts and narratives— are surrendered for the sake of girdling religious communities with the belt of epistemological separation between nature and ultimacy. On the other hand, the arbitrary and speculative qualities of highly meaningful religious narratives— these used to be called their mythical elements—become more and more evident as the narratives enjoy less concrete contact with our increasingly detailed understanding of nature. This manifests the social functions of religious narratives with increasing clarity, which in turn makes them seem useful but theologically arbitrary, and perhaps better criticized by theologians than loyally supported and perpetually reinterpreted.

For example, we can give our best effort in our group narrations about the supernatural souls of human beings—about their origins, journeys, and ultimate destinies—and this furnishes genuine comfort and hope, as well as some measure of true understanding and authentic engagement with ultimacy. But how do we accommodate new information? We can hold fast to our group narratives no matter what we discover about human brains, bodies, and behavior. But then the narratives are only persuasive for those in the group who are most deeply committed to the group's plausibility structures. For those eager to make sense of the whole of nature, and the human condition as a wondrous and complex aspect of the natural world, the narratives stop working, they stop bringing comfort and hope, and sometimes they seem dangerous even if they are also plainly psychologically, socially, and spiritually beneficial within the group that rehearses them. This gradual failure of persuasiveness is what fundamentalists sense that other supranaturalists often do not. But where fundamentalists stubbornly go to war over it, many other supranaturalists loyally continue to narrate their world in terms of supernatural souls and moral laws, confidently explaining what these core features of their religious anthropology express about the intentions and feelings of supranatural deities. Their never-ending stories really do tame the anomic chaos in the name of social order and spiritual comfort, of course, and they do slowly mutate, a century or two after they first confront one or another type of cognitive dissonance. That's all to the good. But a few people keep wondering about the narratives and often wander away, exploring in smaller groups, with widening eyes and broadening smiles.

Religious naturalism, an apophatic mystical view of the ultimate valuational depths of natural reality, and the insights of stakeholder disciplines from the scientific study of religion and religious studies, collectively constitute a deeply compelling framework for interpreting the human being as *homo religiosus*. While I shall not be developing the theological elaboration of apophatic mystical theology in this book, nor arguing in detail for religious naturalism but rather presupposing it, I shall explore many aspects of a religious anthropology in the context of religious naturalism in the chapters that follow.

PART II
Perspectives

CHAPTER 3

Evolution

Introduction

Any religious anthropology worth the name has to ask about the origins of religion in the human adventure. That is a sociological and psychological question, in some respects, but it is also a question about the biological evolution of human beings, and that is the focus of this chapter. Unsurprisingly, the evolutionary origin of religion is not a simple matter. In fact, there has been a lot of tangled traffic at the intersection of evolutionary theory and the scientific study of religion in recent years. This chapter analyzes and interprets this intellectual junction with a view to understanding something fundamental about the kind of creatures we human beings are.

In this chapter and throughout the book I shall take for granted the meaning of several key terms in evolutionary biology and evolutionary psychology. Keeping these terms in mind is particularly important for religionists and theologians. Words such as "fitness" and "adaptiveness" may have misleading connotations in their worlds of thought, suggesting sound psychological adjustment, empirically accurate interpretation of an environment, health-promoting lifestyles, or spiritually efficacious beliefs and practices. As important as these ideas are for understanding religion, they should not be conflated with the differential reproduction advantage associated with the concepts of fitness and adaptive function in evolutionary biology.

Fitness always refers to reproductive fitness, which means the ability of a biological entity (*organism*) to pass genetic information (*genes*) to future generations. This refers not to the number of offspring (which may be infertile or die before they reproduce, after all) but to the spread of genetic material in future generations. A simple (but not foolproof) test of fitness is whether one's offspring themselves are reproductively successful. Fitness is always relevant to an *environment*, within which a population has a *niche* where it is subject to particular *selection pressures* in the form of nutrition, disease, and predators. A key question in evolutionary biology is whether the environment relevant to fitness can include high-level social factors as well as low-level biological factors. Evolutionary psychology's core hypothesis is that social and psychological factors are relevant to evolutionary fitness.

A *trait* is a genetically based characteristic of an organism, such as eye color or a genetic propensity to cancer. I will use *characteristic* or *feature* to refer to aspects of an organism's behavior and function in general. The genetic basis of traits is an extremely complex matter because genes often influence more than one characteristic of an organism, and traits usually depend on many interacting genes. Unresolved questions about the genetic basis of organism characteristics abound, particularly in the context of evolutionary psychology where the concern is with emergent characteristics such as behaviors, emotions, and beliefs. Many behavioral characteristics can be cultivated independently of genetic makeup so it is frequently unclear whether certain behavioral features of organisms are traits in the genetic sense at all. To say that a behavioral predisposition is a trait implies that the behavioral predisposition has a genetic basis that somehow persists through cultural and contextual factors and tends to express the associated behavior in widely varying circumstances. Twin studies and adoption studies can help to decide whether a behavior has a genetic component, and thus whether the associated behavioral tendency is a trait. In human evolution, most key traits were developed in the very long Pleistocene environment of evolutionary adaptation, a hunter-gatherer lifestyle prior to settled agriculture to which I shall refer as the *ancestral environment*.

A *mutation* is a structural, molecular change in genetic material. Many mutations are irrelevant to an organism's function, at least in the short term, though presumably many unexpected things can happen in gene evolution in the long term. The most interesting sorts of mutations produce or affect traits. In evolutionary psychology, the focus is on mutations that affect cognitive and behavioral traits. An *adaptation* is a mutation or a set of mutations that increases individual fitness. Genetic change is *adaptive for a population* when it produces traits that increase the population's average fitness.

Fitness is a relative term, expressing differential reproduction advantage of one organism relative to others of the same species in the same environment, or average differential reproduction advantage of one population relative to a similar population at a different time or place or in a changed environment. There is no absolute measure of fitness. A *niche* is the ecological setting for a *species* of organisms and determines the part of the wider environment that is causally relevant to the species' fitness. A *niche resonance* is a self-reinforcing match between an adaptive trait and an environment that increases both the frequency of the trait in the population and the fitness of organisms possessing the trait. A niche resonance can link genetically distinct traits in such a way that the frequency of both traits increases in the population. This is especially important in sexual reproduction where a male trait and a female trait can reinforce one another and increase in frequency within the population even though neither trait alone would increase fitness. Niche resonances can even occur between species, particularly in *communicative environments* that permit the sending and receiving of signals between predators and prey. Evolutionary psychology proposes that niche resonances might also sponsor *gene-culture co-evolution*, a hypothetical relation between organisms and environment in which genetically linked cultural practices have a genetic influence.

Adaptive function refers to the biological or behavioral function of a genetic trait that causes it to be adaptive. A trait that decreases fitness has a *maladaptive function*; selection pressures may reduce the presence of such traits in the population. A genetic feature can be neither adaptive nor maladaptive if no selection pressure exists in a particular context to affect its presence in the population. The question of the context for assessing adaptive function and maladaptive function is a vexed one in evolutionary psychology. The *original selection context* is that in which a trait first becomes established in one or more organisms within the ancestral environment and then spreads widely through the species because of its adaptive function in that context. An established trait can also have effects other than the *primary adaptive function* for which it was selected. These effects, whether co-present already in the original selection context or appearing only much later as environmental conditions change and new traits are established, are called *side-effects* or *byproducts*. When byproduct effects serve to increase fitness independently of the primary adaptive function, the underlying trait has a *secondary adaptive function*. As with primary adaptive function, there can be *secondary maladaptive functions* and secondary functions that are neither adaptive nor non-adaptive, or *nonfunctional byproducts*.

Traits adaptive in one context can become maladaptive in a new context. Byproducts can be simultaneously adaptive, maladaptive, and non-functional with respect to different selection mechanisms. There is great deal of dynamism here as varying sets of traits interact with diverse environments. Evolutionary psychology proposes that culturally conditioned behaviors can combine with genetic traits to have genetically relevant effects, as when health care policies and technologies create reproductive opportunities for those who would not have been able to reproduce in the ancestral environment. *Sexual selection*, through mate choice, is particularly important in giving genetic relevance to culturally conditioned aspects of organisms. *Communicative environments* vastly expand the range and likelihood of trait side-effects. Some may be potentially maladaptive, as when communication allows human beings to wipe out malaria in some parts of the world, thereby reducing the presence of malaria-resistant genes and exposing larger numbers of people to a future outbreak of deadly malaria under new environmental conditions. Most side-effects are not directly exposed to selection pressures, as when human beings flip coins, cook waffles, and play cricket.

Different types of evolutionary theorists tend to focus on different contexts. Some focus on the original context for a trait's selection, some on the long-term persistence of traits through varied environments, and some on the current observable adaptive function of traits. This leads to quite different conceptual and terminological frameworks, and sometimes to a great deal of confusion. Miscommunication can be mitigated by paying attention to the question of context for claims about the adaptiveness of traits. As it happens, diverse terminological frameworks are evident in the literatures surrounding evolutionary byproducts, so I shall return to terminological and conceptual clarification when I come to that topic, below.

In this chapter I first take up evolutionary challenges to traditional religious anthropology, explaining why some have proved easier to handle than others. I then address the key question of the evolutionary status of religion. I consider the extreme views that religion has no genetic component and that religion is an adaptation rising on the back of one or two traits. I also consider the more plausible view that *religion in evolutionary terms is a combination of side-effects of both adapted and non-adapted features of the human organism*—the hypothesis defended here.

Evolutionary Challenges to Traditional Religious Anthropology

The Authority Challenge

Charles Darwin's theory of evolution confronted traditional religious anthropologies with a series of problems when it first appeared 150 years ago. Considerable uncertainty attended the scientific status of the theory for some decades, and theological reactions were quite diverse. With increasing force, however, evolutionary theory posed deep puzzles for theology.

Some were relatively easy to resolve. For example, evolutionary theory makes a literal interpretation of the Genesis, Qur'anic, Vedic, and little-known Chinese creation narratives unsustainable because of conflicts over the timing, order, and process of creation. The process of reception among religious communities and religious intellectuals of the theory of evolution was not straightforward, by any description (see Glick et al. 2006, Moore 1979). But careful historical work has shown that many religious intellectuals regarded evolution as not essentially problematic for religious assessments of the authority of sacred scriptures, and that some theologians were able to produce compelling syntheses (see Bowler 2001, Brooke et al. 2001, Cantor & Swetlitz 2006, Glick et al. 2006, Livingstone 1984, Livingstone et al. 1999, Roberts 1988). Other scientific discoveries had prepared the way, such as Charles Lyell's earlier work (1830–33) on geology, which had already made an old Earth likely in many minds. Moreover, thanks to historical and textual criticism, mainstream scholarly interpreters of the Bible had already long surrendered any expectation that the Bible could rightly be interpreted literally on scientific questions and they had learned to identify legendary and mythical elements in biblical narratives. These were complementary scientific and theological reasons to question the validity of according absolute authority to every statement in the Bible regardless of considerations of literary style, cultural formation, or historical context. Consequently, evolutionary theory was relatively unproblematic for mainstream theologians in respect of its challenge to literal readings of creation myths found in the Bible. The relationship between evolutionary theory and creation narratives in the Qur'an, the Vedas, and the sacred religious texts of other religions is still an unfolding story. In the case of Christianity in the West, and to a significant extent Judaism as well, the challenge of evolutionary theory to the Bible's authority has been absorbed and positions are now clearly staked out. Naturally, Fundamentalists for whom the absolute authority of the scriptures is an essential component of their communities' religious identities were appalled by the moderate theological consensus (see Numbers 2006).

Some other problems were not dispatched as easily as the problem of the authority of sacred texts. This is partly because there was less preparation for them than in the case of the authority problem just described, and partly because the resulting challenge reached more deeply into the roots of traditional theology and religious anthropology. I shall discuss two in what follows: the challenge to human dignity and the challenge to divine providence.

The Dignity Challenge

Human beings are the object of special divine attention in all theistic religions. The manifestations of this conviction range from Judaism's divine covenants to Hinduism's human-centered strategy for escaping *saṃsāra*, and from Islam's concept of humans as God's viceroys on Earth to Christianity's teachings of incarnation and *theosis*. The same is true of generally non-theistic religions, from Buddhism, which shares the South Asian view that *mokṣa* (liberation from *saṃsāra*) first requires transmigration at least to the point of becoming human, to Chinese religion, where the mandate of heaven is essentially and primarily relevant to human social and personal life. There is no escaping the influence of religion in this regard: universally, religious anthropologies established a lofty estimate of the spiritual dignity of human beings, sometimes to the neglect of wider nature and sometimes in harmony with it. Experiences of forgiveness, salvation, liberation, supernatural communication, and purposeful life, as well as unshakable convictions about life after death or immortal souls, powerfully reinforced this impression of human spiritual dignity, in tradition after tradition, generation after generation, believing mind after believing mind.

By contrast, the most natural interpretation of human beings in evolutionary theory is that we are neither the final purpose of evolutionary process nor its acme but merely one species among uncountably many, destined eventually to be surpassed by better adapted species, at least for as long as the ecological conditions for continued complex life on our home planet persist. This strikes at the very heart of the narratives guiding beliefs about salvation, liberation, and the theological meaning of history and nature in a host of religious traditions. A symbolic touchstone for this is the so-called Scopes "Monkey" Trial, which was documented in newspapers of the time with cartoons mocking the idea that human beings could be descended from apes (see Larson 1997). But this merely scratches the surface; most people have no problem accommodating the evolutionary picture of hominid and ape ancestry, and much older relations to other living beings from plants to bacteria.

The deeper questions about human dignity have to do with the meaning of human life. After all, if religious traditions cannot deliver an unambiguous and compelling message about the point and purpose of our existential situation that is both commensurate with the intense interest we bring to those issues and consistent with everything that we know from the sciences and from our experience, then most people have little use for them. Religious groups overwhelmingly ignore the suggestions from evolutionary theory that are dissonant with traditional religious claims about the centrality of human beings in the divine awareness and cosmic plans. In this way, religious groups deliver what the faithful expect and demand, pointing out that evolutionary theory as a scientific theory cannot dictate to theology how it should interpret the meaning of human life in divine perspective. As a result, this challenge to anthropocentric religious conceptions of human spiritual dignity remains largely undigested—even in mainstream theological work on religious anthropology for which the authority challenge is a non-issue.

The Providence Challenge

With about the same degree of difficulty as the spiritual dignity challenge, evolutionary theory gave rise to a particularly sharp form of the providence challenge. In this case, the issue is not the purpose and meaning of human life but the presence or absence of divine providence as a creative and regulative force in nature, in the history of human civilizations, and in individual human lives. In most theistic contexts, God may have created the system, but evolution requires no divine supervision to run according to its created specifications, so God's providential role is marginalized or eliminated. Non-theistic versions of the providence challenge exist, too. For example, the *saṃsāric* system in South Asian religions is guided and assured by a vast karmic law of moral cause and effect, which is either ultimately vested in the divine nature (as in Hinduism) or a standalone principle of reality (as in Buddhism). But evolutionary theory thoroughly obscures any possible basis for such cosmic moral regulation, just as it obscures the basis for divine providence. The evolutionary system cannot rule out supernatural or even wider forms of natural providence, but it has no use for those hypotheses in its own framework. Nature in the evolutionary framework is self-regulating and oblivious to moral questions of justice and judgment. Once it starts running, the kinds of species that emerge depend as much on chance events as on the natural regularities that give particular shape to the emergent structures of evolution. Focal divine action can still be asserted in this setting, of course, but the providence challenge aims elsewhere—at the very relevance of God to the natural evolutionary process that brings human beings into existence.

As with the dignity challenge, the providence challenge has not been fully unassimilated within traditional religious anthropologies. Religious naturalism greets the providence challenge warmly as helping to deliver us from anthropomorphic conceptions of ultimacy as an attentive and providentially active supernatural being, of course. But mainstream theism still struggles to find a way to make God essential to the evolutionary process, not merely as its creator, but also as an active partner in guiding and directing evolution toward the realization of providential divine ends. Accurately sensing the danger for traditional religious anthropology in the providence challenge, so-called intelligent design theorists attempt to show that evolutionary theory can't live up to its claims of operating independently of specific acts of intentional intelligent design. Their aim is to drive a wedge between evolutionary theory and its otherwise inevitable theological endpoint—which is at best religious naturalism—thereby leaving room for a concept of God as an attentive and providentially active supernatural personal being and for a concept of the human being as the special expression of divine planning and intention.

Meanwhile, theological defenders of so-called theistic evolution strive for a similar theological goal but without the implausible stretching of evidence required in intelligent design. That is, theistic evolutionists affirm the completeness of evolutionary theory on its own terms, against intelligent design theorists, but claim that the evolutionary process contains within itself a native causal intelligence that strives for complexity of the sort that is expressed in ecosystems and that is teleologically driven to produce consciousness and the particular form of spiritual awareness that human beings possess (see the discussion Dembski & Ruse 2004).

While theistic evolutionists are typically quite clear that this telic power would not figure in evolutionary explanations of human beings or anything else, they struggle to express how it should be understood on its own terms. The clearest accounts are the process views of evolution that build telic possibilities and divine providence into the very causal fabric of nature (deriving from Whitehead 1978; see Birch & Cobb 1981, Cobb 2008, Haught 2003). Other panentheistic accounts offer less metaphysical architecture than the process view but strive to affirm something similar (for example, see Clayton 2008, Peacocke 1993, with a related but not as clearly panentheistic account in Russell 1998). But all such panentheistic accounts of theistic evolution, including the process accounts, are vulnerable to the criticism that the actual results of the evolutionary process, with its false starts and design flaws, suggest that the deity in question suffers from serious competence problems.

The ultimate resolution to the providence problem is not protecting traditional claims about religious anthropology by means of intelligent design or theistic evolution but surrendering the ideas of focal divine awareness and self-conscious providential divine action. This is the path of religious naturalism. But that endpoint is firmly resisted by many theologians because of what it portends for religious anthropology. In particular, without focal divine awareness, action, and responsiveness, any semblance of the traditional meaning of divine providence seems impossible to preserve. The valuational depths of nature may be replete with aesthetic and moral possibilities that are explored and manifested in the evolutionary process, but there is no center of consciousness behind it all for the religious naturalist. Human beings are thus no longer the object of special divine purposes and plans but rather explorers in a world of marvels and disasters, making of themselves what they will. For some theologians, this is to go at least one large step too far, evacuating religious anthropology of its essentially religious content. For others, it is precisely the right move because it overcomes the distorting anthropomorphism of theistic (and also some aspects of non-theistic) religions and decisively delivers responsibility for human affairs into human hands, which is where it always properly belonged despite all religiously inspired evasions and deflections.

Evolutionary Status of Religion

If religious anthropology is somehow able to secure traditional theological claims about the centrality of human beings in either the divine attention or in non-theistic conceptions of cosmic plans, then little is at stake in the evolutionary study of the origins of religion. On this essentially conservative theological view, the meaning and value of religion derives from the truth it conveys about human life in ultimate spiritual perspective, regardless of how religion arose in history and nature. At most, knowledge about the evolution of religious traditions and ethical systems would help to explain the particular differences among those traditions, and perhaps alert us to ways that the immutable spiritual truths of religion might be vulnerable to distortions of perception and understanding. By contrast, for the religious naturalist, there is no protected domain of religious truth claims, so the evolutionary story of the origins of religion is directly relevant to assessing the meaning and value of religion, as well as religious claims about human beings.

What, then, is the evolutionary status of religion? Is religion an evolutionary adaptation, increasing fitness in and of itself and originating because of the adaptive functions of religious behaviors, beliefs, and experiences? Is religion a side-effect of a collection of adapted traits, much as language and war and commerce seem to be? Is religion a non-adapted byproduct of the evolutionary process, like the redness of blood, or perhaps a maladaptive byproduct, such as back problems that derive from erect posture? Is it possible that religion has no genetic component at all, either in its unfathomable origins or in its subsequent cultural expressions? These questions lie at the heart of the interpretation of religion within an evolutionary framework and they are also highly significant for religionists and theologians, as we shall see.

Religion as Non-Genetic

We might be tempted to think there is no genetic component to religion, despite its near universality among human beings, because we can find no way to account for the diversity of religious practices and beliefs in terms of genetic traits. Rather, on this view, we should understand religion as a culture-level response to social needs for bonding and legitimation, to the problems of deception and free-loading, and to primal experiences of transcendence, revelation, love, and death. Religion is diverse because cultural practices are genetically underdetermined, leaving lots of room for chance factors to condition the particular practices of a given group. Religion recurs across cultures and eras for the same reason that fire does: it is an effective way to deal with common challenges. We need presuppose no genetic tendency to either religion or fire. How credible is this non-genetic interpretation of religion?

The classic modern sources for the scientific study of religion include early philosophical and theological theorists such as Immanuel Kant, Georg Hegel, and Friedrich Schleiermacher; early sociologists such as Emile Durkheim and Max Weber; early psychologists such as Sigmund Freud and Carl Jung; and early crossover intellectuals such as William James. It is vital to note that these field-defining religionists worked by and large out of the non-genetic framework for understanding religion that I have just sketched. To a very large extent, the non-genetic framework for interpreting religion continues to dominate religious studies today. For example, few religious studies programs offer courses in the evolutionary psychology of religion.

In many ways, this bias toward the non-genetic does not matter much. To study the peculiar changes that crept into Buddhism when it migrated eastwards from India into China, historians work closely with documentary sources. They can do that without paying any attention to evolutionary psychology if they confine themselves to description of the changes, surely a difficult enough challenge. Yet changes in religious beliefs upon such migrations might well be affected by genetically based cognitive structures that constrain the options for how given beliefs are reframed in a new cultural context. If the historian were interested in *explaining* the changes rather than just *describing* them, and most historians do have such interests, then the evolutionary psychology of religion claims a place in the discussion.

Such thought experiments challenge prevailing assumptions in religious studies that religion is a non-genetic, culture-level phenomenon, or that its genetic linkages are irrelevant to understanding it. There is also strong evidence that some aspects of religiousness have a genetic component. (For example, see Bering 2006, Koenig and Bouchard 2006, Koenig et al. 2005.) So religionists need to start paying attention to evolutionary theories of religion on pain of irrelevance. But irrelevance cuts both ways. From the point of view of even the most elementary religious studies, the lack of nuance in evolutionary theories of religion is appalling and makes the affected scientific work irrelevant for understanding religion as such, which in turn compromises the usefulness of such scientific work for understanding even a single dissociated feature of religion.

The disconnect between evolutionary theories of religion and mainstream religious studies is quite profound and must be overcome not only for the sake of theoretical adequacy but also to improve the quality of public discourse about religion. A scientist studying a single feature of religion may not have the broad-based knowledge needed properly to appreciate manifold levels of value in religious phenomena. To have such a person speak in public about a religious controversy can be disastrously insensitive and potentially insulting to adherents of a religion. In fact, we saw unsophisticated punditry from scientists repeatedly in the widespread controversy over the September 30, 2005 Danish publication, and subsequent republication in over fifty other countries, of caricatures of the Prophet

Muhammad. It is religious studies specialists who best understand religions and their internal and external battles. Yet the evolutionary study of religion casts many contemporary religious controversies into a fascinating and informative light that may eventually help to explain group identity struggles better than sociology alone. The quality of public discourse about religion demands that, if hard scientists are not going to learn religious studies, some religious studies specialists need to overcome their "genetics does not matter" mentality and seek to learn about the evolutionary interpretation of religion and the brain.

Religion as an Adaptation

On the spectrum of theories about the evolutionary status of religion, the view that religion is an evolutionary adaptation lies at the opposite end from the non-genetic view. The *adaptation explanation* says both that genetic predispositions to specifically religious beliefs and behaviors increased average fitness in the ancestral environment and that the primary adaptive functions of these beliefs and behaviors are precisely what caused the genetic predispositions originally to become well-established, and eventually virtually ubiquitous, in the human population.

This is a bold claim, considering that we cannot inspect the ancestral environment to check its accuracy. But we are not totally confined to speculative reconstructions of how things went down in the savanna prior to 50,000 years ago. Adaptationists assume that the beliefs and behaviors associated with religion-inducing traits were expressed in ancestral environments in ways similar to today. This assumption is implausible if we think the challenges that originally provoked religious beliefs and behaviors no longer obtain. But it is plausible if we have reason to believe that those behaviors solved similar evolutionary challenges consistently across different evolutionary contexts. In that case, we can indirectly inspect the original selection context by directly examining selected religious beliefs and behaviors in the contemporary world. Research on the evolutionary origins of religion as an adaptation can then be accomplished by studying how tightly connected religious beliefs and behaviors are to genetic traits in the current context. This involves twin and adoption studies to isolate genetic from environmental contributions to religious belief and behavior (for example, Koenig and Bouchard 2006, Koenig et al. 2005). It also increasingly involves neurogenetic studies, though these sorts of studies are currently highly speculative and controversial (for example, Hamer 2004). But it is crucial for the adaptationist's case that the relevant genetic traits induce specifically religious beliefs and underlie specifically religious practices—as against other, non-religious beliefs and practices that might play a role in solving social problems among savanna hunter-gatherers.

In this way, we might try to construct the evidential foundations for a theory of the evolution of religion as an adaptation: religion rides on the back of specifically religious beliefs and behaviors that are tightly linked to genetic traits, with the traits selected for by virtue of the problem-solving usefulness of the associated beliefs and behaviors. Around this core of belief-inducing and behavior-promoting genetic traits there may be a complex accretion of side-effect behaviors and cognitive tendencies that are not as tightly linked to genes and therefore can account for the massive variation in religious expression across cultures and eras. The adaptive functions of core religious beliefs and behaviors would produce observable structural similarities in all religious phenomena, however, and perhaps even specific religious beliefs and behaviors that are universal or nearly universal across the wealth of religious expressions. On this view, we could and should define religion in terms of these core genetically linked behaviors. (Startlingly, we have here the promise of a relatively objective part-solution to the religionist's unending problem of trying to define religion.)

The adaptation explanation is helpfully vulnerable to correction. Simply look for evidence of structural factors that persist through religious phenomena. Religionists have discovered few such universal factors, and most that have been discovered seem not to be distinctively tied to religion but rather seem to be generic features of human cultural activity. For example, religion is universally a group phenomenon, in part, but so is cultural activity in general. This weighs against the adaptationist explanation of religion. But perhaps religionists have not been looking in the right places or for the right universal features. Cooperation between evolutionary theorists and specialists in the study of religion might turn up stronger evidence to support the adaptationist case.

Relatively few theorists explicitly defend in print the idea that religion as a whole or in large part is a genetic adaptation. Yet many evolutionary psychologists attack adaptationism as a theory of the origins of religion as if this view had a lot of supporters. Perhaps this is a vengeful expression of frustration that the adaptationist line is so easy for the general public to grasp that oversimplified adaptationist views, rather then their more complex competitors, typically make the front pages of news magazines and television documentaries. The title of Dean Hamer's (2004) book says everything we need to know about the popular cachet of adaptationist readings of religion: *The God Gene: How Faith is Hardwired into Our Genes*. Even when books do not argue explicitly for religion as an adaptation, publishers often insist on oversimplified titles that suggest the eminently comprehensible adaptationist position, as in Matthew Alper's (1996) *The "God" Part of the Brain*, which comes complete with the neurological modularist's favorite sort of image on the cover: a brain scan with a small patch lit up (presumably with spiritual illumination). A similar adaptationist oversimplification happened in the press's reception of V.S. Ramachandran's work on a temporal lobe brain area that seems connected to religious experiences, reportedly to Ramachandran's great dismay (see Ramachandran 2004; Ramachandran & Blakeslee 1998).

Hamer is more cautious than his many critics often allow, but he does seem to want to argue for religion as an adaptation, so it is worth noting the weakness of his argument (Hamer is aware of the difficulty but risks it for the sake of speculatively articulating a bold hypothesis). He claims to find a correlation between a point mutation on a single gene (VMAT2) and small differences on surveys about self-transcendence experiences (see Hamer 2004 for the details).

But this is not the same as providing an argument for religion as an adaptation. Most obviously, the mutated gene may have evolved for reasons having nothing to do with religion, whereafter its religious significance (such as it is) kicks in as a side-effect, and nothing is gained for the adaptation case. Unfortunately, Hamer does not investigate this alternative, so his argument for religion as an adaptation is weaker than he would like. Not holding anything back, Carl Zimmer in his *Scientific American* review of the book suggests an alternative title for *The God Gene*: "A Gene That Accounts for Less Than One Percent of the Variance Found in Scores on Psychological Questionnaires Designed to Measure a Factor Called Self-Transcendence, Which Can Signify Everything from Belonging to the Green Party to Believing in ESP, According to One Unpublished, Unreplicated Study" (Zimmer 2004). Evidently, we need clear criteria for establishing that something is an adaptation.

Criteria for Adaptation

Steven Pinker (2006) takes up the theme of adaptation as applied to the origins of religion. He helpfully lists four adaptationist explanations for the pervasiveness of religious belief: religious beliefs are adaptive because (i) they truly describe the environment of human life; (ii) they bring comfort; (iii) they forge unified communities; or (iv) they answer our need for moral values. His discussion of these four explanations is brief and mainly serves to indicate that he is more interested in explaining religion as a byproduct of a host of behaviorally linked genetic traits. I agree with Pinker's preferred approach, so I am ready to appreciate his arguments against these four adaptationist perspectives.

In relation to (i), Pinker rightly treats as an empirically testable hypothesis religion's claim that its beliefs describe reality. But he considers only the theistic type of religion and only one type of theism, the one most vulnerable to falsification because it is strongly oriented to moral confidence and hope for a better world (i.e. a personal, caring, judging God). And then he dismisses all religious beliefs because of the empirical inadequacy of this particular worldview. While I happen to concur with Pinker about the empirical implausibility of "a personal, attentive, invisible, miracle-working, reward-giving, retributive deity," I also think it is tendentious to choose this as the only representative of religious belief worth mentioning in the quest to test the empirical claims of religion. I would be glad to see a patient evaluation of the more theoretically persuasive, if less popular, forms of religious belief, the ones historically adopted by intellectuals because of their empirical adequacy, among other reasons. Some of these are broadly theistic, as in Aristotle's and Plato's worldviews, and the philosophical theisms of Neoplatonism and South Asian religion. Others are non-theistic, as in philosophically refined versions of Buddhism, Daoism, and Confucianism. And religious naturalism is another kind of alternative, which (as I pointed out in the previous chapter) can be seen as both theistic and non-theistic depending on the theoretical context. These belief systems are intellectually and existentially profound and empirically far more robust than the one Pinker appoints as the sole representative of "religious belief."

In relation to (ii) and (iii), Pinker allows that religion may bring comfort to some people and may unite communities but rejects these as adaptationist explanations of religion because they do not establish why the characteristics in question are adaptive or, if they are, why their adaptive functions were the cause for the fixing of genetic predispositions to the associated beliefs and behaviors. In other words, the comforting and bonding elements of religion are available to all explanations of religion, including the non-genetic approaches, and all will make use of them to explain why religion persists, so the adaptationist can only make special claim on them if he or she also shows that these features of religion are adaptive in the original selection context in their specifically religious forms. This involves showing that other, non-religious ways of getting access to the same comforting and group-bonding benefits are either impossible or less adaptive than the religious ways.

Unfortunately, Pinker's criticisms of these two adaptationist explanations of religion merely asks for more detail and does not acknowledge that a lot more detail already exists in the literature on the subject. For example, Pinker asserts that we have no reason to think that religious beliefs could induce people to cooperate. But he does not say what is wrong with one of the core assertions of the "religion is adaptive because it facilitates cooperation" position, namely, that religion causes people to believe that their private thoughts are transparent to a supernatural power with an interest in preventing deception and promoting group loyalty (see, for example, Bering 2006). In the right social context, a person demonstrating such beliefs will be trusted by potential mates and the wider community alike, and thus is more likely to have an opportunity to reproduce, passing along whatever genetic component plays into his or her predisposition to this sort of religious belief (see Sosis 2006, which explores this at length). These and related themes recur in the literature on the evolutionary psychology of religion and it is unfortunate that Pinker does not address them but merely assumes they carry no argumentative weight.

In relation to (iv), Pinker argues that the idea of a retributive, human-like deity plays no role in our best explanations of the logic of morality. But this depends on which logic of morality we accept. I think the sociology of knowledge's interpretation of the role of morality in the social construction of reality is highly persuasive, particularly as elaborated in Peter Berger's interpretation of religion as in part a means of legitimation and social control (see Berger 1967). Sociologist Émile Durkheim anticipates and inspires many of the insights of the sociology of knowledge (see Durkheim 1915), including its recognition of religion as the means by which groups codify their core moral commitments. Similarly, Immanuel Kant's account of the natural logic of human moral reasoning demands a religious framework for moral reasoning to be rational and practical: our moral reasoning presumes (but cannot prove) standards of right and wrong vested in an ultimate moral judge who has the power to reward and punish (see Kant 1993). Kant and Durkheim and Berger cannot easily be swept aside. I consider religion's role in moral reasoning and practical moral activity to be one of the strongest arguments for religion as an adaptation, but its strength derives essentially from group-bonding and cooperation considerations, and from comfort considerations having to do with moral orientation and the management of cognitive dissonance—the second and third points on Pinker's list.

Despite these difficulties, the main point of Pinker's argument is well taken. The fact that claims of adaptiveness are challenging to support in any domain makes the idea of religion as an adaptation difficult to establish. He mentions three criteria for a trait to be an adaptation. The first two are more or less obvious: the trait has to be innate and it must increase a population's average fitness in the ancestral environment. Pinker's third criterion is more complex because it concerns the epistemology of evidence as much as biology: arguments for the supposed increase in average fitness because of the putatively adaptive trait do not count if they take the form of suspiciously convenient explanations ("just-so" stories). Rather, the arguments must justify the usefulness of the trait with independently convergent evidence from several perspectives. That is, arguments that some aspect of religion increases average fitness in a population have to be based not only on our ability to imagine their practical usefulness in an ancestral environment but also on evidence from some independent field, such as cognitive science or biomechanical engineering. This criterion quite properly functions as a burden shifting principle, defining what counts as a satisfactory argument for average fitness increase because of a trait, and therefore setting the bar high for claims that religion is an adaptation.

Attempts to clear Pinker's high bar are sometimes made. For example, in one of the more aggressive arguments for religion as an adaptation, Bulbulia (2006) hypothesizes that religiosity is an adaptation for health and cooperation. He makes his case, and meets Pinker's criterion in doing so, by arguing not just on the basis of imaginative speculation about the era of human evolutionary adaptation, but also with reference to anthropological and medical evidence about the health benefits of hypnotizability and dissociative states that religion supposedly promotes in the forms of it that are most relevant to the era of evolutionary adaptation.

Religion as an Evolutionary Byproduct

There is overwhelmingly strong evidence against the extreme view that no aspect of religion is genetically related or evolutionarily conditioned. Similarly, the evidence for religion as an adaptation so narrows the focus to one or two adapted "religion" traits that only a fraction of the varied phenomena of religion are registered in the explanation. It seems highly likely, therefore, that the evolutionary explanation for the origins of the multifaceted reality of religious behaviors, beliefs, and experiences must lie somewhere between these extremes. Religion, in other words, is evolutionarily conditioned, possibly in a few special respects by virtue of the adaptiveness of specifically religious traits, but in most respects by virtue of side-effects of traits adapted for some other, primarily and originally non-religious, purpose. We turn, then, to the endlessly complicated subject of evolutionary side-effects.

Evolutionary Side-Effects

There are many examples of side-effects of adaptive traits that solve problems in ancestral environments, and perhaps also in contemporary cultural settings, and thus turn out to have a secondary adaptive function even though this is not the reason that the underlying traits were originally selected. Language and commerce are standard examples in the literature. In fact, even if side-effects have no subsequent adaptive function, or prove to be maladaptive, they may still be culturally important. For example, war is probably a side-effect of genetic predispositions to violence, especially among men, combined with the challenges of resource scarcity and possibly our inability to control powerful emotions, and it seems mostly maladaptive as a form of behavior, being extremely costly with questionable benefits in most cases.

Such side-effects are very common in evolution, indeed far more numerous than direct adaptations. This only makes sense as follows: as biological systems get more complex and carry more information, the number of potential trait interactions increases exponentially, well beyond the prodigiously high information limits of DNA. It is in this fuzzy world of trait interactions that most of culture comes to life. Cultures are diverse because they explore in different ways the vast space of human behavioral tendencies made possible by trait interactions. They take advantage of the human learning capacity and the opportunities presented by random events to determine quite different beliefs and behaviors, moral norms and social conventions, languages and life patterns. Most evolutionary psychologists seem to believe that it is in this space of possibilities that religion finds its origins. There are many theoretical frameworks for articulating precisely how this occurs, however, and there is considerable controversy within evolutionary psychology over which theoretical framework is correct.

Some of the questions that recur in disputes over the evolutionary origins of religion as a side-effect are as follows. (i) Given the complexity of religion, which features of religion are we are talking about in any given claim about its evolutionary origins? (ii) How can we design experiments to yield unambiguous determination of genetic traits having religious beliefs and behaviors as their side-effects? (iii) Given that the ancestral environment is no longer with us, how can we discern adaptive function in the original selection context of traits subsequently having religious beliefs and behaviors as their side-effects in the contemporary world? (iv) Were secondary adaptive functions of traits having religious beliefs and behaviors as their side-effects evident from the beginning, even in the original selection context, or did those secondary adaptive functions only appear later, in changed environments? (v) Did religious beliefs and behaviors ever have a secondary adaptive function or have they always been non-adapted or maladaptive? (vi) Is it possible that some features of religion directly increased fitness in the original selection context, and thus were adaptive, while other features were side-effects with secondary adaptive functions? (vii) Can we place the entire research enterprise of the evolutionary origins of religion on firmer evidential foundations?

These are enormously complicated questions and the evolutionary psychology of religion is in some disarray partly because of their complexity. Terminological inconsistency plagues the literature, sometimes reflecting unclear concepts. A number of theorists have attempted to come to the rescue, offering key definitions in an attempt to furnish a solid foundation for evolutionary psychology and to tame the zoo of crazy concepts and tangled terms. Stephen Jay Gould has been a particularly important figure because of his coining of the two terms "spandrel" (Gould and Lewontin 1979) and "exaptation" (Gould and Vrba 1982), the latter matching what Charles Darwin (1859) described as the shifting functions of traits over evolutionary history. Gould's pluralistic approach to evolution was aimed at overthrowing what he saw as a selectionist-and-adaptationist-oriented orthodoxy and instilling an awareness of the prodigiously complex space of possibilities opened up by emergent complexity in the evolutionary process. Thus, Gould championed the idea of evolutionary side-effects and pluralism of evolutionary mechanisms, along with evolutionary theorists such as Richard Lewontin, as far back as the 1970s. Since then, tidying-up efforts have improved the conceptual clarity of key terms but some terminological confusion persists.

Buss and colleagues (1998) explain this persistence of confusion by pointing out that sociologists, psychologists, anthropologists, and biologists working in evolutionary psychology—and I add the few religionists with this interest—typically have little or no training in evolutionary biology and can get caught in the terminological difficulties. It is virtually impossible for an outsider to penetrate very far into the extremely technical literature on the subject, with its vast arrays of evidence and intricate argumentation. It is nowhere truer than in evolutionary theory that a little knowledge can be a dangerous thing—of course, religionists would rightly say that a little knowledge of religion is a dangerous thing, also. Terminological differences having potentially serious conceptual implications are common even among evolutionary specialists. This is the case with terms such as exaptation, spandrel, and functionless byproduct, for example. I am sure there are good reasons for any lexicon of terms. For the sake of consistency, and to honor the one who coined most of the key terms, here I follow Gould (1991), as enhanced and corrected by Buss et al. (1998)—though I note the objections to Buss et al. (1998) advanced by Kennair (2002) and others.

The key terms for describing evolutionary side-effects are exaptation, spandrel, and functionless byproduct. Table 1 distinguishes these three concepts from one other and from adaptation, and indicates how common each is in the real world, reflecting the argument above that complexity exponentially increases in space of possibilities for trait interaction.

Table 1 Factors discriminating key terms that evolutionary psychologists use to describe the evolutionary status of a biological or behavioral feature

	Adaptation	**Exaptation**	**Spandrel**	**Functionless byproduct**
Corresponds to a trait with an adaptive function that caused the trait to become fixed in the original selection context	Yes	No	No	No
Corresponds to a trait with a secondary adaptive function in the original selection context or in some subsequent evolutionary context	Possibly	Yes	No	No
Does not correspond to a trait but has a secondary adaptive function in the current context of study	Possibly	Possibly	Yes	No
Relative frequency in human life within the current context of study as postulated by theorists	Rare	Common	Very common	Virtually ubiquitous

Brief discussions of exaptation, spandrel, and functionless byproduct will illumine these distinctions. Gould's definition of exaptation has become the standard for both use and abuse, and I present it here using terms already discussed. An *exaptation* is a feature of an organism that originated not as an adaptation but as a side-effect of an adaptation that proved (often much later) to have a secondary adaptive function (see Gould 1991; Gould and Vrba 1982). Gould spoke of *cooption* to describe the way evolution makes use of a secondary adaptive function.

Named for the more or less unprogrammed parts of an architectural design, Gould defined a *spandrel* as a side-effect of biological features that were never selected for their usefulness even in the original selection context and yet subsequently prove to possess an adaptive function in a new evolutionary context (see Gould and Lewontin 1979). One of his examples is a bridge that was not designed with shelter in mind but subsequently provides shelter to homeless people.

Spandrels and exaptations collectively do not account for side-effects with no adaptive functions in any later environment. Buss et al. (1998), in refining Gould's distinctions, called these *functionless byproducts*. Of course, there are also a host of *random effects* in evolutionary biology, and these play a role in all of these concepts, including functionless byproducts. Similarly, biology and context jointly present *constraints* that profoundly affect evolutionary design (for example, there seem to be only two basic ways of connecting optic nerves to eyes—from behind or from the front), and constraints figure in all of these concepts too.

This lexicon of key terms situates spandrels in a middle space between exaptations and functionless byproducts. On the one side, spandrels share with exaptations the functional characteristic of increasing fitness in some evolutionary environment, but spandrels differ from exaptations in being side-effects of non-adapted characteristics, whereas exaptations are side-effects of adapted traits. On the other side, spandrels share with functionless byproducts the same evolutionary origins as side-effects of non-adapted traits, but spandrels proved to be useful in the sense of increasing fitness in some evolutionary context whereas functionless byproducts never did, or at least do not in the context assumed in a given study.

Religion: Exaptation, Spandrel, or Functionless Byproduct?

The *multidimensional byproduct explanation* for religious beliefs and behaviors has proved important because it is so difficult to show that religion is an adaptation, because it is so implausible that religion has no genetic component whatsoever, and because religious phenomena are so multifaceted. Adaptation arguments for religious behaviors, beliefs, and experiences *as a whole* fail because there is too much to explain. They also fail because genetic predispositions to beliefs and behaviors are not uniquely tied to specifically religious beliefs and behaviors but affect many other domains also. Similarly, genetic predispositions to violence are not uniquely connected with war, genetic predispositions to appreciate beauty are not uniquely connected with art, and genetic predispositions to inquire are not uniquely connected with science. Yet war, art, and science can affect and obviously have affected fitness in a variety ways.

The same applies to religion. One much talked about feature of some religious beliefs concerns supernatural agents, a theme we shall take up in a later chapter. It is extremely difficult to show that the cognitive predisposition to believe in supernatural causes is an adaptation. Rather, this tendency probably derives from more basic cognitive strategies that are demonstrably adaptive but not uniquely tied to religious beliefs—cognitive strategies such as overactive pattern recognition skills and the readiness to impute intentionality to hard-to-interpret natural events. These abilities had an adaptive function in the ancestral environment because they enabled us, for example, to interpret movements in bushes as potentially dangerous and thereby helped us to escape predators. Overactive pattern recognition skills routinely led and still lead to cognitive error, to be sure, including running away from bushes when the wind rather than a tiger caused the rustling, but they can still be adaptive. Religious-cognitive error can sometimes increase fitness, namely (according to Bulbulia 2004, 2006), by furnishing access to health-promoting placebo benefits. It follows that religious beliefs and behaviors grounded in these cognitive capacities can be understood as sometimes adaptive side-effects of traits originally adapted for non-religious functions—that is, as exaptations.

An evolutionary psychologist might conclude that some aspect of religion is a spandrel rather than an exaptation. In that case, the argument concerns the original selection context for the features whose side-effects underlie the religious phenomenon in question. If those features were based in traits that were originally selected for some other adaptive function, and now have a secondary adaptive function in religion, then we have an exaptation. If those features were not based in traits that were selected for some other adaptive function, but rather were combinations of side-effects of evolutionary design, springing from chance events and merely expressing certain design constraints, then we have a spandrel. Of course, if you trace a spandrel back through its chain of dependencies far enough, you do find traits adapted for something somewhere, just as most family trees contain an aristocrat and a criminal. In this sense, the line between spandrels and exaptations is unclear. A good illustration of this difficulty is the possibility of gene-culture evolution in relation to religion (for example, see Ilkka Pyysiäinen 2001, 2006), where cultural practices actually alter the selection constraints on genes. But it is still important to recognize that features of religion can be more and less remote from adapted traits. Adaptations just are adapted traits. Exaptations are side-effects tightly linked to genes, with the side-effect possibly co-occurring in the original selection context, though never the cause of the fixing of the trait. Spandrels are more remote side-effects with secondary adaptive functions.

The distinction between exaptations and spandrels seems to have little bearing on the way religionists understand religion, as fascinating and important as this distinction may be in evolutionary biology generally. Much more important for religious studies is the distinction between both of these ideas and functionless byproducts. The functionless byproduct explanation of religion is a relatively rare viewpoint because most theorists readily grant that religion helps to catalyze group cohesion and to solve social problems ranging from deception to free-loading. The eventual adaptiveness of religion seems obvious at the social level, therefore, even when we cannot agree on whether religion is an adaptation or an exaptation or a spandrel, and even when we can't generate consensus around what are the relevant genetic traits and how closely they are tied to religious beliefs and behaviors. The functionless byproduct viewpoint is most common among those who believe the moral downside of religious beliefs and behaviors outweighs its strategic social benefits. This passionate anti-religious position has an opposing twin in the equally passionate pro-religious view that denies any genetic component in religion at all on the grounds (quite mistaken, I think) that a genetic link would evacuate religion of its spiritual value and sacred character.

The contemporary value of religious beliefs and behaviors is a point of great moment for religionists and theologians alike, and it has enormous political and social significance. Detractors of religion have argued for centuries that we should eliminate religion, or a large part of religion, because it is bad for people. Similar arguments about toxic religion are quite common today among the so-called new atheists (for example, see Dawkins 2007, Harris 2007, Hitchens 2007). One way this is done these days is to argue that the toxicity of religion is a result of its being maladaptive or a functionless byproduct of the evolutionary process. In such cases, the assumption is that adaptive function is valuable and good whereas we can dispose of evolutionary byproducts with no adaptive function without any loss of value. This assumption is pointedly evident when, for example, Pinker (2006) asks how a powerful taste for apparently irrational beliefs could evolve, or Bulbulia (2006) interprets religious beliefs exclusively in the framework of cognitive error.

Religionists and theologians—including scholars with no religious affiliation—tend to find these sorts of characterizations of religious belief outrageous and inexcusable. To be completely direct about this, I think such criticisms are well earned in a few cases. Certainly, the logical problems with such patterns of valuation are obvious. If adapted function really is good and maladaption or non-adaptation really is bad then moral consistency demands a eugenics program to optimize adapted function, understood in some way—no doubt a ridiculous and dangerous way given the abominable history of social Darwinism and eugenics programs (see Kevles 1995). If value accrues through adaptive function but not through functionless byproducts then most cultural artifacts are relegated to the low-value bargain basement bin because they have not been around long enough to have had much effect on human genes. So much for glorious cooking, fabulous new-year fireworks, and awe-inspiring architecture.

I think religionists and theologians should go to war over these issues with the few ideologically extreme scientists guilty of such errors. That is certainly preferable to bending over backwards trying to be tolerant, perhaps because religionists condescendingly think that scientists can't be expected to understand the multidimensionality of value, or because religionists are cowed by science's current cultural prestige—which, I note with concern, is capable of being squandered if a few shrill scientists do not learn to speak in public about religion with greater depth of awareness. It is important to remember at this point that this sharp criticism is being leveled by a religionist and theologian already inclined to see human religion in many respects as a kind of agonized striving against the difficulties and uncertainties of life, full of cognitive self-deception, and typically blissfully unaware of the social forces and cognitive predispositions that drive it. Despite this religious and moral critique of religious beliefs and behavior, I am deeply moved by the empirical fact that religion has genuine value for vast numbers of people. Moreover, this value is assessable independently of any considerations of evolutionary fitness. In other words, my criticism is not religious special pleading but a demand for more intellectual sophistication across the board.

Spleen vented, I note that religionists and theologians still stand to learn a great deal from scientists about the origins of religion by studying its adaptive functions, both in the original selection context and in subsequent evolutionary environments. But little is gained for the religionist or the theologian by mastering the intricate debates over adaptations versus exaptations versus spandrels because little depends on the details of how religion evolved once it is granted that religion is in fact partly the product of evolutionary processes. The general fact that religion is partly the product of evolutionary processes proves to be the most salient point for any religious anthropology.

Religion as a Collection of Multiple Byproducts

One of the most compelling theoretical efforts to determine the evolutionary status of religion is that of Lee Kirkpatrick (2004), who argues that religion is a complex combination of side-effects that have a variety of adaptive functions. He builds this case on the basis of attachment theory, which is the heart of his constructive theoretical viewpoint. For my purposes here, the most interesting point is that Kirkpatrick is particularly good at saying why adaptationist explanations of religion fail.

Kirkpatrick's (2006) attack on adaptationist explanations of religion is entertaining and insightful. He begins by showing how slender the evidence is for the adaptationist view, especially God Modules (Alper 1996, Ramachandran & Blakeslee 1998) and God Genes (Hamer 2004), which I have already mentioned. He then points out that the adaptationist view faces serious theoretical problems. For instance, he shows that adaptationists by the nature of the case have to explain religion through one or maybe two adaptive traits, so that they inevitably end up focusing on certain bits of religion and leaving other pieces out. They might focus on a particular neural capacity for one sort of religious experience but leave out other sorts of religious experience as well as group bonding and morality, or else they emphasize cognitive susceptibility to supernatural beliefs but neglect ritual and compassionate behaviors. Kirkpatrick further argues that adaptationists tend to conflate the psychological benefits of religion with reproductive fitness, they often underestimate the fitness costs of alleged religious adaptations, and they remain tantalizingly vague on the key question of the mechanisms by which religious traits get selected for their specifically religious adaptive function—all elementary mistakes in evolutionary theory. With these problems in view, it is no wonder that Kirkpatrick concludes that religion is an evolutionary byproduct, arising on the back of countless psychological mechanisms whose evolutionary history is largely independent of any special religious purposes.

As I noted earlier, it is more difficult to locate *bona fide* defenders of the religion-as-adaptation view than one might suspect, given the frequency with which they are attacked. Unfortunately, Kirkpatrick (2006) does not cite many, or any, *bona fide* defenders of the religion-as-adaptation view, despite saying often enough that God modules and God genes are "commonly cited" as reasons to think that religion is an adaptation. He mentions Hamer (2004), but even Hamer acknowledges that the case for religion-as-adaptation is difficult to make out, and Kirkpatrick himself notes this. I suspect that this lack of cited opponents is evidence of a difference between what gets published in evolutionary psychology and the way evolutionary psychologists talk—a distinction needed to make sense of discourse in many disciplines. Or perhaps Kirkpatrick is indirectly attacking the media frenzy around the religion-as-adaptation view, which reflects the public's fondness for oversimplified pictures of complex phenomena.

Be that as it may, the case against adaptation is well made. Kirkpatrick's argument definitely shifts the burden of proof to his opponents, showering them with challenges to meet in order to justify any claim that an aspect of religious behaviors, beliefs, and experience is an adaptation.

Conclusion: *Homo Religiosus* and Evolution

Understanding religion in evolutionary terms predominantly as a combination of side-effects of both adapted and non-adapted features of the human organism, possibly with a few directly adapted features, is the hypothesis I regard as possessing the most *prima facie* plausibility, for the reasons I have presented. This hypothesis has pervasive effects in a religious anthropology.

First, and most obviously, this view rules out the oversimplified but popular view of human religiousness as somehow separate from genes, a kind of supernaturally established ability that has nothing to do with our evolutionary heritage and everything to do with our eternal essence. At this point in the development of the scientific study of religion, this extreme view is completely lacking in persuasive evidence and now essentially defunct. Yet it remains quite common in traditional religious anthropologies. For example, mainstream Hinduism, today as in centuries past, interprets the human being as a supernatural soul, or *jīva*, on an exhausting journey of transmigration from which the soul seeks escape (*mokṣa*). While the concept of *karma* makes the entire scheme causally intelligible and morally just, the *jīva* idea supplies the continuity of identity needed to link one bodily life to the next. The Buddhist rejection of *jīva* as a violation of the principle of *anātman* (no own being) obscures the doctrine of transmigration and its karmic underpinnings: what is it that links one life to the next, and what seeks *mokṣa* from *saṃsāra*, if there is no human essence that transcends and outlasts any particular life? This ancient South Asian theological dispute drives home the dependence of the transmigration theory, and the associated religious interpretation of the human condition, on a core metaphysical essence that has nothing to do with evolutionary theory. Much the same is true for religious anthropologies built around supernatural souls where reconciliation and fellowship with a deity rather than transmigration and enlightenment supply the dynamic tension.

The theory of evolution produces such a strong emphasis on human embodiment that it inevitably sits awkwardly with any view that regards the essentially human as something other than bodily in character—a point taken up in detail in a later chapter. The traditional Hindu view of the human as essentially religious by virtue of its ontological character as a supernatural *jīva* was asserted long before evolutionary theory, of course. The same is true of all traditional religious anthropologies that assert an indestructible supernatural soul as the core of human nature—and most do this. So the question is what happens to these traditional views of the essential human nature *after* they confront evolutionary theory. Can they be reframed for an evolutionary context, without difficulty or theoretical artificiality? If not, then the credibility of supernatural theories of the human soul takes a fatal blow. Could this be all that is required to rule out such traditional supernaturalist religious anthropologies—simply pointing out that they contradict evolutionary theories of human embodiment?

As a religious naturalist, I would not be unhappy to overturn supernatural views of a human soul in this or any other way. But in fact some such views have shown considerable resilience in the face of evolutionary theory. For example, within Christianity, the Roman Catholic Church in its official teachings on religious anthropology has made a relatively robust evolutionary adjustment to its traditional view of the human being as essentially a supernatural soul. The current official Catholic position affirms that evolution occurs in whatever way scientists conclude it does, and rules out origins of the human spirit either in emergence or as an epiphenomenon of material organization. It also insists that evolutionary cannot explain the essence of the human being, that supernatural divine action must operate somehow through the evolutionary process to guide it (not in the sense of intelligent design but in the sense of theistic evolution), and that human beings are spiritual fundamentally by virtue of the divine infusion of a supernatural soul (see John Paul II 1996). This accommodation creatively unites traditional religious belief with scientific developments in such a way that the resulting religious anthropology remains unfalsifiable by science and preserves the basis for Catholic moral teaching about human dignity. Similarly, in the South Asian *jīva–karma–saṃsāra–mokṣa* framework, while the interaction with evolutionary theory is relatively new compared to the Catholic case, it appears feasible to regard evolutionary embodiment as a premier instance of karmic entrapment, thereby making a virtue of evolutionary embodiment to *enhance* the traditional *jīva* view of human nature (see Gosling 2007).

Neither of these two moves entirely eliminates awkwardness in the confrontation of traditional supernatural-soul anthropologies with evolutionary theory. The Catholic supernatural soul-infusion view appears to be an hypothesis without any concrete application, and could be dispensed with if some other basis were secured for moral teachings about human dignity (and surely this is possible). And the South Asian supernatural *jīva* view has great difficulty linking the moral cause of one life to karmic effects in the next when it interposes evolution as the basis for embodiment. The causal factors operative in evolutionary theory appear to yield satisfactory explanations of the physical, moral, and spiritual character of individual human beings without any need to appeal to another karmic layer of causal influence. It appears, therefore, that evolutionary theory does not simply eliminate supernatural religious anthropologies so much as decrease their plausibility by showing that they are dependent on theoretically superfluous supernatural premises.

Second, understanding religion in evolutionary terms as a combination of side-effects of both adapted and non-adapted features of the human organism also rules out oversimplified views of religion as determined by one or two genetic features adapted for specifically religious purposes. In recent times such views tend to base religion on one of three types of core evolutionarily rooted traits. First, we see views of human religion that stress the neural capacity for a particular type of religious experience such as union of the self with its entire environment (Newberg et al. 2001), near-death and mystical experiences (Strassman 2001), or feeling the presence of a disembodied being (Persinger 1987). Second, we see views that treat the evolutionary powerhouse of religion as a cognitive tendency to form beliefs about supernatural beings (see Atran 2002, Bering 2006), to learn and pass on stories of a particular counterintuitive kind (see Boyer 2001), or to appreciate God beliefs from some other indeterminate but genetic reason (see Hamer 2004). Third, we see views that base religion on a capacity for a particular type of social interaction such as scapegoating behavior (see Girard 1972), altruistic love (see Post et al. 2002), or social regulation (see Berger 1967).

By itself, this list is self-canceling, undermining the "core of religion" thesis by serving up too many candidates with similar degrees of credibility. It is more useful as an indication of the large number of neural, cognitive, and social elements that combine in religious behaviors, beliefs, and experiences. Adopting a view in the large territory between the implausible extremes throws the theologian developing a religious anthropology into the tangled jungle of evolutionary theory, including evolutionary psychology, animal signaling theory, and the never-ending struggle to discriminate nature from nurture. This is the right place to be because nothing less complex can properly register the intricate diversity of religious behaviors, beliefs, and experiences that religionists have documented. But it is challenging intellectual territory requiring careful equilibration of a large array of features of human religiousness and a rich suite of evolutionarily rooted human cognitive, emotional, and behavioral capacities.

Third, in light of these first two conclusions about extreme interpretations, we can move ahead reasonably confident in the hypothesis that, in terms of its evolutionary origins and functions, religion is an assemblage of adapted and exapted genetic traits constraining culturally variable exploration of a landscape of social and existential possibilities. The nature of religion, and thus of the human being as *homo religiosus*, lies between the two extremes, where adaptations and side-effects mingle in complex ways to provoke the emergence of the varied phenomena we recognize as religious. This complexity of evolutionary origins is commensurate with the complexity of the observable functions of religion, so the middle territory seems about right. It follows that religion can no longer properly be studied in isolation from evolutionary interpretation of the factors that condition its emergence, development, and functions. To put the point perhaps over-sharply, religious anthropology without an evolutionary component is, in some fundamental sense, reductive to the point of irrelevance. There are just too many areas where theories emerging from the evolutionary sciences transform the understanding of human nature within religious studies and theology. Many religionists and theologians will go their own way in the specialized language games of their discourse communities, of course, but their work will be the poorer for neglecting the impact of this emerging literature on religious anthropology.

Fourth, the literature on the evolutionary origins and functions of religion alarmingly displays almost no awareness that there are such things as naturalistic religious outlooks and naturalistic theologies. The emphasis on statistically and historically dominant supernaturalist religion is overbearingly strong, and often defines the core of religiosity. This leaves the reader floundering when trying to make sense of philosophers such as Plato and Aristotle, Śaṅkara and Laozi, upon whose thought vast traditions of religious philosophy have been built. In fact, the emphasis on supernaturalism seems calculated to make human religiosity seem maximally unappealing to that class of thinkers for whom supernaturalism suggests only credulity, superstition, and psychological frailty. Yet many theologians have held—and many living theologians insist—that supernaturalism is the antithesis of authentic religion, because (so they say) it embraces cognitive self-deception for the sake of undeniable communal benefits and immediate but ultimately dubious comfort. There appears to be a profound breakdown of communication between religious naturalists and anti-religious humanist naturalists at this point.

There are plenty of theologians who will reject any naturalist theological outlook as a faithless betrayal of one or another home tradition, regardless of naturalism's historic credentials in the figures and traditions of religious philosophy mentioned above. But naturalism is not a perverse or destructive challenge to conventional religion. Rather, religious naturalism is an iconoclastic theological articulation of a vision of human spiritual and moral maturity. It has a great deal in common with secular humanism and a profound respect for learning in all forms. It functions within all religious traditions, often on the underside or in the interstices of religious sociality, as a challenging goal and a refuge for serious religious people of a particular type. For scientists to marginalize or ignore this intellectually and socially important religious perspective, without any explanation, is bizarre. Be that as it may, it is especially important to note that naturalistic theological viewpoints accommodate scientific insights into the origins and functions of religion easily and constructively. And that should be as interesting to thoughtful scientists studying religion as their scientific work is to religionists and theologians inclined toward religious naturalism.

Those theologians and religionists who engage the scientific study of religion for the sake of a more adequate interpretation of the human being as *homo religiosus* will inevitably seek to make sense of the way that religion engages human beings with ultimate realities. The religious naturalists among them will do this with a view of religion in evolutionary terms as an *ad hoc*, complex, and variable assemblage of adapted and exapted genetic traits that constrain culturally colored exploration of a landscape of social and existential possibilities within an ultimate environment defined by the valuational depths of nature itself. The anti-religious scientists who cavalierly reduce religiousness to self-deluded pining for supernatural fantasies have chosen caricatures for enemies. The naturalist interpreters of human religion are far more formidable opponents. And they are opponents both of anti-religious scientists and of supernaturalist religionists.

CHAPTER 4

Groups

Introduction

Religion has more or less obviously individual aspects, such as experiences, beliefs, meaning, and character transformation. We will take up some of these individual aspects in later chapters. This chapter focuses on the equally vital group aspects of human religion, from its social dynamics to the evolutionary functions of corporate religiousness. Human beings are social animals. Group belonging and corporate security are essential for our physiological development and mental health, for managing daily life, and for creating the cultural achievements that we prize. Human group life is extraordinarily complex and has many negative effects on individuals. But it is essential, and more than that it is also valuable. We strive to protect and nurture our varied forms of social organization for both reasons—we need them and we treasure them. Each chapter of this book opens up one of the many dimensions of meaning to the human being as *homo religiosus*. None more strongly determines the textured particularity of actual religions than the social dimension.

The social character of religion is subject to various levels and types of generalization, each of which is both valuable and contestable as an approach to description and explanation. For example, the field anthropologist may produce elegant ethnographic descriptions of particular religious behaviors within a little known human culture while the sociologist may develop theories of the way that religious behaviors and beliefs condition economic practices. Or the historian may uncover intricate webs of factors conditioning the emergence of a particular group-defining religious doctrine while the theologian may attempt to evaluate the truth and value of that doctrine. The resulting tensions between generalization and particularity have been perplexing aspects of the study of religion for many decades.

Since the middle of the twentieth century, and especially after post-structuralism diagnosed the fabulous overstatements of structuralist theories of human nature, the influence of anthropologists and historians in the academic study of religion has been dominant. The direction of this influence has been away from generalizations about religion, which so often seem futile or fantastically distorted, and toward close study of texts and contexts. With the rise of the scientific study of religion in the late twentieth century, the pendulum is starting to swing in the other direction, in search of stable generalizations about human religion. The tension between the academic study of religion and the scientific study of religion reflects the perpetual mutual wariness between people who love the empathic understanding that can only come through appreciating intricate particularities, on the one hand, and people who are drawn to the theoretical understanding and technologies of control that only generalities can produce.

This kind of tension is common in intellectual life and analyzable much the same way in each case. We can produce no generalizations without particularities from which to generalize. And we cannot describe or even notice particularities apart from the structured categorizations that reflect one or another generalization. We all stand on both sides of this divide and I see no need to choose one side over the other. Rather, the pressing requirement is to learn to pay attention to one's shadow side hovering within the habits of mind of those whose intellectual instincts strike us as alien.

This chapter first approaches religion and group life through a description of the social dynamics of religion. The key disciplinary resources here are from sociology. The sociology of knowledge, in particular, offers a powerful account of the social construction of reality that makes excellent sense of a host of group-level phenomena surrounding religion, including those pertaining to social control and social transformation. The insights generated by the sociology of knowledge describe high-level group phenomena that emerge from more basic group dynamics. These more basic dynamics require evolutionary theory for their discernment and analysis. Accordingly, the second theme of this chapter is the evolutionary functions of corporate religiousness. Finally, in the third section we shall take up the theme of peculiar and bizarre behaviors that seem to defy all generalized theories of human religion in relation to group life. In particular, these behaviors seem to reduce individual fitness and thus seem to contradict the main thrust of evolutionary theory, threatening its account of the low-level social dynamics of religion. The development of costly signaling theory has proved vital for showing that, when situated in the appropriate group context and interpreted in light of the novel fitness strategies made possible by communicative environments, many of these bizarre behaviors prove to be intelligible and consistent with evolutionary generalizations about human groups and religion.

The result of these efforts is a sketch of the social dimensions of *homo religiosus* in terms of both evolutionary theory and the human sciences simultaneously. We do not need to choose between these approaches to describing human group life; they complement one another by focusing on lower and higher levels of an emergent hierarchy of complexity. In its own way, this portrayal of religion from the sociological and evolutionary perspective is as stunning as the nuanced portrayals of the intricate details of particular religious texts and contexts, artifacts and cultures within the academic study of religion. Jointly, these two domains of investigation—the generalized analyses of the social sciences and evolutionary theory, and the particular analyses of ethnographers, archeologists, and historians—present us with a picture of human religiousness that is vastly more detailed and more useful for further research than at any time in the past. What it all means is another question, of course, and the distinctive focus of religious anthropology. But religious anthropology needs a theoretical framework for its interpretation of human religiousness, and sociology and evolutionary theory supply a significant part of that integrative interpretative perspective.

Social Dynamics of Religion

Religion as Means of Social Control and Change Agent

Two of the pioneers in the sociology of religion were Max Weber and Émile Durkheim. Weber (2002 [1904–05]) produced the first compelling sociological theory of the economic impact of religion, which opened many minds to the value of considering religion as a social force. He also generated some deeply insightful comparisons among the religions of East, South, and West Asia that have stood the test of time (for example, see Weber 1951). Among these is his contrast between ultimate realities such as Gods and ultimate ways such as liberative paths. This distinction also appears in Tillich's (1951) dual understanding of ultimate concern as describing both the subjective emotional and practical qualities of deep religious involvement and the objective ontological character of the objects of religious commitment. It appears again in the Crosscultural Comparative Religious Ideas Project, which validated categories of ultimate realities and ultimacy as serviceable for describing world religions with minimal distortion (see Neville 2001a, 2001b, 2001c). Likewise, numerous later sociologists have continued to see validity in Weber's account of the entanglement between the religiousness of groups and their economic behavior. These results show that his instincts were good, which explains much of his influence.

Durkheim produced, among other things, the first compelling sociological theory of the origins and in-group functions of religion and morality based on ethnographic data from ancient cultures that he thought most clearly expressed the elementary forms of the religious life (see Durkheim 1915). He postulated that religion enshrines the core moral commitments of a human group, making those commitments sacred and unquestionable. This transformation of moral practices from mere consensual habits to the sacred deliverances of supra-human realms simultaneously makes religious beliefs morally potent and moral behavior religiously loaded. The implications for the roles of religion in group regulation and social change have been unfolding ever since Durkheim introduced this insight into sociology. In particular, Durkheim's way of thinking about human religion lies behind the sociological account of "social reality" as a reflective construction of human groups in which religion plays key roles.

If Durkheim's insights were especially important for isolating the roles of religion in the maintenance of social order, Weber's theorizing was particularly useful for grasping the generative power of corporate religion to change social and economic conditions. Religion is a pacifying mechanism within social groups, sanctifying operative group norms while safely discharging the confusion and frustration of suffering without rending the social fabric of life. Religion is also a disruptive force, destabilizing the status quo, conjuring visions of a different way of organizing human life, and inspiring people to commit to revolutionary social change, even at the cost of their lives. The regulatory aspects of religion define its basic social dynamics; even much of the disruptive potency of religion functions as one way to equilibrate tensions within a generally functional social reality. But it is all too easy to overlook the generative power of religious behaviors, beliefs, and experiences in both the production of culture and the envisioning of ideal social forms. The human being as *homo relgiosus* is deeply involved in both aspects of the social dynamics of religion.

Religion and the Social Construction of Reality

A widely appreciated account of the role of religion in the social construction of reality is Peter Berger's *The Sacred Canopy* (1967). Firmly within the Durkeim-influenced tradition of the sociology of knowledge, Berger's account focuses on the regulatory social functions of religion. It can be supplemented with an account of religion's disruptive potential to create a satisfyingly balanced interpretation of the social dynamics of religion. Moreover, it can be extended beyond a strictly sociological theory, which is neutral to ontological questions about religious realities, to a component of a philosophical account of *homo religiosus* that can accommodate questions about the meaning and value of religion's social dynamics. I shall supplement and extend in these ways in what follows.

Berger describes the social construction of reality as a process of dynamic equilibrium. He explains how religion both supports this dynamic equilibrium and resists threats to its stable operation, and thus exercises the protective function of a sacred canopy. Berger's presentation is more theoretical than data-driven, but he demonstrates the fruitfulness of his theory in a series of valuable case studies, which in effect manifest the data that drive his interpretation. The equilibrium dynamic is a cycle of externalization, objectivation, and internalization. Externalization refers to the expression of internal ideas in cultural products, whereby human beings build and create, inquire and communicate. Objectivation refers to the social fate of many of our cultural expressions: they become ways of being for our entire group, defining its identity and normal ways of functioning. Internalization refers to the way we absorb this emergent social reality from the time we are babies, speaking the language of our setting, learning its behavioral norms, and repeating in our own lives its values, all more or less unconsciously. This equilibrium dynamic powering the social construction of reality operates reflexively and is more stable and profound for not being noticed. To notice anything is inevitably to render it questionable to some degree; to become aware of the equilibrium dynamic at the heart of the social construction of reality is to interfere with its reflexive efficiency. This perfectly expresses the revolutionary implications of the social sciences: by drawing attention to social dynamics they change them. They burden human beings with running societies whose social dynamics are no longer hidden or mysterious, at least for some. This removes one of the power sources for social stability while conferring greater knowledge about how to exercise social control. Such self-awareness both increases responsibility and complicates its exercise—a common feature of human life.

What the social scientist does more or less comprehensively in manifesting the hidden dynamics operative within the *habitus* of life is accomplished in a less dramatic way by untrained individuals every day. As soon as an aspect of a socially constructed reality stops making sense to someone, the resulting cognitive dissonance arrests that individual's attention and insinuates questions about social reality. Is it just? Should I comply? Can it be improved? These questions are potentially disruptive to an extreme degree, increasing individual anxiety and corporate unpredictability, and blocking the formation of an effective equilibrium state for the social, political, and economic spheres. There is enormous emotional resistance to such disruption and uncertainty, presumably born of evolutionarily rooted instincts to control the environments of human life, taming its uncertainties and calming anxiety. This emotional resistance is the core conservative force in all human societies. It drives social hierarchies that place authority and control into the hands of those most committed to perpetuating social reality as it is. It lies behind marginalization of those who do not fit prevailing social norms, from the mentally ill and socially odd to the stubbornly rebellious and resolutely cynical. It inspires social differentiation that promotes loyalty within ingroups and provokes suspicion of outgroups.

There is a fundamental problem, however. No matter how resolutely the equilibrium dynamic at the heart of socially constructed reality is protected, cognitive dissonance persists. No social order could allay all fears and quiet all questions of creatures as emotionally complex and cognitively alert as human beings are. Social systems always have unwanted side-effects and bring pain to some who did nothing to deserve it. Coercion only amplifies the unpleasant cries of suffering and inspires righteous resistance to a social order. The equilibrium dynamic of social reality as described to this point is, therefore, fundamentally unstable. Optimal stability requires a way of managing cognitive dissonance that inspires willing compliance and minimizes the need for counterproductive coercion. Fortunately for the cultural evolution of human societies, human beings are evolutionarily primed with cognitive and emotional reflexes that make optimal social stability more than a despairing fantasy. The secret ingredient is religion. Whether religion will always be the main way to safely discharge the destabilizing influence of cognitive dissonance remains to be seen as the human project unfolds. But there is no question that it has been an essential component in stabilizing social reality in the past and remains so in the present.

It is in connection with religion that Berger most strongly resembles Durkheim, though the framing of the social functions of religion within the sociology of knowledge reconfigures Durkheim's insights. Religion discharges socially volatile reactions to cognitive dissonance and inspires voluntary compliance with socially embedded moral norms by sanctifying the status quo in a way that brings comfort to the afflicted and meaning to the confused. The historic and cosmic sweep of religious narratives draws individuals into a larger story and gives ultimate meaning both to their lives and to the moral norms embodied in their socially constructed reality. In effect, religion "cosmologizes" social reality, vesting its rules with cosmic significance, interpreting the authority of social regulators as from beyond the human sphere, positing the transparency of human internal life to supra-human scrutiny, stipulating a range of divinely mandated rewards and punishments, and bringing special meaning to each human life. When cognitive dissonance arises, it is easily deflected by weaving it into the larger religious narration of short-term trials in an ultimately meaningful and perfectly fulfilling cosmic context. The social causes of cognitive dissonance are masked in the process instead of manifested as injustice or inefficiency or unintended side-effects of a constructed system of social, political, and economic relationships. The frustration of injustice and suffering is discharged partly through displacing the analysis of causes from social and economic conditions onto cosmic powers and transactions, and partly through experiences of comfort and meaning that seem to allay anxiety, calm aggression, and make sense of the misfortunes of life.

The influence of Karl Marx on sociology of religion is unmistakable here. Religion may not be *only* the social opiate, calming anxiety and inducing compliance, but it certainly is that in part. To grasp what else religion may be, it is necessary to broaden theoretical vision beyond the blinkering effects of Marx's well-earned influence in the social sciences. Without abandoning Marx's insights about religion, it is certainly possible to acknowledge that the complexity of social systems permits many emergent functional roles for religion, well beyond those that Marx theorized. A concrete example will make the point.

Religion was a factor that increased the North American slave owner's control over slaves by pacifying rebellion, displacing resentment, tolerating violence, and rationalizing the institution of slavery. But religion also helped African-American slaves define an identity beyond their social circumstances, retain their integrity and pride in the face of humiliation and violence, deceive slave owners about the extent of slave compliance, envision freedom in a different future, and ultimately inspire the activism of the civil rights movement that ended segregation. Marx's account of the first aspect of the social functions of religion in this case seems right, as does Durkheim's and Berger's. But religion is also social dynamite, and not necessarily in a violent way. With a few notable exceptions, the civil rights movement was substantially a matter of non-violent resistance and raising of consciousness both among African Americans and among the white American majority. It was driven by ideals of universal human rights that were rooted in an essentially religious vision of human relationships under divine authority and love. These ideals may have been useful fictions or they may express the deepest truth about human nature. But the point for present purposes is that these ideals were not those of the *status quo*, as judged by its practices as well as by its self-descriptions; they were competing principles that threatened the *status quo*.

There are many other such examples from all over the world. Religion often fuels the social change and personal sacrifice necessary to modify or overthrow one social order in favor of a new dynamic equilibrium that enshrines religiously envisioned and nurtured ideals. Sometimes the mutation is relatively peaceful and sometimes extraordinarily violent. Intrinsically, religion in the process of social change is an inducement neither to violent revolution nor to peaceful transformation. Nor is religion on only one side of debates over the transformation of economic conditions, political power, and social norms. Rather, religion functions as an inspiring force on all sides of every issue, catalyzing commitment, envisioning the new, and rationalizing both the protection of sacred social orders and their transformation in the name of realizing precious ideals. In fact, on the largest scale of analysis, even the most dramatic of religiously inspired challenges to a social order have as their ultimate goal the smoother running of the equilibrium dynamic, with less cognitive dissonance, less suffering, and less need for coercion. This is why the account of religion as an agent of social change does not contradict the role of religion in the maintenance of social order but merely elaborates that role. It is a complex role with diverse and often paradoxical functions.

Sociology and Theology

The cynical interpreter of religion goes well beyond the hermeneutics of suspicion as it is employed in the theories we have been discussing to the position that there are no genuine religious objects engaged in religious behaviors, beliefs, and experiences. The value (and disvalue) of religion is expressed and exhausted in its social and psychological functions; its truth claims are either false or impossible to assess. Some theologians deem this to be nothing other than crass reductionism and, unwilling to get too close to this extreme, have difficulty accommodating themselves even to the more moderate, theologically more neutral, and deeply persuasive account of the social dynamics of religion. For them, to acknowledge this account of the social dynamics of religion would be to raise the specter of religious pluralism whereby their favored religion no longer has any privileged standing. By contrast with both of these extreme interpretations, naturalist theologians comfortably argue both for the social functions of religion as analyzed here and for the possible reality of religious objects, for the potential authenticity of engagement with those objects, and for the genuine objective value of some aspects of religion. The religious naturalist would suggest that religious objects may not be what most religious people think there are; in particular, supernatural deities and personalized cosmic fates are not typically a part of the naturalist's theological scheme. Nevertheless, there are genuine religious objects—the valuational depths of nature, perhaps—and people can authentically engage them even under descriptions that are in some senses false and in other senses true.

Sociology as such cannot pronounce on such questions. But theories of the social dynamics of religion definitely constrain the answers that a theologian might give to them. For example, if a theological view of a religion and its social roles demands privileged treatment that distinguishes that religion decisively from others in quality or truth, the sociological theories we have been discussing present a sharp challenge to that view. To avoid the ignominy of special pleading, the theologian has to generate a theory of religion in general, and an interpretation of religions in the plural. To the extent that theologians are unwilling to do this, or do it in such a way as to perpetuate traditional special pleading, they exclude themselves from the most serious conversations at the junction of sociology and theology and speak only to the special interests of their ghetto communities. This pattern of inferential relationships is typical of the dialogue between sociology and theology: sociology cannot rule out any particular theological theory but it can make it more or less implausible, forcing a retreat to special pleading or face-saving maneuvers to preserve the theological viewpoint under stress.

A particularly interesting theological question for the theologian who repudiates special pleading is the relationship between human social realities and the ultimate objects of religious commitment. Most religions narrate the sacred canopy of social reality in such a way as to invite personalistic images of ultimate reality as a deity with supra-human characteristics, or as a cosmic process that is intimately aware of and responsive to individual human beings if they direct their efforts toward harmonious interpersonal and cosmic–human relationships. In either case, the prospect of rewards and punishments is preserved. But the religious naturalist hypothesizes that such personal features of ultimate reality reflect human interests and longings more than any objective features of the realities that religious people seek to engage, and see ultimacy instead as the fecund depth-structures of nature that furnish the conditions for the possibility of creative human expression. On this account of the ultimate religious object, the socially potent legitimation narratives of religion really are significantly misleading, despite the fact that they also help people engage ultimacy under manifold descriptions. The sacred canopies of social orders do not just cosmologize social norms and facilitate social control; they also *protect people from awareness of ultimacy itself.* That is, the sacred canopy is as much a religious problem to be solved as it is a religious answer to a social question. When we reflexively deploy religion to legitimate our social orders, we succeed in doing so at the price of promulgating an image of ultimacy that is most easily and conveniently and compellingly narrated—given the cognitive makeup of human beings, those are the highly personalistic images. But all religions in their less well-known resources carefully deconstruct the images promoted in retail religion—they undo what Derrida calls the "forgetting" that is the condition for speaking in such concrete terms about ultimate reality (see Derrida 1982). These deconstructions point toward paths of enlightenment and liberation that take us beyond attachment to religiously saleable images of ultimacy, and thereby seek to overcome the religious problem posed by religion itself, or rather by the salience of religion for legitimating social constructions of reality.

This portrayal of *homo religiosus* as unconsciously using or deliberately deploying religion to maintain and adapt the dynamic equilibrium of social orders does not tell the whole story about the social dynamics of religion. But it certainly introduces its main features and leads us to ask what the evolutionarily stabilized features of religion that make it so well suited to perform its roles in the social construction of reality are. That is the topic of the next section, and along the way we will discover other aspects of the social functions of religion not mentioned to this point.

Evolutionary Functions of Corporate Religiousness

The Meaning of Evolutionary Function

The social aspects of religion discussed above express high-level characteristics (equilibrium dynamics) of an emergent system (social reality) whose components (individuals) are cognitively and emotionally primed (with the appropriate evolutionarily adapted and exapted features) to produce those high-level characteristics when they combine (interact socially). The next chapter takes up some of the individual cognitive and emotional features that make this emergent system possible. For now, my aim is to inquire as to the evolutionary functions of the entire emergent system, of *homo religiosus* as a corporate religious animal.

To recall, in the previous chapter I essentially ruled out the extreme views that religion is an adaptation and that religion has no genetic component. Instead, I defended the view that religion, in evolutionary terms, is as an *ad hoc*, complex, and variable assemblage of adapted and exapted genetic traits that constrain culturally colored exploration of a landscape of social and existential possibilities within an ultimate environment defined by the valuational depths of nature itself. As discussed in that chapter, however, even if religion is not the result of a very few adapted traits and is as complex in its origins as I have claimed, it can still have evolutionary effects. In particular, it can have secondary adaptive and maladaptive functions both in the evolutionary past and in the present. My aim in this section is to present evidence about the evolutionary functions of religion not in the far past where speculation replaces experiment, but in the present where the scientific study of religion and religious people can function through careful studies. This can then guide speculation about the era of evolutionary adaptation, where the origins of religion lie.

Of course, it is difficult to judge whether any evolutionary function of religion that *seems* adaptive at the present time is in fact *truly* adaptive or maladaptive. Such judgments involve assessing many aspects and levels within an emergent system and weighing how adaptiveness in some respects and maladaptiveness in others combine to make a gene-based feature of human beings more or less likely to spread in the population. Evolutionary complexity makes adaptiveness a hazy theoretical issue. Nevertheless, in some cases, the adaptive or maladaptive quality of an evolutionary function is obvious enough to take the risk and make the judgment intuitively without having compelling evolutionary models in hand. For example, if a particular social phenomenon increases the health of people prior to and throughout their childbearing years, it is probably safe to bet that this social phenomenon has a secondary *adaptive* function. By contrast, if a social phenomenon involves the killing of young people with no obvious payoff for the wider population, then it is probable that it has a secondary *maladaptive* function. This is the level at which contemporary scientific analysis of the evolutionary functions of corporate religiousness is working. Hopefully future research will make possible more rigorous evolutionary models that can justify intuitive claims about adaptiveness and maladaptiveness.

Allowing for the problems complicating judgment that I have just described, evidence for the evolutionary relevance of many corporate features of religious behavior, belief, and experience is quite impressive. On the one hand, some features of corporate religiousness appear to promote mental and physical health, and thus appear to have secondary adaptive functions in the present, increasing fitness among individuals and groups with the capacity to produce those features. On the other hand, the role of religion in motivating and rationalizing violence, war, bigotry, and deception appears compellingly to be maladaptive. This remains so even though costly signaling theory promises to show that a number of apparently fitness reducing behaviors may actually increase fitness in the right social setting (the theme of the next section).

Both adaptive and maladaptive functions of corporate religiousness seem to be side-effects of traits originally selected for non-religious reasons, but the behavioral consequences of those traits in religious contexts impacts fitness positively and negatively. We should not forget that a host of other functions of corporate religiousness appear at this point to be neither adaptive nor maladaptive but non-adapted. These functions include some of the most important features of religion such as its role in stimulating cultural expression. Like wonderful cooking and glorious music, features of life do not have to be adaptive or maladaptive in order to be vital and precious to human beings. The evolutionary perspective on religion is extremely important, but far from being the only salient consideration in a religious anthropology's analysis and evaluation of the human being as *homo religiosus*.

I take up evidence for the adaptiveness of corporate religiousness in the bulk of what follows. It is not possible to be comprehensive, but I can mention a couple of important examples. Subsequently I comment briefly on maladaptive and non-adapted features of corporate religiousness.

Gene-Culture Co-Evolution

Ilkka Pyysiäinen (2006) argues that religion has an evolutionary history similar to that of language in one important respect: both are products of gene-culture co-evolution. Like Kirkpatrick (discussed in the previous chapter), Pyysiäinen thinks that religion is not an adaptation or a collection of adaptations in itself. But he emphasizes more strongly than Kirkpatrick the role of gene-culture co-evolution in the origins of religion.

To make this point, Pyysiäinen refers to the late-nineteenth century writings of James Baldwin, after whom the Baldwin Effect is named. The Baldwin Effect as it is used today is actually a variety of mechanisms whereby learned behavior leads to genetic changes. The most obvious examples, which Pyysiäinen does not mention, are learned social stigmas against people with genetic disorders, which limit the spread of the genes in question. A more interesting example is language, which Pyysiäinen does discuss. According to Terrence Deacon (1997), human language is an instance of the Baldwin Effect: it depends on a three-way co-evolution of vocal-tract physiology, the cognitive capacity for symbolic reference, and communicative social environments. Language was not directly selected for in the evolutionary process but it comes to have an adaptive function anyway, once it arrives on the scene, because of its value in group settings. Pyysiäinen thinks that much the same is true of religion. If that is the case, he argues, religion originates neither in cognitive adaptations specific to religious beliefs, nor in simple side-effects of traits that were selected for their non-religious adaptive functions. Rather, religion is a collection of side-effects that changes culture and thereby alters what gets selected in the evolutionary process.

A case in point is the role of religion in sexual selection. Presumably mate selection is guided in part by a preference for partners who are reliable. In many social settings, religious beliefs and practices can signal such reliability, making those who can send such signals authentically more appealing as sexual and child-rearing partners. In much the same way, better language wielders were more attractive as mates at some point in the past (and perhaps also today).

A more elaborate example is the role of moral virtues in promoting group-selection effects. Robert Emmons and Patrick McNamara (2006) use a costly signaling framework (discussed later in this chapter) to explain how character strengths can improve cooperation within a group and thereby increase average fitness of that group. Strengths of character capable of sustaining these effects include honesty, trustworthiness, integrity, and emotions such as gratitude. They contend that religion is a universal feature of human life in part because it is a crucial promoter of such emotions, behaviors, and character strengths. It follows that scientists studying the evolution of emotion and the neuropsychology of character should take into account the role of religion. Emmons and McNamara also argue that religion inculcates in people genuine virtues to the degree that their consistent integrity and generosity are virtually impossible to fake. In this light, religion appears to be an indispensable component in the "gene-culture arms race" to solve social cooperation problems through unfakeable signals of reliability. The unfakeable signals in this case are actually genuine virtues.

Yet another example concerns the adaptive function of religious diversity. Corey Fincher and Randy Thornhill (2008) point out that there are many more religions in the tropics compared with temperate regions. They explain the tropical flourishing of religious diversity in terms of the particular social qualities of religion and the particular health properties of infectious diseases. Infections diseases flourish in the tropics because of the relatively small changes in ambient temperature through the year. To resist contagion, it helps to limit contact to people who share the same immunity profile, to avoid strangers, and not to travel very far. Thus, infectious diseases select for genes that promote ingroup behaviors that promote contact between people likely to have similar immune responses to relevant pathogens.

They also select for genes that produce out-group avoidance and limit dispersal of a population. Religion happens to be excellent at promoting all three behaviors, and so the corporate features of religiousness appear to be adaptive in such contexts. Moreover, once established in such contexts, religions will tend not to interact or disperse, leading to greater religious diversity in the tropics. Fincher and Thornhill's claim, in essence, is that religious diversity is an adaptation in the never-ending war with infectious disease pathogens. Many other factors influence both disease and religion, so this is far from an exhaustive explanation of the origins of religious diversity. But Fincher and Thornhill have certainly brought to light another probably adaptive function of corporate religiousness.

As a final example, consider that brains evolve much more slowly than both languages and religions. Just as languages that children cannot learn do not become important, so religions that fail to make cognitive and emotional sense to children do not get much play. In this way, the framework of gene-culture evolution leads to what I think may be the correct analysis of liberal religion. If a great deal of education is required to make sense of a religious outlook—and this is the case for liberal religion and even more for naturalist forms of religion—its influence is likely to be confined to an intellectual elite and its numbers perpetually small. By contrast, religious outlooks that are readily grasped by children spread more quickly and require less maintenance energy, just as with language. The vital religions of *homo religiosus* are to a large extent determined by the cognitive abilities of our young.

Ritual Healing

Another adaptive function of religion may be its tendency to improve mental and physical health. Many cross-sectional studies claim to show the health virtues of religion (Aukst-Margetic et al. 2005, Baetz et al. 2002, Bartlett et al. 2003, Beit-Hallahmi & Argyle 1997, Bosworth et al. 2003, Braam et al. 2004, Burker et al. 2004, Carlson et al. 2004, Compton & Furman 2005, Comstock & Partridge 1972, Contrada et al. 2004, Daniels et al. 2004, Daugherty et al. 2005, Ellison et al. 1989, Gillings & Joseph 1996, Harrison et al. 2005, Hill et al. 2005, Hixson et al. 1998, Idler 1987, Kinney et al. 2003, Koenig et al. 1998, Koenig et al. 1999, Koenig 2000, 2001a, 2001b, 2001d, 2001d, 2001e, 2002, Kune et al. 1993, Levin et al. 1995, Levin & Vanderpool 1989, Masters et al. 2004, Murphy et al. 2000, Newlin et al. 2003, Oman et al. 2002, Steffen et al. 2001, Strawbridge et al. 2001). A few studies highlight respects in which religion seems to harm health (King et al. 1999) or lacks the predicted positive effect (Idler & Kasl 1992 versus Koenig 2001e, Musick et al. 2000, Strawbridge et al. 1997). To appreciate the evolutionary functions of corporate religiousness in regard to health, however, a large-scale interpretation is needed—preferably one that is explicit about what genetic traits are affected by the health affects of corporate religiousness. James McClenon's (2001) book on shamanic healing practices is a good place to turn for such a large-scale interpretation.

McClenon adopts a sensible strategy. He argues that current-day shamanism gives us the best insight into early hominid life, and therefore that we should study shamanism in order to understand the origins of religion. When we do that, dissociation and ritual suggestion come to the fore as the means by which shamans mediate therapeutic benefits to those with whom they work. Thus, McClenon concludes that ritual healing lies at the origins of religion. Its role is to shape genotypes in the direction of capacities for dissociation and hypnosis—capacities that condition modern forms of religious practice even in traditions with no role for shamans and little interest in healing. McClenon, unlike many other defenders of religion as a byproduct of some trait or traits, actually states what the underlying trait is. Other scientists theorizing about the origins of religion would do well to follow McClenon's example of specificity about underlying traits and clarity about selection mechanisms. In any event, the capacity for dissociation and hypnosis gets established in the human population because its therapeutic benefits give a fitness advantage to those who have it. And its after-effects include social codification of the procedures that maximize those fitness benefits, namely, corporate healing rituals. These practices lead in due course to religion. This is the ritual healing theory of the origins of religion.

McClenon's case is carefully argued. But it tells a plausible story about only one of the evolutionary byproducts that are assembled in contemporary religious beliefs and practices. It is insufficient to theorize about one component of religious beliefs and practices as if this could lead to a theory of the origins of religion. Strangely, despite the flow of McClenon's rhetoric toward explaining the origins of religion, in the conclusion of his essay he straightforwardly acknowledges that his ritual healing theory does not rule out other approaches to explaining the origins of religion, such as group selection theories. And this admission follows right on the heals of a list of distinctive advantages of the ritual healing theory as an explanation of religion, including its genetic basis, which cannot hold true if his theory does not preclude other theories purporting to explain the genetic basis of religiosity. I conclude that McClenon has overstated his case slightly, but that the overstatement only affects the comprehensiveness of his account of the evolutionary origins of religion, not its salience for understanding the evolutionary functions of religion.

Maladaptative and Non-Adaptive Functions

In many ways, as we have seen, religion is an evolutionary boon, increasing fitness in communicative environments—and this regardless of any value religion possesses on its own terms as a means of salvation or liberation, of moral improvement or spiritual enlightenment. In other ways, however, religion can be a disaster for evolutionary fitness—and this quite apart from the very real possibility that it promotes false beliefs and moral values that dubiously privilege ingroups over outgroups. Some of these fitness disasters derive from apparently maladaptive features of religion in its *corporate aspects*. There are a host of such examples, and I briefly mention only a couple here.

First, religion sometimes inspires violence. It is difficult to see how religiously inspired violence increases evolutionary fitness at the individual or group levels. As with all violence, it is young people who most suffer injury and death in religiously inspired group violence. Moreover, it is the healthiest of the young that become warriors and thus many healthy males die before passing on their health-wise robust genes. Assessing adaptiveness in this case is tricky because an aura of attractiveness often surrounds the lucky survivors of religious wars, and also because religious violence may succeed in limiting the spread of genes that foster mentally destabilizing tendencies toward religious enthusiasm and intolerance. But the case for the maladaptiveness of religiously inspired violence is quite strong nonetheless. Religious rationalizations of violence also seem to be a maladaptive feature of corporate religiousness in many cases. Sanctifying a war or even a beating as a holy act by narrating it within a religious framework of fateful inevitability or divine command increases the willingness of mentally balanced and physical healthy young people to risk their lives and their genetic heritage in the name of what they feel is a cause with the highest religious and moral significance.

Second, religion inspires various forms of sacrifice, from sacrificing one's child-bearing potential by embracing a celibate lifestyle to sacrificing one's very life in the name of one or another noble religious ideal. These behaviors are obviously maladaptive at the level of individual fitness in a way that is not as clear in the case of religious violence. An individual might risk involvement in a religious war for the glory that results—glory that may include reproductive opportunities with more attractive mates—should they survive. But self-immolation prior to having children or a faithful celibate existence guarantees that there will be no offspring. At the level of group fitness, the analysis of religious sacrifice is much more complex. The costly-signaling framework casts some light on the question of how such behaviors might in fact increase group fitness. Rigorous evolutionary models of sacrifice and celibacy are needed to evaluate the effects of such behaviors on group fitness.

There are many features of corporate religiousness that seem neither obviously adaptive nor obviously maladaptive at either the individual or the group levels. Examples are the role of religion in structuring economic behaviors and inspiring cultural expressions such as art and music. Religion also helps to define group identity and furnishes existential orientation in the terms of such group identities— functions of corporate religiousness that are difficult to classify as adaptive or maladaptive. In fact, it may be the case that most of the corporate features of religion have little impact one way or another on individual or group fitness. Yet this should not lead to any depreciation of such features. There is often a vast gulf between the evolutionary importance and the intrinsic value of social behaviors. Indeed, much of the richness of human life derives from behaviors that have no apparent impact on evolutionary fitness. To be a "mere evolutionary side-effect" is no slight on a feature of corporate religiousness, but rather testimony to the culture-creating imagination of *homo religiosus*.

Explaining Strange Behavior

To explore further the social dimensions of religion, it is important to address a key objection to the claim that religion requires an evolutionary explanation. This objection runs as follows. "If religion has an evolutionary component at all, then it is maladaptive because it centrally involves behaviors that reduce fitness, such as altruism and self-sacrifice, which would lead to the extinction of religion. Therefore religion has no evolutionary component." Such objections were powerful at one time but they are no longer as persuasive and it is important to understand why.

Costly signaling theory (CST) has proved invaluable in recent years for explaining seemingly fitness-reducing and otherwise hard-to-explain behavioral characteristics, including certain religious phenomena. CST seems to apply only to some aspects of religion and thus its usefulness as an explanation of religion's evolutionary origins is hard to assess with any confidence. Moreover, CST is controversial even in its native domain, as we shall see below. Yet CST also establishes that *costly religious behaviors can no longer serve as straightforward evidence that religion either lacks an evolutionary origin or is maladaptive*. On the contrary, CST explains how such counterintuitive behaviors might actually increase fitness in communicative environments. I begin with a sketch of the main theoretical issues in CST before considering its application to religion.

The Development of CST

In a famous 1975 paper, biologist Amotz Zahavi introduced the *handicap principle* (Zahavi 1975, 1977a, 1977b). Inspired by his long observations of small Arabian Babbler birds, Zahavi was trying to explain how apparently fitness-reducing handicaps could evolve. In the realm of sexual selection, a standard example is the weighty and florid plumage of some male peafowls (peacocks). Such plumage might be sexually appealing to female peafowls (peahens) and a long history of observation confirms this (though feral peahens in a Japanese park appear to have no preference for florid plumage on peafowls; see Takahashi et al. 2008). But such plumage is metabolically expensive to produce, tiring to lift and spread, and increases the peacock's vulnerability to predators, so the male trait seems to decrease fitness. The corresponding female trait also seems to decrease fitness by limiting the number of eligible mates. This doesn't make much sense on the premises of natural selection alone, so how could such an arrangement have evolved? In the inter-species realm, a standard example is gazelle stotting. When a gazelle notices a lion stalking in the savanna grass, the gazelle starts leaping in place, high in the air. Should not the gazelle save its valuable energy for running away and make the most of its time by starting immediately? For its part, the lion tends to avoid high-stotting gazelles and go after low-stotting or no-stotting gazelles instead.

Zahavi's key move in explaining such phenomena was to hypothesize a *communicative environment*, within which evolutionarily relevant *signals* can be sent from *signalers* to *receivers* so as to influence receiver behavior. The peacock's plumage is a trait that "sends a message" about genetic value (in the sense of likely reproductive fitness of offspring), while the peahen's instinctive attraction to florid plumage is a trait that permits her to "receive the message" about genetic value, which influences her mate-selection behavior. The two traits together in the right environment create a niche-resonance that increases the frequency of exorbitant plumage in males and the frequency of attraction to such plumage in females. Males may die sooner but they will find mates more quickly and more often (peacocks are polygynous in the wild and only monogamous in captivity), so their overall reproductive fitness may in fact increase, contrary to initial expectations. Females will have fewer potential mates yet overall fitness may increase because of increased fitness of their offspring.

Zahavi's intuitive (though not experimental) causal explanation of such behaviors promised an analytical framework for understanding their evolutionary origins and significance. At the time when Zahavi made his proposal, the most broadly accepted theory was Ronald Fisher's runaway sexual selection explanation (Fisher 1930). Fisher proposed that there are no selection pressures (apart from peahen mate selection) on peacocks with large plumages so the trait is amplified in the population without limit so long as peahens are attracted to such plumage. Surely runaway sexual selection applies in many cases, but the handicap principal is superior in the case of peafowl because it accommodates the fact that plumage varies tremendously among peacocks. This variation presumably allows it to be used as a reliable fitness signal.

Gazelle stotting can also be explained on the premise of communication between gazelle and lion. The speculative reconstruction of this communication is as follows. The gazelle uses up valuable energy but it shows the lion how strong and fast it must be through the height of its leaping. A lion smart enough to get that message, but not smart enough to realize that gazelles with longest-lasting stotting displays may be more exhausted and easier to catch, will chase down non-leaping or lower-leaping gazelles. This helps the lion because a failed chase is extremely exhausting, making a subsequent chase even less likely to succeed, and risking starvation. It helps the individual gazelle by deflecting the predator's attention to weak or sick animals. At the gazelle population level, this deflection costs nothing in average fitness if the killed animal is old. It may actually improve average fitness if the unlucky prey is genetically prone to weakness. The resulting niche resonance increases the frequency of both the stotting trait in the gazelle population and the cognitive inference trait in the lion population. The careful scientist immediately wonders whether this story can ever really be confirmed, or even experimentally tested, because it depends on the cognitive contents of animal minds.

These explanations of seemingly fitness-reducing traits make evolutionary sense only if the signals in question are reliable indicators of reproductive fitness. Why? Suppose it turns out that low-leaping gazelles can actually run faster and dodge better than high-leaping gazelles. The lion that chases low-leaping gazelles thinking they are more vulnerable is less likely to eat. Its fitness is reduced by its possession of this mistaken cognitive structure and the frequency of that trait will decrease in the lion population accordingly. Correspondingly, the high-stotting trait offers no survival advantage for gazelles to offset the disadvantage of exhaustion when lions do not treat stotting as a reliable signal of strength and speed. In this case, the stotting trait is not relevant to reproductive fitness so it cannot function as an authentic signal and would not become an evolutionarily stable feature of the gazelle–lion–savanna environmental niche.

Zahavi's proposal was not received warmly at first. Evolutionary biologists from John Maynard Smith (1976) and Richard Dawkins (1976) to Robert Trivers (1985) and Mark Kirkpatrick (1986) criticized it because it flies in the face of the principle of natural selection, has no theoretical justification in the familiar terms of game theory, relies on very little data, and seems to oversimplify animal signaling phenomena. Whereas natural selection eliminates fitness-reducing traits, the handicap principle can amplify them. Explanations of strange biological phenomena are welcome, of course, particularly when such phenomena make little sense on the principle of natural selection alone, but the theoretical confusion induced by conflicting principles at the heart of biological evolution was not welcome. In fact, the problem of conflicting principles in evolutionary biology is longstanding. Darwin himself had distinguished the principle of sexual selection from the principle of natural selection and had produced no fully satisfying synthesis (see Darwin 1859 and Darwin 1871). This suggests that the difficulty accepting Zahavi's speculative interpretations of his observations may have been driven in some cases by a selection-oriented orthodoxy in biology that was not nearly as empirically minded as Darwin himself was.

The handicap principle is far more general than Darwin's sexual selection principle because it helps to explain surprising phenomena in sibling competition, predator–prey communication, and a variety of other contexts (see Zahavi & Zahavi 1997). It is really about how the principle of natural selection needs to be modified to accommodate the fact of emergent communicative contexts. *Fitness remains the evolutionary yardstick, but in communicative environments natural selection in the ordinary sense is only one of many possible algorithms for optimizing fitness.*

Alan Grafen's landmark 1990 paper confirmed this interpretation of the handicap principle with game-theoretic formality that was alien to Zahavi's more intuitive observational work (see Grafen 1990). Grafen's mathematical model showed how handicaps understood as a kind of costly signaling could optimize fitness in evolutionarily stable ways. The model also clearly exposed the assumptions of the handicap principle, allowing evolutionary biologists to see how it could complement the principle of natural selection. Grafen's work helped to win broad acceptance of the handicap principle among experts in the field. Some early critics reversed their early judgments (see Dawkins 1989), while others sought to generalize animal signaling theory to include the possibility of non-costly signals as well as the costly signals of the handicap principle (see Maynard Smith and Harper 2003). With Grafen's contribution, the idea of handicap traits making sense in communicative environments had taken a huge step toward theoretical stability and what we now know as CST was born.

The Strengths and Weaknesses of CST

Contemporary critics of CST have isolated weaknesses and oversimplifications in CST-based modeling. They point out that real-world relationships are multifaceted and cannot be reduced to the simple roles of CST game-theory models; that the actual genetic relevance of signals is often assumed rather than shown; that the models rarely accommodate dynamic complexities because of the social realities of cheating and deception, memory and reputation; and that the game-theoretic criterion of evolutionarily stable scenarios oversimplifies the fluidity of evolutionary environments and the endlessly complex relationships that animals form within them. Yet, because of the success of the handicap principle in solving some classic problems in evolutionary biology, scientists have tried to apply CST to other phenomena that they find difficult to explain. In the biological sciences, it is an important factor in theories of sexual selection, kin relationships, and predator–prey behaviors. In the human sciences, it appears in theories of class distinctions, conspicuous consumption, fashion trends, adolescent peer-group dynamics, deception, language development, and ritual. Anthropologists and psychologists use CST to explain dangerous or bizarre human behaviors that reduce individual fitness, from needless risk-taking to painful rituals, and from altruistic acts of sacrifice to exorbitant acts of public generosity. Despite the ongoing challenges to CST, therefore, it is here to stay. The core idea that communicative environments change the way environmental-species niches optimize evolutionary fitness corrects selection-focused biology by pointing out that *complex emergent communicative environments permit many novel pathways to increasing fitness.*

While experts now agree that costly signals are among the signaling phenomena that can be evolutionarily relevant, it is important to ask why costly signals turn out to be important in a given case when there are so many other potentially relevant dimensions of signaling, such as the communicative capacities involved in non-costly cooperation behaviors. In other words, if non-costly signals can enhance evolutionary fitness, why would costly signals ever arise? This is not a difficult question to answer, in principle: costly signals may be able to solve some problems that non-costly signals cannot, such as the *free-loader problem* (i.e. detecting and rooting out animals that take advantage of group benefits without making any contribution). But it is extremely important to keep this question in mind because game-theoretic models often suggest that non-CST equilibria persist alongside CST equilibria for biological signaling systems. In order to be credible, therefore, a CST-based analysis of a behavioral trait probably has to *show* that explanations based on non-costly signaling do not rule out a role for costly signals. But this level of rigor is hard to achieve because evolutionary biology presumes communicative environments that we cannot inspect but only imaginatively reconstruct. The speculation that inevitably results makes it difficult to determine why, given that every imaginable kind and variation of signaling seems to have a role in evolution, one kind of signaling rather than another seems to have paid off in a particular evolutionary niche.

A similar frustration concerns the struggle for terminological consistency and conceptual clarity in this area. Writers sometimes use different words for similar concepts and the same words for quite distinct concepts, thereby reproducing in microcosm the problem plaguing signaling theory as a whole. As just one example, Sosis (2006) and others use the word "index" and its cognates such as "indicator" in multiple ways. Sometimes it describes a causal type of sign, as in the claim that behaviors can "indexically signal" (i.e. functionally signal because causally related to) acceptance of a community's moral norms. In this usage, an index or indicator is a sign that is causally related to that about which it communicates. Other times it means a suggestion, as in the claim that fakeable signals can still be useful "indicators" of belief. In this usage, an index or indicator increases the probability that an observer's assumption about sincerity will be correct. We need both ideas but we have only one term.

Maynard Smith and Harper (2003) directly address the terminological and conceptual problems of signaling theory. They offer a conceptually well-organized survey of animal signaling and propose sharp definitions aimed at eliminating confusions and stabilizing language used to frame theories of signaling. They also situate CST-type explanations in the broader context of animal signaling, allowing us to see how CST can complement other lines of explanation for behavioral traits. Without a conceptually adequate and consistent lexicon of key terms, entering the world of thought of a particular author is a stiff challenge for outsiders such as religionists and theologians, and may lead to misunderstandings and conceptual muddles even among specialist readers.

Through all of these complexities, several points emerge forcefully. First, communicative environments enhance the range of fitness-enhancing evolutionary strategies, permitting fitness-reducing behaviors to persist in particular species-environment niches. The natural selection filter in its simplest form seems to serve as an indispensable foundation for more elaborate strategies, such as animal signaling phenomena. Second, signaling theory helps to shift the focus in evolutionary biology from selection to fitness, which is to move attention from one strategy to the overarching end served by all strategies. It does this by linking the principle of natural selection with sexual selection, the handicap principle, cooperation, altruism, reputation, and other communication-based modes of analysis into a more comprehensive theoretical approach to evolutionary fitness. This promises to resolve the tension between apparently conflicting evolutionary principles that has persisted in biology since Darwin's writings. Third, if we allow that a species can become genetically predisposed to certain behaviors within an evolutionary niche, we also have to allow that those behavioral predispositions may persist in the population even when the niche disappears and the environment changes radically. This can lead to "fish out of water" behaviors that, while expected in the original selection environment, may seem bizarre in a new environment, perhaps because they continue to involve costly signaling when the conditions for overall increase in fitness of a costly signal no longer obtain. This in turn invites explanations of seemingly needlessly costly or otherwise bizarre human behaviors in terms of genetic conditioning.

A CST of Religion

With this survey in place, we come to religion. CST can help to make sense of a number of human behaviors present in religious contexts. For example, CST has been used as an explanatory framework to make sense of costly religious initiations and sacrifices (Pinker 2006), to interpret the pervasiveness of certain sacred emotions in religion (Emmons & McNamara 2006), to understand how religion facilitates group commitment (Bulbulia 2004, 2006), to interpret the link between religion and the promotion of health-increasing placebo benefits (McClenon 2001, 2006), to explain how religion (though not an adaptation itself) functions adaptively as a solution to ever-present existential problems of death and deception (Atran 2001, 2006), and to explain the evolution of religious beliefs and practices (Sosis 2003, 2004, 2005, 2006).

The general pattern of reasoning goes something like this. As outsiders we can observe religious behaviors that strike us as strange because they seem to reduce fitness (for example, Bulbulia 2006 mentions cognitive error associated with religious beliefs) or because they cause pain (for example, Sosis 2006 mentions agonizing and terrifying religious rites)—of course, we also observe that these behaviors make perfect sense to insiders. We reason that the counterintuitive, excessively painful, or fitness-reducing character of these behaviors means that they would not arise spontaneously in a social group unless there were genetic predispositions to perform them. Consequently, we assume the presence of such genetic predispositions—and in some cases there is supporting evidence. But we do not assume that there is a specific genetic tendency to any particular painful ritual because no particular ritual is widespread enough in the species to be an innate tendency expressing a trait. Rather, we assume that there is a genetic tendency to tolerate and seek such behaviors that expresses itself with wide variations in ways specific to culture and circumstance. Some of these behaviors may align strongly with religious rituals, while others may not. After this, we seek to understand precisely what these deeper genetic predispositions are, why they are religiously linked when they are, and how they were formed in the ancestral environment.

Richard Sosis has produced one of the most impressive arguments for a CST of religion. Much of his empirical evidence comes from his careful studies of religion and cooperation in Israeli kibbutzim (Sosis & Alcorta 2003, Sosis & Bressler

2003, Sosis & Ruffle 2003, 2004) and the theoretical work is equally robust (Sosis 2003, 2004, 2005, 2006). Taken together, the empirical and theoretical wings of Sosis's argument show that religion at least sometimes involves costly signaling and that costly signaling can help to explain the origins and persistence of some features of religion. His leading questions are exactly the ones that inspire a CST theory of religion: given the near ubiquity of costly behaviors, why do we spend so much time and energy on them? What is the evolutionary point? And why do costly behaviors vary so dramatically in nature and intensity?

Sosis (2006) offers a summary of his CST theory of religion. He begins with an excruciating description of the torture of boys and young men among the Ilahita Arapesh, galvanizing readers' attention by challenging their moral norms in the way that only anthropologists can—they do this, one suspects, with secret self-congratulatory flourishes of pleasure as they picture their readers' discomfort. But such is life, apparently. Sosis intends his illustration to be a thought-provoking example of the problem he seeks to address. He then frames the problem in religious terms as if he had just been describing instances of religious rituals. But the connection between penis laceration and religion is nowhere established, as it is, for example, in a very different form in circumcision. This would be a minor point except that the fuzzy boundary between religious and non-religious rituals— evident elsewhere in his essay and also in some other writings—endangers the heart of Sosis's argument. If we focus on costly religious rituals we tend to ask about the evolution of religion. But if the relevant evolved traits underlie costly rituals in general, and not merely specifically religious costly rituals, we will not succeed in throwing much clear light on the evolutionary origins of religion by studying costly rituals. So when Sosis analyzes the communicative content of religious behaviors, badges, and bans, it is fair to ask what the evolutionary rationale is for limiting the scope of the question to religion, and whether this way of framing the issue distorts the resulting accounts both of human nature and of religion.

It is not difficult to see how theoretical distortion might occur. Our theory of the communicative content of religious behaviors, badges, and bans may lead us to propose that religion evolved specifically to promote such signaling. Indeed, Sosis plausibly argues that religion promotes reliable signals better than simply announcing promises, but he merely assumes the superiority of religion to all other social mechanisms for establishing signal reliability without offering good reasons to think it is so. What if promise-making was accompanied by some costly, non-religious ritual, such as offering up one's children as a guarantee of sincerity? Indeed, this has happened, as when a slave makes such a suggestion to reassure a master that he or she will return from a journey. Less potentially deadly forms of collateral are common in financial transactions. The result would be a non-religious cultural practice highly conducive to truth-telling, promise-keeping, and reliable signaling. The relevant trait is a cognitive one: we need to be able to count on a promise, in spite of our ability to deceive, and in spite of our *theory of other minds* that allows us to imagine being deceived. But those cognitive traits could promote many sorts of costly ritual practices, even if they were not religious in any recognizable sense. Therefore, we would err if we saw here a reason for the evolution of religion. We have only a reason for the evolution of behavioral traits supporting costly rituals that support reliable signaling. The question of the role of religion in such rituals, and the reasons for its absence in some, is not directly answered in such arguments.

Sosis addresses this difficultly later in this overview essay. He wisely notes that religion is much more than costly rituals supporting reliable signaling that can solve group-bonding problems. It also includes myths and mystical experiences, beliefs and emotions. He focuses on religious beliefs in supernatural agents, the effects of internalizing such beliefs, and their emotional significance. He argues that internalized beliefs in supernatural agents expose one's private intentions to a supernatural being capable of seeing and punishing deception. Such beliefs thus function as an internal goad to honest signaling. Religious practices, as Sosis points out, cause participants to internalize such beliefs, through ritualized repetition and emotional priming. And most religious communities back up these mechanisms for internalizing group norms with an array of punishments, beginning with disapproval and fines, and running through public shaming and physical beatings all the way to banishment, excommunication, torture, and execution.

In this way, Sosis argues that religion evolved as a means of maximizing the reliability of signals in socially complex communicative contexts. But he leaves open the question about whether the underlying traits are tightly tied to religion or rather promote quite general features of human behavior that influence the evolution of religion along with other loci of ritualized behavior and belief. This remains an open question in research around this topic. If we are to apply a CST-based theory, or indeed any other evolutionary theory of religion, to contemporary religious behaviors and beliefs, we need to know what sort of story our theory implies at the trait level. This serves as a check on theoretical adventurousness and may even help to avoid the covert operation of bias in the social and political analyses that evolutionary analyses of religion so readily inspire.

Costly Signaling and Religious Anthropology

The basic significance of CST for religious anthropology is obvious: if CST is correct, traditional religious anthropologies have been overlooking something vital.

This hits home in religious studies, particularly within *ritual theory*, a fascinating and complex interdisciplinary area of study involving many lines of investigation with significant implications for religious anthropology. Ritual theory involves historical study of the origins of rituals and their changes over time, as well as description of the varied cultural expressions of similar rituals— themes less likely to be impacted by CST. But ritual theorists also try to explain the social and religious functions of rituals. The main resources here come from theoretically oriented sociologists and anthropologists who have proposed wide-ranging frameworks for understanding human behavior. Unfortunately, most of the theoretical frameworks in play within ritual theory do not discuss evolutionary psychology, and certainly not CST. As a result, many interpretations of costly religious rituals are currently leaving out a potentially field-transforming insight. CST also deeply challenges theological readings of costly rituals. A theologian typically tries to make sense of the particular rituals that predominate in a single religious tradition as expressed in a particular place and time, being careful to take account of historical developments and the deliverances of sacred texts and traditional wisdom. Some theological interpretations of rituals ignore ritual theory altogether and work intensively within the plausibility structures and resources of a local religious tradition. Neither CST nor ritual studies are likely to induce such theologians to raise their eyes and consider "external" theoretical interpretations of ritual impacting the interpretation of the human being as *homo religiosus*.

By contrast, other theologians attempt to forge interpretations of the theological significance of ritual while absorbing the best theoretical understandings of ritual in general. Such theologians will be fascinated by CST, regardless of their tradition of focus or their religion of affiliation, if they have one. For them, CST raises the question of whether theological interpretations of ritual nurtured within religious communities are compatible with evolutionary psychology's insights into the function of rituals in human groups. What happens to the theological interpretation of shamanic self-flagellation and the Hajj's dangerous crowd-crushing stoning-the-devil ritual, of ancestor reverence and the pouring out of precious milk in Hindu puja, when CST is drawn into the interpretation? Theologians inclined to say that Jewish circumcision expresses a covenant between God and God's chosen people may look at the origins of the rite, which was supposedly among grown men, quite differently in the light of CST. CST may also help theologians used to thinking of the Christian Eucharist as a means of participating in the saving benefits of Jesus Christ's sacrificial death to look upon the historical origins and early social significance of the Eucharist in new and potentially revolutionary ways.

Finally, theologians interested in the theological meaning and social significance of religious groups should scrutinize their working interpretive frameworks in the light of evolutionary psychology, and CST in particular. The sorts of social functions that CST speaks of—such as solving the freeloader problem and increasing the reliability of commitment signals—are rarely mentioned in theological interpretations of religious groups, and yet these kinds of dynamics may be among the most important factors influencing their origins and functions. In short, CST promises numerous insights into the religious behaviors and beliefs of human beings, and thus is vital to any contemporary religious anthropology that aims to be responsive to the scientific study of religion.

Conclusion: *Homo Religiosus* and Groups

We began this chapter with an analysis of the social dynamics of religion, and saw how religious group life facilitates the social construction of reality through cosmologizing social norms so as to legitimate social practices and exercise social control more or less invisibly. We also saw how religious ideas and practices can function as a spark for social change when cognitive dissonance alerts us to incoherent ideas or unjust social arrangements. We then we pressed lower in the hierarchy of emergent complexity to ask about the evolutionary constraints on human group life and the role of religiousness in shaping those constraints, noting that corporate religiousness has both adaptive and maladaptive functions, as well as many functions that seem to be non-adapted. Finally, we considered the costly signaling argument that bizarre religious behaviors can have adaptive functions because of novel fitness algorithms that become possible only in communicative environments. This removes an objection to the thesis that religion is in part a product of the evolutionary process, and also blocks much of the evidence that must be adduced to support the claim that religion is dominantly maladaptive. These themes jointly constitute a persuasive framework for understanding the social dimensions of human religion.

There are many insights into the social character of religion that have not been addressed in this chapter, obviously. Some will be taken up in subsequent chapters. But even this brief treatment covers a wealth of information, much of which was unknown even a few decades ago. This information dramatically reconfigures the evidential and conceptual constraints on a religious anthropology. While it will take the rest of the book to synthesize all of this into an interpretation worthy of being called a religious anthropology, I do want to draw two conclusions about human religiousness based on what has come to light in this chapter about the social dimensions of human religion.

The first concerns reductionism. Let us return to the tension between generalization and particularity with which we began this chapter. I think it is extremely unlikely that we will ever comprehend the evolved diversity and complexity of religious beliefs and practices using a single theoretical framework, whether from sociology of knowledge and evolutionary biology, or from cultural anthropology and history. Nor is it likely that we will be able to prioritize these theories cleanly, ranking the most fundamental ahead of the derivative, and gaining a clear impression of what came first and why. In certain corners of the marketplace of ideas, there are enthusiastic groups hawking their favorite viewpoint as the key to understanding human religiosity. Yet a fair-minded reader of a variety of serious theories must allow that many have the beginnings of a robust empirical basis and impressive theoretical integrity.

The problem with one-sided interpretations among scholars of religion—both scientists and humanists—is reductionism of the varied and complex phenomena of religion merely to what falls within the ambit of the theoretical framework in play. Religious studies specialists and experts in the scientific study of religion must remind one another to honor the complexity of the phenomena they seek to understand. This involves both taking with great seriousness the rich descriptions of particular religious phenomena furnished by anthropologists and historians, and also drawing in the empirically robust generalizations about religious behaviors, beliefs, and experiences produced by cognitive psychologists, sociologists, and evolutionary theorists. Many theoretical frameworks play a role in explaining the origins and functions of religions because religions are too diverse, complex, historically dynamic, paradoxical, existentially vibrant, and socially potent for any one theory to express the heart of human religion, if there even is such a thing, without massive oversimplification. There is no problem with this fact of life, even if it frustrates the eager reductionist. Indeed, it is perfectly appropriate because religion is one of the aspects of human reality that reaches up and down the entire hierarchy of nature's emergent complexity.

Nevertheless, reductionism can be a feasible strategy for studying religion. Achieving this feasibility requires awareness of other approaches and judicious appeal to them, even while focusing on the one approach that produces the sought-after reduction. On the science side, specialists in the scientific study of religion must strive for intelligent selection of salient features of religion and shun simplistic descriptions. It is particularly important for scientists to avoid proposing causal theories of religion that presume data against which religionists effortlessly point out numerous unexplained exceptions. With those caveats, though, reductionist approaches can be highly illuminating. On the religious-studies side, the feasibility of reductionist strategies requires scholars laboring over the minutiae of religion to avoid naively assuming that no larger patterns and forces are at work in producing intricate behaviors in unique contexts. On the contrary, knowing about the social dynamics of religion and the evolutionary constraints on human religiousness helps to make feasible the humanist-reductionist approaches of scholars focused on supplying thick descriptions and intimate ethnographies of particular settings.

The second conclusion concerns constraints on what I have been calling theological elaborations of religious anthropology. What has been said here about the social character of religion, and indeed about human groups in general, presents a serious challenge to theological interpretations of the human condition. Traditional theological anthropologies have ignored or marginalized all three of the major considerations presented in this chapter. We might think that redressing this glaring problem is simply a matter of filling in gaps and extending the scope of traditional theological anthropologies so that they deal with the relevant data. But the situation is more difficult than this. The data relevant to the sociality of religion is highly coordinated and presents a compelling metaphysically minimalist interpretation of human sociality in religion. We require neither supranatural nor supernatural hypotheses (discussed in the 'Preliminaries' of Part I) to account for human sociality in religion. This does not completely disable theological elaborations of the human condition relying on supranatural or supernatural elements, and it certainly does not falsify such elaborations. But the metaphysically minimalist interpretation of human life that is steadily unfolding in the chapters of this book makes increasingly implausible theological elaborations that rely on supranaturalism or supernaturalism. That is a sharp problem for traditional theological anthropologies, and it will only get more pointed.

CHAPTER 5

Brains

Introduction

The human brain furnishes the cognitive, emotional, and motor capacities underlying the extraordinary range of religious behaviors, beliefs, and experiences. To grasp the human being as *homo religiosus*, therefore, we must appreciate the way the particular features of human brains directly impact and indirectly influence personal and corporate religiosity. In recent years, neuroscientists and cognitive scientists have produced spectacular breakthroughs in understanding how the brain mediates religious behaviors, beliefs, and experiences. Surely these are but faint traces of the understanding that lies ahead if research continues at its current pace. But even at this early stage of development it is possible to discern the outlines of what is emerging. Based on that, I expect the neurosciences to have at least as much transformative importance for religious anthropology as the evolutionary sciences have displayed.

The neurological study of human beings is challenging because the brain is an extraordinarily complex organ. The most sophisticated human-made computational systems capable of simulating reality and producing controlled behavior are silicon based. In such machines, diodes and transistors allow for circuit switching that is reliable and complex enough to host useful information processing. But these computational systems use only one switching system, they are digital in the senses that a circuit must be switched wholly on or off and the strength of signaling is unimportant so long as the circuit is activated, and their physical circuitry does not mutate. The brain's complexity begins with the basic facts that its biochemical workings allow for multiple switching systems to interpenetrate, it is an analog system rather than digital so levels of signaling matter, and its physical circuitry is highly plastic and adapts to changing usage requirements. Moreover, the brain is vast in the sheer numbers of component units and connections among them. Its basic structure is genetically rooted and yet experience is necessary to complete the development of most brain features. It has specialized circuitry for key tasks and a certain degree of structural modularity to support such specialized processing, but it also has global integrating functions.

The electromagnetic and biochemical signatures of brain activity can be measured using functional imaging equipment, which is one of the main ways to gather information about brain structures and functions. Another way is the anatomical study of dead brains and structural scans of living brains. A third way is the study of people with localized brain injuries or diseases. Most of these approaches require a human subject to share the contents of his or her consciousness—thoughts, feelings, memories—so that researchers can link up objective behavior and brain function with its meaning to the person being studied. In this way, the brain's capacity for conscious awareness is an indispensable tool for penetrating the brain's meat-like physicality and manifesting the sparkling meanings and mercurial thoughts and feelings that arise within (this presents non-trivial methodological problems; see Revonsuo 2006, Wildman & McNamara 2008). The impact of combining these techniques of study has been a wealth of insights into brain structure and function. These insights are most detailed and the neural models most sophisticated in sensory and autonomic systems, which are relatively convenient to study. The study of emotion, cognition, language, behavior, and dreams is more complex and less convenient, but progress is rapid and much is now known. Religious behaviors, beliefs, and experiences are complex combinations of all of these features of the human brain and thus relatively little is known about their neural realization.

While these dimensions of the brain's complexity are a good thing for brain users, obviously, they present prodigious challenges to those who study the brain. In particular, the most interesting human behaviors, including religious phenomena, are so complex in their neural realization—so multiply connected, so diverse across individuals and cultures, subject to so many constraints, and productive of so many varied effects—that full-scale neural modeling is out of reach at the present time. Rudimentary cognitive models of religious behaviors, beliefs, and experiences are only now becoming possible. Unfortunately, such models are inevitably oversimplified and thus run the risk of unattractive and misleading reduction of religious phenomena to what can be registered within the model. Researchers should embrace this difficulty rather than avoid it while learning to overcome it to whatever degree proves possible. Cognitive and eventually neural models of religious behaviors, beliefs, and experiences may never comprehend the full complexity of the existentially, emotionally, cognitively, behaviorally, and socially potent phenomena of religion, but we can certainly commit to moving in the direction of increasing subtlety and comprehensiveness.

Many chapters in this book inevitably deal with the human brain in one or another respect. This chapter focuses on one of the most prominent brain functions in relation to religion, namely, beliefs. How does the emerging understanding of the brain's role in forming and transforming beliefs impact our interpretation of human beings as *homo religiosus*? The cognitive science of religion has already attempted to answer such questions and it is incumbent upon theologians to build such insights as now exist into religious anthropologies. It is also important to contest hasty or superficial interpretations of the philosophical significance of religious believing, which plague the literature on the cognitive science of religion.

I begin here with a discussion of the brain's role in biasing human beings toward supernatural beliefs. This is a major discovery about human cognition that consolidates what religious skeptics have always said, with far less reason than we now possess. I then take up what is most deeply at stake in this debate over the reliability of religious beliefs, namely, cognitive biases that may yield cognitive errors. Finally, I address the vital practical question, which concerns our prospects for resisting our evolutionarily bequeathed tendencies to cognitive error through a variety of socially borne processes of training and character change. I will argue that we can indeed deploy both religious and non-religious techniques to resist tendencies toward cognitive error, while improving the beliefs we have. The result is a complex appreciation of the brain's role in supporting religious beliefs, with both critical and affirmative implications for the value of religious beliefs and of efforts to believe truly.

Religion and Supernatural Beliefs

Religion is not only about beliefs. But there is no question that beliefs are a big part of religion. Among religious beliefs, moreover, it is clear that beliefs in supernatural agents are especially prominent and deserve special attention. The prevalence of supernatural beliefs inspires us to ask what it is about the human brain that renders us, as a rule, so willing to entertain supernatural causes and agents, particularly when others sustain supernatural beliefs that conflict with our own. This question is partly a neurological and partly an evolutionary one, and has been a focus of creative research in recent decades.

Again, it is important to recognize that there have always been religious people who reject supernatural beliefs as superstitious. From many of the ancient religious philosophers of West, South, and East Asia to the numerous religious naturalists of our own day, this significant minority of anti-supernaturalists will have nothing to do with superstitious beliefs even as they consistently affirm the value of some aspects of religion. Unfortunately, literature on the cognitive psychology of religion rarely even mentions such thinkers as exceptions to a rule (though Dawkins 2007 and Dennett 2006 do mention them as exceptions, after pressure from debate partners over the years). Cognitive theories of religion resulting from identifying religion with supernaturalism strike religionists and theologians as exceedingly fragile. This is an obvious instance where deeper knowledge of religion might help scientists studying religion to deal with powerful contra-indicating evidence. That caveat entered, it is important to repeat that supernaturalism is the dominant form of popular religion. Obviously there is something to be explained here.

Supernatural Beliefs

Jesse Bering's research on the cognitive psychology of belief in the supernatural has enjoyed a high profile, thanks especially to an important publication in *American Scientist* (2006). Bering's article derives from a series of research studies with children. He hypothesizes that their rapid cognitive development can give some indication as to what degree of complexity in the evolution of human cognition would have been needed to entertain the idea of supernatural agents. This makes sense as a research strategy because there are so few avenues of approach to questions about levels of cognitive development in evolution; after all, we have no direct access to earlier hominid species or even earlier versions of evolutionarily modern human beings. Moreover, even if the analogy between cognitive complexity in evolution and cognitive complexity in human development breaks down, Bering's research still effectively illuminates the brain's penchant for supernaturalism.

Bering's experiments were designed to test whether the human tendency to believe in supernatural agents and states is innate or acquired through cultural exposure. His results suggest that even the youngest children are inclined to impute mental states to a dead mouse eaten by an alligator in a puppet play. Yet these youngest of children rarely mentioned beliefs about afterlife prevalent in their culture, which older children tended to do. Bering concludes that belief in an afterlife cannot be entirely a matter of cultural conditioning and that we have here evidence for an innate tendency to treat mental states as fundamental and persistent regardless of bodily state.

There are several problems here. First, Bering's research question about innateness versus social acquisition presumes that the two options jointly exhaust the possibilities. But this omits the alternative that children are born with another innate tendency, namely, to develop a theory of other minds, which initially applies to everything and so often misfires until they learn to apply it only to objects with minds. On this view, the greater cognitive sophistication of later childhood allows children to detect inferential mistakes and thus implicitly to feel the need for a more plausible intellectual framework for mental states beyond death, whereupon they adopt whatever sophisticated framework is ready-to-hand in their environment. This interpretation is quite opposed to Bering's yet consistent with the data he presents. Second, Bering's experiment apparently did not have a broadly crosscultural basis so as to control for the effect of cultural exposure. This ought to be an important check on his interpretation of these preliminary results. Third, a subtler methodological difficulty is that such experiments are notorious for not successfully controlling for extraneous factors, such as the experimenter's interview technique (tone of voice, facial expressions) and contextual factors (young children may enter an "as if" mode of explanation as dictated by the experimental context). This can result in answers that do not reflect authentic metaphysical opinions but rather merely the sorts of answers that ought to be given in the context of the language game currently being played. Despite these difficulties, this sort of research is just getting started and Bering's results are fascinating and useful within limits. Most importantly, he produces persuasive evidence for the general point that human beings have a cognitive propensity to adopt supernatural beliefs.

Bering acknowledges that belief in supernatural entities depends on preexisting traits and so rejects the idea that the corresponding propensity is an adaptation. But he is careful to point out the potential evolutionary benefits of supernatural beliefs. For example, he presents experimental evidence that supernatural beliefs induce a *Santa Claus effect* wherein human beings believe they are being watched, with attendant improvements in behavior and conceivably an increase in fitness. It follows that the cognitive traits underlying the tendency to believe in the supernatural probably have a secondary adaptive function even though they were probably selected originally for a more cognitively basic adaptive function. That makes them exaptations rather than spandrels, in Bering's terminology—in the lexicon introduced in Chapter 3, this only shows that they are exaptations or spandrels but not functionless byproducts.

We can go a step beyond Bering's evidence for a supernatural cognitive propensity to ask about its evolutionary origins. It is not difficult to speculate plausibly about how human beings developed the cognitive disposition to form supernatural beliefs. In fact, there is significant consensus around the following account (see Atran 2002, Boyer 2001, Dawkins 2007, Dennet 2006, Wilson 2002, among others). It is better for survival that an animal run away from a rustling bush even when no tiger is present to cause the rustling, because that is what is required to escape when there actually is a tiger stalking in the undergrowth. The cognitive capacities required for this adaptive behavior are the abilities to detect patterned noise and to attribute the noise to a tiger with food or territorial defense on its mind. The tuning of these capacities should be such that they are operative as often as necessary to cover virtually all instances when a real tiger is involved even if they also operate when there is no tiger, so long as the resulting overactivity does not have worse fitness disadvantages. This is how cognition works in human beings. Our selectively overactive cognitive equipment drives from much older hominid brains, and even pre-hominid brains. But this overactivity worked well for human beings in the era of evolutionary adaptation and is now a part of every newborn human child's cognitive apparatus.

In short, it was (and perhaps still is) adaptive for human beings to have overactive cognitive capacities for recognizing patterns, detecting causes, and attributing intentions. These are precisely the cognitive features that eventually produce the propensity to attribute intentions and causal powers to invisible agents. Such attributions will feel completely compelling to those who make them even if the beings in question do not exist. This is why supernatural beliefs remain so prevalent in the human species. We cannot infer from this that naturalists are correct and that supernatural entities are human fictions. But this account of human cognition is more congenial to the naturalist's ontology, which is awkward for traditional supernaturalist explanations of human religious cognition. The existence of a compelling naturalist explanation for supernatural beliefs means that the conviction with which such beliefs are held can no longer count as supportive evidence for the reality of the putative supernatural beings to which such beliefs refer.

Minimally Counterintuitive Beliefs

Anthropologist Scott Atran has made valuable contributions to the cognitive science of religion. His work has the virtue of registering the importance and value of religion in a multileveled way, thereby oversimplifying religious phenomena far less than is typical in this field. The relative sophistication of his understanding of religion is enormously helpful when communicating with religionists and theologians, and also a prerequisite for responsibly carrying out public commentary duties. Moreover, contrary to the fears of cognitive scientists that registering the intricacy of religious phenomena will make research progress impossible, Atran's work shows that subtlety in understanding of religion need not interfere with a fair-minded and rational scientific approach to analyzing the cognitive and evolutionary roots of religion. This type of analysis is Atran's goal in his (2002) book, *In Gods We Trust: The Evolutionary Landscape of Religion*.

Atran sees the human evolutionary heritage as a landscape that constrains, without determining, the development and function of individuals, cultures, and religions. This leads to an interpretation of religion as a recurring byproduct of more basic evolutionary traits, of course. But the interesting point in Atran's theory is that he claims to account for variations in religious beliefs and behavior as different journeys within the constraining landscape. Does the evolved cognitive architecture of human brains really permit this much freedom to structure religion differently in different cultural settings? Atran gives the impression that the freedom is rather limited when he claims that many fundamental beliefs and behaviors recur in all religions, such as supernatural agents, the appreciation for rhythmic coordination of affective bodily states, and social devices to promote cooperation and deal with deception. Empirically these claims are strained in the sense that they must contend with numerous unexplained exceptions, of which religionists are sharply aware. His argument would be much stronger if he acknowledged the exceptions and explained them. But the non-supernaturalist sub-traditions within the world's religions are in the minority, as are those that shun rhythmic coordination of affective bodily states, and those that have no important social component, so his general point about landscape-based constraints on religious beliefs and behaviors probably survives despite these problematic characterizations.

Atran stresses the point that the cognitive functions associated with supernatural beliefs are present in many domains of human life, including our appreciation for fictional cartoon characters. It is the emotional freight associated with religion that makes all the difference in bonding communities together, solving social challenges of cooperation and deception, and inspiring the willingness to sacrifice that he sees in the Islamic Jihadists he studies (see Atran 2004, 2006, 2008). His question, therefore, is how the neurocognitive architecture of religion ramifies religious beliefs so powerfully that people are willing to die for them. His answer is similar to that of Pascal Boyer (2001) in part, namely, that religious beliefs about supernatural agents minimally violate, and thus memorably contrast with, ordinary intuitions about how the world works. These ordinary intuitions arise within universal cognitive domains, and include what has come to be called folk mechanics, folk biology, and folk psychology. Supernatural entities, like comic book heroes, are the same as other folk entities except that they have one or two strange features, such as a man who is ordinary except that he can fly, or a God who is like a powerful person except for being invisible. Too many strange features and the character is less interesting because the contrast with background folk expectations is too indeterminate. The fascinating and memorable quality of *minimally* counterintuitive beliefs makes them useful for catalyzing unity of groups through compelling stories and thereafter for solving existential problems such as death and deception. For example, a person who is like a supportive human being except in respect of being everywhere at once makes for memorable and intriguing narratives that can yield feelings of comfort as a result of belief in the presence of that person at every moment. If personal experiences and group consensus endorse this narrative, and if it catches on with children, who are the principal carriers of popular ideas, the narrative and its supernatural characters will become vital aspects of the network of beliefs in that group (see discussions of the epidemiology of representations in Fraser & Gaskell 1990, Sperber 1996).

Atran (2006) presents experimental evidence in support of the memorable quality of minimally counterintuitive beliefs. This helps to explain why supernatural religious beliefs persist. It also supplies an experimental basis for interpreting religion as a cultural product passed from generation to generation because it makes sense to children and solves social and existential problems. What is less clear, here as well as in Boyer (2001), is precisely how minimal counterintuitiveness is adaptive, or how it arose from other adaptive features of human cognition. This is crucial for understanding the evolutionary origins of the neurologically rooted propensity to supernatural beliefs, as against its persistence. In any event, what matters most for my current purposes is that this is the way the brain works now, in many diverse individuals and cultures across the human species. Our species' cognitive architecture promotes and nurtures beliefs in supernatural agents and states, and in such a way as to induce powerful emotions that bind people into committed groups, the members of which deploy compelling narratives to manage existential and social problems.

Cognitive Biases and Religion

Cognitive Biases and Cognitive Errors

Brains are amazing organs, in all creatures with central nervous systems but especially in human beings. The brain's autonomic regulation functions are staggeringly efficient and consistent. The sensory system is typically reliable, the motor system is generally superb, and cognition ties sensory and motor activities together in such a way that human beings can navigate enormously complex environments virtually effortlessly. The capacity for emotions, sociality, and intense forms of awareness produce cultures of unending variety and sophistication, and advanced cognitive abilities make us brilliantly adapted to solve problems and generate technologies that transform our habitat.

Given all this, it may seem finicky to point out a few problems with the human brain's cognitive systems. But cognitive error is an extremely important factor in religious belief. Without forgetting the larger success story of cognitive evolution, therefore, I want to explore the way that cognitive biases sometimes produce errors in both religious and secular social settings and how such errors can be diagnosed and corrected when they occur. This will involve noticing that error diagnosis and correction is a process that certain social groups have a vested interest in resisting or neglecting, in some respects, while the very same social groups may furnish resources that support the detection of cognitive errors, in other respects.

The term "error" is a potentially problematic one in that it misleadingly suggests that there is a uniquely correct way in which cognition should work. I do not wish to suggest such a binary opposition. After all, biases exist in the human cognitive system either because they have been selected in the evolutionary process for their survival benefits or because they are side effects of other traits selected for their usefulness. My concern is with the wondrous human discovery that we can analyze our behaviors and beliefs with such precision that we can sometimes detect when our cognitive biases produce mistaken beliefs and self-defeating behaviors. This forms the basis for my contention that cognition can often work better than it does—more accurately, less self-destructively—when tendencies to cognitive error are diagnosed, corrected, and perhaps even systematically resisted using social resources.

The profound irony here is that the very same social groups (secular and religious) with an obvious vested interest in resisting such enlightenment in some respects can also promote processes of discernment and insight in other respects. Existing literature in the cognitive psychology of religion rarely bothers with such subtleties. It is common to assume that simply to notice the operation of cognitive biases in religion—say, in supporting belief in supernatural entities who providentially interact in human affairs, or in establishing and reinforcing people's willingness to defer to certain kinds of religious authority—is at the same time to establish the presence of rampant cognitive error, massive resistance to diagnosing and correcting it, and thus the infliction of pernicious cruelties on young children who have no way of escaping the resulting irrational indoctrination (see, among others, Dawkins 2007, Harris 2007, Hitchens 2007).

This moral reflex to condemn religious groups because of their reluctance to acknowledge the role of cognitive biases in their beliefs and practices is understandable given the irrationality, ignorance, or denial that such reluctance suggests. I frankly acknowledge that I share this moral concern. But the actual complexities of religious practice demonstrate that the situation demands a subtler evaluation. Resistance to awareness of cognitive biases exists both inside and outside religious groups. Economic and political practices have every bit as much to gain from neglecting to enlighten people about their cognitive operations as religious groups do—just consider the techniques employed in commercial advertising and political campaigns. Moreover, religious groups also promote methods of discernment and self-awareness that have historically been, and continue to be, the dominant method by which ordinary religious people diagnose and resist at least some types of cognitive error—particularly those bearing on self-defeating behaviors and distorted perceptions of reality. As usual in life, as well as in the analysis of anything as complex and vibrant as religion, the case can and must be argued on both sides before drawing final conclusions.

Seven Classes of Cognitive Errors

Psychologists have analyzed, isolated, tested, and named dozens of cognitive and perceptual tendencies that predictably produce errors in certain well-understood contexts. Any introductory textbook in cognitive psychology works through this material (e.g. see Baron 2006). An efficient way into this world of commendable self-criticism is psychologist Thomas Gilovich's (1991) survey of the fallibility of human reason in everyday life (also see Piatelli-Palmarini 1996, Plous 1993). This approach involves setting aside the many illusions and misjudgments and imperfections related to the brain's sensory and motor systems, focusing instead on memory, interpretation, and reasoning, which are the parts of human cognition most relevant to personal religious beliefs and practices.

Drawing on a host of psychological experiments in the preceding decades, Gilovich distinguishes between cognitive factors in producing erroneous beliefs, on the one hand, and motivational or social factors, on the other. He discusses three classes of each type, making six factors, to which I add a seventh factor derived from the core hypothesis of cognitive psychotherapy. I illustrate each here in relation to everyday life experiences and in relation to religious beliefs and behaviors. In each case, the point is that well-established cognitive tendencies regularly and predictably produce errors in belief and interpretation, and that such vulnerabilities to error are amply present in religious settings.

The first of the three cognitive factors is our tendency to produce meaningful patterns from purely random data. This arises from a general capacity for pattern recognition in human beings that in many instances is tremendously useful and important for social life, inquiry, and survival. For example, social life crucially depends on facial recognition, our fondness for music requires an embodied sensitivity to rhythmic patterns, and much of advanced mathematics requires people with a prodigious talent for pattern recognition. The error in question arises when our native talent for pattern recognition leads us to misinterpret and sometimes even to misperceive random data. Any psychology undergraduate has seen and probably participated in the entertaining experiments that manifest the turning point at which this enormously useful cognitive tendency becomes a source of errors in interpretation. Statistical analysis of the shooting results of professional basketball players shows that belief in the "hot hand" that supposedly makes them hit baskets in streaks is just such an error (Gilovich 1991 discusses this research and its popularly indigestible but scientifically well established conclusion). Many aspects of a basketball player's game may measurably improve when he or she is in the wondrous flow state—being "in the groove"—but streak shooting is not one of them, on the whole, regardless of the player's feelings about the matter. In the religious context there is a virtually unlimited amount of data available for interpretation as meaningfully patterned, as when an apparent coincidence strikes us as highly religiously significant and evidence of the providential action of deities, ancestors, angels, demons, ghosts, or other discarnate entities. The data may well be random and we may well be experiencing an instance of this cognitive tendency producing cognitive error, but it is difficult to decide whether this is so. In fact, the ontology of religion is such that there is a significant scarcity of information capable of correcting mistaken religious beliefs. As a result, this kind of cognitive error, if it occurs in religious settings, is more difficult to detect and harder to eradicate from the religious domain than from many other domains of human cultural expression where resources for correction may be more readily accessible and analyzable.

The second cognitive factor is our tendency to infer a great deal from too little information. Again, this is a useful aspect of our pattern recognition skills that allows us to interpolate effortlessly and efficiently to produce interpretative hypotheses that guide action plans. When this otherwise useful cognitive bias goes awry, however, we misinterpret incomplete and unrepresentative data. This problem is common in epidemiology, as when people pay more attention to instances of cell phone users getting brain cancer than to cell phone users not getting cancer, or when people feel certain that there is a link between autism and childhood inoculations without ever conducting statistical analyses on what is a prodigiously complex data set to which our personal experience gives us only an incomplete and possibly unrepresentative sample. Such questions remain unanswered until the research necessary to answer them is performed and replicated, but such answers do not convince everyone, such is the strength of this particular cognitive bias. In religious settings, groups and their leaders typically make available only information supportive of preferred religious beliefs and either suppress or make no effort to inform themselves about contraindicating evidence. For example, people notice and report on supposedly answered prayers but do not mention the host of unanswered prayers, or prayers allegedly answered in the form of divine permission of an unwanted tragic outcome. The resulting information sets are incomplete and unrepresentative, which makes more likely (without of course guaranteeing) the occurrence of a cognitive error in the corresponding beliefs about providence and the power and mechanisms of prayer. In respect of the virtues of transparency and full disclosure, unfortunately, religious leaders rarely acknowledge these limitations in data, hopefully because they themselves remain unaware of them rather than because of any deliberate intent to deceive. But this may not be all bad: to point out the human vulnerability to cognitive error in such cases would probably disrupt the sort of positive thinking and enthusiasm that appear to produce desirable physical and mental health outcomes, particularly for people grappling with a health challenge that might be emotionally crippling without supportive social and cognitive resources.

The third cognitive factor is our tendency to see what we expect to see. The linkage between expectations and perceptions is necessary for making sense of the world and for navigating it smoothly without having to attend to every little detail of our environments. Imagine if we had to think about every little movement of our limbs and every potential obstacle in our path while walking! The obvious usefulness of our tendency to see what we expect to see can leave us ill-prepared to detect the error that occurs when something unusual happens and our existing expectations distort our interpretation. When it occurs, this error often involves biased evaluation of ambiguous and inconsistent data, as when scientists interpret mixed data as supportive of their favored hypothesis and discount unfavorable data as aberrant. In religious settings, there is ample opportunity for this error to occur, though again actually detecting the error if and when it occurs is difficult because of the scarcity of convenient corrective resources. For example, religious people may attach an interpretation to a sacred story such as Noah's Ark that conforms to expectations formed in their religious group about a loving God who saves people from disaster and protects helpless animals. This ingroup interpretation makes it almost impossible for a group member to perceive the story as one of divine mass murder and arbitrary cruelty. Does an error occur because of this blindness to unexpected outsider perspectives on familiar precious stories? Perhaps, but perhaps not, depending on the theological outlook and prevailing attitudes to sacred texts and our obligations in interpreting them. In the case of the Noah's Ark Story, the possibility of discerning a vengeful deity is almost eliminated by the "saving God who is kind to helpless animals" reading; against the long run of biblical interpretation and theological reflection this certainly seems to be a serious error. It may also be a serious error in respect of practical considerations such as appreciating how traumatizing this story might be to a young child who hears it for the first time. Religious groups and leaders sometimes do a good job of interrupting people's expectations so that they can see reality as it more truly is—certainly they endeavor to catch some instances of this error in a way that they rarely attempt to diagnose and correct errors of the first two types.

Fourth, and the first motivational or social factor, is our tendency to see what we want to see—note the difference between seeing what we *expect* to see, which is typically a matter of cognitive instinct, and seeing what we *want* to see, which is typically a matter of social-emotional needs. This cognitive tendency can produce errors when our desires seriously distort our interpretation of ourselves, others, and the world around us. For example, almost everyone believes he or she is more intelligent and less prejudiced than the average person—an obvious statistical impossibility. Religious groups and belief systems are particularly vulnerable to this error, as many critics of religion from Feuerbach to Marx and from Nietzsche to Freud have pointed out. This is fundamentally because religious messages encode promises (possibly valid promises) to meet some of our most vital existential and social needs. This predisposes us to see in religious groups and systems of religious beliefs what we most need to see. Is what religious people most need to see really there or are they victims of need-driven self-delusion as the projection critiques allege? While this question is difficult to answer at the best of times, there is no question that the vulnerability of religious groups and religious believers to error is particularly strong at this point. Correspondingly, the question of the obligation of religious groups and leaders to be transparent about the possibility of error is particularly pointed, the resistance to this sort of self-awareness particularly pronounced, and the need for mechanisms to detect and correct cognitive delusions resulting from projection and wish fulfillment particularly urgent.

Fifth, and the second motivational or social factor, is our tendency to believe what we are told. This cognitive tendency makes social life more exciting and reduces the felt obligation to investigate all stories personally—both valuable effects. But secondhand information also has biasing effects on interpretations. In everyday life, most people tend to believe entertaining gossip passed on by friends, regardless of its actual truth. We give our friends special authority to determine what we believe about the world, other people, and ourselves. While that saves energy and increases the richness of our interpretation of reality at low cost to ourselves, it can also lead to serious errors of judgment and mistaken beliefs. Religious settings are ripe for such errors to occur, though as usual it is easier to note the probability of error than it is to demonstrate that an error actually occurs. The vulnerability to error derives particularly from the fact that religious groups often exercise authority in service of potent forms of social control. Members of religious communities tend to believe what their religious leaders tell them, particularly in religious groups that esteem their leaders highly and embrace the role of centralized authority in their common life. In this way, religious groups are frequently able to maintain leadership-defined plausibility structures even in the face of considerable evidence to the contrary. The authority-laced social fabric of religious groups appears to depend to a significant degree on this tendency to believe what we are told, and the outcomes are not always positive.

Sixth, and the third motivational or social factor, is the tendency to imagine that others agree with us. Another energy-saving device, this derives from a social instinct to fit in with a group. We imagine we fit in better if we can sustain the belief that others agree with us, whether or not it is the case. This tendency can also produce incorrect beliefs at times. For example, people who drink alcohol mistakenly assume that far more people also like to imbibe than actually do. In religious settings, the messages and practices of group life promise (and frequently deliver) not only individual benefits but also corporate belonging of a uniquely satisfying kind. The powerful experience of intimate belonging and acceptance makes religious people particularly vulnerable to the expectation—which careful surveys show tends to be mistaken—that their religious beliefs enjoy broad support from the group to which they belong. People rarely pause to check if this is really so, and the need to check is effectively obviated by religious leaders who define the putative common faith of a religious community through preaching and teaching. In fact, people routinely make adjustments to official group beliefs. While a relatively less harmful tendency than the others discussed here, it does appear that religious groups are particularly vulnerable to capitalizing unintentionally on putative near unanimity of opinion and belief for consolidating group identity and the authority of group leaders.

Seventh, and finally, we are liable to cognitive errors in the form of self-defeating thought processes and behaviors that seem obviously stupid to ourselves and to others and yet are surprisingly difficult to change. This is a standard assumption of cognitive psychotherapies. Unfortunately, the errors that result from the tendency to self-defeating thoughts and behaviors can bring tremendous suffering. Consider the woman who needs and wants comfort because she is panicky and afraid, yet pushes away every possible source of help. Or the man who drinks himself out of a job and family and eventually to death despite the fact that he loves his work and his family and at most levels wants to continue living. In both cases, ways of thinking and patterns of self-understanding are entangled in the most destructive way with emotional needs and powerful behavioral habits. In religious settings, unlike in the case of the other six tendencies to cognitive error, there is a wealth of resources for diagnosing and mitigating the effects of self-destructive beliefs and behaviors; this is one of the most impressive aspects of religious groups and one of the recurring reasons why people commit to involvement in them.

The Origin of Cognitive Biases

Why are these tendencies to cognitive error present in human beings? Errors #1, #2, and #3 are results of what I described earlier in this chapter as our innate talent for recognizing patterns and attaching meaning to them. These cognitive skills are apparently tuned within the evolutionary process to be overactive, which is optimally functional for hunter-gatherer survival. This same degree of vigilant tuning can be counterproductive on occasion within many cultural settings. Witch crazes and persecution of minorities—among a host of other human moral disasters—show that overactive pattern recognition, cause detection, and intention attribution skills can give rise to mistaken beliefs, dangerous superstitions, and sometimes terribly violent, fear-driven behavior.

Errors #4, #5, and #6, which are the three classes of motivational and social factors, derive ultimately from the social embodiment of human brains. Sociality is crucial for producing healthy brains that function optimally (see Brothers 1997). The problem is that more intricate forms of social organization and subtler types of belief assessment manifest inferential liabilities hidden within the same cognitive functions that operate well enough for most ordinary purposes.

Error #7 expresses the tragic side of the human condition. Behavioral habits and emotional needs can collide with healthy commonsense in self-destructive ways. People lash out against others, tearing apart the fabric of society and harming themselves. Such stupidity and sin can descend to the level of epic evil, particularly when socially embodied and religiously rationalized. At the level of ordinary personal frustration and failure, self-defeating thoughts and behaviors are a kind of negative culmination of every aspect of human life: evolutionary conditioning, social pressures, psychological needs, and failure of moral imagination and will. Religious traditions have a host of contradictory supernatural explanations for this great problem but no supernatural explanation is needed.

Our default cognitive tendencies may prove highly functional and advantageous for survival and world-making in some social settings and yet practically and intellectually disadvantageous or even disastrous in other social settings. This spectrum of functional evaluations of human cognitive powers confutes any simple binary opposition between useful and useless, or between true and false. Yet we can draw on psychology, medicine, and commonsense to construct feasible criteria for mental, physical, and spiritual wellbeing. Such judgments call on socially stabilized networks of norms. Obviously, it is not always in our interests to expose those webs of normative resources to scrutiny, or even to become fully aware of their operations. It is partly in virtue of this natural resistance to self-awareness that we are sometimes powerfully motivated to neglect the possibility of cognitive errors and resist naming and correcting them. Yet these judgments are also crucial in the human quest for physical, mental, and spiritual wellbeing, so in other respects we are strongly motivated to diagnose cognitive errors and identify ways of mitigating them.

Transformation of Beliefs and Behavior

The Difficulty of Resisting Cognitive Biases

As we learn about our cognitive limitations, we can choose to become aware of them, and subsequently to resist them through forging new habits that are strong enough to contend with the innate wiring, the functional tuning, and the social framing of our cognitive systems. We may not so choose, however, and in fact few people elect to fight for a high degree of self-awareness across the full range of ways that we are prone to cognitive error, let alone volunteer for the arduous work required to forge new habits that overcome those liabilities. The fact that this kind of self-awareness can disrupt some aspects of otherwise smoothly functioning secular and religious groups is added disincentive to take on this sort of moral and intellectual project. Nevertheless, the possibility for pursuing the project exists if we want to embrace it. Perhaps it is awareness of personal moral and spiritual shortcomings that most consistently triggers a quest for transformation in most people, religious or not. There is greater incentive to fight for change in that domain.

If we choose to resist our cognitive biases, resources for change do exist, and are discussed below. But the ensuing transformation is not a simple one. Like trying to win a military war against insurgents who blend in with the general population and are always prepared to wait for a better time to fight, talk of "decisive victory" in the battle with our cognitive liabilities is a category mistake. A steady transformation of habits conjoined with long-term vigilance is a more sensible way to conceive the challenge.

A first measure of the difficulty of transforming default mental and emotional habits is the recalcitrance of those habits. Cognitive and emotional evolution has forged those default patterns and typical social training reinforces many of them so there is naturally internal resistance to change. This means that prodigious levels of energy and imagination, courage and persistence, are required to change default mental habits.

A second measure of the difficulty of transforming default mental and emotional habits is the implacable social resistance to some types of change, which reinforces natural internal resistance. While social groups encourage behavioral changes related to smooth social function, and punish failures to change quite severely, many types of cognitive change are resisted fiercely. For example, even to raise the possibility within some conservative theistic religious communities that there might be a species-wide cognitive bias toward believing in supernatural agents can bring harsh reprisal. And the politician who wants to run a campaign that resists the temptation to exploit voters' default cognitive biases will be mocked by campaign strategists and dissuaded by political advisors.

A third measure of the difficulty of transforming default mental and emotional habits is the heritability of certain patterns of belief and behavior. For example, Laura Koenig and Thomas Bouchard (2006) have shown by means of twin and adoption studies that authoritarianism, conservatism, and religiousness—jointly, the *Traditional Moral Values Triad*—are heritable to a significant degree. This is a challenging finding for traditional religious anthropology and even many contemporary researchers. This genetic element in religious beliefs and behaviors indicates the presence of a selection bias operative in the formation and endorsement of religious beliefs, which subsequently resists change.

Despite these indications of how difficult it is to change habits of belief and behavior, the situation is far from intractable. Many techniques have proved effective to some degree. Schooling can contest superstitious impulses. Scientific research can raise consciousness about mistaken beliefs. Character training can yield artful social engagement. Long experience and deep attentiveness can produce wisdom. Before discussing such techniques of transformation change in more detail, I first discuss five basic transformational resources that support change in beliefs and behaviors, and thus offer a basis for resisting our cognitive biases.

Five Transformational Resources

Self-awareness about the likelihood of cognitive error is depressing and misleading without some understanding of how we can recognize and resist our tendencies to err. In fact, there are several basic transformational resources that are marshaled in both secular and religions methods for promoting discernment, self-awareness, and character change.

The first resource for change is *neuroplasticity*. New neurons (neurogenesis) and dying neurons, changes in number and type of synapses (synaptogenesis), and changes in the biochemical capacities of synaptic receptors alter the brain's functional capacities. Contrary to earlier neurological assumptions that many parts of the brain are anatomically and functionally immutable after the periods of development critical to their formation, the neuroplasticity thesis is that virtually every part of the brain remains mutable long after it is initially formed and functional, not merely the parts related to memory and learning. The evidence for the neuroplasticity thesis is extremely compelling, led by spectacular longitudinal studies of athletes and musicians (see the journal *Neural Plasticity*, as well as accessible surveys in Begley 2007; Doidge 2007; LeDoux 2002; Schwartz & Begley 2002). It is one of the most important contemporary discoveries about human neurology—indeed, about human life—because it implies that the brain has a fundamental capacity for rewiring itself in response to environmental circumstances, training, and traumatic injury. All capacities for cognitive and behavioral transformation of both the short-term and long-term varieties appear to depend to various degrees on neuroplasticity.

A second resource for change is *implementation intentions*. The brain's executive control functions allow ideas, judgments, memory, and desires to impact action plans so that behavior rises above the merely instinctual and reactive to become creative and imaginative. This capacity in human beings is profoundly open to intervention through training, ritualized habit formation, and the deployment of action scripts. In particular, we can deploy behavior-specific implementation intentions to form new habits. This involves stipulating a goal (such as being courteous to family members), imagining circumstances in which the goal is at risk of not being achieved (such as feeling stressed when overworked or grumpy after a midday nap), defining actions that we intend to take under those circumstances (such as reminding ourselves of our likelihood of being discourteous and our desire to show respect for our loved ones), and practicing the implementation intention until we consistently achieve the desired goal. Implementation intentions deployed in this way have been shown to be highly effective in avoiding risky behaviors, in overcoming addictions, in blocking unhealthy impulses, and in changing behavioral habits (see Armitage 2004, 2006, Cohen & Gollwitzer 2007, Galanter 2006, Gollwitzer 1993, 1999, Gollwitzer & Moskowitz 1996, Gollwitzer & Schaal 1998, Orbell & Sheeran 2000, Orbell et al. 1997, Prestwich et al. 2003, Sheeran 2002, Sheeran & Orbell 1999, 2000, Sheeran & Silverman 2003, Sheeran et al. 2005, Verplanken & Faes 1999).

A third resource for change is *ritual*. Socially reinforced rituals can also produce behavior change and character transformation, even when they do not involve specific implementation intentions of the sort just discussed. The explanation for this probably lies in at least two considerations. On the one hand, ritual repetition is intrinsically rewarding thanks to the fact that its neural realization appears centrally to involve the dopamine circuitry of the frontal lobes, which implicates pleasure centers (see McNamara 2002; for a related but neurologically slightly different account, see Newberg et al. 2001). On the other hand, repeated actions reinforce a way of thinking that subsequently more easily emerges into consciousness even under stress when more automatic behavior tends to take over (see Hogue 2003). Once a way of thinking—a worldview, a moral framework, a suite of moral purposes—intrudes itself into a reflexive stream of behavior, we have an opportunity to evaluate our actions and arrest their trajectory if we so choose. Carefully crafted rituals lay down cognitive pathways that then appear within the flow of consciousness more consistently. This helps to decrease automaticity of behavior in problem areas while increasing awareness of behaviors and behavioral consequences, thereby creating opportunities to interpose interpretations and action plans deriving from those ritually established cognitive networks. Underneath the double role of ritual in both maintaining social order (Durkheim 1915) and transforming society (Turner 1969)—a classic tension in ritual studies—participation in specific forms of ritual programming can increase cognitive alertness and moral freedom and thereby both reinforce self-understandings and help to transform behavior.

A fourth resource for change is *unconscious processes*. Some forms of change appear to be rooted beneath the level of conscious awareness altogether. In particularly aggressive quests for self-understanding, it is possible to expose automatic behavioral impulses and cognitive habits to awareness, analysis, and modification. This is not a reference to direct behavioral modification of the sort used in cognitive-behavioral therapies, which more properly falls under the category of implementation intentions, above. Rather, this refers to the kind of therapeutic process prized in the psychoanalytic tradition of psychotherapy, in some types of spiritual direction, and in some types of shamanistic intervention. The premise here is that cognitive and behavioral patterns are often set so early and deeply—sometimes by trauma but more often by ordinary habit formation—that they are beyond the reach of memory and understanding, yet remain behaviorally intrusive. Some of these induce great unhappiness and resist every conscious effort at change. The techniques for indirectly exposing such reflexive ways of thinking and acting vary. Some involve the construction of interpretative narratives that are useful for gaining some reflective control over unwanted behavior sequences—pragmatically speaking, the historical accuracy of such narratives is secondary to their personal intelligibility and potential to leverage change. Some involve the symbolic and often unconscious reenactment in a non-traumatic therapeutic context of the problematic structural dynamics, in the course of which unexpected responses may defuse the causal inevitability of the behavioral and cognitive reflexes and allow new possibilities for behavior and self-understanding to arise. Such therapeutic processes can effectively promote change without the client ever gaining a clear understanding of how the change occurs or why change previously seemed so impossible (for wildly opposed analyses of how this is possible, see the Jungian approach of Young-Eisendrat 2004 and the Shamanistic approach of Sandner 1996, among a host of other works).

A fifth resource for change is *social inducements*. As the behaviorist school of psychology has emphasized, inducements to attempt specific behavioral change, and also to tackle the wider context of character and personality change, help us overcome natural resistance associated with confronting aspects of ourselves that may be painful to contemplate. Escaping existential despair and self-loathing is inducement of a personal kind. Social inducement refers to meeting the requirements of group belonging and social fluency, and involves rewards for appropriate behavior and punishments for inappropriate behavior. Moreover, the three last-mentioned techniques for behavioral and character change—implementation intentions, ritual forms, and unconscious processes—either require some degree of social connection or can be powerfully reinforced by an appropriate social group. For example, Twelve-Step programs crucially deploy group contexts to establish and consolidate implementation intentions, to cultivate healthy ritual reinforcement of cognitive and behavioral programming, and to help people find their way to new spaces of personal freedom even when they do not know how to get there by themselves. Social context is every bit as vital as neural plasticity for facilitating these techniques of behavioral and character change.

This litany of transformational possibilities may suggest that human character is mercurial and readily changes with the slightest effort. But experience indicates that this is not so. While the potential for change is genuine, change occurs most readily at the level of behaviors and beliefs that can be impacted by attentional shifts—shifts that allow us to expose otherwise automatic cognitive and behavioral sequencing to scrutiny and thereby to interpose more desirable alternative possibilities (this is one of the conclusions to be drawn from Kristeller 2007; see below). By contrast, the kinds of change needed to overcome the cognitive errors that are all important in religious beliefs and behaviors are extraordinarily difficult to achieve and require adept-level training. Moreover, fundamental personality change is exceptionally unusual in human beings. Character transformation is thus variously a readily available live possibility, an exceptionally hard-won life goal, and virtually impossible, depending on what type and degree of transformation we have in mind (see Heatherton & Weinberger 1994).

Techniques for Mitigating Cognitive Error

What techniques work best to mitigate cognitive error? This is an important question in a host of contexts, from the comparative evaluation of psychotherapies to the comparative evaluation of religious traditions, and in recent years especially in the assessment of religious versus non-religious techniques for change. My central concern here is to explain why such comparative calculations are formidably difficult to perform. The interreligious calculation has predictably tended to favor the evaluator's preferred religious tradition—a hurdle that the new discipline of comparative theology seeks to overcome—but in fact seems as complex as ever. The religious-versus-secular calculation is straightforward, according to some recent writers (see Hitchens 2007, for whom "religion spoils everything"; also see Dawkins 2007, Harris 2007), but I believe a sound comparison is extremely complicated in this case also.

The reason such comparisons are difficult is chiefly that religion shows up on both sides of the issue. Moral training, ritually implanted worldviews, and social reinforcement are prominent aspects of most religious traditions, so it is safe to say that they have valuable assets to offer people seeking to overcome cognitive errors of at least some kinds—particularly error #7 and to some degree error #3. But religious traditions also unintentionally tend to increase chances for cognitive error. In relation to matters of belief, for example, the interest in rooting out cognitive error is rarely thematized within religious communities and inevitably competes with the many ways in which religion exercises social control to resist group identity dilution in the form of non-authorized beliefs.

Pressing deeper, the reason religion both promotes and resists healthy resistance to cognitive error derives from the entanglement of cognitive error in experiences of cognitive dissonance. When it intrudes, as described in Chapter 4, cognitive dissonance threatens to disrupt the silent social power of religion by calling fundamental beliefs into question. The varied roles of religion in the social construction of reality are most effective when their internal architecture is not evident and cannot be scrutinized. Cognitive dissonance tears away part of the shroud and manifests the inner social workings of religious groups. To maintain their social effectiveness, therefore, as well as to fulfill their self-designated educational and spiritual missions, religious groups must attempt to anticipate and address cognitive dissonance. On the one hand, this involves suppressing awareness sufficient to trigger the unwanted dissonance in the first place, and this is the sense in which religious groups tend to have an interest in perpetuating cognitive biases. On the other hand, because cognitive dissonance arises fastest and most reliably in relation to more obviously false beliefs, religious groups also tend to be invested in eliminating personally idiosyncratic, intellectually fragile, and foolishly false religious beliefs. The result is various forms of education, public speaking, liturgy, sacred scripture study, and group discernment processes. These may not impact subtle cognitive biases but they are effective in detecting gross errors, as when a putative belief is clearly implausible, emotionally unhealthy, and possibly dangerous. Small religious sects that stress intimate mind control forego this function of cognitive error correction in the name of complete conformity to a corporate identity defined by a charismatic leader. But cognitive error correction is an important aspect of spiritual maturity in mainstream religious groups with less intrusive forms of belief cultivation and monitoring.

This suggests a criterion for healthy rather than toxic religious communities: minimizing cognitive error and emotional harm at the same time as maximizing individual change in the direction of lower suffering and greater cognitive insight. Unfortunately, religious groups in practice both promote and interfere with realizing such healthy processes of transformation. And much the same might be true—to a lesser degree I would think—of therapeutic methods for transformation and even for certain types of education.

Both religious and secular techniques have proved effective for mitigating the problems caused by many kinds of cognitive bias, to various degrees depending on the bias in question. I discuss a representative selection of such techniques here: meditation, psychotherapy, and rigorous intellectual training. Throughout I am concerned to demonstrate the complexity of the ways that human groups both furnish resources for dealing with the problem of cognitive error in some respects while simultaneously resisting the requisite self-awareness and corrective resources in other respects.

Meditation and Cognitive Error

First, then, let us consider meditation as a technique for mitigating cognitive error, focusing on the widespread Buddhist practice of mindfulness meditation—*vipassanā*; literally, to see things as they really are. While the cognitive and behavioral consequences of meditation are sometimes overstated by meditation enthusiasts, extensive research has confirmed the correctness of the central claim, that mindfulness meditation supports behavioral and cognitive change.

The most comprehensive survey of psychological research into putative changes due to meditation is Jean Kristeller's (2007) multi-domain model of meditation effects. Kristeller distinguishes six domains of effects: attentional/cognitive, physical, emotional, behavioral, self-relational/other-relational, and spiritual. She then distinguishes within each domain the kinds of changes that can be expected in the initial stages of meditation training, as well as in the intermediate and advanced stages. For example, in the attentional/cognitive domain, beginning meditators can expect to see increases in ability to focus and awareness of their own thoughts, while intermediate meditators can expect to see greater mindfulness, less ruminative thinking, and greater attentional flexibility. In the emotional domain, beginners can expect lower reactivity and higher awareness of emotional patterns, while intermediate meditators can expect decreased anxiety, anger, and depression along with increased positive emotion, stronger engagement in the moment, and sustained equanimity. In the behavioral domain, beginners can expect increases in impulse control and awareness of behavior patterns, while intermediate meditators can expect to enjoy increased ability to overcome bad habits, more compassionate behavior, and decreased addictive behavior. Kristeller presents significant empirical evidence in support of her multi-domain model, including a fairly comprehensive list of relevant research studies. (Also see the neurological studies of Lutz et al. 2004, and the discussions in Begley 2007, Wallace 2007, Benson 1975, 1996.)

The most spectacular, though not necessarily the most robust, neurological evidence for sustained long-term changes as a result of meditation is probably a research study of neurologist Richard Davidson. In response to a personal request by the Dalai Lama, Davidson's research group used EEG equipment to measure the electrical activity in the brains of eight Tibetan Buddhist monks with at least ten thousand hours of meditation practice and ten volunteer controls with a modest week of meditation training specifically for the purposes of the experiment. The widely reported result was that the adepts displayed distinctive and non-typical gamma-wave signaling before, during, and after meditation, while the novice controls displayed no change after meditation whether or not they experienced similar gamma-wave changes during meditation. This was hailed as important evidence for neuroplasticity in relation to high-level cognitive-behavioral features of human beings (see the report in Lutz et al. 2004). Critics were quick to point out that it may merely be evidence that some brains are better suited to intense meditation than others, and that the intricate selection processes of full-time meditators in Buddhist monastic settings inevitably locate the few people with the right neural gear for the job. The longitudinal studies of meditation needed to settle the question of whether meditation produces neurologically detectable changes in brain structure or function are only just now underway.

While meditation is typically the domain of religious traditions, secular forms of meditation practice do exist. Perhaps best known among these is Herbert Benson's reduction of Transcendental Meditation to the simple and thoroughly secular technique of relaxation. The bodily response to this simplest form of relaxation meditation has been shown to have significant health effects, particularly in relation to stress-related illnesses affecting the cardio-vascular system (see Benson 1975, 1996).

Within religious traditions, meditation practices take an enormous variety of forms and enjoy a wide array of legitimating explanations. Some traditions stress meditation as a central aspect of corporate and individual spirituality. Others stress prayer as a relational encounter between a believer and a supernatural entity, but such acts of prayer can often involve elements of meditation such as focused attention, heightened concentration, and wide awareness. Under a host of descriptions, therefore, meditation and its varied effects on cognition, emotion, behavior, and stress have been central to religious practice of many kinds. To date, secular versions of meditation have proved hard to motivate beyond the associated health benefits.

Kristeller's survey and analysis demonstrates that traditions of meditation practice, with widely varying emphases, have a robust claim to confront our vulnerability to cognitive error in several domains. Most notably, some forms of meditation are well suited to confront error #7 by raising awareness about self-defeating modes of thought and increasing the willingness and ability to change the resulting behaviors. Other forms of meditation, when pursued to adept level, are well suited to the task of discerning oneself, one's relationships, and even the world as they are, beneath the distortions of social and motivational factors and behind the biases of the cognitive factors that predispose us to errors of perception, interpretation, and behavior (errors #1–#6). Very few meditation experts reach the adept level necessary to benefit from the full wealth of resources for confronting our vulnerability to cognitive error. But even moderately seasoned meditators understand the point from their own experience: the focus of attention and broad awareness achieved in certain meditation states allows meditators to escape the grip of their self-delusions and distorted interpretations to some degree. It follows that religious traditions have been responsible for promoting one of the very few more or less timeless resources for confronting, diagnosing, and correcting cognitive error.

Psychotherapies and Cognitive Error

Second, religious and secular psychotherapeutic techniques are best suited for addressing the cognitive processes that produce self-defeating beliefs and self-destructive behaviors (error #7). Psychotherapeutic methods promise immediate benefits related to healthy emotional and social function, and even improved physical health, particularly through the reduction of unhealthy stress (see the journals *Psychotherapy Research* and *Psychotherapy Theory, Research, Practice, Training* for an array of empirical research studies, and see the surveys in Norcross et al. 2005; Roth & Fonagy 2004; Wampold 2008). Fundamentally, it is enormously satisfying and intrinsically rewarding as well as socially advantageous to break self-defeating habits of mind, to rise above self-destructive behaviors, and to craft new ways of being that bring greater happiness, peace of mind, and social artfulness.

As with meditation, exaggerated claims on behalf of the efficacy of psychotherapies have been vigorously challenged. The valid criticisms are that psychotherapy lacks an integrative framework of interpretation that allows therapists to generate powerful consensus about which therapeutic techniques to apply to which problems; that there are high dropout rates (47% in the United States according to Wierzbicki & Pekarik 1993); that dropout rates are much higher for minority, less educated, and low-income clients; that it is difficult to tell when success and failure have been achieved; and that it is difficult to distinguish the healing effects of the passing of time from the healing effects of an extended therapeutic process. Nevertheless, the most careful and comprehensive research suggests that, despite these difficulties, a conditionally affirmative assessment of the value of psychotherapies is in order (again, see Wampold 2008).

At this point in western cultures, and increasingly in other world cultures, there exist side-by-side extensive religious and secular traditions of psychotherapy. On the one side, religions are peppered with practices and techniques that fall under the descriptor "psychotherapeutic" broadly construed. For example, there is Scientology's auditing process (involving an interview in conjunction with "E-meter" biofeedback measurement of electrical resistance on the surface of the auditee's finger), more conventional pastoral counseling and Dharma studies, advanced forms of spiritual direction, and group training in spiritual practices. On the other side, secular psychotherapy achieved professional recognition during the twentieth century and now is a large tent filled with hundreds of therapeutic techniques. Dozens of these techniques have been subjected to formal outcome studies by academic psychologists, insurance companies, and professional therapists. Many "standard of care" therapeutic modalities are virtually indistinguishable in religious and secular settings, because the operative norms for health and training of caregivers are so similar. But there are also characteristic differences related mainly to the way spirituality and religiousness are handled: therapeutic relationships can be constructed with or without articulated goals for spiritual maturity as well as mental health, with or without norms for therapeutic success rooted in authoritative spiritual traditions and sacred texts, and with or without the resources and conceptual frameworks of particular religious traditions.

The five basic resources for cognitive and behavioral change—neuroplasticity, implementation intentions, ritual practices, unconscious processes, and social motivations and supports—are leveraged in a variety of ways within the host of psychotherapeutic processes. The resulting psychotherapeutic methods appear to range across essentially the same suite of possibilities in both religious and secular contexts. This is part of the reason that dialogues between religion and psychotherapy are so rich (for Buddhism and psychotherapy, see works such as Epstein 1995, 2005, Fromm & Suzuki 1986, Meckel & Moore 1992, Molino 1999, Safran 2003, Wellings & McCormick 2005; for Christianity and psychotherapy, see works such as Alter 1994, Capps 1983, Clarke 1988, Clinebell 1984, Fowler 1981, Kelly 1995, Kelsey 1982, McDargh 1983, Schlauch 1995, Whitehead & Whitehead 1992). I suspect that the therapeutic relationship and the therapeutic technique determine the mechanisms of transformation more than the religious or secular context—certainly, this is how things appear to the religious naturalist who rejects the idea of supernatural divine beings that can supposedly change people in the blink of an eye. In all cases, therapeutic transformation is as difficult as it is rewarding. It involves painful moments of self-realization and repeated, multileveled failure to realize one's cognitive and behavioral goals. But it also involves deepening awareness of circumstances and one's responses to them, as well as the joy of breakthrough moments and increased freedom of thought and action when under stress. The drama and intensity of the therapeutic process is indicative of a fundamentally spiritual quest, whether or not spirituality is thematized by patient or therapist.

Psychotherapeutic techniques, whether secular or religious, may be best for dealing with the tendency to error #7, but they also appear to be somewhat useful for confronting the social and motivational factors that expose us to cognitive errors #4–#6. A well-conceived therapeutic process enhances self-awareness, reinforces the ability to discern motivations and interests, and heightens sensitivity to the actual complexity of interpersonal transactions. The same research that ascribes overall effectiveness to psychotherapeutic processes suggests that the impact of psychotherapy on cognitive errors #4–#6 should be small but significant. Unfortunately, psychotherapies do not appear to be useful for confronting the cognitive factors that lead to errors #1–#3.

Rigorous Intellectual Training and Cognitive Error

Third, rigorous intellectual training is particularly useful for detecting and resisting all of the cognitive biases that can produce mistaken beliefs, including errors #1 through #6. Effectively resisting such cognitive biases is not the work of a mere few years of education in reading and writing, humanities and sciences, however. It takes many years to ritualize the process of following evidence where it leads rather than where we want it or expect it to lead. Such educational achievements may be of no interest to some and out of reach financially or intellectually for others. But the possibility exists nonetheless that the error-prone aspects of our otherwise eminently functional and generally accurate cognitive instincts can be resisted, ameliorated, and eventually significantly overcome through disciplined education and training.

To the extent that religious groups and leaders do not acknowledge their vulnerability to cognitive error, whether or not actual errors occur—to the extent, that is, that religious groups and leaders do not take advantage of available resources for diagnosing the potential for cognitive error and educating religious people about it—rigorous intellectual training can be and has been seen as the enemy of religion. The so-called New Atheists do not fail to stress this point (see Dawkins 2007, Dennett 2006, Harris 2007, Hitchens 2007), and there is good reason for this interpretation. For example, a 2005 Pew survey (http://pewforum. org/surveys) reports that 42 per cent of Americans believe that "life on earth has existed in its present form since the beginning of time" (this includes almost three-fourths of white evangelical Protestants). Moreover, a further 18 per cent believe that evolution is guided by a divine being and not by natural selection. Thus, a staggering 60 per cent of Americans possess what appear to be profoundly religiously motivated and sustained beliefs about nature and history that are directly challenged by rigorous intellectual education. Notice that the subtle synthetic views in which a *divine being works through natural selection* (classic theistic evolution) are excluded from this 60 per cent, as are atheistic, naturalistic, and religiously indifferent interpretations of evolution. The 60 per cent figure encompasses people with beliefs that directly contradict the most basic elements of evolutionary biology.

The fact that most of this 60 per cent have had some science education and yet still hold these supernatural beliefs about Earth geology and biology indicates the extent to which religious social settings are capable of supporting scientifically erroneous beliefs. The errors in this case are understandable; they derive from failures of imagination in the face of biological complexity and evolutionary time spans, and believing what we want to believe in light of justified worries about what evolution, if correct, portends for the moral intelligibility and existential relevance of a divine being. Correcting and resisting the cognitive biases that yield such errors is evidently extremely difficult. It can take decades for exceptional minds to learn how to combine apparently competing worldviews into intellectually and spiritually satisfying syntheses. The fact that only a few people undertake such arduous cognitive self-reconstruction is one of the reasons that education introduces a genuine hierarchy of expertise into a social system, from Plato's time up to today. It also injects a problematic tone of condescension and defensiveness into debate over social issues whereby some effectively claim (not without significant justification) more objectivity and insight than others.

One of the most interesting features of rigorous intellectual training is how little impact correcting cognitive errors related to belief formation (errors #1–#6) often has on cognitive errors related to self-defeating relational and personal beliefs and behaviors (error #7)—and *vice versa*. Even training in particular disciplinary specializations produces cognitive habits that ameliorate the effects of some cognitive errors more than others. For example, professional historians are enormously sensitive to errors associated with contextual specificity, such as anachronism and abstraction—a species of the "everyone thinks, behaves, and believes like I do" error—whereas natural scientists appear to have little advantage over the general population in overcoming this instinctive flaw in human cognitive operations. Meanwhile, good scientists develop advanced suspicion of their overactive inbuilt pattern recognition and cause-detection skills—a variant of the "too much data underdetermines interpretations" error—which directly mitigates against superstitious beliefs in every domain of life, while humanities specialists typically are not trained in this way and do not have the same sensitivities. This is probably one of the reasons belief in a supernatural divine being is so rare among premier scientists in the United States, as measured by membership in the National Academy of Sciences (7 per cent)—much lower than among US scientists generally (39 per cent) and enormously lower than in the general US population (upwards of 90 per cent) (see Larson & Witham 1997, 1998).

Another fascinating feature of the cognitive effects of disciplined education and training is that, in some forms, it produces cognitive fruits in relation to errors #1–#6 that are quite similar to some that flourish in advanced meditation practice. For example, Edmund Husserl believed that phenomenologists, with prodigious effort and focused training, could penetrate a variety of cognitive and perceptual processes in order to make objective observations without falling prey to the sorts of cognitive errors that routinely produce mistaken beliefs about the structure of consciousness and distorted interpretations of the surrounding world. The two best known techniques for achieving such mastery are *bracketing*, which involves deliberately not taking account of some features of an object of consciousness (say, ordinary assumptions about its ontological status or social function) in order to interpret other features in their own terms (say, its qualitative characteristics and contextual importance); and *variation of parameters*, which involves imaginatively changing conditioning factors in an effort to detect the most salient underlying causal structures and dynamic features of a phenomenon (see Husserl 1931). The phenomenological tradition flowing from Husserl has substantiated these claims to a significant extent. Much the same kinds of claims are made by and about advanced meditation practitioners (see Bhawuk 2008, Bornstein & Masling 1990, Kristeller 2007, Krueger 2008, Rao and Paranjpe 2008, Rinpoche & Napper 1986, Singer & Bonanno 1990, Travis & Pearson 2000, Vyner 2007). It is these features of meditation practices that underlie the wealth of phenomenological observations about states of consciousness in South Asian philosophical traditions, both Hindu and Buddhist, and also in Tibetan and Zen Buddhist literature. There are differences: phenomenological training focuses on describing internal states of consciousness and the surrounding world whereas advanced meditation insight seems most useful for understanding internal states of consciousness and interpersonal dynamics. But the similarities are impressive.

The interpretative powers conferred by advanced phenomenological techniques are not always appreciated. For example, consider Forman's (1999) claim that states of so-called "pure consciousness" permit adepts to discriminate the contribution made to experience by our operative conceptual frameworks and social contexts. Forman argues that this skill enables mystics from all traditions to agree on the ineffable nature of the logical object of mystical experience, regardless of the cultural, historical, religious, doctrinal, or devotional contexts of the mystics themselves. Forman deploys this argument against contextualists (Katz 1978, Proudfoot 1985, Bagger 1999) who argue on essentially Kantian grounds that it is impossible to tease apart the intrinsic content of mystical experiences from its various conditioning factors. Which side is finally correct in this debate remains to be seen, if the debate is in fact tractable. But in attempting to resolve the issue, it is important to contend with the fact that advanced states of concentrated attention permit the discrimination of extremely fine features of cognitive, perceptual, emotional, and memory processing—with far more depth and precision of insight than would be thought possible by a person familiar with only the usual range of states of consciousness, no matter how well educated and highly trained they may be in other respects.

We have important evidence here, therefore, that both religious and secular techniques exist that are capable in principle of confronting most and perhaps all of the cognitive errors #1–#6, just as we saw earlier that there are both religious and secular techniques that address cognitive error #7. Yet the differences matter a great deal. Secular forms of advanced education are far more effective than secular or religious therapeutic techniques in addressing all of errors #1–#6. Moreover, even if advanced meditation practice is year for year just as effective as secular forms of education in addressing errors #1–#6, education is far more widely available, imposes far fewer special requirements on those who pursue it, and remains far more directly relevant to ameliorating the sometimes erroneous effects of our cognitive biases. This defines the sense in which the rise of awareness about tendencies to cognitive error of the first six types is a notable and commendable achievement of secular cultures, often battling against significant resistance from religious groups, and massively outstripping the ancient and limited achievements of religious practices in relation to these six cognitive errors. In relation to the seventh error, pertaining to self-defeating beliefs and behaviors, the story is quite different. Religious means of confronting such tendencies to cognitive error are more widely accessible than secular therapeutic techniques and, roughly speaking, apparently no less effective. These conclusions indicate the sense in which the story about religion and cognitive error is a complex and fascinating one.

Conclusion: *Homo Religiosus* and Brains

For all of the ways we are right to stand in awe of human cognitive powers, we are also wise to recognize that they are quite imperfect. It is not surprising, given the evolutionary circumstances to which human cognition is adapted. The cognitive science of our imperfect brains—including the work of Bering and Atran presented above—has the potential to transform the way religious anthropology approaches phenomena related to religious belief. The field of comparative religious ideas within religious studies and theology is quite young but already it has become dominated by the view that religious ideas are usually too full of richly layered existential and contextual meanings to be significantly compared to one another. While anyone who knows anything about religion finds it easy to appreciate this view, it also seems somewhat defeatist, cutting off a valid line of inquiry before it gets started. I suspect that the landscape constraints that Atran describes, backed by the sorts of experiments that both he and Bering summarize, could provoke a more balanced approach in comparative religious ideas, opening religionists and theologians to the possibility that religious beliefs might be a mix of constraints that produce recurring similarities and unique cultural and chance determinations that produce differences. By the same token, the cognitive science of religion would do well to notice the staggering wealth of detailed information that religious studies specialists have collected about the world's religious beliefs and practices. Most cognitive scientists know less than a rank novice in religious studies about the vast associated literatures on religious beliefs, so cooperation across disciplines seems essential here.

The cognitive science of religion has particularly challenging implications for religious anthropology in regard to the truth of religious beliefs. Theology rarely investigates the truth claims of religion in respect of the evolutionary function of the corresponding beliefs, the neural expression of those beliefs, or the cognitive appeal of their minimal counterintuitiveness. Were theologians to address such issues frankly, they would necessarily make manifest the social and psychological dynamics of religion, which seem to work more smoothly when religious people remain unaware of them (see Chapter 4, "Groups," above, and Berger 1967). Theologians who take it as part of their moral obligation to support the spiritual wellbeing of religious believers, and who begin publicly discussing the cognitive science of religion, may find themselves in an especially difficult situation. They can be understood as betraying their calling and they may be—indeed, have been—resisted both by other theologians and by the very religious groups they seek to serve for essentially social-identity rather than intellectual reasons. Van Harvey (1970) described such a doubly committed intellectual as an "alienated theologian," though he had in mind the impact of historical critical consciousness rather than cognitive neuroscience. It follows that there are powerful incentives for theologians not to engage what the cognitive neurosciences have to say about religious behaviors, beliefs, and experiences with the seriousness these lines of research deserve. Of course, at this point it is important to recall that there are many kinds of theologians, in the broad sense that word has here, and some of them are not so constrained, either because their religious group affords the required freedom, or because they have secular and non-religiously affiliated intellectual projects.

I have argued that the problem of cognitive error is about personal suffering through self-defeating ways of thinking and self-destructive behaviors, as well as mistaken beliefs. Evolution will not solve these problems for us, at least not in the short term, and perhaps not at all, given the demonstrated difficulty of exposing subtle cognitive processes to selection pressures capable of changing our species' gene-based cognitive fortunes. To fix this problem, short of genetic engineering—and where would we begin with that?—we will have to deploy our most creative and rigorous forms of social organization to establish relevant rituals, implementation intentions, training practices, and therapeutic processes. Fortunately, the message of neuroplasticity is that change is possible with respect to overcoming both the instinctive formation of mistaken beliefs and incessantly self-defeating modes of thoughts and behavior.

A lifetime of disciplined training seems necessary to achieve internal resistance sufficient to contend with our cognitive liabilities. We should expect that people will inevitably specialize in one or a few types of cognitive reprogramming. Expert historians immune to cognitive liabilities of the "people in other eras must think as we do" sort may still mistakenly expect a coin almost certainly to come up tails when told it has already come up heads fifty times in a row. Mathematicians who would never make common mistakes in probability may find themselves deeply superstitious because it was never in their professional interest to tame instinctively overactive pattern recognition skills. The highly trained physicist who would never make mistakes in the domain of pattern recognition and thus would never fall prey to superstition may nonetheless be thoroughly ensnared in cycles of self-defeating beliefs and behaviors that make everyone miserable and cause terrible suffering. And the monk who is deliciously free from attachment and the suffering it brings—on the very edge of enlightenment—may still be utterly unable to avoid biased interpretation of incomplete data about the earth's evolutionary and geological history. We do well to spread the word about cognitive error, especially if it prevents people expert in one type of reprogramming from arrogantly supposing that they are thereby immune to cognitive error in every sense.

Spreading the word in this way—regardless of its salutary effects for individual happiness and social understanding—will not delight some representatives of religions. It is in religious groups, after all, that cognitive errors such as superstition and biased appraisal of incomplete evidence find a sanctified home, where they are sometimes set apart from criticism and presented as the height of wisdom. And it is in religious contexts that resources for the diagnosis and correction of tendencies to cognitive error are routinely neglected and the full story about human cognitive processes routinely suppressed. Yet is it also religious traditions that furnish the most widely accessible techniques for personal transformation in relation to self-defeating beliefs and behaviors (error #7). Religion is such an enigma!

We need to recognize that religious groups, as well as economic and political practices, do have vested interests in neglecting resources for diagnosing and correcting tendencies to cognitive error. This suggests that there may be little large-scale change in the human cognitive profile for the foreseeable future. Yet there are always individuals and some groups who seek transparent awareness of human cognitive biases in social practices. Those people should have uncomplicated access to all of the information and techniques relevant for achieving their intellectual and transformational goals. People in a position to assist those who seek help in handling the effects of cognitive bias should speak plainly about it, battling instinctive tendencies toward cognitive error on as many fronts as possible, and fostering as many techniques of diagnosis and correction as are available. This means diverse and disciplined education. It means meditation. It means suitable therapeutic processes.

After that, we must let the chips fall where they may with regard to religious beliefs and practices. Perhaps we come to see some of those beliefs as superstitious. Perhaps we conclude that those beliefs are the height of wisdom despite the constant threat of undiagnosed cognitive error. More likely we will find wisdom hovering within and behind the superstitions and errors. Wisdom lives on despite the abuse it suffers at the hands of cognitively careless mortals whose most intractable form of idolatry is to make ultimate reality conform to their undiagnosed tendencies to cognitive self-delusion. For those who learn to see wisdom there present in the midst of cognitive confusion, however, there is great and simple joy as the world untangles and wisdom shines through clearly. This is a wondrous matter of human brains recognizing their own limitations and deploying socially borne methods for improving their accuracy and reliability—brains in a social nexus transforming brains. And there should be no question that the ensuing transformation is worth the prodigious effort required.

CHAPTER 6

Bodies

Introduction

One of the consequences of the wondrous human capacity for self-consciousness is that we tend to regard ourselves most essentially as what we appear to ourselves to be in moments of clear self-awareness. This is what underlies the instinct to assume that consciousness is somehow housed, or embodied, in human beings, and indeed by projective extrapolation, in other animals and perhaps even plants or inanimate objects or the universe as a whole. This idea of "embodiment" is potentially problematic, for two reasons. First, it threatens to prejudge complex metaphysical questions about human nature by suggesting the en-fleshing of a non-physical soul rather than the presence of soul *within and as* the complex organization of components in a physical system. Second, the instinctive idea of embodiment potentially distracts interpreters of religious anthropology from the vast range of ways in which the body is crucial to human nature. Both problems can implicitly bias the conversation between theology and the sciences and cause religious anthropology to overlook vital aspects of human nature in favor of dwelling on spiritualized abstractions. This is a species of reductionism just as pernicious as that of scientists who neglect the complexity of religious phenomena or frame religion as driven solely by cognitive delusion, emotional pining, and psycho-social deprivation. For example, it is tempting to regard the human condition as most essentially expressed in terms of suffering and the quest to overcome the attachment that produces suffering, or in terms of original sin and the quest for spiritual reconciliation with a divine creator. Meanwhile, bodily aspects of the human condition are pushed to the margins and often completely out of sight.

The significance of the bodily character of human life is discussed throughout the book, including in the previous chapters on evolution, groups, and brains. In this chapter I focus on three domains in which sharp awareness of human bodies and their functions is vital for understanding the human being as *homo religiosus*. The first is sociality, from the brain's facilitation of social behaviors to the role of bodies in structuring social arrangements. This is vital for any consideration of the corporate aspects of religion. The second is morality, from human moral instincts to the reasoning we deploy to make sense of them. Morality has a great deal to do with the regulation of bodies and sustains complex relationships with many aspects of corporate and individual religiosity. The third is the domain of religious and spiritual experiences, understood as stretching all the way from simple Seder meals and church picnics to the mass hysteria of religious revivals, and from ineffable mystical states achieved in *zazen* to moments of luminous inspiration in an encounter with an artwork of exquisite beauty.

In all three areas, bodies make religion, in the broadest sense of the word, not only possible but also inevitable. Bodies influence the cognitive and emotional shape that religion takes in individuals, and the social and moral practices that religions manifest in groups. Traditional religious anthropologies have often attributed the specific forms of religious beliefs and practices to sacred texts or supernatural commands, or perhaps to heretical impulses. By contrast, a religious naturalist informed by the sciences of human brains and bodies looks for an explanation of the shared features and distinctiveness of religious behaviors, beliefs, and experiences in terms of body- and brain-based constraints on culturally specific explorations of a landscape of religious and spiritual possibilities. This interpretative approach is far better positioned than traditional theological anthropologies to make sense of individual and cultural variations in religious expression at the same time as furnishing a satisfying explanation of the commonalities in religious expression across individuals and cultures, locations and eras.

Despite being our evolutionary inheritance, our bodies do not completely determine what we are and how we act, in religion or any other domain of human behavior. But they do constrain what we are and do, how we think and interpret, and how we build civilizations and religions. As with every other aspect of a religious anthropology tuned to the realities of evolutionary theory, neuroplasticity, and social creativity, the relationship between bodies and human life, including religion, is a matter of *constraint without determination*.

Bodies and Sociality

The Bodily Nature of Human Identity, Sociality, and Communication

Neuropsychologists working with primates and social psychologists working with human beings have uncovered compelling evidence that human identity is forged socially. The commonsense version of this assertion is obvious and masks its striking implications. Sociality was crucial for driving the evolutionary process toward what we call modern humans. And sociality is essential for the formation of a brain that we can recognize as human even among modern humans. When human babies are born their genetically engineered brains are incomplete in numerous ways and they require sensory and social experiences to complete the wiring. Experience-based completion and enhancement of genetically guided brain connectivity is a key factor in several developmental processes. In embryonic and infant development, biochemical environment and sensory input affect expression of genetic possibilities. In neural Darwinism, excess synaptic connections in the first half dozen years of life are gradually pared back based on experiential efficacy. In childhood and early adult brain development, myelinization of neurons allows previously unused parts of the brain to become active at different times during the first two or three decades of life. In neural plasticity, learning and habitual practices strengthen some neural circuits while weakening others throughout life. *All of these processes involve social inputs and socially oriented neural processing*, from learning language and social rituals, to understanding our place in the world and deciding how to change it.

Perhaps the most spectacular evidence for the ineluctably social character of human nature derives from apparently relatively hard-wired behaviors with explicitly social dimensions. For example, attachment responses appear to be reflexive and hard-wired in infants of many species, including human beings. Knowing that such hard-wired instincts for social connection must be transmuted and sublimated in order for adults to function in complex societies casts Freud's theory of unconscious dynamics into an intriguing light and helps to flesh out the biological underpinnings of psychological constructs such as object relations theory (see Greenberg & Mitchell 1983) and attachment theory (Bowlby 1982, Kirkpatrick 2004).

As another example, consider that mirror neuron ensembles are primed for social engagement (see Gazzaniga 2008, Iacoboni 2008, Rizzolatti 2008). Mirror neurons enable human beings (and possibly other primate species) to reenact in their own brains some of the circuitry that fires in the brains of observed individuals. For instance, when we watch a soccer goalie strain to reach a ball that is flying toward the goal, our mirror neuron ensembles create for us a semblance of the physical exertion that the goalie is experiencing, but in a way that is almost completely isolated from our motor systems. We don't ourselves strain to reach anything, therefore, unless we are so excited that we lose track of social propriety rules, but we do experience a neural representation of the bodily actions we see. This same process occurs for everything we see and even for things that we hear when the aural information is rich enough to enable us to picture motor movements.

Our ability to grasp what others are thinking has everything to do with mirror neuron ensembles. We can penetrate the minds of those in our own cultures and families so much better than strangers and those from unfamiliar cultural settings because being able to "recognize" what mirror neurons are expressing helps us make correct inferences about behavior and emotion. The function of mirror neurons also underlines the meaning and value of specialized training in physical activities. An expert soccer player will have a far more sophisticated mirror-neuron representation of the goalie's dive than either a novice player or someone who has never before seen a soccer game. An expert dancer will grasp the movements of another dancer not only conceptually but also in enormously sophisticated mirror-neuron expressions of bodily movements. The appreciation of beauty in many forms, it seems, is profoundly an embodied achievement.

Another dimension of the embodied character of human sociality is the ineluctably bodily nature of communication. It is commonly said that more information is communicated through "body language" and tone of voice than through the words actually spoken. In recent years this plausible fact has been studied carefully and confirmed comprehensively: the bodily character of in-person communication is indeed the dominant contributor to the conveyance of meanings (see Brothers 1997). We can learn to write for an unseen audience, of course, but the texture of written communication is far thinner and typically less multivocal than the texture of in-person communication. In fact, we bring our biological priming and cultural training for handling complex in-person communication to listening-only and reading-only forms of communication, which enables these forms of communication to be far richer and more complex than would otherwise be the case.

The Importance of Bodies for Religious Anthropology

Traditional religious anthropologies typically leave the embodied roots of human sociality significantly underdeveloped. To illustrate, consider Wentzel van Huyssteen's account of human uniqueness in *Alone in the World?* (2006). This book is far more attuned to the embodied character of human life and more alert to the natural and social sciences than almost everything that has been published in religious anthropology—in fact, in these respects it is a major intellectual accomplishment. Yet even this work underestimates the importance of the embodied character of human life—and if this is so then so much the worse for religious anthropologies that lack the tremendous virtues of van Huyssteen's approach.

As a first example, consider that van Huyssteen treats ritual throughout the book chiefly as a means of seeking the transcendent. It certainly is that, in part and at times, but it is questionable whether it is *chiefly* that or even *always partly* that. More centrally, ritual is socially framed repetition that soothes through focusing cognitive attention, arouses through inducing rhythmic-affective states, controls through shared cognitions, binds through costly signaling, and triggers psychosomatic healing through promoting dissociation. This means that there are plenty of compelling personal and social reasons to engage in rituals quite apart from any intention to seek the transcendent. It also implies that ritual-promoting social activities such as religion can have enormous significance for the development of human nature through processes of gene-culture co-evolution (see Bulbilia 2004, 2006, McClenon 2001, 2006).

Modern western humans seeking the transcendent within the restrained rituals of suburban lifestyles may offer some insight into the social embodiment of early hominids. But it is equally valuable to look at ritual activities that involve handling snakes, walking on coals, self-flagellation, body modification, entheogen-induced altered states of consciousness, chanting, and dancing to rhythmic music all through the night. Despite van Huyssteen's appreciation for the possible importance of shamanism in the evolutionary origins of religion, his argument's minimization of the more socially charged forms of ritual activity results in a picture of human nature, both past and present, that politely understates the bodily aspects of individual and corporate religiosity, subordinating them to the ultimate end of seeking to engage transcendence. The ultimate aim of ritual, past and present, is more likely the regulation and transformation of bodies—targeting the thoughts and behaviors, states of being and future intentions of both individuals and groups, and using the human capacity to sense "transcendence" as inducement and leverage (see the account of the role of religion in social control in Berger 1967).

As a second example, consider van Huyssteen's account of the evolution of religion. He treats religion as a suite of skills that collectively yields accurate information about God and thereby increases fitness by helping us organize life according to what God reveals about good ways to live. That is, religion is an adaptation every bit as much as our cognitive, emotional, and motor abilities. The naturalness of religion *grounds its rationality* and thus also explains and justifies the relevance of religious beliefs for organizing human life. This is a gentle but persistent claim repeated throughout the book. This addresses a deep worry among theologians. The worry derives from the following objection: *the naturalness of religion as a set of evolved traits means that we are determined to have religious beliefs and so the cognitive claims of religious belief can't be taken seriously.* Van Huyssteen's basic reply is that *the evolved character of religious belief means that it must be adapted to reality, and thus the naturalness of religion is evidence for the rationality of religious belief and the credibility of its cognitive claims.* Van Huyssteen challenges evolutionary epistemologists who accept the above-stated objection to religious belief with a pointed question: "Why should we, so suddenly and only at this point—the development of this metaphysical aspect of our cultural evolution—so completely distrust the phylogenetic memory of our ancestors?" (van Huyssteen 2006: 94). We need to take this "why now?" question and the challenge it expresses with great seriousness.

Unfortunately, van Huyssteen does not consider the possibility—argued in the chapter on evolution, above, to be far more likely than an adaptationist account of the origins of religion—that religious behaviors, beliefs, and experiences may be exaptations, spandrels, or even functionless byproducts. In all of these cases, religion emerges from the mists of time as a set of side-effects of a variety of traits that were adapted for other reasons. The tendencies toward religious believing and metaphysical reflecting are deeply rooted in the human brain and evolutionary theorists normally at least allow for the *possibility* that such "phylogenetic memories" were once somehow adaptive. But most do not accept the adaptationist interpretation of the evolutionary origins of religion because of the sheer complexity and multifaceted nature of religious behaviors, beliefs, and experiences. Thus, the answer to van Huyssteen's "why now?" question is clear in light of recent work in evolutionary psychology and cognitive neuroscience: *We only now, as never before, are developing a compelling understanding of the cognitive and emotional traits whose side-effects probably produced many of the features of religion, so we must revisit our assumptions about the content of religious belief and the reasons we take it to be reliable.* Of course, this side-effect view implies not that religious belief is mistaken but only that the task of securing the rationality of religious belief and the reliability of the contents of beliefs is much more complex than suggested by van Huyssteen's questionable claim that religious belief is in the final analysis a kind of cognitive adaptation.

I think van Huyssteen's restrained approach to human embodiment prevents the "side-effect" position from getting a fair hearing. Moreover, a properly radical view of human embodiment immediately entails that securing the rationality of religious beliefs is extraordinarily complex—more complex than the detractors (e.g. Dawkins 2007) and the defenders (e.g. Alston 1991) of the cognitive reliability of religious belief allow, and also more complex than van Huyssteen's argument suggests. This is because bodies, individually and collectively, have compelling interests—survival, reproduction, cooperation, health, regulation, and coping—that are relatively independent of religious beliefs and human quests for the transcendent. These interests can make hearty use of transcendental sensitivities but they persist even when life circumstances render religious beliefs and rituals beside the point. Being more fundamental in human life than religiosity, bodily interests increase the likelihood that false religious beliefs might still have positive functional effects relative to these interests.

Some theorists make precisely this case, particularly in relation to the health benefits of religious beliefs, regarded as existentially vital and socially borne fantasies. For example, Joseph Bulbulia (2006) argues for the adaptiveness of religion because of the placebo benefits of religious beliefs, even while assuming that religious beliefs are cognitive errors. At the heart of Bulbulia's case is the claim that healing and religiosity use the same kind of cognitive structures, including especially supernatural beliefs. That is, putative supernatural entities both heal and perform religiously relevant functions, such as saving, protecting, and enlightening. Given the way healing mechanisms work through dissociation and suggestion, only those that truly believe with unshakeable confidence can improve their chances of being healed. To be healed, correspondingly, is an unfakeable sign of religious commitment. This kind of costly signaling argument welds ritual healing theory, religious cognition, and the social elements of religion into a flexible and multifaceted theoretical edifice.

It follows that there are sound reasons even in a religion-as-adaptation framework, which van Huyssteen and Bulbilia both endorse, to think that religion could evolve to serve bodily interests and improve fitness even though religious beliefs as such are quite false. I have argued that all human religious and ritual healing behaviors—let alone all of the features of religion unrelated to ritual healing—can be correlated with a few genes so that religion could rightly be described as an adaptation. But the possibility of cognitive error being adaptive in much the same way also persists in the more plausible collection-of-side-effects account of the evolutionary origins of religion that I have defended. Van Huyssteen can only rule out this possibility by underestimating the importance of bodily interests in human life.

As a third example, consider that van Huyssteen, though sensitive to suggestions that genes limit religion, tends to label such possibilities as reductionist, saying that they improperly infringe on the autonomous domain of religion. This claim and counterclaim require careful appraisal. The twists and turns in the ongoing nature versus nurture debate reflect how seriously scientists are taking the roles of bodies in cultural expression. Religionists and theologians tend to lag behind, and admittedly this might be wise given the pace of scientific change, but I think that theologians need to come to terms with the emerging crosscultural picture of human life. Lately, social constructivists (the pro-nurture folk) have been losing ground as neuroscientists, social psychologists, and cultural anthropologists have shown recurrence across cultures of certain characteristics, such as natural categorizations in concepts and language; social organization, social behaviors, moral intuitions; and cognitive operations such as reasoning strategies (sometimes universally mistaken) and interpretation of sensations. This shift toward the nature side of the nature–nurture debate rebalances the scales, which have been tilting toward social constructivism since the collapse of social Darwinism many decades ago. Taking embodiment with due seriousness requires that we recognize the extent to which we may have a great deal in common with people in quite different cultural settings, as a result of the sheer fact of being bodied in our particular planetary ecology with a particular evolutionary heritage.

Limits on flexibility in human nature as seen from cultural anthropology occur at two levels. On one level, structural universals derive from problems that all cultures must solve to exist and survive. Such problems are associated with family or kinship groups, status differences, division of labor, property control, social control, and religious belief or practice. On the other level, cultural universals are culturally specific solutions to structurally universal challenges, such as particular family or kinship structures, particular communication gestures, particular economic arrangements, and particular languages. *Human cultures are constrained but not determined by structural universals.* Cultures explore a landscape of possibilities within the constraints set by structural universals. In fact, cultures can even alter the landscape of possibilities at times (see the discussion of engineered habitat in Chapter 8 below). There is similar evidence of limits on cultural flexibility in many other disciplines, from cognitive science to social psychology.

To acknowledge limits on cultural flexibility is neither political despair nor moral pessimism. It does not necessarily express a philosophy of history that posits futility of human effort. Nor is it succumbing to genetic determinism. Rather, this acknowledgment is based on robust discoveries about the genetically programmed dimensions of bodily human life. There may be deep limitations on the realization of religious ideals. This has important implications for assessing the realism of religious ideals pertaining to individual holiness and social transformation, and for strategizing about how to organize human political life and how to implement religious ideals in a realistic form of social organization. For example, what would it mean to say that the genetic heritage of human beings is now largely fixed because it is dominated by cultural evolution? What if this places permanent limits on how good human beings can be, how well they can learn, how intelligent they can be, whether they can achieve perfection or enlightenment? What if the cognitive canals that bound the mercurial flow of cultural and religious expression can only be redirected through genetic engineering? Can (or must) religious traditions embrace this? *Alone in the World?* evades such questions by treating the framework that leads to them as necessarily reductionist in its approach to religion, by overestimating the autonomy of the religious sphere, and most importantly by underestimating the bodily limits on cultural and religious exploration of the landscape of human behavioral possibilities.

The Ideology of Normalcy

A number of prominent practical questions about human bodies are morally charged and pointedly normative in character. Which bodies are normal and which not? Which bodies are healthy and which sick? Which bodies are socially functional and which socially dangerous? There are many styles of cognition, many types of bodies, many atypical developmental pathways, and many kinds of disease among human beings, which makes these questions complicated and important. There is broad crosscultural agreement over the larger issues surrounding normality, health, and social functionality, deriving from evolutionarily and socially basic needs for functionality. But socially borne and culturally encoded norms for optimal function parse these questions quite differently at the fine-grained level.

To focus the discussion, let us focus on the importance of bodies for understanding what may be its subtlest variation, the meaning of *cognitive normalcy*. A rich awareness of the bodied character of human life stunningly reframes cultural ideologies of the "cognitively normal." I do not refer here merely to supporting the "culture of caring," which ordinary compassion demands. Nor do I refer to eliminating the ideology of cognitive normalcy in the name of compassion and justice by refraining from making value distinctions. Rather, radical embodiment (i) blurs the line between the cognitively normal and abnormal, (ii) recognizes potentially adaptive value in cognitive variations, and (iii) invites value judgments within the domain of the cognitively normal. This is potentially socially explosive.

The human species embraces wide variations in cognitive abilities, in relation to language, sociality, memory, insight, and interpretative skills. From a bio-historical point of view, all human beings are deeply related to one another and there is no basis for decisive cognition-based separations among us. We are they, no matter who they are, how they think, whether they can talk or reason, or how they experience emotion. If our Paleolithic ancestors are us, then certainly autistics, schizophrenics, and the cognitively atypical are us. This realization challenges easy cultural assumptions that the cognitive insights of such people are absent or useless, which in turn leads us to look for the adaptive or cultural or spiritual value in such genetic and experiential variations. It also demands that we take full responsibility for our claims that there is greater value in some cognitions than in others. Specifically, there is no justification for dismissing outright the cognitions of people in psychotic states; if we are rationally to assign less value to the extraordinary cognitions associated with schizophrenia or bipolar mania we need to give reasons.

At the same time, we need value judgments for educational theory, social policy planning, health care, and crime prevention. As suggested above, there is a sound empirical basis for defining genetically based "minimally adequate cognition" among human beings, and this accounts for wide crosscultural agreement on questions of cognitive function. The cognitive challenges posed by psychiatric or neurological conditions make this clear. Psychosis often involves extreme cognitive errors and an inability to perceive such errors and to respond to contradictory information. Abnormal sociality such as that of autistics often interferes with life skills, survival, and mating. Impaired language often prevents effective communication, negatively affecting friendships and cooperation. Minimally adequate cognition among human beings involves avoiding or accommodating these deficits. On this basis, we can make differential value judgments about the cognitive characteristics of human beings without being forced to deny that other forms of cognition possess redeeming qualities.

Such value judgments don't sustain a sharp distinction between the cognitively normal and abnormal because psychosis, sociality, and language vary tremendously in the human population and even within a single person in different stages and circumstances of life. The same is true for body shapes, sizes, and functions. Rather, the continuity of human characteristics justifies extending value judgments into so-called "cognitively normal" humans, with potentially dramatic consequences. Society would then treat genius less as an exception to the norm and more as a task of detection and cultivation. Society would prize high-functioning autistics as wondrous gifts because of their potential genius characteristics. Such people would be diagnosed early, they would be protected from harm and misunderstanding, and their gifts would be identified and nurtured, precisely because they have value that people with normal cognition do not. Society would regard the occurrence of bipolar disorder (e.g. Sting, Virginia Woolf, and a vast array of artists and writers) as potentially hitting the genetic-cultural creativity jackpot. Such people would be nurtured and their sometimes extraordinary gifts deliberately cultivated. Perhaps most dramatically of all, society would regard ordinary stupidity and thoughtlessness in the so-called "normal" population as genetically based problems to be addressed through education, concentration, and care of the afflicted.

Awareness of the special value of non-standard cognition challenges the widespread claim that language is a key (if not *the* key) characteristic of human beings (see Pinker 1994; among theologians offering theological anthropologies, van Huyssteen 2006 affirms this also). Cannot autistic and cognitively atypical humans with little or no language abilities still be gifted artists and appreciate symbols? Cognitive scientists may be profoundly mistaken about the evolution of human intelligence when they extrapolate backwards from the so-called cognitively normal modern humans. They may overlook the special adaptive possibilities of so-called abnormal cognition in certain specific social and cultural contexts. They may fail to see that symbolic forms of understanding (art, music, dance) may precede language by millions of years. They may forget the possibility that what we today would call cognitively abnormal human beings established genetic resources that could be co-opted for language when vocal tract physiology made it possible.

A deeper awareness of genetic variations and functional differences among bodies also challenges traditional theological approaches to cognitive normalcy. Beginning with decentralizing language as the key to human distinctiveness, the body-aware framework questions the centrality of *belief* in human religiosity. What defines a member of a religious group has as much to do with where bodies cluster and what they do together, with mimesis and training, as with beliefs. Moreover, recalling the problem of cognitive error discussed in the previous chapter, the body-aware framework enjoins religious groups to recognize the various ways they exploit cognitive vulnerabilities, and to correct mistaken beliefs when possible, even if this means questioning or abandoning a convenient but questionable kind of absolutized religious authority.

The body-aware framework also highlights the danger of the tendency of religious groups to homogenize human behavior and belief in the name of social control. Surely the interests of social stability can afford a little chaos caused by variations in human cognition and bodies. A particularly problematic variation of this tendency toward homogenization is the articulation and enforcement of theological rationalizations of so-called natural law, whereby created nature is perceived through a socially constructed lens of divine intention. This makes some bodies pure and proper, normal and divinely intended, while other bodies are relegated to the domain of the impure and misshapen, the abnormal and aberrant. The religious linkage between the unnatural, the impure, and the abnormal has been and remains deadly. In the body-aware framework I am endorsing, nothing that occurs in nature can be unnatural, impurity is an occasionally useful artifact of the social regulation of group identity, and abnormality is first and foremost a descriptive matter of frequency statistics.

Finally, the body-aware framework strongly endorses the traditional commitment in most religions to the sanctity of human life and the value of each individual regardless of bodily appearance and cognitive characteristics. Though not perfectly, and never unambiguously, religious people have led the way in finding social homes for those who could not otherwise fit into the flow of ordinary social life because of body-based differences. Whether because of belief in universal divine love or compassion for suffering beings, most religious groups in their day-to-day functioning encourage openness to and acceptance of the bodily and cognitively Other. Relatively few religious people actually achieve such openness and acceptance, such is the ingrained impulse to sameness as the measure of group identity and safety. Nevertheless, the rhetoric of openness and acceptance is prominent in sacred religious texts and liturgies, and it has an effect in structuring the imaginations and behaviors of more empathic religious people.

Bodies and Morality

Moral Psychology

Most of the great problems of human life involve bodies. Violence involves damaging bodies through pain and traumatic injury. Malnourishment involves damaging bodies through strangling the energy input needed to function optimally. Sexism involves controlling bodies as a way, in part, to regulate access to reproductive resources. Racism, ageism, and some other forms of pernicious discrimination involve distinguishing better from worse on the basis of the outward appearance and function of bodies. Ingroup–outgroup, hierarchy, and purity distinctions, with their devastating side-effects, almost always depend on features of bodies, from genetic relatedness to attractiveness, and from residence location to cultural practices. Injustice is almost always about preferential treatment of bodies based on the exercise of available power.

Human moral weakness is often abstracted to the realm of moral decisions and personal character. This is nowhere truer than in religious groups, which generally encourage kind and loving behavior through internal moral transformation, despite their painfully mixed record on matters of violence and justice. The making of individual moral decisions is a relevant factor in addressing human problems, to be sure. But we do well to keep in mind the impact on actual bodies of human moral weakness, whether through deliberate action or through unintended consequences of other actions. Most moral failings translate into kicks or punches to bodies, avoidable infections or diseases in bodies, and torture or neglect of bodies. Without doubt, moral decisions and personal character are significantly about the cultivation of discipline and empathic awareness, but they are also about bodies and one or another type of harm or suffering.

If the bodily impact of moral decisions is a salient measure of their practical meaning, the bodily process of moral decision making is a vital consideration in grasping how to overcome social problems and realize moral ideals. In recent years, social psychology and cognitive neuroscience have made vital breakthroughs in understanding moral decision making. These breakthroughs include constraining some traditional philosophical debates about moral reasoning and establishing a sturdy empirical basis for the reappraisal of both contemporary moral problems and effective methods for moral change (see Greene & Haidt 2000 for a review of cognitive neuroscience contributions to moral psychology, Greene 2003 for a review of the moral implications of neuroscientific moral psychology, and Haidt 2007 for a review of social psychology contributions to moral psychology).

The portrayal of the processes of moral decision making and moral reasoning emerging from this growing field of experimental and theoretical research is compelling and in some ways contrary to commonsense expectations and habitual self-understandings. First, human morality is not completely unified. It involves an uneasy synthesis of several relatively independent cognitive and emotional processes, each with quite different neurological supports. Second, moral decision making involves both emotion and reasoning, in various degrees, depending especially on the perplexing quality of the moral issue at hand. Third, in many ordinary situations, moral judgments are significantly instinctive, with moral reasoning functioning to rationalize a judgment already made. Fourth, people routinely mistake the *post-hoc* rationalizing and self-justificatory functions of moral reasoning for originating reasoning that produces the moral decision itself; thus, they underestimate the preempting role of instinctive moral judgment. Fifth, there appear to be at least five relatively independent domains of instinctive moral judgment, each with its evolutionary back story, its associated virtues and vices, and an accompanying suite of resources to support moral reasoning. These five domains of moral judgment are: harm–suffering (corresponding to the virtue of kindness and the vice of cruelty), fairness–equity (with the virtue being justice, and the vice injustice), ingroup–outgroup (loyalty, betrayal), prestige–hierarchy (deference, rebellion), and purity–disgust (cleanliness, contamination). Sixth, prodigious training is required to intercept the relatively automatic process of moral decision making in order to render it properly responsive to all relevant considerations, and thereby responsive to rational deliberation. Seventh, through lifelong training and social pressure, a cultural context can successfully contest certain instinctive domains of moral judgment so as to weaken their influence relative to other domains, but the default suite of moral instincts includes all five domains operating at roughly equal strength.

Moral decision making, it seems, involves a suite of relatively stable instinctive impulses. They intrude into consciousness as potent convictions (e.g. "be polite to old people!"), which we subsequently might explain to ourselves using *post-hoc* moral reasoning guided by the rational resources available in our social setting and personal training ("other things being equal, old people deserve respect and deference because they are wiser and less able to defend themselves than younger adults"). If we have to address a moral dilemma—for example, the famous "trolley problem" in which someone must decide whether to divert a runaway trolley guaranteed to kill five people onto another track where it is guaranteed to kill only one—we interrupt the normal flow of moral judgment and rationalization. We find ourselves confronting a puzzle. We experience conflicting emotionally charged moral instincts ("Don't cause harm!" and "Don't let harm occur!") and conflicting rational considerations ("I don't want to do anything in my life that causes harm to others but in this case if I do nothing I will allow great harm to occur that I could have avoided"). This account contests Greene's (2002, 2003) analysis that this represents a conflict between opposed emotional and cognitive responses; there are emotionally charged cognitions on both sides of the dilemma. Be that as it may, functional imaging studies of such moral dilemmas show intense activity consistent with processing a conflict and using high-level cognitive processes to resolve it.

Instinctive moral judgments, styles of moral reasoning, and methods of resolving moral conflicts are biologically constrained processes permitting and exhibiting enormous cultural variation. Here again we see the theme of constraint-without-determination that characterizes the relation between biology and culture, between nature and nurture, across all the domains of human life. Haidt's (2007) research into the moral differences between liberals and conservatives in the United States illustrates this beautifully. His generalization, which appears to be fairly stable by the standards of experimental psychology, is that self-rated conservatives tend to stress all five domains of moral judgment and reasoning roughly equally (the evolutionarily default position, according to Haidt), while self-rated liberals tend to stress the harm–suffering and fairness–equity domains and subordinate the ingroup–outgroup, prestige–hierarchy, and purity–disgust domains.

Why does this difference between conservatives and liberals arise? Haidt plausibly conjectures that difference is a result of the demands of cosmopolitan social settings, which involve routine contact with people from multiple cultures. Such settings render the more group-specific conventions (the ingroup–outgroup, prestige–hierarchy, and purity–disgust domains) socially impractical and economically disadvantageous, and this in turn produces patterns of social conditioning sufficient to contest instinctive reactions of xenophobia, umbrage, and disgust. Meanwhile, the more universal moral instincts (harm–suffering and fairness–equity) are extremely useful for establishing empathic and productive relationships with culturally different others. Haidt's main line of evidence for this account of the origins of conservative-liberal differences in moral judgments and reasoning is geographic. He points out that there is a strong correlation between predominantly politically liberal people and predominantly cosmopolitan settings in the United States: both tend to be on the west and east coasts and up and down the traditionally commercially vital Mississippi river. There are other considerations in what makes people liberal or conservative, to be sure—elsewhere I mentioned heritable factors, for example—but Haidt's analysis offers a new and relevant perspective on the question.

Traditional Religious Anthropologies

This line of research serves as a sharp reminder that abstract analyses of moral judgments and moral reasoning are very likely to miss vital information that only enters the interpretative picture when we take full account of the *bodily character of human moral life*. Traditional theological anthropologies have routinely neglected the actual bodily conditions of human morality to the point that they now sit uneasily with the insights emerging from moral psychology.

For example, consider the Neo-Confucian emphasis on widening circles of human-heartedness (*ren*) and virtue (*de*) from the five primary relationships (sovereign–subject, parent–child, elder brother–younger brother, husband–wife, and friend–friend) outwards to the community, the nation, the human realm, other living beings, and indeed all of reality. This widening of the scope of human-heartedness and virtue can be seen as an abstract moral precept reflecting a resonance between human morality and the Dao, the valuational structures and flows of nature that hover beneath the surface of conventional social reality. The sociology of knowledge would point out that this scope-widening also functions to cosmologize and spiritualize principles that work well in the realms of immediate social and political concern, thereby reinforcing those principles and increasing social control, which can be especially valuable at times and in places where they are in question. Moral psychology would add the point that the Neo-Confucian approach furnishes a compelling religious rationalization for emphasizing the more universal domains of moral judgment (harm–suffering, fairness–equity) while subordinating and criticizing the side-effects of the group-related domains (ingroup–outgroup, prestige–hierarchy, purity–disgust). These are persuasive insights stressing embodied economic and political concerns that sit uneasily with an overly spiritualized interpretation of Neo-Confucian ethics.

As a more complex example of the deficiencies of abstract and spiritualized religious approaches to human morality, consider the moral teachings of Jesus of Nazareth, as they are recalled and reconstructed in the writings of the New Testament, and also the mixed fate of these teachings in the Christian churches. Moral principles going well beyond the so-called Golden Rule ("treat others as you would have them treat you")—principles that probably derive from Jesus' own moral vision—include "when you are mistreated, offer to be further mistreated (i.e. turn the other cheek)," "love your enemies and pray for those who persecute you," "recognize strangers and outcasts as your friends and neighbors," "allow for the possibility that the most corrupt person could repent," "accept women and children as valuable and include them in your group," "put loving community before social hierarchy and ingroup–outgroup rules," and "nothing is impure that God blesses, regardless of conventional purity rules." According to the New Testament, these moral teachings were expressed in a lifestyle of radical inclusiveness that challenged prevailing moral norms and displayed what Jesus probably took to be the socially subversive character of divine love. For Christians, the significance of these teachings, and the potential cost of remaining true to them, is symbolized both in Jesus' own unjust execution and in the torture and murder of the martyrs of the church. The vindication of these teachings is symbolized in Jesus' resurrection and in the glorification of the martyrs in heaven.

These moral principles have inspired great works of mercy and courage throughout the history of Christianity. Yet the impact of the biblical Jesus' radical moral example and teaching has been sorely limited in the Christian churches. The New Testament portrayal of Jesus bluntly contesting ingroup–outgroup, prestige–hierarchy, and purity–disgust moral norms is incompatible with a religious identity that is tightly geared to the economics and moral commitments of the encompassing culture, so this picture is reframed and redescribed until what it portrays is rarely seen at all. This is neither surprising nor unreasonable. It makes good sense that Christian identity in practice should be not just about following Jesus but also about believing and behaving in ways that help a local group of Christians forge strong community that can realize the benefits of Christian salvation for its members. Given this, Jesus' moral teachings must coexist and harmonize with other moral principles bearing on the political realities of community life, the stable support and defense of civilizations, and the nurture of complex and captivating cultures.

This obligation to harmonize conflicting moral visions inevitably demanded that the relatively impractical import of Jesus' moral teachings would have to be curtailed to some degree in order to accommodate the demands of society, economy, and politics. Thus, the socially disruptive moral precepts attributed to Jesus in the New Testament are routinely reinterpreted so as to constrict the scope of neighbor love and marginalize the record of Jesus' radical moral behavior, all in the name of ingroup values: identifying outgroup enemies, accepting ingroup prestige hierarchies, and conforming to ingroup purity customs. The themes of compassion and justice are not lost but they are balanced against the group-level requirements of civilization and society. The resulting tension is reconciled differently in different contexts depending on available group resources. For instance, there has been a much discussed aversion to revolutionary social action among conservative evangelicals in western nations during the twentieth century (note: not evangelicals in the wider sense, who have always been quite socially active). For their part, liberal churches in the same settings have stressed social action because they lacked the social vitality to generate and maintain consensus on questions of doctrine and conventions of practice, though their social action generally took the form of compassionate care for the poor rather than radical challenges to the socio-economic system. In all cases, the potentially shocking moral posture attributed to Jesus in the New Testament is effectively tamed and any unwelcome effects eliminated.

The processes serving to limit the impact of this moral vision aptly illustrate the awkward fit between spiritualized moral abstractions and body-aware approaches to morality. On the one hand, full awareness of the bodily character of moral judgments and reasoning requires, and brooks, no dissembling. Our species is equipped with a default moral reasoning apparatus that operates in (at least) five domains. The moral view ascribed to Jesus directly contests human moral instincts in three of these five domains (ingroup–outgroup, prestige–hierarchy, purity–disgust), while relentlessly emphasizing the other two (harm–suffering, fairness–equity). This is an intolerable posture in principle, however, given the social and civilizational obligations of Christian religious communities. So the radical Jesus morality will have to be carefully hedged about with conditions and restrictions so as to mitigate the effect of its unreasonable dismissal of group-level moral considerations bearing on the organization and maintenance of social orders. On the other hand, the "spiritualized moral abstractions" approach cannot afford to recognize why the radical and socially disruptive character of Jesus' moral teaching is relatively ineffective in the history of Christianity. To acknowledge this plainly would be to disrupt the practically valuable processes of group bonding and moral legitimation on which most Christian communities depend for their effective functioning. Therefore, instead of lifting the veil of ignorance and disclosing the inner workings of authority and conformity on which human group life depends—instead of properly absorbing the full force of the conflict between two moral visions—it is expedient to reframe Jesus' moral teachings, through preaching and teaching and socially reinforced habits of behavior, so that they appear to support what the group actually does. Co-opt to curtail conflict. Reframe to achieve harmony. Spiritualize to mask incoherence.

As a third example of the uneasy fit between traditional theological anthropologies and insights from moral psychology, consider the virtually universal religious ideal of moral goodness. This ideal takes very different forms in South Asian saṃsāric settings and in western theistic settings, to name but two variations, and the ruling norms vary tremendously in expression and conceptuality. Nevertheless, religions do tend to assign moral obligations to individuals and groups, they do potentiate human behavior with an awareness of better and worse governed by an ideal of goodness and justice, and these ideals are significantly compatible for most purposes. Not surprisingly, the fact that human life falls short of such moral ideals is a prominent theme in traditional theological anthropologies, with elaborate narrations of the human condition explaining why we are the way we are and what we can hope in regard to improving ourselves or at least escaping the disasters into which our bad behavior leads us.

Strikingly different spiritual paths, behavioral prescriptions, moral laws, and metaphysical frameworks are deployed to make sense of these narratives, yet many core themes recur across traditions. For instance, the futility of effort is balanced against the indispensability of effort in one or another way in most traditions. The social and individual aspects of moral goodness are held together in most traditions in a variety of ways. Most traditions present inducements and penalties for complying with and disobeying moral rules, respectively. Most traditions make ample use of guilt to increase the likelihood of compliance and also to sanctify the power of the priestly or saintly castes that channel forgiveness and wisdom. And moral improvement to the point of perfection is widely held to be impossible without supernatural means of assistance in the form of spiritual power, supportive ancestors, divine forgiveness, or countless lifetimes in a wearying spiritual journey.

These shared features of religious narratives about morality in the human condition leverage great changes in many human lives through inspiring devotion to morally compelling ideals. Such effectiveness is consistent with insights from moral psychology and social psychology. But some insights from these fields sit awkwardly with religious narrative portrayals of the human condition and their systematic, metaphysical theological elaborations. Most important among awkward insights from the field of social psychology is the role of moral discourse in enhancing social control over groups of people and the deployment of theological frameworks to legitimate such mechanisms of social control. This valid insight does not refute the truth claims that theological anthropologies advance about human morality, of course, but it may cast those truth claims into an unfamiliar light. After that, their plausibility comes to seem a matter more of socially constructed habits of mind than of intrinsic intellectual value.

Profoundly important among awkward insights from the field of moral psychology is that human beings are built a certain way, namely, equipped with a default hodge-podge of somewhat inconsistent moral instincts and cursed with a poor native awareness of how the processes of moral judgment and moral reasoning work. To see *this* may be more relevant to changing human behavior than any amount of repeating the narratives of the human condition in either metaphysically naïve or theologically sophisticated ways. To see *this* is immediately to know how to address many of the seemingly intractable problems facing human beings—namely, through education, increased self-awareness, and self-critical assessments of processes of moral reasoning—perhaps with far greater efficiency than afforded by the many conflicting strategies for moral transformation promoted by the world's religions. These comparative claims about efficacy are yet to be tested, of course. Meanwhile, the empirically grounded character of such awkward insights earns them the status of basic truths with which thoughtful religious people are obliged to deal in their distinctive ways, regardless of the conflict that may ensue.

Fully recognizing the bodily character not only of moral behavior but also of processes of moral judgment and moral reasoning has simple and yet potentially far-reaching consequences. I have sketched some of them here but many of these consequences are yet to be manifested. In particular, while traditional religious narratives are proven ways of maintaining social stability and solidarity, could a more thoroughly bodily approach to morality of the sort I am endorsing ever possess the same practical efficacy for regulating and streamlining human group life? And can a thoroughgoing bodily approach to morality ever achieve the same symbolic potency for individual spiritual moral transformation that traditional religious narratives routinely demonstrate? Can we answer such questions in part by devising inquiries capable of rendering them empirically tractable and testable? However these possibilities unfold, there is no question that a bodily approach to human morality demands more self-awareness in the social engineering challenges of human life. This self-awareness is ill-suited to a species that is cognitively and neurologically optimized for moral reflexes, *post-hoc* moral reasoning, supernatural religious narratives, and obliviousness to all of the above. In the final analysis, this particular lack of fit—between empirically derived theories about embodied human morality, and what actually works for moral regulation and transformation—may define the ultimate moral challenge for human beings.

Bodies and Religious Experiences

Mapping the Territory

As with human sociality and morality, a thoroughgoing bodily approach to religious anthropology transforms our conception of religious and spiritual experiences. This transformation begins by bracketing religious and theological claims *about what religious and spiritual experiences are supposed to be*—usually these are implicit in normative stories that effectively guide religious practices—and attending to *what religious and spiritual experiences are in fact*. The transformational significance of a bodily approach to religious and spiritual experiences does not stop there, by any means, but getting the data of religious and spiritual experiences descriptively clear is by itself an enormously important first step.

Describing religious and spiritual experiences as they actually arise in people's lives is complicated, thanks to the varied ways in which terminology is used and the difficulty of extending and checking phenomenological descriptions across cultures. In previous work (Wildman 2010), I have argued for a descriptive approach that combines clearly defined categories (corresponding to relatively sharply delimited phenomena) with loose and potentially shifting categories (where usage is highly variable). Thus, we begin with defining *experience* in an inclusive way along naturalist lines as (inevitably) neurologically embodied and (inevitably) socially mediated states of mind of which a person is at least partially aware; this rules out fully unconscious states while admitting partially conscious states with subconscious elements. Within this vast field of experiences, we focus on a small territory within which religious and spiritual experiences occur, territory identified by means of several further distinctions.

First, we can define *anomalous experiences* as the realm of unusual and strange experiences. While judgments of unusualness and strangeness are subject to some degree of cultural variation, they follow the broad outlines of species-wide cognitive functions so I follow Cardeña et al. (2000) in estimating that there is actually less variation than one might suspect in crosscultural conceptions of anomalous experiences. Among anomalous experiences, Cardeña lists hallucination, synesthesia, lucid dreaming, out-of-body experiences, alien abduction, anomalous healing, past-life, near-death, psi-related, and mystical experiences. Other anomalous experiences include mental phenomena associated with drugs, psychiatric disorders, extreme circumstances, ecstatic states, group frenzy, snake handling, fire-walking, possession, as well as more marginally anomalous experiences such as dramatic self-deception and uncanny insight. Anomalous experiences tend to feel out of the control of those who undergo them, some are reliably reproducible under specific conditions, most are emotionally and cognitive potent, and many have little or nothing to do with spirituality or religion.

Second, we can define *ultimacy experiences* as the realm of existentially and spiritually significant experiences. These are experiences that a person feels are of vital importance for his or her life. They bring orientation and coping power, inspire great acts of courage and devotion, underlie key life decisions, and heavily influence social affiliation. They overlap with anomalous experiences but anomalous experiences can occur without the subjective judgment of ultimate importance and ultimacy experiences can occur in recognizably normal fashion, so the overlap is significant without being dominant. A useful distinction within the class of ultimacy experiences is between short-term states and long-term processes (see Wildman & Brothers 1999). Short-term states are tied more directly to discrete brain episodes whereas extended experiences usually require a rich social context to sustain them. It is discrete ultimacy experiences that overlap most significantly with anomalous experiences.

Extended ultimacy experiences arise in two ways, as "dynamic, socially embedded processes of orientation and control in relation to the cosmos, the social world, and one's self" (Wildman & Brothers 1999: 359); and as "gradual and chronic experiences of personal change or self-transcendence, such as Confucian self-cultivation, Christian sanctification, and possibly also character changes having little explicit connection with religious symbols and practices" (361). These are social and transformative ultimacy experiences, respectively. Four elements recur in both types of extended ultimacy experiences: (i) existential potency, (ii) social embedding, (iii) transformation of behavior and personality, and (iv) transformation of beliefs (362–365).

Discrete ultimacy experiences have different characteristics, which is to be expected given the association with short-term brain states. They involve the following five recurring elements (358–359): (i) sensory alterations, including perceptions that are incongruous with the current environmental situation; (ii) self alterations, including out-of-body experiences, loss of the sense of the individual self, union of the self with an entity such as God or the Infinite, or the self as profoundly threatened by judgment or annihilation in the presence of a being of enormous power; (iii) presences, including non-physical beings, either benign or evil, such as angels or demons, and being invaded, inhabited, or controlled by such beings; (iv) cognitions, including sudden illumination, increased awareness, a sense of unreality, sense of sin or weakness, assurance of salvation or healing, and powerful convictions; and (v) emotions, including feelings of ecstasy, awe, dread, guilt, safety, tranquility, or utter darkness and despair.

An evolutionary interpretation of human experience could perhaps set aside many anomalous experiences as bizarre side-effects with no cognitive or existential value. But *ultimacy experiences of both the discrete and extended varieties have to be placed front and center in any evolutionary account because of their potent functional effects on human self-understanding and behavior.*

Third, we can define *religious experiences* as any experiences that people are willing to call religious. This is the very opposite of a precise category and allows a range of usages to coexist vaguely. This procedure admits mundane experiences into the class of religious experiences, such as simple shared meals in a religious setting or committee work on behalf of a religious organization, as well as more vibrant experiences, such as ecstatic ritual participation or encounters with deities. In all usages, the domain of religious experiences overlaps with the region of ultimacy experiences but there are both religious experiences that are not ultimacy experiences (such as the committee meetings just mentioned) and ultimacy experiences that are not religious in any normal usage (such as a peak athletic or sexual or artistic performances).

Fourth, we can define *spiritual experiences* as a superset of ultimacy experiences that includes some non-ultimate religious experiences, the range of included religious experiences depending on usage. That is, all ultimacy experiences are spiritual experiences (all experiences in the realm of significance are rightly designated spiritual even if some are not willing to call them religious because they have nothing to do with organized religions), a certain range of non-ultimate religious experiences are also spiritual experiences (such as participation in religious ritual acts that are not felt to be especially important or significant), and the remaining non-ultimate religious experiences (probably including the committee meetings once again) would not normally be considered spiritual experiences. The realm of "religious and spiritual experiences" thus encompasses all ultimacy experiences, all religious experiences, and all spiritual experiences. Note, too, that the realm of anomalous experiences overlaps with all of the above subsets but is not exhausted by them and does not exhaust them. That is, there are anomalous experiences that are neither spiritual nor religious, and only some spiritual experiences and only some religious experiences are anomalous.

This approach to mapping of part of the territory of human experiences is well suited to gaining an appreciation for the diversity and range of religious and spiritual experiences. In particular, it allows for the locating of several other types of experience that have prominent places in the phenomenological and research literature surrounding religious and spiritual experiences, in such a way as to indicate that there are a lot of other religious and spiritual experiences that are not discussed as often as they might be. The much discussed experiences include meditation experiences, mystical experiences, and intense experiences. The intense experiences have been treated under a variety of descriptions, including liminal, profound, numinous, extreme, transcendental, traumatic, sublime, Samādhi, vipaśyanā, ānanda, non-dual consciousness, wide awareness, flow, and so on. Figure 1 offers a graphical representation of the territory as I have sketched it here, including overlaps and subgroups.

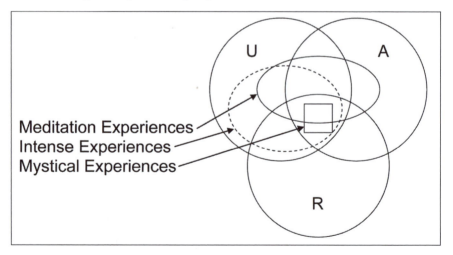

Figure 1   Relationships among all types of experiences discussed: religious [R], ultimacy [U], and anomalous [A] experiences, meditation experiences, and two subclasses of ultimacy experiences: intense experiences and mystical experiences

Almost all human beings undergo ultimacy experiences, which are a part of the domain of what is here called spiritual experiences. Quite a few undergo (or endure) anomalous experiences at some point in their lives. And whether people are willing to call any experience "religious" depends on setting and inclination. The experiences people are willing to call "religious" are incredibly diverse and the study of religious experience has typically fallen far short of fully recognizing this diversity. Perhaps the lure of the mystic's anomalous ultimacy experiences is too tempting to resist, or perhaps the strong philosophical interest in the cognitive reliability of religious experience is the cause for almost universally one-sided treatments. But a great deal of religious experience involves embodied practices, often mundane and often simple, that structure life and strengthen individual coping skills. These ordinary social experiences are of profound importance for grasping the way that religions help people implement their moral intentions and transform their behavior, as well as the way religions achieve the social effects that the sociology of knowledge attributes to them (see Chapter 4, 'Groups', above).

This mapping of the territory of religious and spiritual experiences not only challenges the minimization or neglect of their diversity in the extant scholarly literature on the topic. It also serves as a reminder of what we human beings are, in our bodies, as experiencing creatures. The diversity of these experiences reflects the human cognitive, emotional, and social equipment that is native to our species. This is who we are because this is how our ancestors evolved. A properly body-aware approach to religious and spiritual experiences recognizes that the associated capacities are part of our evolutionary birthright. The diversity of those experiences may not comport well with the sorts of experiences that people in a particular religious community are supposed to have. Experiences narrated within a particular group as completely unique may turn out to have close analogues or exact replicas in other traditions, with people on all sides claiming unique authenticity of their experiences. And aggressive skeptics may dismiss all of these human capacities as profoundly misleading side-effects of an imperfect cognitive-emotional system. Nevertheless, it is vital for a religious anthropology, whether of the religious naturalist kind pursued here or of a more traditional supernaturalist variety, to recognize fully what we actually are, with our bodily capacities for religious and spiritual experiences, and with no dissembling or avoidance.

Intense Experiences

Having charted the territory of religious and spiritual experiences and insisted on keeping their diversity in mind as a signal of our actual bodily character as human beings, it is important also to raise questions about the authenticity of religious and spiritual experiences and the truth of the beliefs that seem regularly to spring from them. Particularly important in this regard are the ultimacy experiences, and within them the intense experiences.

Ultimacy experiences include both some religious experiences and all spiritual-but-not-religious experiences. In all cases, they have enormous existential meaning for people, to the point that they are in some sense ultimately important. Intense experiences are a large subclass of ultimacy experiences, combining ultimate meaningfulness with powerful emotions and wide cognitive awareness that seems to make every part of life meaningful. The combination of strength of feeling and interconnectedness of ideas, memories, and emotions that characterizes intense experiences is what makes them important and leverages significant personal and social effects. To have a moment of such intense love that one feels irrevocably bonded to people and places outside one's own familiar world is to be launched into new possibilities for behavior, new visions for social life, and new values. To be flooded with sharp awareness of a pattern of meaning in one's life history forges resolve to face what lies ahead and sparks confidence in one's life calling. To be struck down with the terrible realization that one is utterly dependent on processes beyond one's control is to experience grace and gratitude, if it does not collapse the psyche completely.

My hypothesis is that the capacity for intensity in the special "depth of significance and breadth of awareness" sense that this term has here is a species-wide characteristic, present in almost all individuals, rooted in evolutionarily stabilized neural capacities, profoundly modified in activation and expression by cultural context, and yet recognizable to the careful observer beneath the more prominent cultural and circumstantial variations, and detectable with properly tuned psychometric instruments. These qualities *open a pathway to a species-wide understanding of the nature, functions, and value of a large subset of religious and spiritual experiences.* This understanding encompasses their evolutionary origins, their cognitive structure, their emotional texture, their neurological embedding, their bodily and social effects, and their existential and cultural importance. (See Wildman 2010 for a full statement of this argument.)

A persuasive case can be made that intense experiences are evolutionarily more fundamental and primitive than religious experiences. Intense experiences possess some degree of internal diversity, as the host of names for such experiences (mentioned above) demonstrates, but they are far less diverse and have more in common with each other than is the case for religious experiences (again, see the phenomenology of intense experiences in Wildman 2010). Being far less diverse than religious experiences is an indication that giving a coordinated evolutionary account of origins will be far easier for intense experiences than for religious experiences. The fact that intense experiences arc through the entire range of human endeavors, from physical activity to aesthetics, from creativity to religion, further suggests that they reflect very basic neurological processes much as cognition, emotion, and sensory processing do. And the fact that intense experiences appear to be a species-wide capacity also suggests that relatively basic neurological processes are implicated. It certainly is possible that religion derives part of its operative machinery from a pre-existing and much older capacity for intense experiences. I conjecture (in Wildman 2010, tentatively guided by such evidence as exists) that the neural capacity for intensity in this particular sense arrives early in the evolutionary history of modern humans, probably about

50,000 years ago, and that this capacity for intensity is a vital component feature of religious and spiritual experiences when they arose in due course. This has quite striking implications for philosophical and theological interpretation, of which I discuss two here.

First, the evolutionarily and neurologically basic character of intense experiences, and the fact that they are experienced as existentially important even while often not associated with religion, *makes everything in reality potentially spiritually significant*, and not merely those things so deemed by the authority and conventions of religious groups. Excellence in a host of fields can induce flow experiences of effortless skill, which are a type of intense experience. And almost any type of activity can give rise to ultimacy experiences that underline the value of that activity in our lives. This serves to explicate the meaning of spirituality in the religious naturalist framework even when spirituality does not align itself with any existing religious tradition. That is, it furnishes a genuine biological basis for the social possibility of being "spiritual but not religious." Human life in every aspect is vibrant with spiritual possibilities and intense experiences make those possibilities count for our existential orientation and for the meaningfulness of life.

Second, the phenomenological qualities of intense experiences suggest that they often involve an intensification of ordinary sense-perception. Indeed, this may be an indication of the evolutionary and neurological origins of the capacity for intensity in the human species. Perception is not about things appearing to us out of nowhere or somewhere, after which we just need to decide whether perceptual objects are real or hallucinations. It is about dynamic engagement with an environment in which we learn to negotiate its physicality with our bodily capacities and to register its value structures with our axiological sensitivities. We know sense perception goes wrong from time to time so we are always trying things out, on the lookout for errors, capitalizing on feedback from our exploratory efforts, and seeking the kind of ecological mastery that allows us to navigate our physical and social surroundings effortlessly and at times perhaps even stylishly. Everything we know about the neurology of human cognition suggests that religious cognitions are forged in and through the same processes that produce ordinary sense-perceptual cognitions.

In a supernaturalist cosmology, the ecological-bodily factors in religious and spiritual experiences are the media for cognitive content that derive ultimately from, or at least refer to, one or another supernatural being, such as a personal God or a bodhisattva. On a naturalist cosmology, the encounter with ultimacy occurs in the valuated depth structures of the ecology of perception itself. In either case, the ecology of perception is the same and our various belief-forming (doxastic) practices differ simply by virtue of their different perceptual inputs and cognitive outputs. Sometimes eyes and ears function as input channels and the output is beliefs about perceptual objects. Sometimes the input channel is a complex bodily synthesis of senses, emotions, and cognitions and the output is beliefs about what is ultimately important in life—which cultural and group conventions then further specify in religious narratives and sometimes metaphysical beliefs.

As an ecological-bodily elaboration of sense experience, intense experiences are our best way of engaging and assessing the valuational depth structures of reality. Indeed, this is the primary means by which human beings engage ultimacy on the religious naturalist account. As such, it is important to ask whether intense experiences, when conjoined with judicious interpretation, permit (without guaranteeing) cognitively reliable perception of, and imaginative engagement with, the valuational depths of nature. This is a large and important question that goes directly to the cognitive reliability not only of intense experiences, but also of religious and spiritual experiences when they are also intense experiences. I claim that there is a case for the cognitive reliability of intense experiences to be made here. This claim is controversial outside of theological circles (it is dismissed without significant argument in a number of recent writers such as Dawkins 2007, Harris 2007, Hitchens 2007), and it has even proved controversial inside theological circles (see the debate triggered by Swinburne 1979 and by Alston 1991). But this claim is quite modest in the form it takes here because there is no *guarantee* of cognitive reliability, which is so often the aim in theological arguments about the evidential value of religious experience, as if the true meaning of such experiences could somehow simply be read off of the experiences themselves without taking account of contextual and interpretative complexities.

To express the epistemological claim precisely, I argue (in Wildman 2010, with key elements also in Barrett & Wildman 2009) that observing three basic conditions—a naturalistic cosmology, an ecological-semiotic account of perception as dynamic engagement with a world (described above), and a symbolic account of religious cognitions—increases rational entitlement to presume cognitive reliability of religious and spiritual experiences, insofar as they are intense experiences or derive substantially from intense experiences. I also argue that no stronger claim for rational entitlement is possible. This argument does not cover all religious and spiritual experiences, by any means, but it does implicate a significant subset of them. Moreover, the kinds of interpretations that can be attached to intense religious and spiritual experiences on this account would not suit the interests of most religious traditions because their working commitments are incompatible with one or more of the three conditions that are jointly necessary to increase rational entitlement to trust the resulting cognitions. Nevertheless, this line of argument demonstrates the philosophical importance of the fact that there is a type of human experience—the intense experiences—that draws on a species-wide, evolutionarily basic bodily capacity.

Our bodily abilities, it seems, engage us with ultimacy in such a way as to open up the valuational depth structures of nature to our understanding and exploration. They do this regardless of whether or not we call ourselves religious, and whether or not we are in conventionally religious settings. There is wonder in every moment and in every aspect of life, as often as intense experiences allow us to perceive it.

Conclusion: *Homo Religiosus* and Bodies

This chapter has extended the religious naturalist interpretation of the human condition by demonstrating how we bear in our own bodies the fundamental capacities that make us the beings we are, socially, morally, and experientially. As in previous chapters, we saw again here how the bodily character of human life constrains without determining cultural and religious expression. Social connectivity is made possible by bodies that are peculiarly well equipped for it, with innate attachment instincts, specialized circuitry that permits an elementary kind of mind-reading, and exquisitely sensitive facial musculature and cognitive-perceptual-motor systems that facilitate rich communication through and also parallel to language. Human moral life is driven by basic moral instincts and patterns of *post-hoc* reasoning, as well as neural mechanisms for resolving the conflicting emotionally charged cognitions of moral dilemmas. Religious and spiritual experiences arise from a suite of bodily capacities with neurological and sensory roots and vast existential and social impacts. Yet, despite these profound forms of bodily conditioning, human life projects are enormously diverse and their navigation demands deployment of traditional resources, corporate wisdom, and individual ingenuity. The result is a riot of cultural and spiritual diversity, driven by creative explorations of the landscape of possibilities laid down for us in our biological, bodily heritage.

The principle of constraint without determination may seem innocuous when first stated, particularly because it does not appear to limit unduly the possibilities for cultural and personal creativity. But we saw repeatedly in this chapter that awareness of bodily constraints stands in tension with many core principles of traditional theological anthropologies. It follows that taking seriously the bodily constraints on religious self-understanding has revolutionary implications for theological anthropologies. There are no knock-down proofs in this business, naturally, but there are burden-of-proof shifts and there certainly are changes in plausibility structures. Any thinker offering a religious anthropology in our time, regardless of traditional framework or theological commitment, must honor empirically derived insights into the human condition. This is not to privilege science over theology, thoughtlessly or otherwise. It is to privilege experience over speculation, and both science and theology make use of both in their ordinary workings. Nor is it to privilege empiricism over rationalism, for there is no understanding without reasoned interpretation just as there is no applicability to the world as we know it without empirical testing of rational hypotheses against all-important real-world details. In other words, there is no easy way for traditional theological anthropologies to escape this burden-shifting argument, short of simple sub-rational withdrawal from the conversation.

In the previous chapter I focused on human cognition and its role in religious belief, whereas in this chapter I focused on bodies and their material importance for human sociality, morality, and religious experience. The contrast between brains and bodies is somewhat artificial, since both are important in all that human beings are and do. Yet the difference remains meaningful because the actual shapes, capacities, and behaviors of bodies are crucial for interpreting human beings as *homo religiosus*. This emphatic dependence of religious anthropology on the details of human bodies is underlined even more strongly in the next chapter on sex.

CHAPTER 7

Sex

Introduction

Human beings are sexual creatures, through and through. This point is appreciated in a variety of scientific inquiries, including evolutionary theory, but tends to be underemphasized in religious anthropologies, and also in most forms of religious belief and practice. This chapter aims to show why and how sex and the biology of sex differences are important for an interpretation of the human being as *homo religiosus*. This will take us through the territories of sexual politics, sexual ethics, and the theology of sex. An adequate account of these themes crucially depends on knowledge about the relevant biological, hormonal, neurological, and social factors that condition sexuality in human beings.

Oppression of women and sexual minorities are social facts, even in so-called post-Enlightenment cultures prizing equality and the intrinsic value of all individuals. Both kinds of oppression have frequently been rationalized by reference to the biology of sex differences. For example, claims of male superiority in biological contexts purport to justify social hierarchies dominated by men, thereby perpetuating oppressive treatment of women. Claims of strict sexual dimorphism at the biological level support the cultural construction of strict gender dualism and an interpretation of sex linked solely to reproduction, with a host of oppressive consequences for both women and sexual minorities. These biologically enabled rationalizations are paper thin, but their cultural prominence has understandably led feminist and queer theorists to attack the cultural ideologies of male superiority and strict gender dualism at the level of psychological conditioning and cultural authority, while generally avoiding the biology of sex differences, in order to avoid playing into the hands of their opponents.

While avoiding the biology of sex differences may have been expedient, new discoveries in this area offer valuable intellectual resources, with important implications for political strategizing, moral reasoning, and theological interpretation. These biological discoveries include non-strictness in biological sex types, prodigious diversity of sexual behavior among animals, and a new understanding of the reasons for male dominance that supplants the age-old mythic paradigm of male and female "types" with a nuanced analysis of sexual behavior, social relationships, and parental investment in a flexible evolutionary framework of diverse fitness strategies. When combined with the discoveries by cultural critics of socially protective and privilege-conferring power dynamics at work in the cultural mindsets of gender dualism and gender inequality, these scientific resources become potently disruptive resources.

Can we or should we treat these new scientific insights as a nature-based rationale for a cultural revolution toward gender polymorphism and gender equality? Perhaps. But such a revolutionary approach is intellectually ineffective, and probably strategically futile as well, because of the inherent flexibility of natural-law ethical arguments. That is, where one person draws on the sexual fecundity and diversity of nature to support social change in the direction of openness toward the acceptance and celebration of diverse expressions of human sexuality, another person can apply a "disease" or "deformity" model to anything in nature that does not fit pre-established norms for sexual behavior. Both take the zoological and biological data seriously but they draw opposite normative conclusions. The "disease" and "abnormality" paradigms appear persuasive enough to perpetuate resistance to large-scale social change in sexual ethics.

Nevertheless, this new biological and cultural awareness does restructure imaginative possibilities for the interpretation of human sexuality, and thereby the ethical and theological justification of desirable social norms. This restructuring of imaginative possibilities does not suddenly overcome the ambiguity of natural-law and natural-theology approaches for attacking and for defending prevailing norms in sexual ethics, for the reasons just described. But it does create conceptual space for a less anthropomorphic theology, one more compatible with our bodily realities and less vulnerable to unconscious distortion for the purposes of legitimating cultural ideologies of gender by making strict gender dualism the expression of a divine intention or of the moral depths of nature. This kind of naturalist theology treats nature as the fecund source of valuational possibilities, and thus as furnishing avenues of exploration by means of which human beings may engage ultimacy, thought of as the valuational depth structures and dynamic energies of nature. On this approach, anything possible can have a kind of value, and human beings decide, both alone and in groups, which kinds of value they will prize. This approach sanctifies the diversity of sexual biology and sexual behavior and places responsibility firmly in human hands for determining social norms and making moral choices.

One important difficulty here is that classic feminist analyses made the same core assumptions about sex and gender as their traditional opponents. That is, all sides in the early feminist debates presupposed a sharp distinction between biological sexes in nature (I refer to this as "strict sexual dimorphism") that maps cleanly onto the cultural construction of two distinct human sexes (which I shall call "strict gender dualism"—note that I regard hybrid terms such as "gender dimorphism" as containing a category confusion, unhelpfully mixing cultural and biological terminology). Both strict sexual dimorphism and strict gender dualism have proved to be problematic, even though two genders is by far the most common arrangement in all known human cultures and distinct biological sexes is by far the most common arrangement within each of the numerous mammalian species. Thus, I am concerned to show that discussions about the ethical and theological significance of the biology of sex differences need not propagate the unempirical essentialization of biological or cultural categories pertaining to sex differences and gender.

We should acknowledge from the outset that this is a sensitive topic for many feminists, as well as for those with concerns for gay, lesbian, bisexual, and transgender individuals. Not only does talk of the biology of sex differences conjure the memory and continuing reality of specious arguments for male supremacy and the abnormality of intersex and transgender realities, it also threatens to sideline cultural analysis, which has traditionally been the strongest intellectual resource for conceiving human sexuality more adequately, creatively, and justly.

With these sensitivities in mind, I shall proceed first by discussing sex types and gender roles, introducing the information that problematizes the widespread habitual reification of sex and gender categories. I shall then discuss the meaning of male dominance, a variety of psycho-social explanations for it, and the biological contributors to it. This involves addressing the political, ethical, and theological significance of the biological analysis of sex differences. Finally, I take up the equally important themes of intimacy and sensuality, which have wide relevance and do not depend on how questions of sex types, gender roles, and male dominance are settled. By the end, I hope it will become clear that biological explanations of sex differences need not undermine the just aspirations of women and sexual minorities to overcome continuing discrimination and violence, and to disrupt the corresponding social realities of hidden privilege. On the contrary, biological awareness can support such aspirations, and a rich understanding of intimacy and sensuality can create empathic awareness of the "sexual other" (see Gudorf 2001).

It should also become evident that this kind of interpretation of human sexuality has profound implications for understanding human beings as *homo religiosus*, in at least the following two ways. On the one hand, the space between the "is" of nature and the "ought" of morality—which is far more complicated than some approaches on both the conservative and revolutionary sides suggest—is religiously volatile territory. Our religious groups and personal theological-moral commitments do a lot of the work needed to traverse the space between is and ought, and they often do this work surreptitiously. Knowing this helps to estimate the actual social and moral power of human religiosity, at both corporate and individual levels, in regulating the sexual thoughts and activities of human bodies. On the other hand, knowing more about sex and its varied roles in human life demonstrates that there can be no neat separation between sexuality and spirituality. The two domains significantly interpenetrate and either one can function as the engine that drives the other. Indeed, as the intensity of experience increases, it can be difficult to discriminate the two.

Sex Types and Gender Roles

The Complexity of Sex and Gender in Human Nature

Throughout I shall use the term "sex" in a biological, not cultural sense. The adjective "sexual" and the noun "sexuality" will be embracing terms, with both biological and cultural connotations. The terms "male" and "female" are biological sex types and here refer to the members of a sexually reproducing species that generate the smaller gametes (sperm) and larger gametes (ova), respectively. Some yeasts and algae reproduce sexually using two same-sized gametes (isogamy), but the focus here is on mammals and primates, where anisogamy is the rule, in the form of oogamy: few, large, non-motile, metabolically expensive ova and numerous, tiny, motile, metabolically cheap sperm. There are individuals in anisogamous sexually reproducing species that produce neither type of gamete, that produce both types of gametes at the same time or at different times, or that are otherwise not classifiable as completely and permanently male or female (Roughgarden 2002 provides a catalogue of examples). Their existence cleanly refutes strict sexual dimorphism. Thus, the terms "male" and "female" are understood here to apply if and as long as the gamete-based distinction is relevant, and thus possibly both at once. Similarly, species that can reproduce both sexually and asexually (e.g. some types of sea anemones) are understood to be male and female only in the context of anisogamous sexual reproduction based on the production of large and small gametes.

"Non-strict sexual dimorphism" is understood in a statistical sense to apply to any species for which the very large majority of members are completely and permanently either male or female—that includes all mammalian species, for example. Among human beings, the rate of exceptions to sexual dimorphism is estimated to be between 0.018 and 1.7 per cent or even 2 per cent, depending on the strictness of the definition. Sax (2002) argues for a stricter definition and the lower rate, against Fausto-Sterling (2000) and Blackless et al. (2000), who produce the higher rate by including syndromes where chromosomal sex is clear and secondary sex characteristics largely match chromosomal sex.

I shall use the term "gender" in a cultural, not biological sense, and strictly in relation to the human species. A number of species have social lives with sufficient complexity to warrant speaking of "gender roles." But I require a term to discriminate the social peculiarities of sexual behavior in the human species, and shall sequester the term "gender" for that purpose. Thus, "gender" here refers to the social construction of individual human identity in relation to sexual behavior and sexual self-understanding. Though non-strict sexual dimorphism applies to all primate species, including human beings, the cultural creativity of human beings promotes numerous gender roles, for which many descriptive categories are used. The most common of these gender categories are "man" and "woman." This pair is cross-culturally universal, presumably because it closely matches the (non-strict) sexual dimorphism of the human species.

This diversity of gender roles corresponds to a fabulous variety of sexual behaviors, which is present in numerous mammalian species as well as in human beings (again, Roughgarden 2002 is a standard reference for the diversity of sexual behaviors in animal species). For example, according to the University of Oslo's Norwegian Natural History Museum's 2006–07 exhibit of homosexual behavior in animals, homosexual behavior has been observed in 1,500 species, varying from occasional to frequent, and from episodic encounters to life-long relationships. Masturbation has been observed in numerous species, also, as has virtually every imaginable arrangement of sexual partners. Nature is wild, sexually speaking— contrary to the prudish assumptions of early zoologists from the ancient Greeks until very recently, who denied that such behaviors existed, or described them in ways that suggested they were atypical outlier phenomena, even when they were common. The numerous creative forms of gender construction among human beings are continuous with this broad picture of sexual reality among animals (see Butler 2004).

Human cultures have traditionally made gender assignments based not on gamete production but on the appearance of externally visible genitalia. The fact of ambiguous genitalia produces many confusing situations in which gender assignment is not automatic or obvious, and parents must make a decision about how to raise a child. The long and painful history of so-called hermaphrodites makes clear how confusing these situations have always been (see Dreger 1998). In our day, surgeries to disambiguate genitalia are possible, and typically are recommended by doctors and decided on by parents based on genetic information about gamete production. Blackless et al. (2000) estimate the rate of so-called corrective genital surgery at between 0.1 and 0.2 per cent of live births between 1955 and 1997, which indicates that the rate of ambiguous genitalia is at least that high. Some advocacy groups urge that parents wait until the child can make an informed decision on the matter, not least because an early decision in the wrong direction complicates later surgery (see the review of ethical issues in Beh & Diamond 2000). In relatively rare cases of strict intersexuality, sex disambiguation is exceptionally controverted, either because sex chromosomes (XX female and XY male) do not match secondary sexual characteristics more or less dramatically, as in Swyer's XY female syndrome and similar situations; or chromosomal markers for male and female are not present, as in syndromes involving XXXX, XXX, XXY, XYY, and XO chromosomes (see Fausto-Sterling 2000 for a review).

The biological capacity to produce gametes is accompanied by a host of sex-typical biological features of an organism, from hormonal profiles to genitalia and from sexual preferences to distinctive neurological features. These suites of characteristics are usually correlated for males and for females. But development *in utero* is extremely complex and subject both to genetic particularities and to environmental conditions. As a result, there are many developmental pathways that produce non-typical combinations of sex-typical features at low frequency. Among human beings the most obvious examples are the ambiguous genitalia just mentioned, and also atypical matches between chromosomal sex and secondary sexual characteristics. Subtler examples involve atypical combinations of neural features and chromosomal sex type (see the review in Hines 2005). This can be intensely confusing for individuals as they seek to forge a coherent personal and sexual identity. These facts of biological life further complicate the social process of gender assignment or reassignment.

In a culture that prizes individual expression sufficiently highly, social space can be created for numerous hybrid or novel gender identities, the transformation of gender identity, and the exploration of transgender space in a host of ways. These cultural creations often reflect an individual's highly personal way of equilibrating the various biological, experiential, social, and emotional factors relevant to sexuality. In cultures where strict gender dualism is taken for granted and socially or legally enforced, these dualism-defying cases are suppressed and individuals have to be men or women, at least outwardly, in order to survive. On the one hand, this can produce enormous emotional hardship. On the other hand, challenging gender identity roles can be unsettling to the majority culture, in most members of which sex-typical characteristics are strongly correlated and spontaneous anxiety produces resistance to the sexually unfamiliar long before reason is called upon to rationalize those emotional responses (as discussed in the previous chapter; see Haidt 2000). The social reflex to regulate sexual behavior produces moralizations of gender dualism. This in turn makes challenges to gender dualism morally charged and potentially quite dangerous to those who mount them, thanks to the potential of anxiety to flourish into violent reactions to the "different."

Religion traditionally has reinforced the linkage between morality and gender identity. The Durkheimian tradition of sociology of religion (discussed in Chapter 4, 'Groups') describes how social groups unselfconsciously use religions to give their moral principles cosmic significance (see Berger 1967, drawing on Durkheim 1915). In this way, religion inscribes human conventions about gender identity onto the divine will or into the depths of nature. After that, the social control for which religion is justly famous or infamous is used to articulate culturally dominant gender roles as "normal" or "abnormal," as "good" or "evil," as "natural" or "unnatural." The fact that religion works this way is fairly clear at this point in the academic study of religion. The correctness of any particular religiously cosmologized rationalization of gender roles is another question entirely.

Modified Natural Law Approaches to Sex and Gender

The most common way of arguing for the correctness of a traditional theological construal of gender roles has been an appeal to natural law. This is true in both theistic and non-theistic frameworks. The Abrahamic traditions vest gender dualism with the authority of intentional divine design by means of the Genesis creation narrative. Chinese religions vest gender dualism with the authority of the depths of nature by means of a sexualized interpretation of the yin–yang cosmology, which permeates every kind and level of religious and social thought in that cultural context. In these and many other examples of rationalizing gender dualism, the male and female are understood to be complementary and fecund by combination, but the "twoness" of the underlying principles persists.

The evidence for the non-strict distinction between biological sex types is overwhelming at this point. The strictest kinds of natural-law approaches are bluntly refuted by this evidence, because on those strict views the kinds of evidence biology has produced should not even be possible in nature. A modified natural-law ethics can still accommodate these discoveries, however, and in spectacularly opposed ways.

In one direction, modified natural-law ethics proposes that any human individual not fitting the biology of strict sexual dimorphism at the gamete level or not conforming to the most commonly correlated sex-typical features is a biological miscreant. This is the view, for example, of early modern Catholic natural law, which developed into official Roman Catholic moral teaching in the early decades of the twentieth century. This body of teachings proposed a fixed human nature, strict sexual dimorphism, strict gender dualism, and cultural universality of sexual norms. It is also the view of the small minority of scientists and therapists who promote the sexual orientation treatments advocated by the US National Association for Research and Therapy of Homosexuality and other such groups (also see Whitehead & Whitehead 1999). The analogy here is with so-called birth "defects" such as deafness, with bodily "deformities" such as vestigial limbs or cleft palates, or with "disease" whereby normal bodily function is disrupted. The presupposition in all cases is that there is a "natural" template against which any phenotype can be assessed. When there is a mismatch between a particular organism (hereafter, a "phenotype") and that organism's template, we have on this view something "misshapen." Misshapen individuals deserve care and are entitled to corrective help, technology permitting, because their condition occurs through no fault of their own.

With regard to gender roles, the same modified natural-law approach invokes categories of willful moral badness to explain why some individuals explore gender roles other than the two supposedly divinely created or naturally occurring roles of gender dualism: man and woman. These people require correction and retraining. The analogy here is with criminal activity: even if circumstances contribute to the decision to behave badly, individuals are still responsible for their behavioral decisions and should be punished and rewarded accordingly. In this way, modified natural-law ethics can accommodate recent biological discoveries about the non-strictness of sexual dimorphism and still produce the resources necessary to uphold existing religious rationalizations of strict gender dualism.

In the other direction, modified natural-law ethics can take its bearings not from a template supposedly arising from the divine mind or from the metaphysical depths of nature, but from what actually appears in the observable plants and animals of the natural world (for example, see Jung & Coray 2001). That is, once our biological knowledge advances to the point that we know sexual dimorphism is far from being an absolute rule of nature, then our concept of the natural mutates, and no single template is possible. Newly informed about what actually occurs in nature, we accept that the possibilities for human sexuality are diverse both at the biological level and at the cultural level. In other words, the spectacular diversity of sexual structures and behaviors in nature legitimates any kind of possibility for gender roles that we desire, subject to whatever moral norms we consider essential. Natural sexual diversity also inhibits any anxious tendency to intervene decisively to reconcile ambiguous genitalia with socially prevalent gender roles. Such surgical interventions may be attempted, but not in order to correct anything supposedly unnatural so much as to help a child live happily in a social environment that takes gender dualism for granted.

In its most extreme forms, modified natural-law ethics developed in this direction invites a cultural revolution in regard to sexuality. In this imagined revolution, everybody comes to understand that sexual dimorphism is not strict and that the sexuality-related elements of human bodies—morphology, neurology, endocrinology—are diverse and not always neatly correlated along sex-typical lines. While the need to reproduce makes it difficult to envisage such a revolution in sexual understanding actually occurring, there is no question that this type of modified natural-law ethics supports it because it is present first in nature.

Of course, various intermediate versions of modified natural-law ethics complicate this simple portrayal of extreme opposed alternatives. For example, categories such as "evolutionary stabilization" can furnish a concept of a teleological template for body plans and sexual functions deriving from the evolutionary process itself. This allows the *telos* of nature to be interpreted as matching the *telos* of a putative transcendental source of morality, such as a divine mind (for example, see Porter 2000). The evolutionary emergence of such a template can be ascribed to divine intention using theistic evolution or the deep structure of the laws of nature, and thereby infused once again with transcendental authority sufficient to uphold existing religious rationalizations of strict gender dualism.

Such possibilities show that the moral linkage between the biological fact that there are two numerically preponderant sex types among human beings and the cultural fact that gender dualism is universal among all known human societies is anything but simple and obvious. I suspect that there is no way decisively to settle questions of the morality of gender roles. While we can draw the obvious conclusion that the strictest forms of natural-law ethics are contradicted by the not-strictness of sexual dimorphism, that still leaves plenty of room for modified forms of natural-law ethics both to support and to disrupt conventional interpretations of gender roles.

At root, these questions may be matters of social organization and political power, driven by the vital principles that we should uphold social stability and also honor the irreducibly valuable experience of individuals. Both principles are sacred, in any religious perspective, but they are also vague and to some extent in opposition, so they allow religious people to disagree authentically. And disagree they do, often dramatically. The way forward in a given social context is therefore not by force of argument alone, but also by the structuring of moral imaginations. The side that best controls the moral imaginations of those in power, of those who elect those in power, and especially of a new generation of children will be the side that gets most of its vision of human rights and social organization realized. The victors in this fight are also those whose moral reasoning comes to feel most persuasive because of its harmony both with evidence and with the most prominent plausibility structures.

Male Dominance

Cultural Explanations for Male Dominance

Having surfaced the biological, cultural, moral, and theological complications surrounding the issue of sex types and gender roles, we are in a position to frame questions about male dominance. I have pointed out that sexual dimorphism is strict neither in nature generally, nor in the human species, and that the variety of sex-typical biological features can combine in diverse and surprising ways to complicate the biological basis for culture-level gender-role assignment. The idea of male dominance does not require either strict sexual dimorphism or strict gender dualism, however. As an emergent feature of groups of sexually reproducing organisms, male dominance requires only that two sex types with correlated sex-typical traits (and matching widespread gender dualism in the case of human beings) occur at statistically overriding frequencies. Regardless of how male dominance has been interpreted in the past, therefore, in our time we need not assume that it entails strict sexual dimorphism (or strict gender dualism among human beings). This opens the way to discussing traditional feminist concerns without essentializing two sex types or two gender roles.

The social fact of male dominance in human societies is broadly agreed upon, though very differently defined, explained, and evaluated. Male dominance here means (i) that men can coerce women through threats, inducements, and physical violence into behaving in ways that suit men, and (ii) that men can establish or control forms of social organization that co-opt women into supporting men's interests and that regulate the options of women so as to give some men what they want even when many women would rather not give it to them. Female dominance may arise in some relationships and even in a few social settings, and there certainly are dominance hierarchies among women that may include having authority over adult men. Generally, however, and particularly when constraining the view to the upper reaches of social power relationships, it appears that men tend to be dominant in all human societies.

To apply to other species, the definition need only be adjusted to match the cognitive level of the species in question, gradually muting intentional features and leaving only behavioral features as cognitive complexity simplifies relative to the human case. With those modifications, this understanding of male dominance applies to many species other than human beings, including almost all mammals and the large majority of primates (but not all—for example, bonobos have a matriarchal social order that effectively regulates male aggression; see de Waal and Lanting 1998).

My concern at this point is primarily to understand male dominance among human beings, using male dominance in other species as a test of the adequacy of explanations in the human case. The definition of dominance is loaded with moral significance, of course, yet I wish to bracket those moral considerations temporarily in what follows in order to identify the biological causes of widespread male dominance. In particular, as I pointed out in the case of the deconstruction of gender essentialization above, my own ethical and theological argument against gender inequality requires protecting space between the "is" of the male dominance so prevalent among mammalian species and the "ought" of moral judgments about male dominance among human beings. There is a lot of conceptual and inferential space between is and ought and proceeding carefully is crucial. Otherwise, we may end up *approving a nature-based inference from the erosion of sexual dimorphism to the rejection of discrimination against sexual minorities* (see Gudorf 2001) that subsequently *traps us when we seek to argue against male dominance and in favor of gender equality*. No wonder turning to nature for norms is so problematic. Nature's ways point toward sexual diversity and also toward male dominance, especially among mammals. Feminists arguing on behalf of the liberation of sexual minorities appear to be caught between a rock and a hard place: the very appeal to nature in one case seems to undermine the other case. And their opponents are in the same position, but in reverse.

In recent decades, scientific and political efforts to realize the vision of gender equality have demonstrated skepticism about attempts to move from the "is" of biological description to the "ought" of morality. As in the case of gender dualism just discussed, strict natural-law ethics permits the following argument: male dominance is good and proper, and ought to be accepted and respected just because it is the way things are; "is" implies "ought." It takes more work to get from is to ought within nuanced modified natural-law ethics, but it can be done in the case of male dominance just as in the case of gender dualism. In all cases, these arguments ultimately depend on creation mythologies or philosophies of nature that vest existing social hierarchies with the authority of divine design or its functional equivalents in non-theistic settings. The is-to-ought move was once common among intellectuals and it persists even now in popular discourse, as well as in the moral reasoning of some conservative religious communities in many parts of the world. Male dominance is so widespread among mammalian species that it is easy to understand why a nature-based approach has not commended itself to social reformers seeing gender equality.

Theistic feminist theologians have aggressively attacked the conceptions of God or nature underlying is-to-ought arguments on behalf of male dominance, invoking the traditional term "naturalistic fallacy" to describe the conceptual error involved. Theistic feminist theologians have almost universally sought to affirm the reality and relevance of God while distinguishing divine intentions from social facts. For example, they point out that male dominance may reflect selfishness rather than

God's will for human societies. For their part, scientists these days tend not to ask whether male dominance should be accepted and respected, because they regard such moral questions as lying beyond their purview as scientists. Rather, while sometimes being transparent about their moral opinions, they focus on trying to answer the question about how male dominance arose in the evolutionary process and why it is a universal feature of human societies and so prominent in other mammalian species. And they endeavor to produce explanations that naturally accommodate the few fascinating exceptions to the pattern of male dominance.

Ethicists, theologians, scientists, and activists writing on male dominance today do not rely on morally laden concepts such as male superiority. The many respects in which one thing can be superior to another make this concept difficult to work with in constructing fair-minded explanations, regardless of the subject matter. Moreover, the value-laden quality of talk about superiority means that it is ill-suited to the kind of explanations that careful scientists and careful theologians and ethicists seek. Unfortunately, this was not always so. The assumption that male superiority, in some sense, explains male dominance has deeply affected scientific practice, from the design and execution of research studies to the judgments inevitably made about which facts seemed most relevant to reflection on a scientific problem. For example, when primatologists observe a troupe of animals in the wild, they frequently notice females wandering away from the troupe. Believing that the interesting activity is with the troupe, which is where the dominant male does his thing, they may assume that a female's wanderings are not important and so they do not follow her to see what she does. But if they followed her they might discover that she mates with a male outside her troupe, thereby making her departure far more interesting and relevant to troupe social life than they had assumed.

In the last few decades, the quality of observations of human and other animal behavior has improved enormously. Objectivity is always a problematic goal in zoological observation because interpretation is such a complicated and contestable blend of awareness and empathy and understanding. But there is no question that these kinds of observations are now far more closely scrutinized for casual assumptions that reflect biases of social imagination than was ever the case in the past. In particular, having detected the assumption that "male superiority explains male dominance" lurking in their scientific work, scientists have gone to great lengths to adjust their practices and assumptions. They started to follow female primates who wander away from the group. They started to analyze forms of competition among females and between females and males, whereas formerly they had only paid close attention to male competition. And they started to take cooperative behaviors as seriously as competitive behaviors. We do not yet know the ways in which current zoological observations reflect undetected ideological bias but we do know that correcting past mistakes has produced surprising new information that is directly relevant to interpreting the biology of sex differences and explaining the social fact of male dominance in human societies.

If we are unwilling to rely on is-to-ought arguments, and if we have given up on the conveniently loose concept of male superiority, what avenues remain for explaining male dominance? The literature on this subject is dense with analyses of gender inequality at the cultural level. In her 1981 book *The Woman that Never Evolved*, Sarah Blaffer Hrdy discusses five prominent psycho-social explanations for male dominance (Hrdy 1999a: 4–7).

First, in the Marx–Engels framework, subsistence produces egalitarian social relationships, but a surplus of goods spurs warfare, which gives the social upper hand to testosterone-infused men with their large bodies and willingness to take risks, leading to male dominance.

Second, in the psychoanalytic framework of post-Freudian theory, each person is closely bonded with his or her mother and must struggle against the mother for independent identity. For boys this supposedly requires a repudiation of all things female in a way that does not apply to girls, thereby producing processes of socialization that create and sustain ideologies of male superiority and corresponding behaviors of male dominance.

Third, in one kind of structuralist framework, reminiscent of the yin–yang cosmology, women are associated with receptive and darkly mysterious nature, particularly because of the internality of their reproductive organs and the hiddenness of their reproductive functions. Meanwhile, men with their significantly external reproductive organs are associated with the assertiveness of culture. After this, the technological superiority of culture over nature serves to legitimate men's superiority over women, and leading to male dominance. (Note that this view is particularly vulnerable to the collapse of strict sexual dimorphism.)

Fourth, in one behaviorist framework, the advent of big-game hunting led to a prestigious testosterone-related role for men as the providers of protein and fat, and thereby to male dominance.

Finally, in one kind of feminist rethinking of sexual division of labor in subsistence lifestyles, women rather than men are the cultural innovators, the toolmakers and educators. Men enjoy social dominance merely because they are large, aggressive, and violent; there is no basis for male superiority underlying the social fact of male dominance beyond higher male body mass and aggression.

Hrdy acknowledges the illumination brought by these five psycho-social explanations for male dominance, but she is not convinced. She writes:

> Each of these theories may contribute to our understanding of the human case, but even taken together, they are insufficient to explain the widespread occurrence of sexual inequality in nature, inasmuch as they account for only a small portion of known cases. They cannot explain sexual asymmetry in even one other species. Yet male dominance characterizes the majority of several hundred other species that, like our own, belong to the order Primates. ... Logic alone should warn us against explaining such a widespread phenomenon with reference only to a specialized subset of human examples. (Hrdy 1999a: 6–7)

Anthropocentric explanations of male dominance are implausible because male-dominance is extremely widespread in nature, and almost universal among primates. This directs our attention back to the realm of biology, in search of an explanation for male dominance that can account for its appearance in so many varied species. Apparently, psycho-social factors condition the way that male dominance is expressed among human beings, but those factors modify something more fundamentally biological.

Biological Explanations for Male Dominance

So what is the best explanation of the biological aspects of male dominance in human and other primates? And how does it relate to the biology of sex differences? Scientists first raised this question in its modern form in late nineteenth-century England under the impact of Charles Darwin's theory of evolution (see especially Darwin 1871). It is to be expected that cultural conditioning of the scientists working in that environment would express itself in the assumptions made and theories propounded (the same is true now, of course). Indeed, most scientists at that time assumed that women were delicate flowers, social butterflies, sexually passive, intellectually receptive, coy, pure, and above all devoted mothers—all in accordance with Victorian mores. Individuals who did not live up to this dubious standard for women sometimes paid a heavy price; they were subjected to enormous pressures to conform and frequently ostracized if they did not.

Darwin himself lent support to this view of women. Though he clearly recognized the evolutionary significance of mate choice, stressing the role that women play in choosing mates from among men competing for reproductive opportunities, he seemed to overlook the equally obvious fact that women must compete for resources and opportunities just as men do, and must therefore be selected for competitive skills to the extent that such skills are genetically linked. He also overlooked the degree to which cooperation occurs in the complex processes of mate choice, and the equally important fact that sexual activity is far more diverse in apparent purpose and function than merely reproduction, especially among mammals. A few early evolutionary biologists pointed out some of these lapses in consistency and thoroughness (for example, Hrdy cites Antoinette Brown Blackwell's (1875) critique of Darwin's neglect of female competition in her 1875 *The Sexes throughout Nature*; see Hrdy 1999a: 12–13, 189). But broadly Victorian assumptions about sex differences mostly remained in place until the feminist movement helped to provoke a more disciplined observational approach to animal sexual behavior. The outcome is far more empirically and theoretically robust than early efforts to grasp the biology of sex differences. Many points are still contested, but the biology of sex differences is coming into clearer focus—clear enough to understand how it might affect theological and ethical ruminations on male dominance, as well as political strategies to disrupt it.

First, the idea of an innate nature determining the personality characteristics of women (such as the coyness Darwin mentioned) has disintegrated almost completely. The biological continuities among women constrain without determining a woman's interests and desires, her personality and behavior. This means that virtually every kind of activity and behavior is possible for women—in the sense that, for any activity or behavior we can think of, a significant number of women are good at it, whether or not they like to do it. It also means that distinctively female drives and interests are expressed in and through however wide a range of behaviors cultural circumstances permit. Cultural norms for female behavior and personality are overlaid on this basic biological and behavioral flexibility. This produces angst and frustration among women who resist prevailing norms and an unearned feeling of superiority among those women who flourish under conformity to those norms. Much the same is true for men, of course, but male dominance means that men play a larger role than women in determining (though not necessarily in enforcing) social norms for women. Conclusion: we cannot explain male dominance with reference to male–female "personality types" in the way that Darwin and many others tried to do.

Second, women's biochemical and hormonal realities vary tremendously across the life cycle, but they do so in more or less predictable and consistent ways for most women. Louann Brizendine's presentation of these realities in *The Female Brain* (2006) is a masterpiece of accessible writing that shows just how pervasive are the effects of estrogen, progesterone, testosterone, oxytocin, cortisol, vasopressin, and several other hormones and neurochemicals in women's lives. Much the same is true for testosterone in men, as James McBride Dabbs shows in his analysis of testosterone and behavior in *Heroes, Rogues, and Lovers* (2001). Yet this emerging biochemical picture does not finally confirm the caricatures of a male nature that indulges an irresistible urge to mate with as many females as possible, and of a female nature that passively accepts whatever sexual and reproductive fate males assign. The sex-typical hormonal characteristics of men and women influence bodies and brains, and modify behavioral style, but are not specific enough to determine "personality types." Rather, a wide range of behavioral possibilities is available to both men and women, and they express sexual interest, intellectual creativity, physical aggression, and social connectivity in a variety of hormonally related sex-typical ways, and *at different times* during the life cycle depending on endocrinal realities. Conclusion: we cannot explain male dominance based on hormonal differences alone, but endocrinal factors certainly condition the way primate social relationships unfold.

Third, in virtually all primate species, both males and females compete within their own sex for resources and opportunities and they also cooperate within their own sex for the sake of efficiency and protection. But males compete and cooperate differently than females do. Males typically specialize in large networks of relatively less intimate relationships, *which is consistent with their evolutionary need to maintain and control access to reproductive resources*. Females specialize in smaller networks of relatively more intimate relationships, *which is consistent with their evolutionary need to preserve networks of protection and care for offspring*. The careless scientist, used to thinking of competition in typically male terms, may fail to notice competition and ambition among females. What is true of males and females generally among primate species in regard to competition and cooperation also applies in the human case. Conclusion: we cannot explain male dominance in terms of male competitiveness alone.

Fourth, the most prominent aspect of the "innate female nature" myth in both its Victorian and contemporary forms is that women are innately devoted mothers, blessed with an all-consuming love to the point of self-sacrifice. Hrdy's portrayal of primate mothers in her controversial but widely respected *Mother Nature* (Hrdy, 1999b) is profoundly at odds with the myth of the devoted, self-sacrificial mother. She presents compelling evidence that females combine maternal devotion and survival instincts in an intricate calculus fitted to the daunting challenges they face in child rearing. This produces a wide range of behaviors, from sharing maternal responsibilities with other females (Hrdy calls it allomothering) to maternal infanticide when circumstances are sufficiently desperate. This network of behavioral possibilities is present among human females, also. Awareness of this fact is of great practical value because it helps women cope with the taboo subject of ambivalent feelings toward their offspring, to manage depression, to give measured rein to their ambitions, and to explore possibilities for creative self-expression. Conclusion: we can't explain male dominance with reference to the ideal of females as nurturing mothers alone.

Correcting these deficient biological explanations for male dominance yields a portrayal of women as intelligent nurturers, calculating protectors, ambitious controllers, and creative competitors—a far cry from Victorian sensibilities, or indeed those of almost any particular cultural setting. This portrayal has the great virtue of not limiting the range of possible or fitting female behaviors, so much as describing the distinctive interests that women express when they nurture, protect, control, and compete. It is a fundamentally liberating insight, even though many women and men in our own day are not ready to embrace it.

An Integrated Evolutionary Explanation for Male Dominance

This portrayal of women and sex differences is thoroughly intelligible in an evolutionary framework—a point that deserves more than the brief discussion that follows. The evolutionary process increases the frequency of genetic variations that help organisms be reproductively fit. The principles of random variation and natural selection are the engines that make fitness relevant. But fitness strategies turn out to be incredibly diverse. In fact, the simplest fitness strategy for sexually reproducing species—mate as often as possible and produce as many offspring as possible—is far from optimal in many species, particularly when offspring require high parental investment, because most offspring just die. As the complexity of organisms increase, the factors relevant to fitness strategies multiply exponentially. Consider neural complexity, for example. Neural complexity sufficient for communication within and between species makes possible fitness strategies based on communication. Neural complexity sufficient for aesthetic preference makes possible fitness strategies based on plumage or displays. Neural complexity sufficient for social life opens a world of fitness strategies based on cooperation and competition. Neural complexity sufficient for emotions relevant to friendship and enmity produce a host of fitness strategies relevant to sexual behavior.

The useful parts of Darwin's sexual selection theory (Darwin 1871) as it has been refined and critiqued up to the present (see Cronin and Maynard Smith 1993, Roughgarden 2002) can be coordinated into the larger analytical framework of fitness strategies, as can signaling theory (see Maynard Smith and Harper 2003), group-selection theory and altruism theory (see Post et al. 2002, Sober and Wilson 1999), and a host of other analyses of parts of the vast, multidimensional domain of evolutionary possibilities. The arguments among evolutionary theorists about particular selection mechanisms do not threaten the basic framework of interpretation, in which fitness is what counts. This framework allows for a plethora of fitness strategies relevant to the emergent properties of species-in-environments, as well as a host of side-effects of adapted traits that may or may not contribute to novel fitness strategies in mutating environmental niches. In the context of human sexual behavior, the array of possible fitness strategies and side-effects is so extraordinarily rich and intricate and the organism in question so cognitively complex that a mind-boggling host of diverse sexual behaviors results (see Baker 2006, Buss 2003, Miller 2001, Ridley 1993).

This is the correct biological context within which to theorize about the origins of male dominance in primates. There is an obvious correlation between dominance and body size: in virtually all sexually reproducing species capable of displaying dominance behaviors, the larger sex is the dominant sex. This is so strong a correlation, in fact, that interpreters have been apt to overlook the few exceptions to the rule that point us deeper, such as the dik-dik or the Weddell seal (see Hrdy 1999a: 19–21), in which the dominant male is smaller on average than the female. The most robust correlation of all is not between body size and dominance but between body size and extended reproductive control over members of the opposite sex. If the male of a species can control reproductive access to several females simultaneously, it is because it can hold off competitive males, for which a large body mass is crucial. In relatively monogamous species, males and females tend to be similar in size.

These realities point to the fundamental biological reason for male dominance. Whatever sex makes the greatest parental investment will be the sex over which the opposite sex competes, producing larger bodies and higher aggression in that opposite sex. *This biases the social system in the direction of dominance of the low-parental-investment sex.* Biologically, the female mammal is almost always committed to greater parental investment at every stage of the process of producing and nurturing offspring, from the precious nutrients in the relatively few ova awaiting fertilization to life in the womb and lactation after birth. Males will compete for access to those limiting resources, without which they have no genetic heritage. Males will tend to have the larger body mass and greater level of aggression commensurate with the need to compete for access to precious reproductive resources. *Then* we get male dominance. *Parental investment comes first, logically, then competition over limiting resources, then body size differences, then dominance behaviors.*

Recognizing the fundamental role of parental investment helps to explain fascinating exceptions and complications in dominance patterns among species. Anne Campbell's magisterial study of the evolutionary psychology of women, *A Mind of Her Own* (2002), is particularly insightful here. In some species, particularly primates, the offspring are so developmentally complex that without male investment in offspring, the probability of infant survival is greatly reduced. Thus, males must invest in rearing offspring—not as much as females, to be sure, but it is in their own genetic interest to contribute food and protection. This is a mitigating factor in male dominance patterns in those species because males and females must cooperate, just as females have to cooperate among themselves, to ensure the survival of offspring.

Females also compete, usually among themselves, so body mass larger than the average female body mass and calculated aggression greater than the average for females is advantageous for bullying. But large body mass is a bad idea for surviving and nurturing offspring when food is scarce. The same considerations do not apply in the same way to males because body size and aggression are all-important for reproductive access, and most males never succeed in reproducing anyway. In fact, in a recent address to the American Psychological Association entitled "Is there anything good about men?" social psychologist Roy Baumeister reported on a study analyzing the genetic diversity of humans alive today (see Baumeister 2007). This study purports to show that about twice as many women as men through the history of our species have reproduced. On that basis, Baumeister estimates that about 80 per cent of women find a way to reproduce, whereas only 40 per cent of men reproduce. He concludes that men are evolution's disposable experiment, risky, extreme, diverse, with a wider separation between majestic winners and pitiful losers, and more often than not genetic dead ends. So what do males have to lose? Apart from their own need to contribute some degree of parental investment to protect offspring, for which too much aggression is a bad thing, there is less evolutionary resistance to the increase of body size than there is for women.

Just as an intelligent species imposes the requirement of lengthy development and heavy parental investment, thereby affecting dominance relations, so other species-specific characteristics can influence dominance. Hrdy discusses hyenas, one of the very few mammals in which females are clearly dominant (1999a: 31–32). She repeats the standard speculation that this is because of lack of inhibition toward cannibalism within the species, which means that mothers must be capable of defending young against all comers, male and female. The resulting trajectory to large body size in females apparently outpaces the impulse to large body size in males, who only have to compete with other males for access to female reproductive resources. If correct, this explanation shows how sensitive mammalian social arrangements are to relatively small changes in cognitive makeup. Alter just one element in the complex mix—reducing inhibition toward cannibalism in a significant percentage of the population—and the social structures and dominance relations change dramatically.

With this biological explanation of male dominance in place, it is important to return to sex differences. The social fact of male dominance imposes extra burdens on females. They must navigate social challenges with great care, lest their elaborate efforts to reproduce and to secure resources for their offspring be defeated by an angry male with the power to assert his whims and impose an unwelcome fate. For example, in some primate species, paternal infanticide is a one method that a troupe's newly dominant male may use to remove the offspring of a former competitor and thereby to clear the way for mating with females previously busy with child rearing (see Hausfater and Hrdy 1984). In these contexts, females may simulate estrous and mate with the newly dominant male in order to protect existing offspring and convince him that future offspring may be his. Male dominance often requires females to walk a tightrope between creative self-assertion and calculated submission if they are to produce and provide for offspring, and the most imaginative and intelligent females just do it better. Fertility by itself is useless in evolutionary perspective if females cannot also convince males and other females to help protect offspring and provide for their prodigious caloric and social needs. These are the fundamental conditions determining what is adaptive for female primates, including humans.

If the Victorian picture of the submissive, coy, pure woman is a culturally potent myth then so is the more contemporary picture of women as innately social and cooperative, lacking competitive instincts and ambitions. And so is the fiction of Amazonian women running society on their own terms. There is no basis for any of these. Moreover, Hrdy points out that "The female with 'equal rights' never evolved; she was invented, and fought for consciously with intelligence, stubbornness, and courage" (1999a: 190). And because these cultural inventions arise on the back of an evolutionary heritage of male dominance, they are constantly vulnerable to collapse, and thus require vigilant protection. This kind of protection is every bit as much a religious task as it is a political one. The way sex differences are handled in a religious anthropology determines whether theologians can lay claim to the valuable social commodity of scientific credibility when promoting and implementing a religious vision of sexual equality.

Intimacy, Sensuality, Fantasy

The Science of Touch and Love

In the movie *Life as a House* (2001), Kevin Kline's depressed, cynical, and lonely character George is stricken with terminal cancer and finds himself lying in a hospital bed, miserable and emotionally trapped. In the course of performing her duties, Sandra Nelson's character, a nurse, touches him. The effect is staggering, as George is swept away by the simple feeling of being touched by another human being. He suddenly realizes that it has been many years since anyone touched him. He tells the nurse this, and she is overwhelmed with sadness and dismay. "People have to be touched. Everyone gets touched by somebody they love," she says.

The science of touch is fascinating. Under the right circumstances, the simple grazing of a finger along an arm can trigger a spectacular cascade of neurochemicals that feels overwhelmingly wonderful and welcome. Intimate touch is necessary for children to be psychologically and socially well-adjusted and for establishing a clear sense of body boundaries. Touch is vital for establishing trust and friendship, whether this involves pressing hands or chests or faces together in a given cultural and social context. Because of the potency of touch, its social effects can be unpredictable and thus touching is tightly regulated in all human and primate societies. Even apparently subtle actions can violate social norms around touch, and thereby be intended or interpreted as extremely aggressive acts. Such acts can be threatening or inviting, and can trigger tsunami-like social effects, from devastating violence to thrilling sexual encounters. The desperate overtones of words such as solitary confinement and isolation, banishment and shunning, are coded with visceral memories of deprivation and unfulfilled longing, of needing but not receiving a kind touch. The warm overtones of words such as home and hearth, belonging and acceptance, are coded with visceral memories of comforting touch, which establishes and nurtures feelings of safety, relaxation, and unconditional love.

So it goes for all primate species and every human society. But human beings add a degree of imaginative complexity to the neurocognitive mix that sponsors symbolic linkages around touch and entirely new dimensions of meaning and behavior. Consider the phenomenon of accidental touch. Human bodies are buffeted every day by a thousand objects and sometimes by vast crowds of people. The brain cannot afford to be attentive to every touch or the organism would be bogged down in a slew of irrelevant processing tasks. Unless these contacts are painful or unexpectedly intimate or display some sort of repeating pattern, therefore, they are typically reduced to background noise by the human sensory system and go mostly unnoticed.

Now, introduce into this mix an individual whose imagination is primed and who wants to touch or be touched under the shelter of ordinary sensory noise. Then a simple brushing of an arm on a crowded sidewalk simultaneously remains totally within the limits of normal background touching for one person while proving to be utterly arresting for the other. Or perhaps a person's imagination is so tuned to anonymous accidental touching that every small bump and buffet dominates attention. This is a recipe for emotional overload in people with sensory integration disorders who have difficulty establishing functional baselines for eliminating most touches to the realm of the negligible and unimportant. In other people this can be the doorway into exquisitely enchanting states of mind, where stories are privately woven from the touch of strangers, unbeknownst to them.

Human beings bring such worlds of fantasy to everything they do, but nowhere more than to emotionally charged activities such as intimate touch. A measure of human distinctiveness relative to other species, this union of cognitive, emotional, and physiological capacities yields dimensions of meaning that vastly complicate social contacts. At times the world of fantasy can imbue personal relationships with all-or-nothing existential significance, leading to obsessive or possessive behaviors, to high-risk attempts to make contact and win favor, or to the establishment of internally narrated standards of blissful union that no actual relationship can ever achieve. The fantasy-laden longing for intimate touch is an essential component in the vast engines of cultural creativity that leverage enormous economic and social effects. Popular culture from novels to music and from movies to plays narrates the fantastic promise of intimate touch, constructing expectations and longings for relationships, defining norms for desirability and beauty, and establishing stories that we readily absorb and make our own. Female chimps do not have to contend with endless racks of magazines defining how they are supposed to look and act in order to be the object of desires for intimate touch. Male chimps do not have to contend with being assessed based on how closely the females with which they are physically intimate resemble a culturally articulated norm. Chimp preferences and prestige hierarchies are very real but they are nowhere near as fantasy fueled as in the human species, and they do not produce such heights of rapture and depths of despair.

The impact of fantasy on human self-understandings and social relationships may be clearest in the social construction of intimate touch between lovers. The architecture of love fantasies and love narratives depends on the constraining foundations of the neurology of love. The emerging picture of love from social neuroscience suggests that it is not one thing. In fact, it probably involves at least three overlapping but distinguishable neurological systems, which appear in various combinations and with various strengths for different lovers at different times of a relationship. These systems are species-wide, and thus culturally universal, but their cultural expressions and regulation differ markedly. In the remainder of this section, I first sketch the neurochemical and evolutionary foundations of intimacy and sensuality (see Buss 2003, Fisher 1992, 2004, Janov 2000, Landis 2000, Numan & Insel 2003, Walsh 1991). I then discuss the way fantasy elaborates the intricate cultural architecture of sex atop these biological foundations. I conclude with a discussion of what all this portends for a theological anthropology that seeks to take science seriously.

First, lust is what drives us to seek sex, which can produce offspring if lust leads to sex between a fertile man and a fertile woman and the timing and other circumstances are suitable. Given the way lust seems to work in the animal world as well as in human beings, pregnancy seems to be a side-effect of a more basic and powerful desire for sensual touching and orgasm. The sex hormones testosterone and estrogen are the dominant players in lust, but there are many subordinate factors. People experience lust differently with different people, depending on functional but typically mostly unconscious templates that specify desirable physical and behavioral characteristics. Pheromones sometimes play a role in triggering lust but only some human beings appear able to produce them and it is not clear how they are registered by potential mates. When present, pheromones offer subtle cues about a potential mate's immune system. There are also built-in systems that inhibit lust between people with whom we cohabit most closely from an early age—this is the biological basis for the incest taboo.

Second, romantic attraction is neurochemically and behaviorally quite different than lust. Its evolutionary function is to attract people (and indeed other animals in the tiny subset of mammals that form human-like family groups) together so that they will want to bond with infants and go through the arduous process of rearing offspring as a parental team. Romantic love is the feeling of being "in love"—complete with the excitement, intoxication, addiction, obsession, and poor judgment that being in love is famous for producing in otherwise quite balanced and rational people. The dominant neurochemicals in this case are dopamine and endorphins, which produce addictively strong pleasure. Along with increased norepinephrine and decreased serotonin, they trigger a cascade of effects from increased heart rate to sweating and nervousness, from sleeplessness to loss of appetite, and from contraction of concentration onto one object to irrational idealizing of that object. Sometimes romantic love occurs without lust, or at different times from lust. Indeed, it is possible to be romantically attached to someone for whom feelings of lust are relatively weak, and *vice versa*. Infatuation seems to be at its most feverish when lust and romantic love line up and reinforce one another. The problem with the irrational heights of infatuation is that people can be attracted to, and fall in love with, people who do not make good life partners, and make precipitous decisions while in an irrational haze of chemical, emotional euphoria. It is easy to see how this might arise. The evolutionary process is most useful for producing mechanisms that keep partners together up until the point that offspring are independent; evolution is ill-suited for guaranteeing lifelong commitment. When social freedoms exist, therefore, couples will often disentangle from one anther, usually when the early years of child-rearing are over.

Third, if lust gets people to have sex and romance bonds them first to one another and then to the helpless babies that sex can produce, then committed attachment helps to keep couples together for as long as possible—from an evolutionary point of view until children are independent and capable of bearing offspring of their own. The neurochemicals in this case are oxytocin and vasopressin. A multipurpose hormone, oxytocin produces feelings of comfort and belonging and increases trust and devotion. Vasopressin is a contributing factor to monogamous bonding in animals such as voles, and seems to be important for the same behavioral outcomes in human beings. Together, oxytocin and vasopressin induce people to commit to making a relationship and a family work. Sex, especially of the romantic kind, helps to release these hormones, producing the desire to cuddle for comfort and pleasure after the frenzied heights of orgasm pass. Familiarity interferes with the strongest feelings of lust, whose evolutionary function is all about having sex with strangers to propagate the species. And the intoxication of romantic love fades within a few short years, just long enough to get through pregnancy and rear children to the point that they can walk and talk. So the neurochemistry of committed attachment is often the dominant feature of relationships after several years. Sex is crucial to keeping those attachment hormones flowing, as are trust-building and simple friendship behaviors.

The Economics and Psychology of Touch and Love

Social neuroscience is thus beginning to chart the neurochemistry of love in considerable detail and with ever-increasing experimental support. But human societies have been rationalizing, controlling, legitimating, and explaining the realities of love and sex from time immemorial. Social regulation of sex is one driving factor in these narrations but our capacity for fantasy is just as important. I already mentioned the cultural reality of mass-circulation magazines that heavily impact norms for women who other people (men and women) most desire to see and touch—norms that determine prestige hierarchies among men who desire women and women who desire women, as well as among women themselves. I have also mentioned popular culture's role in articulating narratives of sex and love, of intimacy and sensuality. This is particularly true of mainstream movies and popular music, in which a dominant theme is romantic love—getting it, keeping it, losing it, longing for it, having too much of it, and so on. The upshot of these popular images in contemporary western cultures is complicated and ambiguous.

There is space in these narrated norms for individual expressiveness and for the uniqueness of each person and relationship. There is space for unconventional sexual relationships into which we are led by "following our heart" and ignoring social conventions. In fact, there are numerous variations on the central story of love and sex that are elaborated culturally and made available for individuals, couples, and groups to incorporate into their fantasies and self-articulations (see Sternberg 1998). But the dominant message is all about eternal true love, everlasting infatuation, and perfect commitment. This is quite oppressive to the majority, who nonetheless clamor after the goods promised in the story of true love even if it means subjecting themselves to deforming stress, artificial behavior, feelings of inferiority and failure, and consuming grief when the ideal fails. When trying to make important life decisions, friends ask one another whether they "truly love" the person in question, carefully gauging the fit between feelings and story, but they typically remain unaware of how unclear and unhelpful the question is for guiding rational decisions. Middle-aged people throw away hard-won economic and social-status privileges, as well as the benefits of friendships and family, because long-lost feelings of infatuation suddenly reappear in their lives in relation to a much younger person, allowing a failed fairy tale one more chance at fulfillment. And many people never experience love that answers to the story's description of how it is supposed to be.

These are the terrible fruits of an economic juggernaut driven by the addictive hormones of infatuation—longing for them, seeking them again and again, and wistfully remembering them long after they last occurred. To some degree the economics of love in western cultures is cynical and exploitative. In most respects, however, it is the reflexive product of insufficiently analyzed social effects of powerful hormones that play indispensable roles in making human existence meaningful. Many cultures never allow these possibilities to arise and hyper-vigilantly suppress freedom of sexual and emotional expression in order to channel the social potency of love in less disruptive directions. But this often produces miserable marriages, particularly for women who feel trapped in cycles of neglect and abuse. There may be a terrible downside to social permissiveness around sex and love, but the upside is that people, and especially women, have improved chances of fighting for authenticity and happiness in this realm. Such is the perpetual moral and existential ambiguity of most western cultural and economic achievements.

Private fantasies around sex and eroticism go well beyond these mainstream forms in a host of directions. Initially fueled by adolescent longings and psychologically both constructive and destructive formative childhood experiences of sensual touching, sexual fantasies are richly present in the emotional and cognitive fabric of most people's lives. These fantasies explore the promise of what is desired, explore the threat of what is feared, and toy with taboos. They produce states of arousal akin to actual sexual encounters and so frequently accompany the self-touching of masturbation and the self-exploration of day dreaming. Another entire wing of the sex and love economy derives from such fantasies, producing pornographic exploration of fetishes and fantasies of every imaginable kind. In this case, however, the primary driving force is not the infatuation cocktail of neurochemicals but the sex hormones that excite us to lust. The true love industry may be far larger but the pornography industry is extremely large with probably hundreds of billions of US dollars (industry revenues are difficult to estimate in this case) invested in it worldwide every year.

Fantasy and Theology

As with the science of sex types and gender roles, theology and ethics is not determined by the science of intimacy, sensuality, and fantasy, but the science does affect the plausibility of theological and ethical accounts of human nature. We have seen this pattern of constraint without determination arise throughout this book and it properly expresses both the mutual relevance and substantial independence of science and religious thought. In the present case, the alarming feature of theological and ethical approaches to human sexuality is how little the actual realities of intimacy, sensuality, and fantasy are engaged in detail. Traditional theological anthropology is frequently desperately weak at this point, a mere pawn in the hands of massive social processes bent to the legitimation of preferred moral norms and the perpetuation of powerful economic practices.

There has been impressive resistance from a very few theologians in the form of particularly feminist and queer theorists discussing the wonders of the body, of intimacy and sensuality, and of eroticism and lust-filled fantasies (see Althaus-Reid 2001, 2003, Burrus & Keller 2006, Eisler 1995, Hollywood 2002,

Loughlin 2007, Marion 2006). The double contention of traditional theological anthropology—that marriage sanctifies sex and that the moral purpose of sex is procreation—has dominated almost all traditions, and certainly most branches of all theistic traditions as well as Chinese religion. But the scientific account shows that procreation is a usually unconscious and accidental side-effect of acting on lustful feelings, and that procreation is a tiny corner of human intimacy, sensuality, and fantasy. By itself this does not contradict and cannot overthrow the traditional view. But it does leave the traditional view struggling for plausibility because it shows how that view asserts a fantastically simple moral norm against a wealth of complex and intricate behaviors without taking any detailed account of what the norm is supposed to govern. Like the simple forms of strict natural law theory, it has to pretend that nature is other than it is in order to find basic applicability. In the case of sex, both in humans and among other animals, nature is thoroughly and decidedly nothing remotely like the norm that traditional theology seeks to impose. The norm is alien because its primary purpose is less to articulate the good, the true, and the beautiful in the realm of touching and sex, than to legitimate social practices that religions are heavily invested in supporting.

While this is by no means a knock-down criticism of traditional theological anthropologies on the theme of human sexuality, it does leave the thoughtful theologian pondering norms for intimacy, sensuality, and fantasy; for human physical and mental health bearing on touching and being touched; for associated behaviors such as sexual relationships, marriage, family, and child-rearing; and for governmental regulation of various dimensions of the economics of love from pornography to romance novels, and from Valentine's Day gifts to women's glossy magazines. I am arguing that the valuational depths of reality are deeply ambiguous at the scale of human moral interests. A modified natural-law approach can be truly revolutionary in that it pays attention to the sexual fecundity and diversity of nature without pretending that norms can simply be read off nature. Nature is not just one thing, sexually; it sings not in a solo aria but in a florid chorus in which vast harmonies complexly emerge from and disintegrate back into a kind of raucous cacophony. We pick out a tune or two and sing them in the company of others, typically blind to alternatives except insofar as our partially suppressed fantasies alert us to the richness of the melodies not voiced. Group by group, culture by culture, civilization by civilization, we thus plot a path through these valuational depths of touching and sexuality.

This social construction of sexual reality is the way it has always been among human beings and the way it will always be for creatures with our degree of cognitive and emotional complexity. We choose, but we fear to take responsibility for our choice, so we rewrite our choices on the divine sky and pretend to read them from there instead. It is as Nietzsche said: we are not ready for full awareness of the degree to which we are responsible for the construction of our social reality (see Nietzsche 1907, 1954). Now as then, to say this is to speak too soon, winning only resistance and confusion. So we smash out the lantern of self-awareness and grumpily stomp off into the night (Nietzsche 1974). Meanwhile, repeating and defending prized sexual norms, the confused and resistant masses continue to harbor secret knowledge that sexual fantasy enlivens within them, and that erotic touch awakens in their bodies. Most of us sense the sexual wildness of nature, and of ourselves, instinctively. And most of us suppress this knowledge out of deference to social norms. So let the grand social and civilizational experiments with intimacy, sensuality, and fantasy continue at their own pace, with the norms that they declare come from God's own hand. And let private fantasy and spontaneous subcultures of sexual realism flourish underground and realize alternative norms for intimacy, sensuality, and fantasy away from majority scrutiny. Theological anthropologies attuned to the social construction of sexual norms need not pronounce on the issue, need not cause trouble, and need not deconstruct the dominant fantasy with disruptive winking or relentless critiques.

Yet there are patterns in the normative depths of sexual reality, so the one who wishes to say more can do so. Humans are not truly human without touching and being touched. Children are unhealthy and violent when they are not protected and intimately touched. Sexual touching of children by those charged with their care is often traumatic. Sexual violence often destroys lives. Guilt over the suppression of natural fantasies often produces bizarre and unhealthy behavior. And one of the greatest spiritual and emotional challenges in human existence is to bond with another person for life—body and soul, sexually and intellectually, buoyed by fantasy and checked by reality, sparked by hormones and guided by wise mentors, relentlessly seeking happiness and resisting mere settling for what is practical. This challenge is testimony to an almost incredible possibility for human beings that both mobilizes and profoundly transcends every capacity that evolution creates for human relationships, beginning with intimacy, sensuality, and fantasy. Such lifelong relationships may or may not involve marriage or children or even other people, in an endless variety of ways. But its aesthetic brilliance and the norm for emotional health and spiritual maturity that it expresses are irreducible to cultural containers and deeply resistant to painfully simple norms that insist against the evidence that the point of sex is procreation and that monogamous marriage is the only sanctified locus for good sex. This is not the only aesthetically staggering sexual norm for human life but it is one that most people understand because in some barely traceable way it still lingers within the miserable distortions that blight human social interaction through the ambiguous economies of love and sex.

Sexual creativity will flourish, suppressed or encouraged, in fantasy and in reality, within human life. This theological anthropology welcomes attempts to sanctify the creativity of touching under a host of descriptions and ruling norms. If we so choose, however, norms for sex can be constructed to optimize mental and physical health, emotional development and spiritual maturity, and possibilities for aesthetic genius in the exploration of the endless space of possibilities for human touching and bonding. I have shown how taking responsibility for sexual norms propels a multifaceted criticism of traditional theological anthropologies, of underground sexual practices that defeat basic norms for health, of meek theological compliance with social legitimation expectations, of the cruel albeit mostly ignorant economic exploitation of the biology of love, of fearful denial of sexual fantasy, and of the failure of nerve that makes people choose safety or surrender in relational misery rather than risk everything to fulfill the astonishing calling of wholehearted intimacy. Taking responsibility for sexual norms also involves plumbing the normative depths of sexual and social reality, becoming aware of the way we make choices both privately and for public consumption about our sexual thoughts and practices, diagnosing how traditions stand ready to legitimate our sexual decisions, and calling us to make those decisions in fully informed and self-aware fashion.

Finally, taking responsibility for sexual norms involves recognizing ultimacy in the normative possibilities surrounding intimacy, sensuality, and fantasy. We engage the divine when we touch, when we are touched, and when we dream of touching. We engage the divine as we peel back the endless layers of sexual rationalization by which we narrate our social and existential location. There is no "there" there, really, because we are nothing ultimately but what we construct ourselves to be under the constraints of our biological and bodily birthright; this is the power of human nature. But to behold this emptiness without recoiling in horror, to see ourselves ultimately as the bundles of constrained guesses and practical habits that accrue in a lifetime, is precisely to appreciate our bodies and the touches that can grace and harm them. It is, in short, to see the divine intimately, sensually, and fantastically present in our very flesh.

Conclusion: *Homo Religiosus* and Sex

Human beings use religion to legitimate social arrangements, as discussed in an earlier chapter. Gender dualism, male dominance, and norms for intimate sexual behavior have repeatedly been the object of rationalization by means of the dictates of sacred religious texts, the pronouncements of religious authorities, or the deployment of religious concepts such as the will of divine beings or the intrinsic metaphysical structures of reality. In fact, behaviors and beliefs related to human sexuality are so closely regulated and rationalized that such rationalizations have often been supplied even in the absence of any threat demanding defense of existing norms. Thus, most of the legitimating work that religion does in relation to human sexuality is powerful precisely because it is not controversial. The cultural ubiquity of the legitimating perspective constructs social reality in such a way that individuals experiencing cognitive dissonance around sexual norms naturally regulate themselves to a significant degree in order to fit in and readily submit to externally imposed strictures aimed at rectifying behaviors and beliefs.

In our time, at least in some cultural settings, everything about sex is controversial and religious legitimation of preferred sexual norms is sometimes forced to exchange silent effectiveness for heavy-handed authoritarianism. For example, though dominance-talk is out of fashion in many places these days, religious rationalizations for male privilege remain common. Witness the arguments for solely male priests and leaders in many religious sects, or the religious reasons supplied for the unequal value of testimony of men versus women in some legal traditions. This flushing into the open of religious rationalizations for sexual norms makes them vulnerable to assessment in a way that they can evade when operating in stealth mode. I have argued that the ethical import of the biology of sex differences and male dominance is ambiguous. But it is equally the case that the scientific background to gender dualism and male dominance makes existing religious rationalizations seem bizarrely antiquated and disconnected from reality. For example, religious arguments on behalf of male privilege typically do not mention biologically rooted parental investment patterns as the reason there is competition over limited reproductive and nurturing resources, followed by sex-based differences in body size and male dominance. To that extent, such religious rationalizations appear to be *ad hoc* and often partly mythological and superstitious rationalizations with little staying power as empirical knowledge increases in depth and precision. The science of male dominance cannot rule out any particular religious rationalization but it certainly can manifest many such rationalizations as implausible and as deriving their importance not from their truth but from their comportment with privileged interests.

The human being as *homo religiosus* does not just legitimate what exists. I have argued that religion is also vital for picturing alternate social realities and for motivating social change to realize those alternative visions. For example, in relation to sex types and gender roles, some religious visions of natural fecundity and perfect divine acceptance of every created being inspire people to embrace non-standard combinations of sex-typical features and exploratory approaches to gender roles. In relation to male dominance, some religious visions of divine love and yin–yang complementarity inspire the diagnosis that male dominance is a social distortion of the most profoundly good and beautiful possibilities for human life. In relation to intimate sexual practices, the flow of power beneath the surface of human life and the intimacy of divine love inspire protection of a space of privacy within which loving human beings can and should freely explore their sacred longings for physical pleasure and emotional intensity.

In such interpretative frameworks, scientific information makes an invaluable contribution by drawing attention to salient causal factors and marginalizing peripheral details. This helps theologians articulate religious visions for human sexuality in relevant ways, and also diagnose the ways in which the good is distorted, the true hidden, and the beautiful marred in the social management of sex. The result of such collaboration between science and religion can be a kind of strategic intelligence whereby the science instructs us how to frame religious rationalizations for the social visions we want to create.

To see how this works, consider one of many possible examples of the political and religious relevance of the biology of sex differences. Hrdy became an outspoken advocate for childcare services for women on the basis of her discoveries about the importance of allomothering in other primate species. The take-home political message is fellow Wellesley College student, Hillary Clinton's widely discussed phase, "It takes a village to raise a child" (see Clinton 2006). Allomothering is the condition for the possibility of women finding a satisfying way to balance parental longings and professional ambitions, and withholding these services is one of the key strategies for preserving male dominance. Keeping women at home raising children allows men greater control over a mate's sexual behavior and psychological state. For example, it inhibits the ambitions that might lead women to choose to have fewer children. Thus, promoting allomothering, including childcare, is one of the most efficient ways to disrupt male dominance and to promote women's self-realization. Theologians with a religious vision of liberation and self-actualization for women will find in this scientific information the key to a persuasive political strategy for making a concrete difference in the lives of many women, and also vital ingredients for a theological rationalization of that strategy. Such theologians will describe motherhood in more corporate and less individual ways, they will challenge the norm of family constituted by two oppositely sexed parents using religious imagery drawn from theories of ultimate reality, and they will celebrate the beauty of alternative norms that stress completeness of self-actualization rather than conformity to existing dominant social arrangements.

There are many other ways in which the biology of sex differences, and the social patterns of dominance that accompany them, impact religious anthropology. I discuss four in closing this chapter.

First, feminist theologians for the most part are not yet engaging this material at depth. The ideology-laden myths of women's identity are burdensome. It is not easy to live down to the Victorian woman, morally pure, sexually passive, and innocent of ambition and competitive intelligence. And it is equally difficult to live up to the idealized contemporary picture of women as experts in cooperation, sensitive and utterly selfless. The evolutionary picture of women and men both evolving under partially different environmental pressures to optimize intelligence, competitiveness, ambition, and social skills as well as high fertility and robust immune systems is exciting and liberating. It will take many years and many books to unfold the theological significance of the insights that this scientific research has uncovered, and to coordinate those insights with the existing approaches to religious anthropology supported within feminist theory and feminist theology. The concern that the familiar tools of cultural critique will be lost in a renewed focus on the biological factors leading to male dominance is significant; some care is needed to avoid a new kind of biological reductionism and to uphold appropriate distance between moral norms and naturally occurring behaviors, as I have tried to do here.

Second, this scientific material problematizes the famous feminist distinction between typical male and typical female sins in the context of Christian religious anthropology. Valerie Saiving's (1960) take on this, *contra* Reinhold Niebuhr (1941), was that men tend to be sinfully selfish and women tend to be sinfully vulnerable to underdevelopment and negation of the self. There is something to this in Saiving's cultural context, of course, and also in ours several decades later. But the very formulation of it is disempowering. In particular, Saiving's analysis presupposed a basic feminine character structure, and thereby perpetuated the myth of the innate feminine type. By contrast, it is empowering to realize that women and men can all sin in much the same ways, because they have much the same intellectual and moral capacities. Just as sex-typical interests modify the typical ways that men and women compete and cooperate, so sex-typical interests modify the typical ways that men and women sin. But the full range of competitive and cooperative activities and also the full range of sins are available to both sexes, with differences determined by interest, opportunity, and cultural circumstance. For example, even criminal activity, traditionally the domain of men, can become a woman's interest under certain circumstances (see Campbell 2002: Ch. 7).

Third, the contemporary outlook on the biology of sex differences profoundly complicates the theological interpretation of creation, morality, and ultimate reality. If theists are correct to say that divine creation is good, then this blesses the very conditions for the possibility of the emergence of our most prized values. We prize empathy, intelligence, cooperation, skillful management of complicated pressures, and spirited independence as desirable virtues. But the conditions for the possibility of the emergence of these virtues in human beings, men and women alike, are sometimes brutal life events, competition among men for access to precious reproductive commodities, competition among women for access to scarce nutritional resources, carefully negotiated cooperative arrangements, and complex social hierarchical environments. Do we really want to say that these conditions are unambiguously good, or that the resulting male-dominance of human societies is likewise good? I do not. If we want to defend a morally uplifting vision of relations between the sexes, then we need to take responsibility for asserting our moral vision in some respects *against the evolutionary tide*, even as our rebellion is borne up by evolutionary conditions. I think this commits us to acknowledging what the apophatic mystics have always known, and what Nietzsche preached, namely, that God is far beyond human moral categories of good and evil (see Nietzsche 1907). Fundamentalists resist evolutionary theory especially because they sense that the idea of a good personal God is at stake. They are quite correct about this, and nothing makes that clearer than our growing understanding of the evolution of sex differences. For the religious naturalist, God is the creative and fecund ground of nature's being, its valuational depth structures and dynamics; the moral dimensions of the ground of being are not scaled to human interests. The solution is not Fundamentalist enforcement of personal theism and all that means for moral determinateness in a religious anthropology, however, but the relentless theological deconstruction of blatantly or subtly anthropomorphic conceptions of God.

Fourth and finally, the literature on the biology of sex differences shows that our idealized or mythical images of women and men are not only illusions, not only means of social control, and not only convenient rationalizations of male dominance. They are all those things but they are also expressions of our tendency to mold theological accounts of ultimate reality in the image of our existential needs and the ethical requirements of familiar forms of social stability. These projective and legitimating tendencies are the driving forces behind anthropomorphism in theological reflection. The sooner we give up inappropriately anthropomorphic conceptions of ultimate reality, the sooner we will be able to bear the morally impenetrable truth about the evolution of sex differences, and take responsibility for our moral stances instead of pushing responsibility for them onto an ultimate reality that is beyond convenient interrogation and constantly vulnerable to manipulation. We can thus live together in our many explorations of sex- and gender-space without any illusions either about what are the evolutionary facts or about what kind of society we want to support. A religious anthropology that supports this type of realism about human sexuality is revolutionary indeed.

CHAPTER 8

Habitat

Introduction

The human project arose and continues to unfold within an extraordinarily intricate habitat. This habitat has many obvious features that humans in every era have been familiar with, such as nourishment and beauty, predation and disease. Our habitat has subtle aspects, such as microorganisms and meaning—no less important for being invisible to the naked eye—that have come to light only as human cognitive capacities and the social organization of inquiry made it possible. Our habitat is also mutable and subject to the creative force of human imagination as well as to the unwanted side-effects of our efforts to manage our surroundings. This chapter concerns the human habitat and its importance for interpreting the human being as *homo religiosus*. I shall focus on three representative aspects of the issue.

First, human life is utterly dependent on a basically hospitable ecosystem that allows human beings to evolve, survive, and flourish. We only need to consider the surface of the Moon or of Mars to realize how precious Earth's ecosystem is. Its intricate network of relationships is relatively robust, as its continuation despite a number of mass extinction events shows. It is sometimes highly responsive to quite subtle changes in physical circumstances and behavior. One of the best ways to appreciate the ecosystem's intricacy is to examine the living beings that have dominated its history and still function as its living tissue: microorganisms. It has not been common for religious anthropologies to describe human nature in relation to microorganisms, but the benefits of doing so are notable, as we shall see.

Second, from its earliest beginnings, the human species was marked by its technological prowess, developing tools and controlling environments far more effectively than any other single Earth species. Long before the advent of large manufacturing machines and electricity, human technology changed the ecological landscape and made possible utterly unprecedented forms of human life. Fire made for warmth, cooking, and community; hunting devices made protein and lipid more accessible; sticks and stones and plants served as building materials; wheels promoted transport; fences helped to domesticate animals; and writing made possible the analysis of regularities necessary for effective agriculture. Modern technologies have continued this pattern, though at such a rate of change that concern for the future of the human project naturally arises. Do human beings really know enough about their environment to engineer it safely and responsibly as they see fit? What is the religious significance of the human drive to control the circumstances of life and to exploit every opportunity for comfort and protection, for creativity and power?

Third, the most subtle aspect of the human habitat is also the most important: the realm of value. Axiological features of reality are accessible to human beings in a uniquely nuanced way among Earth species, thanks to our distinctive cognitive and emotional makeup. Indeed, the marked differences in sensitivity to aesthetic and moral values among human beings yields insights into the vast axiological differences that must obtain between human beings and other species. The world of values awaits discovery, just as the possibilities for engineering living environments lie dormant until creatures arise with the dexterity and intelligence to realize them. Access to the manifold axiological structures and dynamic possibilities of reality, as we are able, is the most precious gift that evolution has bequeathed to us. The territory for axiological exploration is so varied and complex that our efforts to grasp it and chart it often produce confusion. Our social need to control perception of the axiological world is so pronounced that we often shut down possibilities of aesthetic and moral expression for the sake of securing group interests or fending off individual anxieties. Yet the full range of axiological possibilities always lies in waiting, engaged by the bold more often than by the controlling, and celebrated by the alert more often than by the dull-minded among us. If managing group life gives the river of religion its bed and banks, the realm of values is the untamable wellspring of that river, luring generation after generation of individuals to seek the meaning of their lives in what the axiological depths of nature manifest.

Environment and Ecosystem Habitat

Microorganisms

Surely one of the most neglected themes in religious anthropology is the location of human beings in the context of the microbial ocean that births, supports, threatens, and reabsorbs them. It is even somewhat neglected within some branches of the biological sciences, much to the frustration of specialists in microbiology. I shall ask what this aspect of the habitat of human life tells us about human nature and the axiological manifestations of nature's ecstatic ground. I shall also ask what the dawning human understanding of and technological control over this microbial ocean might portend for the meaning of human nature. We shall see that perceiving nature through the lens of microorganisms can have a profound affect on the way we interpret the subterranean structures and flows of nature, its human surfacings into the realm of self-consciousness, and its abysmal ecstatic depths. Somehow, this wider awareness of living nature has to be rendered richly coherent with the character of human beings.

Philosophers and theologians have barely begun to explore the potential of knowledge about the microbial ocean to revolutionize conceptions of the human person, the religious depths of nature, and images of ultimate reality. Perhaps this is not surprising. After all, supranaturalist and supernaturalist theologians effortlessly distance the character of a divine creator from the particularities of created nature;

they do not have to match. But naturalist theologians understand ultimacy as the self-transcendence of nature, and so discover the determinate features of ultimacy in the intricately structured and chaotic dynamics of nature's axiological depths; the character of nature and of ultimate reality do have to match. For religious naturalists in particular, therefore, there is a wealth of insight to be gained from the fecund diversity of biological life, almost all of which is played out in the microbial ocean.

In areas of the world with high standards of public health and good medical care, it is now widely known that indiscriminate use of antibiotics can accelerate the reproduction of "super-bugs" that are resistant to antibiotics. We are taught to wash our hands after visiting the bathroom, and also after moving through public places especially when a contagious disease is known to be spreading through the population. We know we should cover our mouths when we sneeze, shower regularly, watch the expiry dates on the food we buy, and be careful whom we kiss. But these are merely droplets from the salty spray of the microbial ocean's waves as they crash against the shores of our experience. This ocean remains uncharted, except in a few convenient havens, and even there we usually only have rough sketches of the territory. Its sheer vastness in time, space, complexity, and contextual variation beggars the imagination. Microorganisms dominate the evolutionary story of life on Earth—they dominate in terms of length of temporal span, diversity of species, importance for development of cellular mechanisms from metabolism to reproduction, and sheer numbers of life forms.

A microorganism, or microbe for short, is an organism too small to be seen by the human eye. Microorganisms were discovered with the invention of the microscope in the late seventeenth century. Since that time, microbiologists have worked out increasingly intricate classification systems for microorganisms. Shockingly, the discovery of entirely new realms of microorganisms is still common, such is their diversity and the difficulty of finding and studying them. Their morphology is relatively simple, in the sense that many are unicellular and some have few or no organelle substructures such as a nucleus. But their diversity and metabolic complexity is unmeasured, and their ability to evolve quickly through horizontal forms of gene sharing makes them the engine of rapid evolution. From this perspective, multicellular organisms such as plants and animals seem to be spectacular compilations of the biochemical themes already laid down and explored in every conceivable variation within the world of microorganisms, like a greatest hits album. Unicellular microorganisms were the only forms of life on Earth from roughly 4 billion years ago until a relatively recent half-billion years ago, when simple multicellular animals emerged, many of them still microorganisms.

Microorganisms are living entities, according to the generally accepted criteria for life: independent metabolism and reproduction. Viruses are not cells, and need the cellular machinery of another organism for metabolism and reproduction, so they are generally deemed nonliving, though they do have genetic material and do evolve. The concepts involved in the definition of life are blurry in application. For instance, the meaning of "independent" is problematic. Some microorganisms need other microorganisms to reproduce and to carry out some metabolic functions, and so are not completely independent. The obvious example is sexual reproduction in microorganisms but there are other examples: some species must cooperate for movement, feeding, or thermal regulation. For our purposes, precision is less useful than appreciation of the diversity of microorganisms. Vagueness of descriptive categories used to classify them is helpful for that purpose. For convenience, I shall include nonliving viruses as honorary residents of the living microbial ocean.

The diversity of microorganisms is best appreciated by considering some of the major types. In 1735 Carl Linnaeus founded the modern taxonomic approach to the classification of organisms in terms of a hierarchy of groups. For example, human beings can be classified as follows: kingdom: *animalia*, phylum: *chordate*, class: *mammalian*, order: *primates*, family: *hominidae*, genus: *homo*, species: *sapiens*. This hierarchical, taxonomic approach has its difficulties but remains serviceable today. Its use in classifying microorganisms is especially problematic, however, because horizontal gene transfer creates morphological similarities among evolutionarily distant species. As a result, the shift to phylogenetic approaches, which trace out evolutionary dependence, is becoming increasingly important. This is especially so now that genomes can be sequenced more quickly, and so evolutionary heritage can be traced more precisely. Of course, even phylogenetic approaches have difficulty contending with horizontal gene flow across microorganism species.

To illustrate the difference between taxonomic and phylogenetic approaches to microorganisms, consider the three main classes of them. Taxonomically speaking, bacteria and archaea are prokaryotes, or cells without a nucleus; their genetic material is organized into a circular genome and floats in the cytoplasm (the watery environment enclosed by the cell membrane). These morphological similarities led microbiologists until recently to place them in the kingdom *monera*, which they jointly exhaust. The two prokaryote groups are morphologically distinguishable from the eukaryotes, which envelop their genetic material in a nuclear envelope and do not have circular genomes. Phylogenetically (that is, evolutionarily) speaking, however, archaea are more closely related to eukaryotes than to bacteria. For instance, eukaryotes and archaea share similar DNA transcription and translation machinery, which is quite different to that of bacteria. As phylogenetic approaches take over, taxonomic conventions are routinely overthrown in just this way. The result is a clearer picture of the evolutionary history of life on Earth.

Bacteria, Archaea, Protists, and Viruses

The proportion of bacteria and archaea that have been named and studied is negligible—a mere 5,000 out of apparently millions of species. Only 300 of the 500 species of bacteria found in the human mouth have been named and described (see Freeman 2002: 484; much of the information that follows can be found in that book, or in any other elementary textbook covering the subject). Despite the morphological similarities already noted, bacteria and archaea vary tremendously in size and shape, mobility and metabolism. They show ample evidence of horizontal gene transfer, whereby chunks of foreign genetic material are absorbed and then passed on to new generations. Bacteria reproduce asexually, which means that the offspring have the same genome as the parent. But even this is an approximate statement; as cell division is not reliable, some genes are transferred between bacterial cells, and even genetic recombination (a crucial phase of sexual reproduction) can occur in bacterial cell division. All of these features make bacteria incredibly flexible; they mutate fast, toss genetic material back and forth, and multiply quickly in a reckless exploration of the vast space of genetic possibilities. Less is known about the way archaea reproduce but they seem to have about the same degree of evolutionary agility.

Bacteria and archaea use a wide variety of energy and metabolic mechanisms, many of which are quite different from those in animals. Some species of bacteria and archaea synthesize organic compounds (autotrophs) and others absorb organic compounds by consuming other organisms (heterotrophs). Some species derive energy from light, others from processing organic molecules, and yet others from processing inorganic molecules. The biochemical pathways involved in producing energy are also diverse, involving many different kinds of chemicals and producing many different chemical products. For example, some generate energy from methane and oxygen, producing carbon dioxide. Others generate energy from ammonia and oxygen, producing nitrogen-oxygen compounds, while yet others take hydrogen and carbon dioxide into methane, or hydrogen and sufates into hydrogen sulfide. Only one metabolic pathway for energy production took off in animals but numerous alternative pathways were explored in the world of bacteria and archaea, and *these alternatives are still ecologically crucial today.*

To appreciate the importance of these alternative forms of metabolism, consider that the Earth's oxygen atmosphere is a direct result of ocean-borne cyanobacteria using photosynthesis to produce oxygen. Prior to about 2 billion years ago, the half-way point in the history of life on Earth, there was no free oxygen, but after that time, oxygen was freely available, first in the oceans, and eventually in the atmosphere. This is a crucial point in evolutionary development because an oxygen-based metabolism produces far more energy than other types. Higher-pitched metabolisms allow for more complex creatures, so it is at this time that multicellular organisms such as algae, some of which were macroscopic, first appeared. This was the era in which microorganisms first produced macroorganisms, and the key was the creation of free oxygen by means of cyanobacteria and photosynthesis. Human beings owe the possibility of their high-metabolism existence to those bacteria.

Another example of the ecological and evolutionary importance of bacteria and archaea is nitrogen fixation. This process is carried out by diverse species of bacteria and archaea, and is crucial for making organic nutrients available to plants and animals. No nitrogen fixation means no energy, which in turn means no fish in the rivers, no plants in the earth, and no food for land animals. We can see the importance of this in polluted rivers. On the one hand, if the bacteria and archaea needed for nitrogen fixation are killed by pollutants running into rivers, the organic chemicals needed to sustain river plants and animals are not produced, leading to disaster. On the other hand, ammonia-based fertilizers are sprayed onto crops significantly increasing yields, because the nitrogen feeds microorganisms needed to convey nitrate compounds to plant roots. But then the nitrates produced by the hearty plants run off into rivers. Once in the rivers the ready supply of nitrates cause vast numbers of cyanobacteria to bloom, and these in turn become food for oxygen-consuming heterotrophs. The result is that all the oxygen in the river is used up and there is a dead zone for river plants and animals. This example also serves to show that human beings deploying technologies affecting bacteria and archaea routinely underestimate the complexities involved and sometimes produce ecological disasters.

While no archaea are known to cause disease in human beings, a few species of bacteria do. Considering how many species of bacteria there are, it is surprising that so few cause disease. Bacteria-based diseases and conditions include acne, cholera, diphtheria, dysentery, ear infections, eye infections, food poisoning, genital tract infections, gingivitis, gonorrhea, leprosy, meningitis, plague, pneumonia, scarlet fever, sepsis, strep throat, syphilis, tetanus, tooth decay, tuberculosis, typhoid fever, and urinary tract infections. These diseases work in many different ways, from consuming cells for bacterial food to producing poisons that kill other cells.

Most species of bacteria that negatively affect human health have numerous strains as a result of mutation and gene sharing, and some of these are more virulent than others. Evolutionarily speaking, the most virulent strains tend to kill their hosts before they can pass to a new host, while less virulent strains survive in their host for long enough to be passed on, so environmental conditions determine whether virulent strains will be able to survive. In particular, if public health is poor in densely populated areas—say, if human excrement finds its way into drinking water—then virulent strains will easily thrive because they can find new hosts easily. This is how deadly forms of dysentery operate. Where public health is good, by contrast, the virulent forms die off because they never find new hosts, and the inconvenient but not deadly milder forms are the only ones that can survive. In this way, bacterial realities set the conditions within which it is adaptive to worry about the purity of food and anything else with which we come into contact. This is probably the origin of purity rules and regulations in all human cultures, which is an extremely important theme in human religion. It probably also describes the origins of purity-based moral judgments, which are side-effects of an adaptive cognitive feature of human beings and other animals— side-effects that are massively extended into cultural and religious practices where they no longer possess their original biological point.

The other part of the microbial ocean is the domain of eukaryotes. All eukaryotic cells have organelles, including a nucleus that encloses genetic material, and an intricate cytoskeleton that gives structure to the cell. The microorganisms among the eukaryotes are mainly protists, which are all eukaryotes that are not green plants, fungi, or animals; there are also microscopic plants, fungi, and animals, however. The protists are diverse, though not to the degree that bacteria and archaea are. They survive by eating smaller organisms, especially bacteria; by scavenging nutrients from dead organisms; through parasitic or mutualistic relationships with other organisms; or through photosynthesis. Some use tails (flagella), hairs (cilia), or protuberances (pseudopodia) to move and hunt and scavenge, while others sit still and wait for food to come floating or crawling by. Some reproduce asexually as bacteria do while others reproduce sexually. Some can use both means of reproduction depending on environmental conditions.

How did protists evolve from archaea? Microbiologists can determine the character of the first eukaryotes after the common ancestor with archaea by looking at the oldest eukaryotes in the fossil record. These were single-celled organisms with a cell membrane, a cytoskeleton, and a nucleus but lacking the cell wall that later was to become vital for giving structure to multicellular eukaryotes such as plants. The endosymbiosis theory proposes that these early eukaryotic cells absorbed bacterial cells, some of which survived in the cell as energy-producing mitochondria rather than being consumed (see Margulis 1981, who made this older idea prominent). This symbiotic event happened around 2 billion years ago, in the same era that saw large quantities of free oxygen produced by cyanobacteria. The same endosymbiotic event prior to that era (doubtless it occurred countless times) would not have been fruitful because mitochondria use oxygen to produce energy. In the presence of oxygen, however, mitochondria were able to supply high levels of energy that could support previously impossible levels of metabolic activity, in return for protection. It was a happy symbiotic arrangement. The same theory is also used to explain the appearance of photosynthesis in eukaryotes, as protists absorbed photosynthetic bacteria. There is compelling biochemical, structural, and genetic evidence to support these endosymbiotic theories of how eukaryotes obtained the mechanisms for supplying their vast energy needs. Thus protists, and all other surviving eukaryotic organisms from microscopic unicellular creatures to human beings, were from the beginning hybrids made from vastly different elements in the microbial ocean.

Protists affect ecology on much the same scale that bacteria and archaea do. The key here is the sheer numbers of protists. There can be millions of protists in a cup of pond water. The oceans are full of protists, from large kelp forests to microorganisms, particularly near the surface where photosynthesis is possible. This is vital for the Earth's carbon cycle. Carbon moves around quickly in the oceans because of the feeding patterns of protists and bacteria. In this process, it is absorbed into the shells of protists that, upon dying, sink to the ocean floor, gradually forming limestone sediments. This oceanic carbon sink is about 50 per cent responsible for the reabsorption or fixing of atmospheric carbon dioxide, and thus one of the keys to keeping global warming in check.

A very few protists also cause diseases in human beings, including amoebic dysentery, Chagas disease, Chlamydia, some forms of coronary heart disease, diarrhea, malaria, paralytic shellfish poisoning, reproductive tract infections, sleeping sickness, spotted fever, and typhus. In immune-compromised people such as AIDS patients, protists cause diseases and infections of the nervous system, digestive system, and respiratory system. And protists can wipe out human food sources, which is how the Irish potato famine in 1845–47 not only killed 1 million Irish but also brought Irish culture to many parts of the world as 2 million Irish emigrated in search of food for themselves and their children.

Since we are also tracking the roles of non-living viruses in the microbial ocean, it is important to say a word about them here. Viruses are the original parasites, in the sense that they cannot reproduce or carry out any important metabolic functions without using the machinery of a host cell. So they invade cells, reproduce themselves, and spread in search of new hosts. They possess genetic material in the form of amazingly diverse DNA or RNA genomes, reproduce in host cells at a fearsome pace because they are relatively simple, and use gene sharing and genetic recombination to evolve rapidly, allowing them to adapt efficiently to changing environments. They are orders of magnitude more numerous than bacteria, archaea, and protists in many habitats, such as ocean waters. For every kind of microorganism that evolution has produced, and for every kind of cell in every animal, fungus, green plant, and macroscopic protist—that is, for every kind of life form on the Earth—there appear to be viruses that can invade and exploit the internal metabolic capacities. Specifically, viruses can invade virtually every kind of cell within the human body.

It is not easy for a virus to infect a host cell, particularly in a multicellular organism. There are cell membranes and often cell walls to contend with, and in sufficiently complex organisms there are also flexible immune system hunters that gobble up most viruses they encounter. Invasion is possible when there is a perfect fit between the virus and a protein in a cell membrane, so that the virus can simulate another chemical and gain entrance to the cell under false pretenses. Once inside, coopting a cell's metabolic and reproductive services is comparatively easy. Some viruses are more harmful than others. Some cause dangerous diseases in human beings, including adenovirus, dengue, ebola, encephalitis, Epstein-Barr, erythrovirus, hantavirus, hepatitis, herpes, HIV, influenza, measles, pappiloma, polio, rabies, rotavirus, rubella, smallpox, variola, West Nile, and yellow fever. Some viruses are essential for organism survival, such as the so-called endogenous retrovirus whose immune-system depressing features allows embryos to be implanted in the uterine wall of many mammals without being attacked as invaders by the host body.

Human Beings in Ecosystemic Perspective

All of this is a fair description of the microbial ocean in general but it is quite misleading in respect of the human relation to it. There is much more to be said than describing ecological factors and listing diseases. We saw that symbiotic events lay at the evolutionary root of all surviving eukaryotic organisms, from protists to human beings. All larger organisms benefit from symbiotic arrangements with thousands and probably millions of distinct species of microorganisms. Symbiotic relationships on this massive scale are not optional for human beings; they are *absolutely necessary for survival and flourishing.* There are over 500 species of microorganisms in a healthy human mouth, as mentioned above. There is an even larger number of species of microorganisms living in a lining up to several millimeters deep throughout a healthy human gut. These microorganisms perform numerous valuable functions from synthesizing chemicals to fermentation, and from training the immune system to inhibiting the growth of pathogens. There are upwards of ten times as many such organisms as there are cells in the entire human body. Among its other virtues, breast feeding is the main way that this beneficial gut flora is established early in human life. Every external part of the human body is covered with microorganisms and every internal part sustains symbiotic relationships with them. Microorganism-based disease is extremely rare relative to these facts of human life in the microbial ocean.

In fact, it appears to be deeply misleading to think of human beings, or any complex organism, as a distinct species independent of environmental factors such as the microbial ocean. *Human beings are a walking, feeling, thinking superorganism, an entire mobile ecology of organisms.* The Gaia Hypothesis speculatively supposes that the entire ecosphere is a superorganism (see Lovelock 1965; for more recent works, see Capra 1996, Harding 2006, Lovelock 2000, Margulis 1998). We need not commit to so grand a viewpoint in order to acknowledge that human beings are superorganisms, profoundly dependent on an astonishingly complex ecology of microorganisms, including bacteria, archaea, and protists, and even viruses. This gives the true measure of human dependence on the physical aspects of their habitat.

German theologian Friedrich Schleiermacher (1928) developed an entire theory of the human being as *homo religiosus* around the idea of dependence. Writing in the European Enlightenment, he did not know about the microbial ocean and how it manifests the intimacy of that dependence but he did have in mind the physical conditions of life as well as the emotional and existential aspects of dependence. He probably underestimated the extent to which the human habitat is a web of mutual dependencies and symbiotic relationships. But what we have learned since Schleiermacher's time only reinforces his insight: human beings are absolutely dependent on the depths of nature for everything from our quests for happiness and justice to the very conditions of our physical survival. This insight must remain front and center in any adequate religious anthropology.

An important corollary of the idea that human beings are a mobile ecology of organisms is the displacing of the human soul or *jīva*, however understood. As we can now see, the soul-centric views of human beings—whether conceived as "body plus soul" dualism or as "body whose form expresses a soul" monism—abstract an essential "soul" from the actual superorganismic character of human nature. But we might equally well see the essence of the human not neatly as soul but far more messily as a "mobile distributed ecology hosting some centralized processing and a limited degree of self-awareness." This point has enormous importance for the ontology of human nature, obviously. It is even more salient for reassessing the kinds of symbolic constructions that religious traditions deploy in narrating human life in varied social settings. Human beings instinctively project centered personhood onto ultimate reality because it is the most precious part of themselves that they can recognize, thanks to self-consciousness. And it certainly is precious. But self-consciousness is only a part of human life, a transient achievement gained after birth, compromised in sleep and by disease, and often lost prior to death. Centered self-consciousness is an achievement of the entire superorganism, with its host of distributed processes and symbiotic collaborations. *The human essence lies as much in the potential for cooperative creativity that pervades the human superorganism in its ecological habitat as in the transient wonder of self-awareness.*

Technology and Engineered Habitat

The Technological Animal

Some living beings are not mobile but just sit where they are and let life come to them, bringing food on currents or nutrients through soil and light. They have little power to change their environment or to improve their prospects of survival and flourishing. Nothing could be less apt as a description of human beings, however. On the whole, human beings have not just waited around passively to see what fate brings. They have made their own luck. Their transformation of the planet expresses their power to claim it as their home. It began with tools and techniques to improve efficiency of hunting and manufacturing. Then came settled agriculture, based on observation of seasons and weather patterns and implements for taming soil and clearing land. That made towns and cities possible, with all of the rock moving and cutting and piling up that they require. And all along the way there were technologies of war, technologies of water and food storage and transportation, technologies of animal husbandry, technologies of healing, technologies of information, technologies of energy, technologies of artisans, technologies of political control, and technologies of economic management.

Modern life is defined as much by the human technological animal as by any other facet of human beings. Thanks to the understanding of nature won by the sciences, and by virtue of the control that understanding places in the hands of eager human toolmakers, we have seen an unprecedented acceleration in technological transformation in the last century. Manufacturing technology uses robots. Information technology uses the internet. Medical technology uses designer drugs and non-invasive body scans. Energy technology uses everything from dead fossils to processed vegetables, from light to tides, from atoms to wind, and from garbage to cow manure. To focus what would otherwise be an unwieldy discussion of engineered habitat, and since we discussed the microbial ocean in the previous section, I shall confine the discussion to some aspects of biotechnology, regarding this type of technology as representative of everything that human beings do to engineer their habitat.

Microorganisms and viruses are of enormous importance in human economies and inspire fabulously innovative technologies. Human adventures in the microbial ocean have not always worked out well. For example, scientists have speculated that it was probably careless handling of a dead primate carrying one form of the HIV virus—perhaps humans consuming an infected chimpanzee for food without thorough cooking—that allowed the virus to cross to human beings. There are similar stories to be told about human technological explorations of the microbial ocean: the desire to master the environment is virtually unstoppable and we often plunge ahead heedless of danger. For the most part, however, technological interventions in the microbial ocean have been quite fruitful. Microorganisms such as eukaryotic yeast fungi have been used for centuries in fermentation and baking—imagine human life without bread, cheese, or wine. Bacteria have been successfully used for waste processing, from the remediation of oil spills to the treatment of raw sewage. Microorganisms are increasingly important in industry where they are used to produce pure chemicals, to manufacture numerous products, to extract specific minerals in mining refinement processes, and to manage industrial waste. In the latter case, research efforts strive to find microbial processes that can reduce harmful environmental toxins to chemicals that can safely be reused or released into the environment.

Microorganisms also appear in more speculative technological ventures. For example, they are used in agriculture as targeted solutions to infestation problems, with the aim of killing only unwanted insects while leaving the plants, other insects, and human beings unharmed. In biotechnology they are used to produce medicines from insulin for treating diabetes to the antibodies used in vaccines. These and many other applications of microbiology inevitably depend on knowledge of possible side-effects that we simply do not possess. The biochemical interactions between a microorganism and a wild environment are incalculable. Experiments do not necessarily manifest the relevant features in a detectable or timely way. This is why vaccines and biological pest control are such controversial technologies, with both being blamed for larger waves of human suffering such as rising rates of autism and cancer. The evidence for these kinds of negative side-effects is merely circumstantial, and systematic studies of the alleged autism–vaccination connection have come up empty. This frustrates those trying to get government agencies to take more seriously the environmental risks of biotechnological adventures in the microbial ocean.

In medicine, defanged and reengineered viruses are used as delivery vehicles to insert segments of genetic material into target cells. The long-awaited targeted treatments for diseases such as cancer, which we dream of as replacements for indiscriminately destructive chemotherapies and radiation treatments, depend on technologies such as these. But it is clear neither that *only* the targeted cancerous cells would be affected, nor that the proteins produced after the genetic material is delivered would have no unplanned effects. Other medical technologies such as xenotransplantation—the use of organs from non-human animals in human beings—are extremely valuable from a short-term health point of view but may also unleash viruses or microorganisms that are harmless in the source environment but eventually harmful in the target environment. The HIV virus is a classic example of this kind of viral threat; though it was not medical technologies that caused that virus to jump species, it might have been, and something like this could still happen. The military applications of such technologies in any number of forms are especially worrying.

Just as there is virtually no end to the microbial ocean, including the world of viruses, so there is no end to the potential technological uses to which creative and mischievous human beings can apply the special powers of microorganisms and viruses. Unfortunately, in this area as in some others, our ability to devise novel interventions far outstrips our understanding of the emergent interactive effects of our interventions in real environments. Literature and film have been quick to point this out. In Francis Lawrence's film *I Am Legend*, one of three films based on Richard Matheson's 1954 novel of that name, a very minor event produces a deadly plague that destroys almost all human life in a variety of ways. In John Wyndham's 1951 book *Day of the Triffids*, a few superficially unlinked events produce a massively amplified effect, wiping out most of humanity. Almost every science-aware zombie film and book is premised on carelessness in relation to the microbial ocean and waste chemicals that might affect it. The target in all cases is human arrogance and greed in the face of necessary ignorance. Taking dangerous steps for attractive economic reasons is understandable, but prudence dictates that such steps should be taken only with much more complete knowledge already in hand or as calculated gambles in circumstances of great desperation.

This, it seems, is another aspect of the human condition. Enough of us dream dreams and long to realize them so strongly that some are willing to fudge the risk-reward calculus. Meanwhile, other human beings, many of whom may benefit from the upside of technological innovation, may also be negatively affected by its downside. And the greatest tragedy of all is the social management of the upside–downside contrast. Some gambles affect everyone, such as the human contribution to global warming, though the wealthy have options that the poor lack. But the downside of most technological innovation is typically felt mainly among the poor, confined to communities with small voices or desperate nations with little diplomatic clout or military might. This allows the economic juggernaut to roll on, unhindered by having to face on a daily basis pointed distributive justice questions. Given the way human groups legitimate their most questionable practices, there may be no practical way to avoid this miscarriage of justice. And if the price paid for moral scruples is limiting technological progress that benefits everyone in the long run, perhaps the price is too high.

If there is a middle way that equally prizes aggressive technological creativity and responsible care of the most vulnerable, it is hard to discern. Perhaps medical research lights the way in this regard. Having been responsible for appalling disregard of human dignity in the past, from Nazi medical experiments to the Tuskeegee syphilis study, the medical community at least in the West has sought a compromise. The compromise clears the way for aggressive research while protecting human subjects through careful regulation and informed consent rules. The problem with transferring this model to other domains, however, is that research often does not directly involve human subjects, even if it affects them indirectly, so the monitoring and evaluation processes are comparatively difficult to define.

Ethics and Nature

The engineered habitat of human life is potentially the graveyard for human beings and possibly for most or all other Earth species. But it is also the avenue toward the treasured Shangri-La of long lives, just societies, and amelioration of most forms of human suffering. Our exploration of nature has opened up these starkly opposed and strangely intermingled possibilities for the human and planetary future. Can our knowledge of nature also help us identify ethical principles that can guide us through the wondrous possibilities and spectral dangers associated with engineering our own habitat?

The answer to this question appears to be yes and no. The depths of nature manifest moral possibilities and the workings of nature constrain ethical reasoning. For the religious naturalist, however, there is nothing to determine moral principles—no divine moral personality, no definitive revelation of moral laws, no natural moral law. Once again, this is a situation of *constraint without determination*, and human beings must gird themselves to design the future of their engineered habitat as they see fit. On many issues there is wide consensus, making decisions easier to make. Over some issues there is deep conflict between stakeholders because interests do not align. In all cases accurate information helps to manifest disagreements over ethical principles, after which they can be discussed subject to proper constraints and with appropriate empathic seriousness.

The natural law tradition in ethics at one time provided the ideal basis for such ethical debates because of its promise to provide guidelines for moral decisions that conform to nature's own ways. In the broadly theistic contexts that mark the origins of the natural law tradition in both Aristotle and the Stoics, conformity with natural law implies conformity to the divine nature or will. That entailment held good for the mainstream of medieval Jewish, Christian, and Islamic thought. The ideal of living in conformity with the moral structure of nature appears in South Asian and Chinese ethics as well, and in the spiritually charged worldviews of many tribal cultures.

It is easy to understand the prevalence of natural law's two-fold conviction that nature has a moral deep structure and that action in accordance with that deep structure determines the good. But growing awareness on three fronts—of cultural diversity, of the conventional character of social practices, and of the sometimes bizarre and harsh ways of nature—has spurred attempts to explain the prevalence of natural law convictions without presuming that they literally hold truth. Utilitarian ethics, in deploying cost-benefit analysis and the principle of maximization of happiness, typically treats natural law ethics as an unduly speculative extrapolation of ethical principles that utilitarianism explains in terms of pleasure and pain. Sociologists of religion in the tradition of Émile Durkheim and the mainstream of the sociology of knowledge interpret natural law ethical principles as dramatic philosophical objectifications of ordinary and universal social processes in which operative norms receive legitimation and rationalization. Sociobiologists and evolutionary psychologists interpret the most useful natural law ethical principles as optional and changeable moral ideals whose viability consists in the promotion of differential survival and reproduction advantages in populations that hold them, or in their easy comportment with human cognitive predispositions.

Natural law ethics ran aground on another problem, namely, the loss of untroubled access to its fundamental categories, such as nature, law, reproduction, conception, birth, death, intelligence, soul, and the like. As I have tried to show above and in earlier chapters, few ideas are unquestionably "natural" and "obvious" when examined closely. The rise of evolutionary biology caused much of this disruption, and biotechnological innovation also played a part, but the most important factor has been the descriptive work of historians and anthropologists that documented historical and cultural variations. "Is" no longer dictates "ought" but merely describes a messy mass of minute details.

For all these reasons, therefore, the natural law tradition in its Aristotelian, Stoic, and medieval western forms broke down. Official Roman Catholic moral teaching presents an essentially countercultural continuation of the natural law tradition, and theoretical defenses of that tradition are still offered. But most intellectuals have had to satisfy their ceaseless struggle for moral bearings in other ways. Some abandon the comfortable, natural "ought" of the old days in a bold assertion of the power of human beings over their own destiny (will-to-power ethics), as Friedrich Nietzsche proposed. Others relinquish the "ought of natural law" in return for the vaguer "ought of virtue" (virtue ethics), in hopes that everyone can agree on desirable virtues even if they can never agree on exactly how we should express these virtues in particular cultural settings. Any of these new approaches might help supply moral orientation to people. But each approach also reminds us that we may never again have the moral confidence of past eras; the natural law tradition really has broken down.

We need to consider human adventures in engineering habitat against this historic sea change in moral theory. Only when we fully appreciate the degree to which the natural law tradition has formed our moral imaginations can we begin to understand why the ethics of human technology proves so problematic. Here as above, I focus on biotechnologies to keep the discussion manageable.

Biotechnology has grown human ears on the backs of mice. It can reattach hands and limbs in a functional manner, and even connect machines to brains in functional ways. Biotech firms sell sheets of artificially produced human skin. Pigs with hybrid pig-human genes are used to grow organs for transplant that human beings will not reject. Human and other embryos remain in cold storage all over the world, ready for implantation. Scientists have cloned mice, sheep, cows, and pigs, and cloned humans are in the works. DNA analysis permits the reliable prediction of the occurrence of diseases in human beings, which leads to cases of revocation of insurance coverage and subsequent government legislation to regulate insurers and employers. Drugs exist that prevent disease through targeted genetic manipulation rather than merely treating the symptoms of disease. Intrauterine surgery corrects genetic defects. People may select the sex and other desirable characteristics of their children. Two women can combine genetic material and egg cell to make a daughter without the use of sperm cells. Scientists discover a massive overlap between the genome of human beings and evolutionarily close species—and a significant overlap with evolutionarily remote species.

What on earth are humans now? Natural-law intuitions live on in the shock associated with realizing just how many mistakes we made in thinking about human nature, even after the apparent disintegration of natural law ethics. It makes no sense simply to decry all of these developments as disgusting and wrong, appealing in so doing to assumptions about what is natural. After all, as in the previous chapter, *if the natural law tradition in any of its classical forms were correct, none of this would even have been possible.* But it is possible, and it is happening. Many other things, even more confusing for conceptions of human nature, can and will happen—from research in artificial intelligence as well as in biotechnology.

Principles of a Modified Natural Law Ethics

The conception of the "natural" in the sense of traditional natural law ethics seems unavailable for public debate over ethical principles bearing on human beings as engineers of their own habitat and bodily existence. If consciousness of historical and cultural variation has shown the extent to which concepts of the "natural" are socially constructed then evolutionary biology, artificial intelligence research, and biotechnologies have challenged the very meaning of natural kinds. Yet the concept of the natural can be retrieved, and with it a modified form of natural law ethics that respects the constraint-without-determination relation between nature and moral principles. This requires us to stipulate the "natural" independently of our moral compunctions and aesthetic inclinations, which tripped up earlier interpretations of the "natural" in systems of natural law. The obvious approach begins with descriptions of nature that contemporary science offers. The method of the natural sciences promises to diagnose bias in our account of the "natural" and also remains as close as we can come to a global language for ethical debate, despite the fact that the sciences themselves are never purely objective. Scientific descriptions of relevant subject matters, such as those furnished in this book, are far from sufficient for moral decision making. As we have seen, however, they offer a solid starting point by supplying information that experts can readily contest on the way to generating strong consensus about the relevant constraints on moral reasoning.

This radically modified approach to natural law ethics yields not a moral foundation, as if foundationalist ethics were still possible; nor perfectly certain moral conclusions, as if fallibilism in ethics could any longer be avoided; but a compass. This compass reflects the constraints of nature on ethical reasoning while resolutely refusing to evade the human responsibility for engineering a habitat that affects most Earth species. It detects the objective moral magnetic field of right and wrong, to the extent that one lurks in the depths of natural processes, while remaining vigilant about the human tendency to rationalize moral instincts with reference to the ways of nature, which almost always ends up unfairly marginalizing some people in the name of a culturally specific moral norm. It helps us formulate judicious social policy by keeping the relevant scientific descriptions in the picture along with knowledge about cultural variations in moral practices. It gives us the best chance for winning near-universal consensus across cultures on technological questions with global implications. But this compass does not determine moral principles by itself; it merely constrains them by pointing us in a somewhat indeterminate direction. The analogy with the compass detecting the Earth's magnetic field is quite exact here: Earth's planetary magnetic field mutates and shifts its orientation, and on rare occasions may even have reversed its polarity. In other words, human beings must still decide together what moral principles they want their human civilizational project to express, and this may involve fighting opponents when efforts to generate consensus fail.

What moral principles should human beings embrace for regulating the engineering of their bodily and planetary habitat? Some moral principles should alert us when we have gone too far with our engineering efforts. Moral principles effectively performing this alert function include (i) prudence about experimenting with elements of habitat that may have extensive or irreversible negative side-effects, which requires staying alert to the full reaches of human depravity and the sometimes terrifyingly thin veneer of human civilization; (ii) human dignity and human rights, as well as the dignity of other species and the sanctity of nature; and (iii) distributive justice considerations including fair access to therapeutic technologies or preferential treatment for those with the greatest suffering. The global dialogue over human rights and ecology suggests that each of these principles enjoys significant if not yet universal crosscultural support (on human rights, see United Nations 1948, 1979, 1981, 1990; on the Earth Charter see Corcoran 2005; also see Wildman 1999). Moreover, religious naturalists who reject the idea of definitive supernatural sources for moral norms can heartily affirm all of these principles.

Other moral principles should furnish positive criteria that can serve as premises in ethical arguments on behalf of public policy options over human efforts to engineer habitat. Where theists might at this point introduce concepts of "created co-creator" as permitting and even obliging human habitat engineering adventures (see Hefner 1993), religious naturalists operate without categories that presume a morally determinate and consciously aware creator being, and thus tend to appeal to categories that emphasize natural processes and human responsibility to decide on a moral course. The following moral principle furnishes for the religious naturalist much of what the "created co-creator principle" delivers for the creation-oriented theist: *Subject to criteria of prudence, dignity, and justice (i.e. the "alert" criteria just mentioned), human beings should explore the entire space of technological possibilities, as they are able, as they understand the relevant ramifications, and as they so determine through inclusive processes of scientifically and culturally informed debate.* In biotechnology, this criterion licenses everything from genetic experimentation and therapy to the creation of new species and the recreation of extinct ones, while closely constraining such efforts. In fact, it obliges human beings to explore where their technological prowess leads, subject to the demand for a profound degree of awareness of self, other, and nature. The "as they are able" and other caveats recognize persistent limitations of human wisdom and knowledge. Yet the criterion is essentially permissive, ruling out nothing as unnatural from the outset, but resolutely regulating technological ventures by means of the "alert" criteria.

This announcement of a positive criterion does not end a discussion over moral principles but only begins one. Deploying the norm of exploring the entire space of technological possibilities subject to ability, awareness, and desirability, as this principle does, requires us to take responsibility for designing what the evolutionary process has always handled without our guidance—adaptiveness in a variety of potential habitats. Natural selection figures out adaptiveness by trial and error in a messy and drawn-out process. If we use human biotechnologies self-consciously to achieve the same end, then we must be reasonably sure that changes made will improve adaptiveness in the ways we want. That applies especially with regard to the ordinary adaptiveness of biogenetic germline changes but also to the adaptiveness associated with changes in the treatment of human beings at the sociocultural level (e.g. good medical care allows many otherwise poorly adapted people to reach child-bearing years and pass their genes along) and changes in ecosystem management (e.g. methods of energy production have a profound impact on global climate, changing the fit between local niche habitats and the organisms that can survive there).

We have difficulty in knowing with confidence what qualifies as adaptive, especially for human beings, who create their own environmental niches to a considerable extent. The knowledge required to make such decisions responsibly staggers the mind. For example, while scientists understand some effects of many proteins, few scientists will claim that we can know for sure that a particular protein has only the functions we know it to have. How could we ever know such a thing? The side-effects of changing protein expression by modifying DNA prove extremely difficult to assess. Complete knowledge of the human genome does not help in this, because protein function is relative; a protein may be known to have a destructive function in the liver, but another vital function of the same protein in the brain may go undetected. We do not have the luxury of nature's trial-and-error approach to discovering what is adaptive and functional for pleasant lifestyles.

As social and habitat engineers, and increasingly as bioengineers, human beings are gaining control over both organism features and habitat features. If knowing what qualifies as adaptive is the ultimate bioengineering challenge, then deciding on and creating the life niches for which human beings want to be adapted is the ultimate social engineering challenge. The following four considerations for public debate about this challenge point in potentially quite different directions.

First, species survival in a variety of circumstances matters. The concerns here include especially survival of our species in a wide range of unpredictable circumstances, such as after the collapse of culture following massive devastation resulting from rampant disease, nuclear holocaust, or a collision between the Earth and an asteroid. Adaptiveness in this case means strong, fast bodies with flexible immune systems and high fertility.

Second, species flourishing matters. This involves cultivating the moral intelligence necessary to take responsibility for our lives and to preserve culture stably for future generations of human beings (or whatever genetic beings we would choose to occupy the future we create for them). For that, strong bodies are less important than genetic selection for intelligence, responsibility, fair-mindedness, and creativity.

Third, individual flourishing matters. This connotes a range of possibilities. For instance, it might involve customizing genetic makeup to maximize the potential for individual fulfillment, say, by selecting for cultural roles such as musician, artist, scientist, or politician (this requires sophisticated diagnostic and genetic engineering technologies). It might also involve creating a welcoming home for every being that comes into the world within our sphere of influence regardless of its genetic makeup (which requires sophisticated therapeutic technologies).

Fourth, individual survival matters. This would involve biotechnological therapies to help people live longer lives and also to give everyone who wants it a chance to pass on their genetic heritage, perhaps using unfamiliar reproductive technologies if necessary.

Imagining the Technological Future

The complexity of the positive criterion I am defending should now be evident. Figuring out what qualifies as adaptive so that we can run the evolutionary process ourselves, deliberately and responsibly, is daunting. Figuring out what kinds of life-niches we want to be adapted for remains a less complex matter at the level of biogenetic knowledge, but it leads to an enormously complex cultural engineering project. What I am talking about, as much as I hate even using such terminology, are the conditions for doing eugenics right. Pragmatically, I do not see how we can avoid the specter of eugenics in our shared future. We humans use the technology we have, and bans on particular biotechnologies prove ineffective even in the short term; the ethical reticence of bioengineering researchers only ever seems to mean that someone else gets the credit and infamy associated with new discoveries. It is a permanent feature of any technologically driven human future. Eugenics in the past has depended on ideals of racial purity and distorted science. Without ever forgetting that sordid corner of the pock-marked history of human depravity, we need to get past the association of eugenics and racial purity if we are honestly to face the bioethics challenges steadily piling up around us.

Public policy debate of these visions of the human future and how to balance them is vital, particularly for biotechnologies that call for germline changes in human beings or in creatures that define the environment for human life. Human beings must also take responsibility for these same life-niche questions on behalf of the animal and plant species over which they have control. Backing into a bioengineered future may not produce the disasters that alarmists envision but it might—experience shows that if anything can go wrong in human technological explorations, it probably will. The prudent approach demands self-consciously taking responsibility at each step of the way both for the adaptiveness of the genetic changes that human beings make and for the life-niche decisions presupposed in every judgment of adaptiveness.

The compass for guiding human habitat and biotechnological engineering promises to tell us which way to go; that is the daunting positive criterion, and I have given a modified natural law ethical argument in favor of moving ahead with every form of technological experimentation subject to rigorous constraints. The compass also promises to tell us when we stray off course, with vigorous reminders that we cannot afford to forget human corruption and arrogance. We need to refine this compass, not least because it is a dynamic indicator of opportunities and dangers, which implies that the tension it maintains between permissiveness and restraint needs constant revision. The ensuing debate needs to be global, and we do have a part model for the production of Treaties and Declarations in the achievements of the United Nations since 1945. But there is every reason to expect that the debates gaining momentum around biotechnology and habitat engineering will be disruptive and destructive at times. We can also expect the moral corruption of humanity to appear in full force around the issue of technology. Power has always been the most sought-after social commodity on Earth. It used to go with physical might, then with property, and in our own time mostly with financial resources. The ability to modify the human genome and to create novel life niches holds a dizzying kind of power not reducible to any type of power we have known in the past. The battle over access to such power will prove brutal and unrelenting. This situation will only grow more intense with more at stake as technology achieves each new level of sophistication. The battle over technological control will be as fierce as the power is god-like.

Biotechnologies and habitat transformations will forever change the future, inevitably for both better and worse. Those changes will affect human beings, other species, and as yet nonexistent species. The vagueness and fluidity of species boundaries has now reached beyond the realm of biological evolution and into the realm of cultural decision, where it is taking root in the imaginations of a new generation of children. We already raise our children on computer games where they learn how to manage cities and ecosystems, and where they must create, rear, and educate genetically engineered life forms, as well as bioengineer new and hybrid life forms. The human beings who currently cannot even defend and feed millions of human children or rid themselves of the threat of nuclear weapons are certainly not ready for so profound a degree of self-determination. On the whole, we remain morally weak and confused, with neither relevant wisdom from our ethical traditions nor the courage of true moral self-reliance to depend on. So we can tell already what will happen. Ecological conditions permitting, our future will prove more dangerous and at times more depraved than ever and also more full of wonder and health than ever. Hopefully the future will also prove merciful toward us while we continue to struggle to use the moral compass we design to accompany the habitat we engineer.

Symbols and Value Habitat

Speaking of Values in Nature

There are many ironies in contemporary science. Perhaps most impish among them is the corporate rewriting of great episodes in the history of science. It is striking how often vast and complex intellectual struggles, complete with deep methodological uncertainty and great controversy, are reduced with a flourish of textbook elegance to simple stories that narrate the power of the scientific method to produce breakthroughs in knowledge, free from the taint of political ideologies, religious beliefs, funding resources, or impure personal motivations. The actual story is always far more interesting and ambiguous with respect to every kind of potential tainting. But, much as in the case of religion, the simpler and profoundly distorted story serves the legitimation needs of the scientific community much better. When philosophers and historians of science began to notice this pattern, they even offered arguments for the validity of such fairy-tale narratives based on the functions they play in educating scientists and in clarifying appropriate or preferred methods. Meanwhile, the grim beauty, blessed boredom, and everyday creativity of scientific research lies beneath the shiny short-story accounts, undiscussed and unmourned except by historians. Groups that pursue scientific research, it seems, have as much at stake in legitimating their social worlds and practices as any other human group, despite the pervasive rhetoric about science as an ideology-free and legitimation-free zone (here "ideology" is used in the descriptive sense of Eagleton 1991, Freeden 2003; on the question of a more adequate theory of inquiry see Wildman 2009).

Another irony, not unrelated to the first, is of great concern to religious naturalists, who heavily rely on science for an account of nature but worry that science yields a biased account of what there is in nature. It is this: scientists virtually never display any interest in giving an account or even acknowledging the presence of values in natural reality, as manifested in their own scientific work. Even strictly materialist scientists, who should be thrown into a fit of anti-metaphysical panic by the dawning awareness that they presume values for which they have no account, casually slumber in their scientific work, operating in a world of values and value-laden judgments. A number of scientists in their private conversations and public roles will expand on their beliefs about reality—what is in it and what it all means—and a few will go public under the right circumstances (see Richardson et al. 2002). They do this fully cognizant of the fact that they are moving outside the limited domain of scientific inquiry, which is commendable. Most are generous and sensitive interpreters of wider reality beyond their own scientific backyard, even if they lack philosophical sophistication.

Unfortunately, a few scientists venture into the public domain less gracefully. Some fall prey to scientism, an updated form of positivist grandiosity that supposes there is in reality nothing but that which science can recognize and study. Some extend the useful technique of reductionism outside the scientific domain to produce flattened-out accounts of profound human experiences, as when they pretend that love is nothing but the brain processes that realize it in human beings. Some boldly decry religious objects as nothing but superstitions for which we have excellent naturalistic explanations, and then baldly offer poetic flourishes about the wondrous depths and patterns and energies of nature with no apparent concern that in so doing they reconstitute an ontological basis for the very religious objects that they so vociferously reject. It may be unreasonable to expect philosophical sophistication among scientists. But it is not unreasonable to expect modesty when scientists venture opinions about domains of knowledge and types of reasoning that lie outside their fields of expertise. Such manifold failures of modesty are the unmistakable markers of cultural hegemony. Religious leaders once made the same mistakes out in the open with no traces of shame.

The consequence of this vast irony in contemporary science, construed broadly as the activities of scientists speaking as experts on any topic whatsoever, is widespread paralysis around recognizing and speaking about values, particularly in naturalistic ways. The straightforward views are mistaken, according to the religious naturalist. On the one side we have supernaturalist ontologies with souls and discarnate entities who transact ideas and values regardless of bodies and groups and ecosystems. This metaphysically demarcates another world beyond nature, a world that science can neither access nor evaluate, a super-nature that appears to be entirely dispensable in explanations of the nature we can and do experience. But it also establishes a sturdy basis for talk about values in our everyday experience. In popular theistic contexts, values are rooted in God's own being and life, and we are able to engage and appreciate them because God creates us as hybrid beings with souls and bodies. On the other side, the religious naturalist finds the equally mistaken view that there is materiality only, and everything complex is merely an assemblage of material components, with properties derived strictly from the way components are arranged. This metaphysically austere view is profoundly disabled when it comes to giving a persuasive account of values and consciousness. Apparently human beings invent values and experience consciousness, but the question of how these feats are possible in a materialist framework is routinely finessed. Even to know how the brain realizes conscious states would tell us very little about how such a thing as consciousness is possible. And the same goes for values such as goodness, truth, and beauty.

Religious naturalists universally reject a super-nature. But they divide among themselves according to the degree of ontological complexity they are willing to allow in their approaches to the value question. At the first and simplest level, religious naturalism is nature romanticism, in the sense of testimony to the wonder and terror we feel in the face of natural reality. This may lead to speaking of goodness or truth or beauty, but this is a kind of "as if" speech. What matters is not the ontological standing of such transcendentals but the human emotional reaction to the natural world that evokes description in these terms. This kind of naturalism is ontologically diffident but appears committed to there being in nature features (such as beauty) that evoke emotional and intellectual reactions (such as awe and curiosity) in suitably attentive human beings.

At the second level of ontological complexity, religious naturalists endeavor to take theoretical responsibility for the talk about values that arises within nature romanticism. There is a sequence of relevant questions here. Is our feeling of reverence in the face of the night sky in any sense caused by the phenomenon we behold? Yes, indeed—but the cause is what is at stake in the debate over the ontological status of values. Is our feeling of fascination in the face of an intricate natural phenomenon caused merely by our ignorance? No—because a deeper understanding of intricate phenomena often increases appreciation and wonder. Is our feeling of unaccountable fear as we look down into deep, dark ocean water caused merely by evolutionary cognitive reflexes? No—because, quite apart from not having genes that code for particular feelings, our evolutionarily formed cognitive and emotional predispositions are activated by actual experiences of the natural world. Finally, can we deliver a theoretically satisfying account of the basis in nature for our value talk that denies that nature exhibits features that contribute to causing such value talk? No—our value talk arises as a combination of features of nature and human cognitive-emotional capacities to engage those features.

Values, therefore, are not merely human fantasies imposed on value-free nature but collaborative achievements of organism-world engagement. An adequate theory of values must account for both sides of the collaboration. When we write $F=ma$ we must understand *both* that nature displays mathematizable regularities *and* that we have the cognitive capacity and social inquiry skills necessary to detect the regularity and model it. When we feel guilty for being needlessly cruel to another living being we must understand *both* that the other being possesses a wondrous integrity that obliges us *and* that our cognitive-emotional capacities register this in the form of guilt and remorse. When we lie beside the magnificent body of a precious lover we must understand *both* that nature contains beauty in its shapes and angles, shadows and light, movement and warmth, *and* that we are primed to sense and respond to these features of beauty. At this level, therefore, the religious naturalist theorizes that value is a matter both of objective natural features and of human appraisal and creative response. The associated ontology must therefore allow for the objectivity of values—not simplistically as features of nature that we simply read off its surface but complexly as the objective basis in nature of that which we appreciate as valuable in our varied engagements with the environment of life.

At the third level of ontological complexity, religious naturalists venture a theological account of values in nature, though still without falling prey either to supernaturalistic portrayals of souls and miracles or to supranaturalistic portrayals of divine beings. The core hypothesis at this third level is that the axiological features of nature are one of the wellsprings of religious behaviors, beliefs, and experiences; they are the ultimate referents behind and beneath the elaborate symbolism of religious traditions, prevailing theological interpretations of religious language to the contrary notwithstanding; and they are that with which (most) human beings are ultimately concerned. Embracing theological categories is a complicated undertaking because most key terms (such as "God") are firmly in the grip of ontological frameworks inimical to religious naturalism. But on the underside of any religious group boasting a sophisticated tradition of philosophical debate persists an awareness of the world of nature that is strongly evocative of religious naturalism and substantially consistent with its views of nature, values, and ultimate reality. To invent the needed terminology to discuss the valuational depth structures of nature in theological ways would be vain and, at least as important, impractical. The theologically minded religious naturalist is thus faced with the unappetizing prospect of perpetually distinguishing the naturalist deployment of theological categories from their usage in other religious contexts, while simultaneously building bridges to those places within many religious traditions where there is common purpose and shared insight. But to eschew theological categories altogether is worse, at least for the philosophically minded theologian, for it confines discourse to poetic expostulation without any possibility of thinking systematically about the religious dimensions of the natural world.

The second level discussed above flows from the first level as a matter of *philosophical completeness*: rational criteria of consistency and coherence, adequacy and applicability demand philosophical articulation of the axiological presuppositions of nature romanticism. The third level currently under discussion flows from the second level as a matter of *pragmatic necessity*: we need concepts to address the significance for human existence and social life of nature's valuational depth structures and the adequate concepts are theological in character, in the broad sense that theology has here. This difference in logical relationships between levels is vital for grasping what is at stake in theological articulations of religious naturalism. Whereas first-level nature romanticism holds off second-level axiological ontology only through stubborn refusal to take theoretical responsibility for functional premises, second-level axiological ontology resists third-level theology of nature by fighting over whether theological categories are really needed for the guidance and interpretation of human individual existence and social life. While this must remain an argument for another place, my sense is that refusing third-level theological categories altogether is problematic in either of two forms. On the one hand, refusing theological categories while also trying to address the ultimate concerns of human individuals and groups commits the religious naturalist to a type of intellectual parasitism. This involves silently capitalizing on lines of awareness and categories shaped by theological language while refusing to acknowledge or use such theological language. On the other hand, refusing theological categories and also refusing to address the ultimate concerns of human individuals and groups is more consistent but morally questionable and leaves the full existential meaning and social significance of religious naturalism undisclosed.

The Roles of Symbols

I have argued that religious naturalists are obliged, for reasons of philosophical completeness and pragmatic necessity, to embrace the ambiguities and complexities of the theological task. In so doing, they can address the way that the valuational depth structures and dynamics of nature are objects of ultimate concern in individual lives and human groups. They can describe the way religious traditions are built up around perspectivally governed and tradition-guided forms of engagement with these axiological depths. And they can trace the way engagement with natural reality at all levels and in all modes evokes metaphorical, symbolic, and other forms of tropic speech. What is it about the axiological character of nature, the religious naturalist theologian might well ask, that demands anything other than relatively literal forms of language in our quest to express our ultimate concerns? Is poetic indirection a mere conceit, an aesthetic flourish gesturing toward the wonder of our natural life environment? Or is there something inescapable about indirection in theological language?

The issue about indirection in theology, about the status of symbolic language, is one over which religious naturalist theologians might legitimately disagree. After all, theologians of other stripes disagree on the same question. For some theologians, religious metaphors and symbols derive such inevitability as they possess exclusively from the cognitive style of human beings, which is through-and-through metaphoric and symbolic to various degrees (see Lakoff & Johnson 1980, 1999). In this framework of interpretation, literal speech is a social achievement of the first order. It depends on crystallizing categories from the flux of ordinary metaphorical expression and then stabilizing these categories in linguistic systems and technical discourse communities. I believe this is compelling as an account of the origins of literal speech, of the inevitability of indirection of ordinary speech about complex subject matters, and of the way that theologians can sometimes approach literalness in their technical discourse communities (see Wildman 2009). But I shall argue that this is an incomplete account of the reasons for the unavoidability of indirection in theological speech.

It is at this point that some religious naturalist theologians may part company with me. There is a similar split among other types of theologians. In all cases, the issue has to do with the final intelligibility and expressibility of ultimate realities, which for the religious naturalist theologian are the axiological structures and flows in the depths of natural reality. The *apophatic* theologians hypothesize that ultimate realities are finally inexpressible, not just for human beings, but for any and all forms of cognitive-emotional engagement anywhere and anytime in reality. They venture such a bold claim not just on the basis of their experience, which cannot establish the claim in anything remotely like its full generality, but for the theological reason that the basis of nature, however conceived, must surpass the cognitive reach of any being within it. The *kataphatic* theologians, by contrast, reject the apophatic hypothesis and assert any number of alternative accounts of how it is that ultimacy is not finally incomprehensible and inexpressible, even if it is difficult for us to grasp and understand.

To locate my religious naturalist theological project in the coarsest and most direct way, I affirm the apophatic hypothesis. In fact, I suspect that religious naturalists must affirm the apophatic hypothesis on pain of inconsistency, because only supranaturalists have the conceptual resources necessary to maintain a consistent kataphatic approach to theological speech about ultimate realities. To the extent that ultimacy is not a being with determinate features, as it is in most forms of traditional theism and as it is decidedly not in religious naturalism, ultimacy escapes the net of cognition and interpretation. Ultimacy is not thereby entirely beyond cognitive address because it is still reflexively manifest in the valuational features of nature that we engage and can describe—the religious naturalist's version of revelation. But the overall character of those axiological structures and flows necessarily surpasses cognitive grasp. For the apophatic religious naturalist theologian, this is the driving force behind religious symbolism—not merely human cognitive style, that is to say, but the character of ultimacy itself demands indirection in speech and concept. While this fact of nature need not militate against clarity of philosophical concepts in every sense, it does interfere with a certain type of conceptual clarity consisting of definitional definitiveness, which under the circumstances is shown to be an intellectual ideal ill-suited to theological purposes.

This apophatic standpoint has important consequences for my account of human symbol wielding. I shall describe some of these consequences beginning with the practical level and moving to more theoretical considerations. The valuational depth structures and flows that engage our ultimate concerns cannot be comprehended all at once. It is helpful to conceive these valuational depths as a multidimensional landscape of axiological possibilities. Human beings, and indeed on the apophatic hypothesis any and all creatures, are confined to engaging this multidimensional landscape of axiological possibilities not by viewing it somehow all at once but by traversing its territory and sensing what we see and touch from where we are while using our memory and imagination for the rest. The paths we take are inevitably limited in perspective and typically worn into the landscape thanks to the steps of many feet that have gone before. That is, we conceive what we encounter in contextually specific ways, and our engagement with the axiological environment is experientially specific and guided by tradition. Most importantly, it takes a long time—the investment of most of a lifetime, in fact—to understand the axiological meaning of the paths we walk. These paths unfold for us slowly and depend on the building of character and the transformation of group priorities in accord with the principles we affirm in light of what we engage. We often have to fight for those principles but provisional and ever-mutating group consensus is usually within reach.

It is in such groups, formed by the journeys they take, that we learn to describe what we see and build our insights into satisfying self-interpretations. It is in the encounter with other such groups that we learn about the specific and perspectival qualities of our own ways of thinking and speaking and living. This complicates our perception of and engagement with the multidimensional landscape of axiological possibilities. Ways of speaking that we took for granted are problematized in such encounters, as we realize that our estimate of their literal truth was exaggerated. Yet authentic engagement with the valuational depths of nature still occurs despite the perspectivally limited and tropic nature of our conceptual approach. Religious symbols, it seems, can truly engage us with ultimacy even when they are broken, in the sense of being misleading as literal descriptions of that which is our ultimate concern (this is the central claim of Neville 1996 and a key feature of the argument about the scope and truth of theology in Neville 2006).

If all ultimacy talk is necessarily symbolic and if all ultimacy symbols are necessarily broken, where is the basis for distinguishing better from worse theoretical formulations of ultimacy? Some theologians have essentially given up in despair in the face of this question. They resort to affirming the rational sufficiency of religious life worlds with their distinctive language games, supposing that every group plowing paths across the multidimensional axiological landscape has equally excellent and efficacious interpretations of ultimacy, at least insofar as resources permit evaluation. But this is an alarmingly regressive and reactionary theological posture. Rationality is always complex in human beings, and nowhere more so than in theological inquiries, but theological inquiry is still possible. Specialized discourse communities exist to make it possible and such inquiries can be undertaken with better and worse resources and carried off more and less expertly. There are good reasons to say that the religious naturalist account of ultimacy as the axiological depths of nature is rationally superior to supranaturalistic accounts of ultimacy as a divine being. This book does not intend to make that case, of course, but the case can be made quite effectively in a hypothetical fallibilist manner (see Wildman 2006b, 2007a, 2007b, 2008a, 2008b). This fallibilist approach to inquiry in general and theological inquiry in particular (see Wildman 2009) does not satisfy the epistemic foundationalist, for whom certainty of argumentative conclusions is the only relevant standard. But it does permit discrimination of better from worse in theology, enough to make clear the rational stakes in affirming any particular theological hypothesis, including the kinds of implausibility that it must confront and its particular theoretical virtues.

Engaging and Creating the Good, the True, and the Beautiful

The necessarily symbolic character of ultimacy talk, even in the peculiarly strong sense of the apophatic hypothesis, does not interfere with theological theory building. Rather, it renders such theoretical inquiries precisely as complicated as their subject matter demands. Moreover, more and less authentic forms of engagement with the axiological depths of nature persist in and through all religious symbol usage. The relevant criteria for authenticity are arrived at in complex, socially mediated explorations of moral and aesthetic possibilities for human life. This aspect of the valuational dimensions of the human life habitat demands an account not merely of registering values but of creating them—that is, creating values not from nothing but through selectively engaging the axiological possibilities that nature affords. We never simply encounter the good, the true, and the beautiful somehow abstracted from our interpretations, groups, habits, and choices. Rather, we create the good through generating and nurturing moral traditions. We create the true through birthing and deploying traditions of inquiry. And we create the beautiful through inventing and savoring aesthetic traditions.

The supranaturalist account of ultimacy as a divine being comfortably roots the transcendentals of goodness, truth, and beauty in God's personality and preferences. Valuational questions are as clear as that divine personality and those divine preferences. The supranaturalist framework conceives ultimacy in so centered and unified a manner that there never is a question in principle about the determinate meaning of these transcendentals no matter how complicated judgment may become in practice. For the religious naturalist, by contrast, the univocity of goodness, truth, and beauty is deeply questionable. As an empirical question (inevitably, for the naturalist), it certainly seems that the three famous ideals are subject to different degrees of univocal treatment.

First, the most clear-cut appears to be truth, which in its commonsense meaning reflects the value enshrined in a match between a proposition and a state of affairs. We may not be able in every case to determine when a proposition is true, but most of us, and even most philosophers, do not have to struggle endlessly over the very meaning of truth. Nevertheless, our daily engagement with the valuational depths of nature invites us to acknowledge that truth has other meanings as well, and meanings that are far less clear-cut. Specifically, authenticity, fidelity, exemplification, and even authority also fall under the domain of truth, considered most generally rather than in the narrow terms of propositional matches with states of affairs. We do not have the same difficulty in perceiving the breadth of meanings in relation to goodness and beauty that we have in relation to truth, but this is an asymmetry that we can and should overcome (see the discussion of a variety of senses of religious truth in Neville 2001c).

Truth is far from a univocal concept with norms as definite as a putative divine mind that knows or simply defines the truth. This is so despite the fact that the simplest and most abstract cases of truth are definitive. In other words, we do not just read truth off of nature's manuscript but we fight to discern it through creating systems of inquiry, we hopefully grasp after it when we formulate provisional hypotheses that might be subject to helpful correction, and in some cases we create it in the name of curiosity and self-expression. There may be one way to speak truly of most scientific subject matters but there is not one way to speak truly of ourselves, of our loved ones, or of our enemies, such is the complex and perspectival quality of human relationships. There certainly is not one way to speak truly of ultimacy, such is the nature of symbolic discourse and the superfluity of meanings that must be present in any subject matter corresponding to the logical designation of *ultimate reality*. And beyond the realm of propositional truth, there is enormous creativity involved in living authentically and faithfully, in exercising authority and in being an example. Despite initial appearances, truth in its richest meanings does not amount to a univocal concept. It is created as often as it is discovered through processes of inquiry that seek correction of hypothetical ideas.

Second, crosscultural comparison of moral practices and ethical systems quickly drives home the point that goodness is also not a univocal concept. As with truth, and even more so, we create the good as we journey in our groups across the multidimensional axiological landscape of possibilities. We notice the valuational structures and flows, we compile wisdom about what creates and what destroys in the short term and in the long term, and we make our moral decisions in light of everything we know about reality, prioritizing what we care about according to our own creative preferences. If the narrowest meaning of propositional truth might lead us to expect that the axiological depths of nature speak in a single voice in that respect, this certainly seems not to be so in the case of morality. Moral goods routinely conflict, at least around the margins, and sometimes they are directly opposed, such that each side decries the opponent as evil in a transparent manifestation of the constructed quality of the values that guide our behavior—it would be comical if it were not so often deadly.

Even so, we do not just create the good arbitrarily. There really are patterns and flows in the axiological depth structures and dynamics of nature. Some behaviors are routinely self-defeating or cruel and deserve to be called "bad" while others reliably increase kindness and fairness and deserve to be called "good." We make our choices about the good and the bad in relation to the objectively structured features of natural axiological possibilities and those features genuinely and sometimes brutally constrain how things work out for us afterwards. Conflicting moral values show how implausible it is to suppose that the good has a univocal meaning, as it would have if it were derived from a singular determinate divine personality. The importance of moral values in our lives shows how implausible it is to suppose that we merely invent moral values free from any constraints. We invent them, yes, but constrained and informed by the landscape of axiological possibilities.

Third, we create beauty, too, but once again we do so in relation to, and enabled by, a potently tradition-guided appraisal of the axiological possibilities of nature's depths. Here we arrive at what appears to be the least constrained and least determinate domain of nature's axiological depths. Where we find actual truth conflicts (as against conflicting truth claims) hard to conceive, and actual moral conflicts (as against conflicting moral postures) deeply disturbing, most of us appreciate and savor the actual multivocity of beauty (as against conflicting norms for the beautiful). So long as it does not lead to epistemological or moral chaos, therefore, we can readily accept a high degree of aesthetic chaos.

Put differently, we are comfortable with the view that ultimacy is so aesthetically dense with possibilities that we could not possibly express it fully in any one aesthetic work or tradition. Strangely, though, we do not comfortably apply the same insight to the domains of morality and inquiry. Why should not ultimacy be so dense with moral possibilities that we would have to take multiple perspectival approaches even to begin to register its complexity? And why should not ultimacy be so cognitively rich as to demand multiple conflicting theoretical models?

One way to understand the human condition is in terms of its enormously variegated exploration of the multidimensional landscape of axiological possibilities. If on our journeys across this landscape we only ever encounter and realize in our own experience one form of the true, the good, and the beautiful, and if this form were determinate in the way that a divine personality might be determinate, the case against supranaturalism and for religious naturalism would be immeasurably weaker than it is. Theoretical parsimony would make it almost irresistible to interpret the ground of nature's values as a deity with a determinate personality that furnishes clear-cut truth, clear-cut moral laws, and clear-cut aesthetic norms. But this is not what we find, and indeed not even close to what we find.

The toxicity of religious exclusivism and violence is one measure of the anxiety we feel as nature manifests its irrepressible axiological multivocity in our lives and groups. Personal disorientation and failure of moral and aesthetic creativity is another measure. But human beings need not be paralyzed by a vision of axiological possibilities that is more complex than a divine personality, nor terrified by the realization that nature's valuational depths are more perilously conflicted than any one person or social expression of ultimacy could possibly tolerate. We discover in our own experience, in our own bodies and in our own groups, that ultimacy is perpetually beyond our complete cognitive and emotional grasp. Yet we can and do engage it more and less authentically and truly, more and less lovingly and beautifully, as our journeying groups venture such norms— venture them as living invitations for our own creative responses.

Conclusion: *Homo Religiosus* and Habitat

This discussion of the multidimensional habitat for human life has far-reaching implications for any theological consideration of human nature, and here especially for the central claim of this book that human beings are *homo religiosus* not only historically, culturally, or circumstantially, but also ontologically, essentially, and inescapably.

We have seen that the microbial ocean surrounds and suffuses human beings, and that they are profoundly dependent on it. As noted, the microbial world was where the lion's share of adaptation occurred, producing simple organisms with virtually all of the biochemical processes that are needed to make functional multi-cellular organisms and eventually sensate and intelligent life forms who visit restaurants, read fashion magazines, and worry a lot. Microorganisms are the basis of every food chain. They play essential roles in the health of every organism. Bacterial symbiogenesis lies at the root of the energy-processing capabilities of all animals and plants. That is what makes glucose work efficiently as fuel energy;

why we have livers with the energy-sequestering power to transform glucose into fats and back again, making us adaptable and mobile; and how we are able to sustain the metabolically expensive brains that enable our emotional, mental, and spiritual lives.

Every large organism is thus a mind-bogglingly complex ecology of organisms whose viability represents a kind of negotiated settlement between the fortuitously enabling features and the mindlessly destructive properties of the microbe-dominated environment. The negotiated settlement crafted through evolutionary adaptation sometimes breaks down, bringing disease and untimely death. Most of the time, however, it works well enough to allow hours or months or decades of healthy life activity, depending on the species. Human beings can count on optimal adult function for several decades—more when sound public health practices allow us to keep at bay the parts of the microbial ocean to which we are poorly adapted, thereby delaying the inevitable microbial reclaiming of our bodies as their adaptive harmonies yield to the chaos of sickness, decrepitude, and death.

This entails that *sickness, decrepitude, and death are natural parts of human life.* Contrary to the religious narratives of a variety of traditional theological anthropologies, they are not penalties for sin, though they can be the results of foolish choices surrounding food, behavior, and technology. Nor are they to be escaped, in the way suggested by the legendary encounters with sickness, decrepitude, and death that spurred the young Buddha's quest for enlightenment. But sickness, decrepitude, and death are not pleasant, either. The fact that the superorganism ecology of the human person can sustain dynamic balance within the microbial environment for a few decades is a stunning achievement of the evolutionary process. It gives us time to contribute to the building of cultures, to create technological marvels, and to lay down treasured memories. Equally importantly from a religious point of view, this dynamic balance creates opportunities for us decide how we will regard the ultimate realities manifest in and through the wealth of our life experiences. This evolutionarily negotiated window of high-functioning allows us to dispose of our lives creatively, for the sake of projects larger than ourselves. We can bend our embodied minds to the purposes of self-cultivation, responsibility, and harmonious acceptance of our actual life-context. We can frantically throw our energies about in self-dissolution and crazed denial. Or we can focus our efforts in acts of great selfishness and violence, powered by displaced fury at our life situation.

We do all this together, in groups, of course. We narrate our existential situation to one another using the symbolic resources sequestered in sprawling wisdom traditions. We rehearse the importance of the fundamental moral and spiritual choices that we face. We deploy technologies of healing and compassion to bring comfort in the face of trouble and where possible to restore optimal functioning when it is compromised. We handle cognitive dissonance between the world as we narrate it and the world as we encounter it by adapting our stories and technologically taming the parts of the world that we can manage. This socially networked process of technological, moral, and religious exploration is not mere delusion. Mechanisms of social control and self-deception are increasingly obvious once we learn to identify them. But much more is going on here than merely management of terror in the face of anomic chaos.

We sincerely engage the spiritual depths of nature through our moral and religious exertions, through our religious narrations and moral legislations, and by means of technological ingenuity and healing methods. This is human life in its multidimensional habitat, properly understood: it is spiritually charged with luminous possibilities of authenticity and engagement with ultimacy. And we dance out our options in the company of story-telling companions along the knife edge of transient dynamic stability that is biological evolution's gift to us. Beset on all sides by mindless microbial consumption, enabled by microbial ecologies to which we are well adapted, and creatively deploying technologies of habitat engineering, we claim a few decades from anomic chaos and flourish with emotional intensity, intellectual curiosity, spiritual meaning, and moral creativity.

While the supranaturalist theologian tries to discern a divine being behind all of this, and distances the purported divine nature from this account of the human condition in order to preserve a morally intelligible deity, the naturalist theologian takes another route. Indeed, it can be with enormous relief rather than any sense of grief that the religious naturalist shakes off the dust of tired religious narratives transparently legitimating social orders and sets out on a different road. The new road brings vistas of ultimate reality lying within the axiological depth structures and dynamics of nature—and not just a convenient selection of them that reinforces our reality-evading biases toward the pleasant or our alienated biases toward the unpleasant, but nature as a whole. On this road, we celebrate the discovery of the network of ecological relationships that suffuses our lives, historically and bodily, and we become increasingly intentional about habitat engineering projects to relieve suffering, increase justice, and to enjoy the possibilities that life presents.

Religious naturalists see the staggering fecundity of life, and can effortlessly picture a post-human biological future. They are amazed that anyone could still give nature and evolutionary history anthropocentric meaning. Religious naturalists see the chaotic consumption, the formative symbiotic events, the horizontal and vertical transmission of genes, and the preservation of structural achievements across generations, and are amazed that anyone could know any part of this and still embrace anthropomorphic pictures of an aware, intentional, providential, active deity behind it all. In fact, the vast majority of those who really do know these things have long surrendered the supranaturalist narratives of deities with feelings and plans and powers to act (see Larson & Witham 1997, 1998). Of course, religion is often about the human condition at levels other than the biological, the evolutionary, and the technological. Thus, these stories really do help people to engage ultimacy, and to that extent they possess goodness and truth and beauty. But serious knowledge of evolutionary biology, and particularly of the microbial ocean, also unmasks supranaturalist narratives as transparent mechanisms of social control and renders them implausible.

What are the ultimacy images that religious naturalists conjure in the depths of the microbial ocean and at the heights of habitat-engineering creativity? Ultimacy is chaotic, fecund, and also emergently ordered. Aristotle had it half right when he conceived God as the principle of natural order that knits together the natural purposes of every living creature into bodily, moral, social, and intellectual harmonies. The half he underplayed is that ultimacy is also the morally impenetrable chaos of mass feeding, the blind chance of random symbiotic events, and the heartless opportunism of viral parasitism. We can narrate one side of this great natural truth about the depths of nature and convince ourselves that we are telling the whole story. We can invent theodicies and other conceptual deflections to manage the painful cognitive dissonance that results. We can organize communities that make it virtually impossible to hear any other narrative and so bind ourselves together in creative exercises of social power. There is real value in all of that, especially because the overriding existential concern of religions is to manage the human condition, not to understand it. And I freely acknowledge that there is real danger in seeing all of ultimacy together rather than just the anthropomorphically intelligible bits that best support such communities. But the whole story of ultimacy, of the structures and flows in the abysmal depths of nature, is still there to be told.

Perhaps only those who feel truly thankful for the miracles of knife-edge dances of life and transitory islands of ecological and stability in the fecund wilds of the human cosmic and planetary habitat will be motivated to tell the whole story of human beings in the ambit of ultimacy. Seeing the whole and being willing to attest to what we see requires a love not only of what we enjoy but also of what we fear. For nature manifests abysmal depths that pass understanding, that absorb mindlessly and hunt mercilessly, that defy moral taming and remain oblivious to the predictable interests of social orders. The apophatic mystics of all traditions have seen this. They may not have known about biological or cosmic evolution. But they sensed that, from an existential point of view, ultimacy is both *pro me* and *contra me*, supportive of and also hostile toward our bodily and spiritual interests. The authors of Job knew it, as has every commentator who saw through the fragile and ultimately self-deconstructing way that this story of an awesome encounter with the depths of nature is framed as the result of a bet between two prideful supernatural beings. Even a preliminary awareness of the complexity of the human habitat drives home this abysmal insight with renewed force.

If ultimacy is groundless abyss, it is also ground of being and power of being. And here we have to take account of the structures and flows of nature that swirl up out of cosmic processes and then in and through the microbial ocean and finally seemingly almost beyond it. These structures and flows are not intelligible as anthropomorphically scaled intentions, and so are not commensurate with supranaturalist aspirations to detect intelligent design. Rather, they are interplays of chaos and order, of chance events and emergent patterns. They create layers of complexity, with each layer repeating the entanglement of chance-like and law-like components that give rise to the next most complex layer. What are we entitled to infer about the character of ultimacy from this entanglement of form and dynamics in layer upon layer of emergent complexity? Two misleading suggestions and a theoretically more stable interpretative option exist.

On the one hand, the layering of complexity reaches downwards in complexity and backwards in time to cosmic origins that settled the regularities of quantum chemistry, which in the right ecological context yield biology and life. It is likely that our universe of regularities is one of infinitely many in an endless multiverse. This judgment of likelihood already flows from the standard version of inflationary big-bang cosmology (see Guth 1997, Vilenkin 2006), and does not depend on the more speculative multiverse proposals arising in quantum cosmology, such as the multiverse landscape of string theory (see Susskind 2005) and brane-world theory (see Steinhardt & Turok 2007)—but if correct these more speculative quantum cosmologies deliver the same result. It is conveivable that each universe within the multiverse expresses different regularities and emergent patterns, which is why Susskind calls his (2005) book, *The Cosmic Landscape: String Theory and the Illusion of Intelligent Design*. No basis for resuscitating the comfortable and subtle anthropomorphisms of supranaturalistic ultimacy theories is to be found in this direction. But we do find ample basis for wonder in the layering of emergent complexity that spontaneously organizes and channels the chaotic flux of nature into life forms, beginning with the incredible microbiological complexity of bacteria and archaea and extending upwards from there.

On the other hand, the layering of structures and dynamics reaches upwards in complexity and forward in time to the emergence of persons with potent emotions and existential problems, with intellectual abilities and spiritual yearnings. Surely the ground of being, however else it is understood, must be at least as complex and centered as the complex and centered creatures it produces, and thus at least as personal as human persons. But this line of reasoning also fails. Partially hidden within it is an anthropomorphic conception of creation, in which we design and make what we first conceive. This kind of creating presupposes envisaging and planning, and thus requires both centered attention and focal action. But there is no basis for applying to ultimacy this analogy from human creation. In particular, there is no basis for it in the structures and flows of nature. Centeredness sufficient for attention and focal action is a transient achievement of dynamic harmony, constantly under threat from, and profoundly indebted to, the living microbial ocean. The supranaturalist impulse is to generalize this transient achievement to an eternal state of a divine being, which involves the anti-naturalist move of arbitrarily splitting off centered attention and focal action from its actual roots in natural processes. The only way the analogy can be sustained is with a developmental, emergent view of the divine life, such as Georg Hegel and others have proposed, but properly adjusted to accommodate the emergent patterns of nature as well as the emergent patterns of history. Indeed, this continues to be an option for a metaphysical account of ultimacy in the context of self-transcending nature, though perhaps not in Hegel's historical-logical way. The alternatives to emergent centeredness within ultimate reality involve diffuse intentionality, superorganismic fecundity, and a plenitudinous yearning that supplies power for indiscriminate exploration of an evolutionary landscape of ontological niches. But there is slender basis in nature for ascribing centered personhood to ultimate reality.

Finally, then, with two misleading suggestions set aside, we are left with a theoretically more stable picture of ultimacy as at once impenetrable abyss and partially intelligible ground. The co-presence of the two in every aspect and dimension of nature is manifest in the entanglement of chaotic and order-producing elements within the structures and dynamics of natural processes. Both abyss and ground are distinguishable from the sheer nothing that is the ultimate contrast to everything determinate and from everything as determined as a center of consciousness. Ultimacy in this portrayal is simultaneously gracious in respect of its fecundity and its receptiveness to creative human effort, and untamable in respect of its ceaseless challenge to all forms of order, including all human achievements. It is because of our dawning awareness of the cosmic, evolutionary, microbial, and ecological habitat that births us, sustains us, threatens us, and receives us—because of this awareness more than our knowledge of the vicissitudes of history and of the psychic chaos of our personal lives—that human beings are able to perceive ultimacy in these terms.

PART III
Findings

CHAPTER 9

Homo Religiosus

Introduction

This inquiry is almost at an end. All that remains is to enter testimony concerning the findings of the inquiry, at least as I make them out to be. But what can an ending mean in this case? As described in the first preliminary chapter, the type of multidisciplinary inquiry pursued here combines insights from as many stakeholder disciplines as are relevant and requires synthetic interpretation governed by a dual commitment: to the widest possible conversation among qualified partners in inquiry and to the ceaseless quest for correction wherever it may be found. The hermeneutics of such an inquiry are a matter of art. A written record is a snapshot of an ongoing process, at a moment when emerging consensus or conviction warrants public testimony about findings. But the testimony is perpetually provisional and the conversation never ending. After all, how could any conversation about the ultimate meaning of human life come to a definitive end? Endings, therefore, are creative impositions. Just as the artist arrests a process momentarily to press determinate creativity into space and time and imagination, so we end inquiries, to see what we have wrought, and to testify to what it all means, so far. As with art, so with complex multidisciplinary inquiries: people see things differently. So the inquiry must end to make one synthetic interpretation sufficiently determinate that others may view it, appreciate it, critique it, and do their own work better because of it.

Some inquiries, such as those pertaining to the nature of ultimate reality, are relatively free from stakeholder disciplinary constraints—not entirely free, by any means, but far freer than this one has been. In inquiries centering on ultimate realities, therefore, we expect many artistic products testifying to many possible interpretations. These will fill metaphysical museums of art, gracing the walls with complementary perspectives and passionate paradoxes. I have argued that this is not the result we should expect for an inquiry into religious anthropology, at least not in our time. Rather, the natural sciences from physics to evolutionary biology, the human sciences from sociology to psychology, and the scientific study of religion furnish perspectives on human beings and human groups that are significantly consonant. None of these disciplines is univocal, of course, but their provisional conclusions collectively constitute the basis for a powerful interpretation of human life that is characteristically modern, secular, and interdisciplinary—I shall call it the *modern secular interpretation of humanity* (MSIH). Despite disagreements in stakeholder disciplines and the large tracts of human nature that remain poorly understood, the MSIH is sufficiently determinate to impose strong constraints on any wider theological interpretation of the human condition, as I have demonstrated repeatedly in this book (this point is also affirmed, though with a greater tendency to scientific reductionism, in Slingerland 2008).

While an interpretation of human beings, and thus somewhat philosophical in character, the MSIH is a minimalist interpretation in the sense that it extends beyond the results of the scientific disciplines that furnish its major insights only by consistently coordinating those insights. It is a theory in the sense of a seeing-together of scientific insights into human beings. Its force derives from the compatibility of those insights, notwithstanding a few tensions here and there. Its intellectual and aesthetic appeal derive from this coherence and also from its modest posture with regard to other interpretations of human life. That is, the MSIH does not claim that it includes every worthwhile insight into human life but it does demand that consistency with it should be a goal of any more adventurous interpretation. For example, the MSIH presents human beings as religiously concerned in various ways but does not venture a position on the reality of Gods or on the efficacy of paths of liberation that correspond to those human religious concerns. Other interpretations of human beings may well take up such normative or metaphysical questions—indeed, the religious anthropology of this book does precisely that—but MSIH *as such* does not.

This posture of relative neutrality and the policy of staying close to virtually unanimously held and highly credible scientific results are the main reasons why the MSIH is simply assumed as a minimalist starting point in much contemporary intellectual life. And why not, after all? MSIH covers a lot of territory in spite of its minimalist approach and is a truly impressive cultural and intellectual achievement. Any wider interpretation of human beings that values consistency of knowledge or seeks a public forum ought to treat consonance with MSIH as a criterion of adequacy.

I contend that the constraints from the MSIH are sufficient to determine a uniquely adequate religious naturalist interpretation of the human being as *homo religiosus*. This is most definitely a theological interpretation, one going beyond the MSIH itself. It presents a pointed challenge to other theological interpretations of the human condition, insisting that they, too, strive to take full account of the MSIH. And it claims that the theological framework of religious naturalism permits a degree of harmony between religious anthropology and the MSIH that no other theological framework can match. This is the essence of this book's argument on behalf of religious naturalism: not a metaphysical case but an argument based on quality of results relative to the emerging portrayal of human beings in stakeholder disciplines. The metaphysical case can wait for another inquiry and another book.

This inquiry purports to describe human beings as *homo religiosus* in every cultural setting and in every social context. This is a hypothetical conclusion subject to correction, as is every other conclusion of a process of inquiry according to the fallibilist pragmatic theory of inquiry. But it is a conclusion with excellent credentials, thanks to its consistency with the MSIH, which also has this universal intent. It is unfashionable to speak of universal features of the human condition in an era dominated by sharp awareness of cultural and individual differences—

particularly in the humanities, in cultural anthropology, and in history, where intricate differences are all-important. But many of the social sciences and all of the natural sciences relevant to the human condition have continued their attempts to describe universal features of their subject matter. This inquiry has attempted to synthesize these two impulses, describing the universal while honoring the particular.

Two recurring themes have expressed this. The first is the idea of *constraint without determination*, which we have seen repeatedly in previous chapters. The second is the analogy with landscapes, whereby constraints describe structured possibilities corresponding to universal features of our species that cultures and individual human beings then explore (and sometimes even modify) in their uniquely creative ways. Once the vast multidimensional quality of the landscape of structured possibilities for human life is properly appreciated, there really is no problem recognizing both the constraining structuralist elements of the human condition as described in the MSIH and the mind-boggling diversity of ways in which human beings explore this space of possibilities. Universality and particularity are only at odds when there is a fight for honor and recognition. With enough space in the multidimensional landscape of life possibilities, universality actually requires particularity for its articulation, and particularity demands universality for its meaningfulness. In this way, many persistent debates between structuralist and post-structuralist impulses are honored and also held at bay, if not rendered superfluous.

This final chapter formally ends this inquiry by presenting a synthetic portrayal of the human being as *homo religiosus*. This is not so much a review of findings as a knitting together of the strands of inquiry into a frankly theological portrayal of the human condition. I then step back slightly from the inquiry itself to discuss the standing of alternative theological and anti-theological interpretations of the human condition that similarly prize consistency with the MSIH, as well as those that reject this as an appropriate goal for inquiry in religious anthropology. Finally, I step all the way back and ask about the meaning of this approach to religious anthropology in relation to the longstanding project of theologically interpreting the human condition. This involves comparing the approach of this book to the ways religious anthropology has been pursued in the past. It also involves estimating the significance of the multidisciplinary comparative approach implemented here for future inquiries in religious anthropology. All of these methodological issues warrant discussion at much greater length than is possible here. But that is not the purpose of this book. Methodological self-awareness and reflection is, in this context, quite secondary to the material findings of inquiry.

Homo Religiosus: A Synthetic Portrayal

The Cosmic and Evolutionary Backdrop

We human beings are the complex, provisional products of an ongoing process—a process channeled by law-like regularities in nature and open to chance events. This process is driven by chance variations in the genetic makeup of organisms, competition for resources within niches that make such variations relevant to the probability of reproducing healthy offspring, and then the natural selection of genetic variants that best succeed in reproducing. Realizing this about ourselves is one of the greatest intellectual achievements of all time, regardless of culture, and it has far-reaching implications for our self-understanding. The discoveries go on. The modern synthesis's assumption of one-way influence from genes to proteins has collapsed with the discovery of situations in which environment influences gene expression and proteins modify genetic structure. The ability of creatures to modify their environments in ways that alter the probability of successful reproduction by providing for novel fitness strategies has proved more widespread than formerly supposed; it is particularly obvious in builders such as beavers, hive insects, and human beings. There are selection effects across multiple species simultaneously, demonstrating the interconnectedness of animal and plant life. Communication, cooperation, and altruism are vital factors in generating novel fitness strategies at the kin-group and species levels.

Despite the fact that life is more complex than it was 1 billion years ago, there does not appear to be a clear-cut directionality in the evolutionary process. It seems to lack either a determinate goal or any kind of transcendent foresight until such foresight arises in creatures capable of deliberately influencing the evolutionary process. There is an impulse toward complexification, perhaps, but it appears to be a side-effect of emergence in complex ecologies. After all, an ever-broadening, niche-filling process of speciation entails a certain amount of increasing complexity on some evolutionary fronts. Though difficult to be sure, that statistically predictable increase in complexity may be sufficient to account for the intricate phenomena of nature. This lack of clear directional teleology underlines the fact that we are contingent through and through. Our appearance is the result of a combination of chance-like and law-like events, our physical form might have been quite different, we might not have appeared at all, and we will be superseded by better adapted species for as long as the biosphere remains habitable.

This evolutionary story takes place against a vast cosmic backdrop in which apparently independent fundamental features of nature are fine-tuned to permit life of the sort we know. Our entire universe may be one of many, perhaps infinitely many, in a multiverse, and the fact that the cosmological settings of our universe are fine-tuned for organic life may depend on that wider scheme of universes. In our own cosmic neighborhood, several generations of stars need to live and die before fusion in the heart of stars produces sufficient quantities of the heavier atoms necessary for biology and life. Even then, ecologies seem to depend on unfathomably complex interactions between variables we barely understand. However it happened, we inhabit a spinning jewel of life, rich with plants and animals, stabilized and fueled by dynamic geological processes, and built atop and within a teeming frenzy of rapidly mutating microorganisms. This, and not any spiritualized heavenly or saṃsāric abstraction, is our home.

In this planetary home, the surface feeds on the sun, continents drift atop molten rock, the watery oceans host the emergence of the biochemical machinery of life, and multicellular plant and animal species come and go. We have come and we, too, will go, though whether our species perishes at our own hand or is superseded by another remains to be seen. Love is a luxury in this home; civilizations and cultures, as old as they may seem to us, are brand new experiments in excess given the wider scheme of things. Fecundity and predation are the rules of the game and survival of our evolutionary heritage the meaning of winning—the simplest and most compelling meaning that word, winning, can have. Most of our evolutionary birthright comes directly from bacteria, archea, and protists, the microorganisms that have always dominated life in our home and that bequeathed to us the staggering city-like intricacy of intra-cellular biochemical mechanisms. The smaller but no less vital part of our evolutionary birthright comes from the large animals, mammals, and primates that are our direct evolutionary ancestors. Microorganisms are our ultimate direct ancestors, and they are still with us, but none of our immediate evolutionary ancestor species has survived. The best means we have of finding out about those long-lost direct descendents is by studying our primate cousins, a few close but most rather distant cousins.

What we learn from our animal cousins is that we have a more advanced form of the central nervous system that we observe operating in them. Watching them is like watching ourselves in a faded mirror: it is not quite the same but a lot of the behaviors seem eerily familiar. Some kind of neural breakthrough—possibly a series of protein changes that sent neuron production into overdrive, expanding cortex and multiplying neural connections—lies at the origins of our earliest recognizably modern human ancestors, probably about 50,000 years ago. These may have been people with whom we could have shared a cup of tea and enjoyed one another's company because they were cognitive sufficiently like us, though not yet cognitively the same as us. Put them in our environment from the time of birth and it is possible that they grow up much like we grow up, speak much like we speak, and probably drive cars and fly planes and eat in restaurants as well. Though evolutionary changes in human beings have continued, including in cognitive domains, the difference between them and us is mainly cultural. By about 10,000 years ago, with the onset of organized agriculture and domesticated animals, the culture and civilization engine sparked into life and has massively outpaced evolutionary change ever since. There have been significant human genetic changes in the last 10,000 years, mostly related to digestion and disease. These changes derive from human modification of natural environments such as the domestication of cows that yield milk and the clearing of land that yields mosquitoes and malaria. The few genetic changes that impacted brain function probably did not affect intelligence or personality in dramatic ways. While it is important not to overstate the point, because it is difficult to be sure, modern humans appear to have cognitive, emotional, sensory, and motor equipment that is quite similar to that of hunter-gatherer tribal people from 100 centuries ago. Human cognition has been relatively quiescent while time marches on, so now we deploy much the same brains to operate civilizations we barely understand and create technologies we can barely control.

Under these circumstances, it would not be surprising if our species were not to survive for long in this wondrous home, at least compared to the species with real staying power such as sharks and lizards and birds. But we certainly seem destined to make a difference while we are here. In the last century alone we have transformed our home ecology far more than in all of the previous 500 centuries combined. We are only just now scrambling to figure out how we did it and what price we may be doomed to pay if we push our planetary ecology too far from the comfortable center of its equilibrium dynamics. This ability to change our home profoundly burdens us with responsibility we seem ill-equipped to bear. How afraid would our evolutionary cousins and our more distant animal and plant relatives feel if they had to capacity to grasp the degree to which their fate is in our unsteady, eager hands?

The Brain–Group Nexus

How we got this way is enormously difficult to reconstruct because we cannot watch it happening and we have no other examples of life-supporting planetary ecologies to study. The neurosciences and cognitive psychology yield rich insights, though, so it is not absolutely necessary to answer the "where did we come from?" question in order to figure out who we are and how we work. It turns out that the amazing capacities of animals are a result, at least in part, of the amazing chemical properties of the brain and especially of those properties arising within, and at the synaptic clefts between, neurons. This necessity of neural processes for mentality marks an impressive advance over previous disembodied conceptions of human mental life. It has yielded tremendous advances in understanding of human development, movement, sensation, cognition, emotion, and communication.

The mysteries of mental life remain, in some ways, because the mercurial qualities of our thoughts seem so different than the physical properties of brain functions. Is biochemistry sufficient to account for everything that brains are called upon to do, including serving as the basis for personality, for responsible freedom, for the qualia of self-conscious experience, and for every other aspect of mental life? Apparently, yes. But some demur. The disagreement underlines the extent to which we remain a mystery, even and perhaps especially to ourselves. Nevertheless, we know how our state of mind changes when we crack our heads, and we can study how people's personality, cognition, memory, and behavior changes with neurodegenerative diseases, localized strokes, tumors, or medication. The brain-mind might be complicated and surprising, but it seems to be a single unit rather than two correlated processes. More generally, we appear to embody gapless continuity from the lowest, least complex level of organization of matter to the highest, most complex level of conscious experience and value awareness. Our conscious feelings are a surprising but still biological characteristic of sufficiently complex central nervous systems; no supernatural soul is necessary to explain what we are and how we work.

We understand ourselves with folk-psychological concepts, based on intelligent extrapolation from our experiences. Some concepts in our folk psychological self-descriptions appear to match natural kinds at the level of brain function, in the way that the folk concept of "learning something until it becomes second nature" neatly corresponds to the processes by which various kinds of non-declarative, non-cognitive memories are established. But others seem to find no natural correlate with brain processes and functions. For example, emotions (except fear and one or two others, perhaps) seem too diffuse in terms of brain function to be a meaningful natural kind at the neurophysiological level, and our folk concepts appear not to register the neurological fact that memory is several distinct processes rather than just one.

Apparently our folk-psychological self-understandings are often misleading. This is especially evident when we live in cultures that permit and encourage exceptionally careful evaluation of the accuracy of perceptions and beliefs. We observe visual illusions with delight, as they disclose to us the weaknesses of our perceptual-cognitive apparatus, alongside its amazing strengths. We observe limitations in our ability to form accurate beliefs with less pleasure, particularly when we find out that we are inclined to believe false things just because we want to or because others around us believe them. The mystery that we are also includes emotional impulses that we are ashamed of and try to keep secret, usually in vain because our behavior makes most of them obvious sooner or later, at least to those who know us best.

With careful attention, then, we learn that we are adaptable, anxious, and curious; led by powerful psychological drives and needs for communal identity; liable to violence, disease, and fantasy; and embodying ultimate and preliminary commitments in linguistic habits, symbolic systems, and social organizations. Our beliefs are always socially located, sometimes trivially so as not to interfere with the public standing of such knowledge, but sometimes in profound ways that make allowing for socioeconomic factors and personal motivations in assessing knowledge claims extremely difficult.

Our needs for orientation in the world and for legitimation of social practices find in our wondrous imaginations and in our capacity for symbolic manipulation a perfect match. This marks the birth of the *brain–group nexus* in its modern human form, with groups necessary for brains that recognize and brains necessary for forms of group life that we prize. In the brain–group nexus we construct complex, symbolically potent worldviews that permit many cultural activities to carry on undisturbed by questions about their legitimacy. Such automatic legitimation processes produce greater stability of economic and social systems and render us psychologically calmer and better placed to handle stressful events. All of this promotes the uninterrupted advance of scientific inquiry and a wealth of creative expression from art and architecture to zoology and Zen meditation. The hand-in-glove fit between our needs and abilities sometimes has negative consequences, such as an inhibited or perhaps repressed capacity for cultural self-criticism, fear of those beyond the boundaries of our social group, and intolerance of those within our group who do not conform to its active processes of legitimation.

At this point, insights into our ways of being in the brain–group nexus are more and more difficult to achieve and few people really understand them. This is because folk-psychological self-understandings work well for most purposes whereas more elaborate forms of self-awareness are actually disturbing in some ways; they leave us confused and worried and not sure that we can trust our own instincts. For those with the will to dig deeply into the mystery of who we are, however, these discoveries are tremendously exciting and the rewards of self-discovery far exceed the discomfort of unwelcome self-awareness. One of the more exciting-yet-disturbing discoveries is that we use the brain–group nexus to make our worlds in groups using the resources of traditions, and that the presuppositions of our world-making are received from others and usually not capable of decisive justification. We have even achieved a partial vision of the motivation for world-making: it is a matter not merely of a need for existential orientation but also of a struggle to ensure genetic self-perpetuation. This drive to genetic self-perpetuation is expressed first psychologically, in the drives for personal survival and reproduction, and then socially, in the drive for kin-group and species survival. These constraints on the brain–group nexus do not prevent enormous creativity in cultural expression, however. Indeed, it appears that the existence of biological constraints actually enhances our freedom to create cultures and build civilizations.

Awakening to the Axiological Landscape

Understanding the brain–group nexus allow us to see ourselves, and our lives in this planetary home, as journeys through a multidimensional landscape of possibilities. Evolutionary biology and our home ecology set up the landscape and constrain the possible individual and group movements within it. Our cognitive-emotional equipment makes some behavioral problems common and other behavioral possibilities desirable, and in this way we establish ideal norms for behavior. We enshrine these ideals in our groups, along with techniques for achieving or approximating them, and that wisdom is passed along through traditions much as knowledge of how to weave baskets or catch fish is passed along. We thus open up a world of values, which is where we derive so much of the meaning of our lives. This axiological world constrains the landscape of life possibilities just as physical environment and evolutionary heritage do. Beauty, goodness, and truth inspire us and lure us, and we are fascinated by the particularity of these transcendental ideals. A particular person is beautiful to us, or a particular landscape; beauty in general seems to escape our grasp like sand running through fingers. We are also fascinated by the diverse particularities of values, as when we have moral disagreements over right and fair behavior.

Our landscape of life possibilities is suffused with value. The complex, multifaceted quality of those values is ultimately what we mean to refer to when, in a host of ways, we declare that life is somehow sacred or mysterious. Sometimes the mystery is awesome, like a cavernous abyss that would blindly swallow us up without a thought for our welfare. Other times the mystery seems attentive, almost customized to our interests, and reality feels gracious to us. Our cognitive-emotional makeup tends decisively to produce fear of one and love of the other, and readily personalizes and cosmologizes these open-ended aspects of the axiological depths of nature as demonic and divine.

It is at this point that we need to heed the critiques of the projective and illusionist elements of ethics and religion. All of these critiques rightly portray us as bundles of drives and impulses grouped in dense relational networks with other such bundles, possessing both the need and the means to construct interpretations of the world that are good for orienting ourselves within it and for managing our group life. The projective impulse leads us to anthropomorphize our experiences of the axiological depth structures and dynamics of nature, in an attempt to gain a kind of cognitive handle on them. This is how we get so deeply invested in religious worldviews, myths, and rituals. Our psychological needs for orientation to the world and for social stability arise from our evolutionary drives and depend on our projective impulses operating within the brain–group nexus for their satisfaction, so we have little incentive to deconstruct these projective and illusionist processes. Our religious concepts of ultimacy—God, Karma, Dao, Enlightenment—are born in these processes and have a profound regulative effect on social life. They legitimate religious-moral rules by weaving them into narratives that are broad enough to embrace ideas about nature and history. Such narratives effectively furnish existential orientation and comfort as well as group purpose and identity.

Some of us naturally wonder whether it might ever be possible to show somehow that the concepts of God, Karma, Dao, or Enlightenment correspond to the real structure of the axiological depths of nature that we engage as we generate our value-laden social worlds and meaning-infused life journeys. A few make philosophical arguments about this greatest of spiritual questions. But most of us access such concepts unreflectively, automatically making use of whichever of them our local environment supplies in order to cope with life challenges and to enjoy life opportunities. Some rebel prophets want to raise consciousness and deliver all of us from the grip of illusions sustained by narratives built around our anthropomorphic ultimacy concepts. But most of us instinctively sense that the critiques are too strident. They betray a hidden agenda of painfully scrupulous asceticism, and we would prefer to have more fun than these passionate prophets would allow. Meanwhile, we all journey, in our groups and in some respects alone, in limited bodies with astonishingly creative and self-transcending imaginative powers, across the multi-dimensional landscape of value-infused life possibilities. We engage the depths of nature as we go, taking it all in through our bodies, our senses, and our sensitivity to value. We act to transform our habitat and mold the world after the fashion of our dreams, all the while wondering what it all means.

It follows from this that human beings are religious and spiritual creatures not only historically, culturally, and circumstantially, but also ontologically, essentially, and inescapably. In this sense, therefore, we are *homo religiosus*, and we will remain so as long as the axiological depths of nature afford us opportunities in the brain–group nexus to exercise creative self-expression as we engage those depths. Our species started to become *homo religiosus* as we gradually awoke to the axiological depth structures and dynamics of our natural environment, transforming it into home and playground. We became *homo religiosus* more decisively about 50,000 years ago with the crucial neurological changes that gave birth to modern human beings. We will remain *homo religiosus* even if the statistically and historically dominant supernatural and myth-laden forms of religion eventually decline at the hands of its currently subordinate religious naturalist symbiotic partner. And we will remain *homo religious* even if supernatural and myth-laden forms of religion in the conventional, narrower sense always remain historically and statistically dominant. We are *homo religiosus* not because of what we do in religious groups or in our spiritual solitude but because of who we are in evolutionary and axiological perspective.

The Standing of Alternative Interpretations

Varieties of Synthetic Interpretations of the Human Condition

Implied throughout the book, and now made completely explicit in this concluding chapter, is the distinction between the impressive (though not perfect) consensus around a modern secular interpretation of humanity (the MSIH) and theological elaborations of this consensus that address questions about the ultimate meaning and value of human life. This is not a completely sharp distinction, because keeping description and evaluation entirely separated is not feasible. For instance, I count the description of the axiological realm engaged in human experience as part of the MSIH even though it pertains to values—surely a grey area expressing my bias toward keeping the humanities in the interpretative picture with the biological and human sciences in trying to forge multidisciplinary understanding of the human condition. But recognizing the presence of values in human life is not the same as evaluating the ultimate meaning and value of human life. Thus, the distinction between the MSIH and theological elaborations of it is sharp enough to justify its use.

We would do well to invoke the distinction between MSIH and theological elaborations of it more often. In particular, anti-religious interpretations of the human condition are sometimes treated as following immediately and trivially from acceptance of the MSIH, to the point that the distinction is suppressed. The hastiness of such approaches can be demonstrated by positioning the MSIH in religiously positive theoretical contexts. I have offered a bivalent (religiously positive and religiously critical) theological elaboration of the MSIH, within a religious naturalist framework, but there are other religious anthropologies in quite different frameworks. All of them go beyond the scope of MSIH by venturing judgments about the ultimate meaning and value of human life, which the MSIH as delimited here does not do. The presupposed worldviews of the class of theological anthropologies so defined is rather diverse and includes some that many traditionally religious people might find alarming or distasteful. They range from profound atheism to Qur'anic monotheism, from Nietzschean perspectivalism in a meaningless world to traditional Buddhist accounts of suffering, no-self, and liberation.

As a religious naturalist, I do not hesitate to regard all such ventures as theological, even when they are bluntly anti-religious, because theology in my framework is not God-talk but ultimate-concern-talk. This reclassifies as "theological" all of the most interesting anti-religious anthropologies, such as the atheistic-existentialist ones heavily invested in the concept of authenticity. Religious people may judge it Trojan-horse foolishness to speak of theological anthropology so generously, since it brings anti-religious critiques into the theological city walls. But this is a matter of indifference to a religious naturalist. Moreover, this approach effectively draws attention to the theological commitments of anti-religious interpretations of human life. More than that, this richer scenario for theological anthropology enables us realistically to register the power and delicacy of the best of the so-called anti-religious views. For example, we find in some atheist existentialists an impressive kind of authentic fury or resignation, directed toward or at least caused by a cosmos that condemns us to an unfulfillable desire for fulfillment (as in Jean Paul Sartre). This is as profound a response to the environment of human life as can be found and, in respect of criteria bearing on ultimate concern, it is as religious as the most spiritual worship. More recently, the anti-religious or partially anti-religious views of the human condition expressed in Richard Dawkins (2007), Daniel Dennett (2006), and most others among the so-called new atheist writers are theological views because to some degree they address evaluative questions about the ultimate meaning of human life.

Having opened the floodgates to every type of synthetic theological extension of the MSIH that registers ultimate concerns, regardless of presupposed worldview, is there any way to conceptualize the variation of possible viewpoints that result? I suspect there is, and in at least the two ways discussed in what follows.

First, it is possible to parse the range of theological anthropologies that prize consistency with the MSIH in terms of their characteristic weaknesses. The weaknesses in extant syntheses tend to fall into several categories:

- the failure to register traditional religious wisdom about the human condition, as when the problems of human suffering and weakness are neglected;
- the failure to register the impact of the biological sciences, as when too much directionality in the evolutionary process is assumed to ease theological pressure for a purposeful natural order, or the roles of bodies in defining the meaning of the human condition are minimized;

- the failure to register the insights of the social sciences, as when the demonstrated realities of projection, delusion, and social legitimation are minimized for the sake of uncomplicated theological access to the testimony of religious experience and tradition;
- the failure to come to terms with the diversity of competitive theological anthropologies, as when one account does not acknowledge competitor accounts.

The first three problems represent failures of disciplinary integration of a specific sort, focused on the humanities, the biological sciences, and the social sciences, respectively. It is striking how clear the judgment of a religious anthropology typically is in respect of whether or not each of these three weaknesses occurs. It seems that, once the theologian begins confronting the relevant questions—say, about directionality in the evolutionary process, about embodiment, or about the social construction of reality—the effect on the religious anthropology is quite pronounced and predictable. In short, theologians typically press to minimize the meaning of the brain–group nexus and maximize cosmic and evolutionary intelligence. Both moves are fundamentally evasive. This is evidence that the MSIH exercises a reliable and consistent impact on religious anthropologies, and also that striving for consistency with the MSIH should induce some degree of convergence within religious anthropology.

The fourth problem is extremely widespread. In fact, it is rare to see a religious anthropology engaging a wide range of alternatives from across the world religions (but see Ward 1998, a welcome exception to this trend). The problem exists partly because theological projects that include comparative and multidisciplinary components have only recently been attempted. This is an historical circumstance that can be changed with appropriate shifts in interest and training.

A second and more positive way to conceptualize the variety of religious anthropologies is to parse the approaches that prize harmony with the MSIH in terms of major approaches to this synthesis. Each approach involves provisional acceptance of one of two theses, which are listed in what follows with several sub-theses attached to each one.

Thesis I: *The essence of humanity is expressed in its world environment and relations, so the MSIH gives accurate and indispensable insights into human life and human nature.* This approach appears in at least these two forms:

- IA. All nature including humanity is oriented to a mystery that has the qualities of a super-nature (found in some varieties of the following: divinization approaches, philosophical Taoism, process versions of panentheism, …).
- IB. All mystery is limited to nature and its ground—there is no super-nature (found in some varieties of the following: secular humanism, religious naturalism, …).

Thesis II: *The essence of humanity is not expressed in its world environment and relations, so the MSIH gives a misleading account of human life and human nature.* Synthesis in this case consists in accounting for MSIH in the process of laying out a more complete interpretation of human beings. Again, there are at least two approaches here:

- IIA. Proper discrimination discloses a higher purpose for humanity to which theological anthropology should testify (found in some varieties of the following: perennial philosophy, supernaturalistic liberation schemes, most tribal traditions, …).
- IIB. Proper discrimination discloses that humanity has no essence, is nothing finally namable and nothing in particular; simply to realize this fully is to free oneself, to be happy and at peace (found in some varieties of the following: Buddhism, Advaita Vedanta, …).

The first sub-thesis in each pair (IA and IIA) posits a super-nature in one or another form while the second posits no super-nature, giving the four options a grid-like quality as shown in Table 2.

Table 2   Classification of broad types of religious anthropology

	Super-nature: YES	Super-nature: NO
MSIH accurate, indispensable	IA	IB
MSIH limited, misleading	IIA	IIB

These theses and the classes of major worldviews they configure draw fresh attention to a problem of arbitrariness in religious anthropology. It is genuinely difficult to justify one approach decisively over the others. Scant attention has been paid to this problem among theologians who articulate large-scale interpretations of the human condition. All of these ways of interpreting human life have good prospects of rendering themselves consonant with the MSIH, though in the quite different ways required in each case. And each type of approach has good prospects of achieving consistency with traditional religious wisdom, at least as such wisdom expressed in a single religious tradition (consistency with multiple religious traditions is more difficult). Each would find, however, that some parts of the MSIH are easier to absorb than others and that the harder-to-digest parts would make less plausible some aspects of familiar religious wisdom while not affecting others. Tracking such plausibility shifts may offer leverage on the extremely difficult question of how to resolve disputes among the varied approaches to religious anthropology (this approach is defended in Wildman 2006a, and its efficacy demonstrated in Wildman 2008a).

For example, can the MSIH can be consistently combined with the implications of such religious ideas as soul (or *jiva*), reincarnation, creation in the image of

God, *anatta* (no-soul), spirit possession, exorcism, or the veneration of ancestors? This would be extremely difficult, at best, but some may facilitate compatibility more easily than others. What about religious experience, sanctification, holiness, spiritual bliss, the dark night of the soul, prayer, spiritual gifts, prophecy, *wu-wei* (active non-action), flowing with *ch'i* (energy), healing power, prophetic knowledge, or extra-sensory perception? Is MSIH consonant with being under the command of God, receiving the law of God, being in harmony with the mandate of heaven, or encountering the Word of God? What about sin, salvation, *saṃsāra* (the process of reincarnation), *mokṣa* (liberation), *duḥkha* (suffering), *nirvana*, atonement, or divine forgiveness? Each list of religious ideas, in addition to being internally inconsistent, seems profoundly at odds with the MSIH. Any quest for consistency would be challenging but it is likely that some sets of ideas will fare better than others.

Synthesizing the Modern Secular Interpretation of Humanity and Traditional Religious Wisdom

It is worth asking at this point why we should pay any attention to such religious ideas in the process of trying to formulate adequate interpretations of human beings. Why not follow Dawkins and Dennett and resolve the problems of mutual inconsistency and dissonance with the MSIH simply by discounting traditional religious anthropological ideas as nonsense or fantasy, toxic or functional as the case may be? Theologians are well acquainted with the way religious symbols function in the lives of people and this typically leads them to an intriguing conclusion: religious symbols express significant wisdom about human nature, even if sometimes in arcane or fantastic language. Moreover, the competent use of such symbolic resources transforms human lives in impressive ways. The transformative and orienting power for billions of people worldwide of such religious symbols is *prima facie* evidence that their claim to express wisdom should be taken seriously, even if the various metaphysical vehicles should be reformed. Indeed, out of their familiarity with the wisdom of religious traditions, theologians throw their own challenge at anyone developing wider interpretations of human beings: can the virtues, including the efficacy, of traditional religious wisdom be registered, even if in dramatically translated and revalued terms?

The usefulness of the MSIH for resolving seemingly intractable disputes among religious anthropologies depends fundamentally on its public and crosscultural character, together with its relative religious neutrality. Consistency with the MSIH is a criterion for theoretical adequacy that promotes rational discriminations among religious anthropologies. For example, the joint message of physical cosmology and evolutionary biology is that religious anthropologies electing to centralize the human species in a cosmo-historico-theological narrative (such as most forms of Christianity and Islam) will have a harder time with the MSIH than those that do not (such as some forms of Hinduism and Buddhism). Obviously, the criterion of consistency with the MSIH will not prove useful in every situation.

Nor is it the only available tool for making progress on apparently intractable theological conflicts, as the growing technologies of comparison and the long-standing effectiveness of criteria such as internal consistency and theoretical economy demonstrate. Nevertheless, the MSIH promises to be especially useful because it selects out aspects of religious anthropologies as preferable regardless of tradition, and because any one tradition is unlikely to be decisively favored in this process of discrimination. The challenge then becomes how to coordinate the MSIH-preferred insights into a coherent religious anthropology. That has been one of the tasks of this book, though the dialogue with the specific details of theological traditions has been relatively less developed than the dialogue with stakeholder disciplines.

An appeal to the plausibility structures of the MSIH, even as prudently minimal as they are, can be contested. That is the point of the second thesis, above. But even in that case the theologian must explain the core insights of the MSIH, if only to say in detail how they are misleading or how they define a conventional reality that masks some other, truer reality. For example, theological anthropologies that assume a non-physical basis for human personhood under the aegis of concepts such as soul or *jiva* will have a hard time with the MSIH's bet on physicalism. But this tendency of the MSIH allows intelligible dissent in the form of a counter-bet that physicalism is mistaken. Indeed, the religious naturalist theological anthropology presented here dissents from the strictest forms of physicalism in insisting on axiological components of reality. But dissenters need to show, as I have here, how the MSIH's reasons for its physicalist propensities can be taken account of while still resisting strict metaphysical materialism.

Organizing these major interpretations into categories highlights some of the choices that need to be made—or that are made unawares—when a theologian attempts to synthesize a religious anthropology with the MSIH. The main choice is between Thesis I and Thesis II, obviously. The key to understanding this choice is the fact that the conflict between the two major approaches is a dispute not over the truth of the MSIH but over its status as knowledge. Thesis I holds that the MSIH is accurate and straightforwardly true and demands nothing less than consistency from any religious anthropology. Thesis II, by contrast, argues that the most discriminating account of human nature takes the MSIH to be a valid but preliminary insight for which one must account without being misled into according it definitive status. On Thesis II, therefore, it would be enough to explain why the world *appears* in such a way as to make the MSIH so persuasive.

In practice, many who hold views consistent with Thesis II display little interest in questions of consistency of their theological anthropologies with the MSIH. This is for the obvious reason, as the Buddha himself might have put it, that when the house is burning and you finally realize that you need to flee, you don't pause on the way out in a fit of scientific curiosity to analyze yourself in the mirror. Nevertheless, these views would be much strengthened if a persuasive account could be given of why the world shows up for us humans in the way that the MSIH recounts, an account that does more than preemptively appeal to "suchness" (i.e. "that is just the way things are") or similar inquiry-stopping concepts. The omission of any treatment of so powerful a view of human beings as the MSIH seems deeply suspect, though in some cultural contexts it may be the result merely of lack of interest. The lack of interest in Buddhist circles has begun to change in recent decades; witness the descendents of the Kyoto School and Msao Abe, and the western followers of the Dalai Lama. The Abrahamic traditions, especially most branches of Christianity, have a long history of tangling with the sciences.

The problem of choosing between Thesis I and Thesis II can only be resolved, I think, by hypothetically adopting one or the other in order to test the feasibility of each. As Hans Georg Gadamer might put it, in a situation such as this, the energy of personal perspective is necessary for driving the process by which horizons are fused and thereby (in this case) the character of humanity disclosed. For my part, the religious anthropology presented here sought a synthesis of traditional theological insights with the MSIH in provisional conformity with the first thesis. In other research, I try to develop a more fundamental theory of human knowledge and ultimate reality that is capable of explaining how the dispute between the two theses can continue to seem intractable. My heart is with the approach of Thesis II, but I believe that I can use a Thesis II approach subsequently to reframe the preliminary Thesis I approach presented in this book, without loss or inconsistency. That, however, requires an account of ultimate reality to complement the account of the human condition furnished here, and that is deferred to a companion volume.

Everyone, surely, no matter which approach is to bear the effects of their energies, should carefully consider the arguments on behalf of striving for a detailed synthesis of traditional religious and modern secular wisdom about humanity. We may decide that the retrieval of a few scraps of traditional religious anthropology is finally the best we can do because MSIH sets so demanding a standard. Or we may try to relativize MSIH as a limited vision of human beings. We could then reintroduce souls perhaps as supervenient or emergent or even supernatural characteristics of sufficiently complex organisms, after which we may be able to retrieve a good deal of traditional religious anthropology. I certainly will not attempt such aggressive projects of tradition retrieval. Religious naturalism does not require it and in fact aims to challenge such metaphysically elaborate viewpoints on the grounds that they do no explanatory work.

The Relentless Difficulty of Synthesis

The MSIH, as construed here, is formally neutral to the question of the reality of religious objects and the ultimate meaning of religious life, concerning itself only with the function, efficacy, and causal properties of religious feelings and ideas, languages and activities. At least the MSIH intends to be neutral to such questions, and surely realizes this intention to a significant degree. Yet, precisely because of the relatively impressive way it handles what is in its domain, the MSIH can be used in theoretical valuations of religion to argue both that religion is *nothing other than* mental states, social dynamics, natural functions, and causes;

and that people only ever think differently by mistake. The MISH can also be used to mount religiously affirmative evaluations of human life. Or, as in the case of the argument of this book, the MSIH can be deployed both to critique religion and affirm it, in different respects.

This account of the relation between the MISH and wider theological interpretations of the human condition might suggest that religious anthropology can yield as much ground as necessary to MSIH without any fear of contradiction or conflict. After all, the final and all-important interpretative step of theological evaluation still remains open for either religiously affirmative theological anthropology carried off in the name of some home religious tradition, or reductionist critiques of religion carried off in the name of fidelity to the values of secular humanism. This finding would be reassuring to those who develop religious anthropologies by articulating and defending the core commitments of one or another religious tradition. They might rejoice in the way theological elaborations of the MSIH seem to divide into distinct language games. Their only obligations would be to make sure that their tradition-guided theological anthropologies are consistent with the most strongly attested points in MSIH and to conduct courteous dialogue with those defending alternative theological anthropologies. They would be safe from the specter of conflict and free from the awkwardness of logical traction between opposing theological interpretations.

In fact, this way of seeing matters is correct up to a point. A sufficiently sharp distinction between the descriptive value of the MSIH and the evaluative purposes of theological interpretations of the human condition really does serve to allow each theological interpretation a degree of independence from competitor views, so long as consistency with the MSIH is first achieved. But it is tempting for theological interpreters—both pro-religious and anti-religious—to claim this independence hastily. Throughout this book I have tried to show that the MSIH imposes quite stringent requirements on theological interpretations of the human condition, requirements that are rather difficult to meet. In fact, I pointed out numerous ways in which traditional theological anthropologies, including even contemporary efforts, fail to meet the requirements of the MSIH. I also pointed out the failure of some anti-religious, reductionist religious anthropologies (recall that this is what they are in my broad sense of the term) to take proper empirical account of the axiological structures of reality that are engaged and created in human endeavors. The MSIH is a demanding dialogue partner and consistency with it or even reasoned resistance to it is difficult to achieve. Taking this point seriously helps to avoid the trivialization of both properly reductionistic critiques of religion and insights about the human condition encoded in longstanding religious wisdom traditions.

One of the ways traditional religious anthropologies attempt to secure an account of the ultimate meaning and value of human life is to define some essentially religious or spiritual aspect of human reality that is somehow secure from invasion by insights from the MSIH. Correspondingly, one measure of the awkwardness of the MSIH is that it offers a provisional account of *every* aspect of human reality and religion—from pious feelings to rational belief, from personal conversion to corporate rituals, from ethical power to achieved sainthood. This leaves no *special* ground for traditional theological anthropologies to stand, be they cognitive-metaphysical visions of souls and salvation, or pragmatic-epistemic processes of transformation.

Western Enlightenment critiques of religion left ground open for nineteenth-century religious romantics to build reactionary theological anthropologies on, say, feeling rather than thinking, or subjectivity rather than objectivity. But MSIH leaves no ground untilled. Neither the domains of emotion, will, or intellect, nor the loci of individual or society are left as distinctive turf for specifically religious anthropology. Neither Kierkegaard's radical subjectivity of religious awareness nor Lovejoy's objectivity of the human position in the great chain of being is left untouched, so neither can be promulgated as the characteristic, "non-secular" heart of theological anthropology. Neither Tillich's ecstatic reception of revelation, nor Rahner's apprehension of an infinitely mysterious horizon, nor Śaṅkara's cultivation of discrimination, nor Bhavaviveka's process of liberation from the illusions of conventional reality, nor the Qur'anic portrayal of humanity submitting to the command of God, nor the Jewish conception of a covenant expressed in the giving of the law to Jews, nor the Chinese ideal of harmonious existence in the flow of the Dao, nor the mystic's supra-rational experiences—none of these ideas has proved impervious to analysis and explanation within the MSIH. The MSIH's invasion, if it must be so called, has been spectacular and comprehensive and there appears to be nothing to prevent this invasion from being exhaustive as well. Though it must be admitted that the MSIH can handle objective features of human existence with more comfort than subjective ones, and causal features more easily than axiological features, not even the most inward subjectivity or the most complex value structures are beyond its interpretative reach, at least in *some* respects.

It follows that there is no simple strategy for checking the MSIH, or for blocking reductionist critiques of religion, as there might be if religious anthropology could be given some distinctive locus in human nature, out of reach of the MSIH. It also follows that the force of properly reductionist critiques of religion as an aspect of the human condition does not depend on contradictions between religious and modern secular readings of human nature that might later be overcome. The purveyors of these critiques are happy enough (and usually right) to point out the respects in which traditional religious anthropologies express ignorance of, or mistaken judgments about, human nature (as perhaps in the case of traditional theological usage of the concepts of "soul" or "ecstasy" or "revelation"). Moreover, the most viable critiques of religion no longer need religion for their very self-definition, as atheistic or anti-religious views did at one time. Rather, these critiques derive from stable and independent interpretations of reality that can be turned to the criticism of religion or not, as desired. Ironically, then, reductionist critiques of religion have outgrown their shrill, anti-religious origins to become mere components of large-scale interpretations of human life with enough poise to appreciate and absorb the wisdom of certain aspects of traditional theological anthropologies, subsuming what is deemed valuable and dispensing with the rest.

Given these features of the MSIH, how should we assess the relative strength of traditional theological anthropologies and the anti-religious theological extensions of the religiously neutral MSIH? On the one hand, anti-religious theological interpretations of humanity, being valuational, normative, and recent elaborations of the MSIH, achieve consistency with that well-attested vision more easily. Traditional theological anthropologies, being far older and thus bearing many concepts that are foreign to the MSIH, must painfully struggle toward a new synthesis. Moreover, anti-religious interpretations of human life are able to a considerable extent to subsume the traditional wisdom of their religious counterparts. And they can explain the existence of religiously supportive theological anthropologies as intellectually framed legitimation of the processes by which religions shield humanity from full awareness of the stark truth about itself: that religion is a by-product of the self-referential entanglement of humanity in its confused need to secure protection from the chaos and boredom of life. Traditional theological anthropologies are significantly marginalized in contemporary intellectual life, to the point that asserting them appears arcane or reactionary or even completely arbitrary, because these theological interpretations struggle to achieve even minimal consistency with the MSIH. It is the comprehensiveness of the MSIH in conjunction with the appeal of Ockham's metaphysically minimalistic razor that makes the critiques leveraging the MSIH so potent. No wonder so many contemporary religious anthropologies with allegiance to particular religious traditions withdraw from the fray and depend heavily on a Wittgensteinian language-game strategy or on the fundamentalist reversion to forms of absolutized authority to justify their terminology and assertions.

On the other hand, traditional religious anthropologies embody a tremendous amount of wisdom about spiritual life, the agonies of suffering and guilt, the cultivation of personal maturity, and the honing of human consciousness and behavior. Anti-religious interpretations of human beings have not yet found ways to incorporate enough of these vast bodies of wisdom because the MSIH has not either; both are behind the curve in this respect. Moreover, if traditional theological anthropologies could be rendered in terms compatible with those of the MSIH—a virtue the recent anti-religious interpretations possess more easily in virtue of their being born in the era of MSIH and often spurred into life by the MSIH—the advantage of the anti-religious theological visions just described would be neutralized. Given the pervasiveness of the MSIH in scientifically informed cultures, therefore, traditional theological anthropologies have a lot riding on forging and testing syntheses with the MSIH.

Religious Anthropology, Past and Future

The demonstration of a close fit between the religious anthropology presented here and the MSIH answers the challenge articulated in the preceding section, namely, that religiously affirmative theological anthropologies are at a disadvantage, and culturally largely irrelevant, until they demonstrate consistency with the MSIH. But the religious naturalist framework of this religious anthropology is not directly supportive of the institutional interests and intellectual projects of established religious traditions. Indeed, even though the religious naturalist framework supplies a humanistic and spiritual basis for speaking of the ultimate meaning and environment of human life, as befits a theologically serious religious anthropology, traditional critics would happily argue that my approach to religion, which is sometimes quite critical, indicates a failure truly to recognize religious wisdom about the human condition. While I would reply that criticism of religion is not at all opposed to recognizing wisdom in religion, I do recognize a more serious point in this criticism, which I shall address in what follows.

The profound question that religious traditions present as a challenge to a religious anthropology of my naturalist sort is this: Is there not grave danger in synthesizing religious anthropology and the MSIH? The attempt at synthesis mistakenly presupposes that religious anthropology and the MSIH are commensurable accounts of human nature, if only because they can be deemed to be consonant or dissonant with one another. Under this false assumption (so goes this strong version of a Thesis-II viewpoint), seeking a synthesis with the MSIH may well induce even the most faithful religious people in ever-widening circles to regard the traditional theological anthropologies of their religious groups as arbitrary and intellectually unattractive, even though the legitimacy of religious anthropologies should be established by their efficacy within the life worlds that support them. That is, seeking a synthesis with the MSIH would be both intellectually wrongheaded and needlessly destructive of sacred and vital religious life worlds. Preserving the integrity of the religious life world is the overriding value.

On this view, it would be better in religious circles to reject the criteria for rational discourse that force theologians to pay attention to the MSIH if that is what preserving the integrity of the religious life world requires. Doing that rationally is quite easy, given the way that the MSIH encodes an ideology of secular reason without proper argument. The secular academy's way of thinking about the human condition cannot justify its own foundational premises, and similarly circular community-oriented theological interpretations of the human person should not be held to a higher or different standard of rational discourse (an argument expressed forcefully in Milbank 2006). According to this critique, therefore, we must reject the assumption of the value of a search for a synthesis between the MSIH and religious anthropology. Instead of a synthesis, what is needed is the maintenance of an alternative life world, one not in thrall to the science-oriented worldview that is expressed in the minimalism and even in the religious neutrality of the MSIH, and one in which religious wisdom about the human condition can be spoken of freely and with conviction, regardless of what other interpretations of life are offered elsewhere. Both the MSIH and religious anthropology have their place within cultural-linguistic life worlds and the effectiveness of the orientation to life thereby achieved is the only criterion for adequacy of such life worlds.

I am skeptical about this argument. Such an approach to the preservation of religious wisdom about human life will have diminishing returns because life worlds leak: they are never the secure, insulated bubbles of discourse that this argument ultimately requires. On the contrary, some degree of intersubjective debate and conversation is the only way to keep any particular bubble intact and viable for defining a life world for groups of people. Historical accounts of communities bear this out. A critical consistency with MSIH is therefore a *practical necessity*. Moreover, this argument gives up too quickly on inquiry, supposing that it is pointless even to seek a critically consistent coordination of sometimes divergent worldviews. But how can this be known in advance? The possibility of a synthesis can only be assessed through extensive attempts to forge one. Thus, the synthesis of religious wisdom with the MSIH is an important goal for all kinds of religious anthropology. The MSIH and religious anthropology are commensurable *enough* that anything less than synthesis will not be intellectually or practically viable.

The final reply to this important criticism from traditional theological anthropologies is the most direct but potentially also the most thought-provoking. The religious naturalist anthropology offered here is not ventured on behalf of any particular religious tradition past or present. Its social context is the secular academy, which is increasingly a global social system with shared standards for excellence, and its disciplinary identity is a form of philosophy of religion conceived as multidisciplinary comparative inquiry. Even if the critique from traditional theological anthropology was sound—and I have argued that it is not— it has slender claim on this project.

It follows that this project articulates a possibility for theological reflection that is profoundly different from the options evident in almost all extant theological work, without being directly opposed to that body of work. Theology is normally done within a religious tradition, by members of that tradition, and in support of that tradition's institutional and intellectual interests. The theology developed in this book belongs not to a religious tradition but to the secular academy, and the theology proceeds by means of multidisciplinary comparative inquiry rather than by confessional elaboration of a deposit of faith or constructive extension of a tradition of theological debate. This kind of theology is not thereby free of institutional obligations and potential blind spots; on the contrary, the secular academy throws up challenges to inquiry of this sort regularly. In this case, the most obvious gamble and the most obvious potential problem is the commitment to consistency with the MSIH, as discussed in the previous section. Subtler but no less important is the danger that full recognition of the axiological dimensions of the human life habitat will be suppressed because they are more awkward topics for scientific treatment. But the secular academy includes humanists as well as social and natural scientists in part to prevent such a disaster from occurring.

It may seem odd to use the word "theology" to describe this type of inquiry. Indeed, I confess that this is an intentionally provocative usage, though not thereby inaccurate. Elsewhere, in an extensive methodological treatment of this type of inquiry (Wildman 2009), I use the phrase "religious philosophy" instead. There I discuss the relations between religious philosophy, understood as multidisciplinary comparative inquiry, and each of philosophy, theology, and religious studies, drawing out the affiliations and differences in each case. This book steers clear of methodological discussions about the feasibility of this type of inquiry and rather simply exhibits it. On this basis, at the end of this book, I venture to suggest that theological anthropology, in the mode of religious philosophy as multidisciplinary comparative inquiry, opens or reopens a vital avenue of discourse within the secular academy. This is an important possibility for inquiry in a social context that has too often neglected the full range of questions that pertain to the human condition. It promises to produce integrated interpretations arcing across the humanities and the sciences, joining theoretical disciplines with the professional crafts of law, medicine, and divinity. Most importantly, it also promises to create appreciation—both among religions for the value of secular interpretations of human life and among secular university researchers for the value of wisdom encoded in religious traditions.

Conclusion

I have presented a religious anthropology that exhibits thoroughgoing consistency with the modern secular interpretation of humanity (MSIH) in a naturalist and humanist framework. This theological elaboration of the MSIH takes with complete seriousness both the accrued wisdom that tradition-specific religious anthropologies attempt to preserve and the critiques of religious behaviors, beliefs, and experiences that arise in anti-religious theological anthropologies. The fundamental hypothesis of this theological anthropology is that the human being is *homo religiosus*. This means that we are oriented to primordial, ultimate mystery in our experiences, our social practices, our drives and projective impulses, our longings and failures, our malevolence and love; and that we are so not only historically, culturally, or circumstantially, but also ontologically, essentially, and inescapably. The religious naturalist framework delivers an interpretation of this primordial mystery as the valuational depth structures and flowing dynamics of nature, which we engage in a host of ways in every aspect of our lives. I attempted to evaluate and justify this hypothesis against both extant religious wisdom and the MSIH.

The result is not a spiritual narrative on a par with those that gave us the Four Noble Truths of Buddhism, the Four Spiritual Laws of Evangelical Christianity, the Five Pillars of Islam, or the Ten Commandments of Judaism. The anti-*supra*naturalist framework of this view rules out the conception of ultimate reality as a determinate divine entity just as its anti-*super*naturalism rules out discarnate entities, so the resources available for narrative construction are sorely (but pleasingly) limited relative to those of traditional religious traditions. This religious anthropology sponsors a narrative nonetheless, as laid out earlier in this concluding chapter. To those with ears to hear, this is a more deeply satisfying story, both intellectually and spiritually, because of its exceptional realism, its full recognition of the manifold ways that human beings navigate their biologically constrained and socially conditioned life landscapes, and its refusal to stipulate one way of salvation or liberation so as to consolidate religious authority.

Nevertheless, given what has been said throughout the book about the role of religion in legitimating the social construction of reality, exercising powerful mechanisms of social control to do so, this approach to religious anthropology, and to theology generally, appears far from ideologically innocent. The religious naturalism of this viewpoint, as well as its cautious demand to tear away the socially constructed and religiously maintained veils of ignorance that obscure full self-awareness, make it politically and religiously potent. Who deploys this viewpoint, as well as how it is deployed, must therefore remain questions of the first concern for anyone who has learned the lessons of the past and remains vigilant about the effects of powerful ideas and the masking of power under the guise of neutral descriptions.

In particular, I frankly acknowledge that many theological representatives of religious traditions, while possibly interested in the argument of this book, might hesitate to commend it to their own intellectual communities in good faith as an example to follow. Its naturalistic religious framework is too awkward a metaphysical partner for theology in most forms. Despite this, I remain cautiously confident that full theological engagement with the rousing consensus around the modern secular interpretation of humanity will produce tendencies in any religious anthropology that harmonize with the tendencies this engagement has inspired in the present religious anthropology. For the manifold reasons discussed in this book, religious naturalism is highly unlikely to win the day in competition with the religions of our world, at least for the foreseeable future. But I dare to hope that the view of human beings as *homo religiosus* that it sponsors can exercise a healthy influence both on religious traditions resistant to naturalism and on secular research institutions resistant to religion.

Cited Works

Alper, Matthew. 1996. *The "God" Part of the Brain: A Scientific Interpretation of Human Spirituality and God*. New York: Rogue Press.

Alston, William P. 1991. *Perceiving God: The Epistemology of Religious Experience*. Ithaca, NY: Cornell University Press.

Alter, M. 1994. *Resurrection Psychology: An Understanding of Human Personality Based on the Life and Teachings of Jesus*. Chicago: Loyola University Press.

Althaus-Reid, Marcella. 2001. *Indecent Theology: Theological Perversions in Sex, Gender and Politics*. New York: Routledge.

—. 2003. *The Queer God*. New York: Routledge.

Armitage, C.J. 2004. "Evidence that Implementation Intentions Reduce Dietary Fat Intake: A Randomized Trial." *Health Psychology* 23: 319–323.

—. 2006. "Evidence that Implementation Intentions Promote Transitions Between the Stages of Change." *Journal of Consulting and Clinical Psychology* 74: 141–151.

Atran, Scott. 2001. "The Cognitive and Evolutionary Roots of Religion," pp. 181–207 in McNamara 2006.

—. 2002. *In Gods We Trust: The Evolutionary Landscape of Religion*. New York: Oxford University Press.

—. 2004. "Mishandling Suicide Terrorism." *The Washington Quarterly* 27/3 (Summer): 67–90.

—. 2006. "The Moral Logic and Growth of Suicide Terrorism." *The Washington Quarterly* 29/2 (Spring): 127–147.

—. 2008. "Who becomes a Terrorist Today?" *Perspectives on Terrorism* 2/5 (March): 3–10.

Aukst-Margetic, B.; Jakovljevic, M.; Margetic, B.; Biscan, M.; Samija, M. 2005. "Religiosity, Depression and Pain in Patients with Breast Cancer." *General Hospital Psychiatry* 27/4: 250–255.

Baetz, M.; Larson, D.B.; Marcoux, G.; Bowen, R.; Griffin, R. 2002. "Canadian Psychiatric Inpatient Religious Commitment: An Association with Mental Health." *Canadian Journal of Psychiatry* 47/2: 159–166.

Bagger, Matthew C. 1999. *Religious Experience, Justification, and History*. Cambridge: Cambridge University Press.

Baker, Robin. 2006 [1996]. *Sperm Wars: Infidelity, Sexual Conflict, and Other Bedroom Battles*. Revised edition with new preface. New York: Thunder's Mouth Press.

Baron, Jonathan. 2006. *Thinking and Deciding*, 4th edition. New York and Cambridge: Cambridge University Press.

Barrett, Nathaniel F.; Wildman, Wesley J. 2009. "Seeing is Believing? How Reinterpreting the Direct Realism of Perception as Dynamic Engagement

Alters the Justificatory Force of Religious Experience." *International Journal for Philosophy of Religion*. Published online December 17, 2008. See http://www.springerlink.com/content/e7737tm607216745/fulltext.pdf, retrieved March 3, 2009.

Barth, Karl. 1975. *Church Dogmatics*, 2nd edition. G. W. Bromiley and T. F. Torrance, eds. Edinburgh: T. & T. Clark.

Bartlett, S.J.; Piedmont, R.; Bilderback, A.; Matsumoto, A.K.; Bathon, J. M. 2003. "Spirituality, Well-being, and Quality of Life in People with Rheumatoid Arthritis." *Arthritis & Rhematism—Arthritis Care & Research* 49/6: 778–783.

Baumeister, Roy F. 2007. "Is There Anything Good About Men?" American Psychological Association address, August 24, 2007. See http://www.denisdutton.com, retrieved November 1, 2007.

Begley, Sharon. 2007. *Train Your Mind, Change Your Brain: How a New Science Reveals Our Extraordinary Potential to Transform Ourselves*. New York: Ballantine Books.

Beh, Hazel Glenn; Diamond, Milton. 2000. "An Emrging Ethical and Medical Dilemma: Should Physicians Perform Sex Assignment on Infants with Ambiguous Genitalia?" *Michigan Journal of Gender & Law* 7(1): 1–63.

Beit-Hallahmi, B.; Argyle, M. 1997. *The Psychology of Religious Behavior, Belief, and Experience*. New York: Routledge.

Benson, Herbert. 1975. *The Relaxation Response*. New York: Morrow.

—. 1996. *Timeless Healing: The Power and Biology of Belief*. New York: Scribner.

Berger, Peter L. 1967. *The Sacred Canopy: Elements of a Sociological Theory of Religion*. Garden City: Doubleday.

Bering, Jesse M. 2006. "The Cognitive Psychology of Belief in the Supernatural." *American Scientist* 92: 142–149.

Bhawuk, Dharm P.S. 2008. "Anchoring Cognition, Emotion and Behavior in Desire: A Model from the Bhagavad-Gita," pp. 390–413 in Rao and Paranjpe 2008.

Birch, Charles; Cobb, John B. Jr. 1981. *The Liberation of Life*. Cambridge: Cambridge University Press.

Blackless, Melanie; Charuvastra, Anthony; Derryck, Amanda; Fausto-Sterling, Anne; Lauzanne, Karl; Lee, Ellen. 2000. "How Sexually Dimorphic are We? Review and Synthesis." *American Journal of Human Biology* 12: 151–166.

Blackwell, Antoinette Brown. 1875. *The Sexes Throughout Nature*. New York: B. Putnam and Sons.

Bornstein, R.F.; Masling, J.M., eds. 1990. *Empirical Perspectives on the Psychoanalytic Unconscious*. Washington DC: American Psychological Association Press.

Bosworth, H.B.; Park, K.S.; McQuoid, D.R.; Hays, J.C.; Steffens. D.C. 2003. "The Impact of Religious Practice and Religious Coping on Geriatric Depression." *International Journal of Geriatric Psychiatry* 18/10: 905–914.

Bowlby, John. 1982. *Attachment*, 2nd ed. New York: Basic Books.

Bowler, Peter J. 2001. *Reconciling Science and Religion: The Debate in Early Twentieth-Century Britain*. Chicago: University of Chicago Press.

Boyer, Pascal. 2001. *Religion Explained: The Evolutionary Origins of Religious Thought*. New York: Basic Books.

Braam, A.W.; Hein, E.; Deeg, D.J.H.; Twisk, J.W.R.; Beekman, A.T.F.; VanTilburg, W. 2004. "Religious Involvement and Six-year Course of Depressive Symptoms in Older Dutch Citizens: Results from the Longitudinal Aging Study Amsterdam." *Journal of Health & Aging* 16/4: 467–489.

Brizendine, Louann. 2006. *The Female Brain*. New York: Broadway Books.

Brooke, John Hedley; Osler, Margaret J.; van der Meer, Jitse M. 2001. *Science in Theistic Contexts: Cognitive Dimensions*. Osiris : Second Series, vol. 16.

Brothers, Leslie. 1997. *Friday's Footprint: How Society Shapes the Human Mind*. New York; Oxford: Oxford University Press.

Bulbulia, Joseph. 2004. "Religious Costs as Adaptations that Signal Altruistic Intention." *Evolution and Cognition*,10(1): 19–38.

—. 2006. "Nature's Medicine: Religiosity as an Adaptation for Health and Cooperation," pp. 87–121 in McNamara 2006.

Burker, E.J.; Evon, D.M.; Sedway, J.A.; Egan, T. 2004. "Religious coping, psychological distress and disability among patients with end-stage pulmonary disease." *Journal of Clinical Psychology in Medical Settings* 11/3: 179–193.

Burrus, Virginia; Keller, Catherine. 2006. *Toward a Theology of Eros: Transfiguring Passion at the Limits of Discipline*. New York: Fordham University Press.

Buss, David M. 2003 [1994]. *The Evolution of Desire: Strategies of Human Mating*, revised and expanded edition. New York: Basic Books.

Buss, David M.; Haselton, Martie G.; Sheckelford, Todd K.; Bleske, April L.; Wakefield, Jerome C. 1998. "Adaptations, Exaptations, and Spandrels." *American Psychologist* 53/5: 533–548.

Butler, Judith P. 2004. *Undoing Gender*. New York: Routledge.

Campbell, Anne. 2002. *A Mind of Her Own: The Evolutionary Psychology of Women*. Oxford: Oxford University Press.

Cantor, Geoffrey; Swetlitz, Marc, eds. 2006. *Jewish Tradition and the Challenge of Darwinism*. Chicago: University of Chicago Press.

Capps, D. 1983. *Life Cycle Theory and Pastoral Care*. Philadelphia: Fortress.

Capra, Fritjof. 1996. *The Web of Life: A New Scientific Understanding of Living Systems*. New York; London: HarperCollins.

Cardeña, Etzel; Lynn, Steven Jay; Krippner, Stanley, eds. 2000. *Varieties of Anomalous Experience: Examining the Scientific Evidence*. Washington DC: American Psychological Association.

Carlson, L.E.; Speca, M.; Patel, K.D.; Goodey, E. 2004. "Mindfulness-based Stress Reduction in Relation to Quality of Life, Mood, Symptoms of Stress and Levels of Cortisol, Dehydroepiandrosterone Sulfate (DHEAS) and Melatonin in Breast and Prostate Cancer Outpatients." *Psychoneuroendochrinology* 29/4: 448–474.

Clarke, T.E., SJ. 1988. "Jungian Types and Forms of Prayer." In R.L. Moore (ed.), *Carl Jung and Christian Spirituality*, pp. 230–249. New York: Paulist.

Clayton, Philip. 2008. *Adventures in the Spirit: God, World, Divine Action*. Minneapolis: Fortress Press.

Clinebell, H. 1984. *Basic Types of Pastoral Care and Counseling: Resources for the Ministry of Healing and Growth*, revised edition. Nashville: Abingdon.

Clinton, Hillary Rodham. 2006. *It Takes a Village*, 10th Anniversary edition. New York: Simon & Schuster.

Cobb, John B. Jr., ed. 2008. *Back to Darwin: A Richer Account of Evolution*. Grand Rapids; William B. Eerdman's Publishing Company.

Cohen, A.L.; Gollwitzer, P.M. 2007. "The Cost of Remembering to Remember: Cognitive Load and Implementation Intentions Influence Ongoing Task Performance." In M. Kliegel, M. McDaniel, and G. Einstein (eds.), *Prospective Memory: Cognitive, Neuroscience, Developmental, and Applied Perspectives*, pp. 367–390. Mahwah, NJ: Erlbaum.

Compton, M.T.; Furman, A.C. 2005. "Inverse Correlations Between Symptom Scores and Spiritual Well-being among African American Patients with First-episode Schizophrenia Spectrum Disorders." *Journal of Nervous & Mental Disease* 193/5: 346–349.

Comstock, George W.; Partridge, K.B. 1972. "Church Attendance and Health." *Journal of Chronic Disease* 25: 665–672.

Contrada, R.J.; Goyal, T.M.; Cather, C.; Rafalson, L.; Idler, E.L.; Krause, T.J. 2004. "Psychosocial Factors in Outcomes of Heart Surgery: The Impact of Religious Involvement and Depressive Symptoms." *Health Psychology* 23/3: 227–238.

Corcoran, Peter Blaze, ed. 2005. *The Earth Charter in Action: Toward a Sustainable Future*. Amsterdam: KIT Publishers.

Corrington, Robert S. 1992. *Nature and Spirit: An Essay in Ecstatic Naturalism*. New York: Fordham University Press.

—. 1994. *Ecstatic Naturalism: Signs of the World*. Bloomington and Indianapolis: Indiana University Press.

—. 1996. *Nature's Self: Our Journey from Origin to Spirit*. London, Boulder, New York, Oxford: Rowman and Littlefield.

—. 1997. *Nature's Religion*. London, Boulder, New York, Oxford: Rowman and Littlefield.

—. 2000. *A Semiotic Theory of Theology and Philosophy*. Cambridge and New York: Cambridge University Press.

Cronin, Helena; Maynard Smith, John. 1993. *The Ant and the Peacocke: Altruism and Sexual Selection from Darwin to Today*. Cambridge: Cambridge University Press.

Dabbs, James McBride. 2001. *Heroes, Rogues, and Lovers: Testosterone and Behavior* (with Mary Godwin Dabbs). New York: McGraw-Hill Companies.

Daniels, M.; Merrill, R.A.; Lyon, J.L.; Stanford, J.B.; White, G.L. 2004. "Associations between Breast Cancer Risk Factors and Religious Practices in Utah." *Preventative Medicine* 38/1: 28–38.

Darwin, Charles. 1859. *On the Origin of Species by Means of Natural Selection, or the Preservation of Favoured Races in the Struggle for Life*. London: John Murray.

—. 1871. *The Descent of Man, and Selection in Relation to Sex*. London: J. Murray.

Daugherty, C.K.; Fitchett, G.; Murphy, P.E.; Peterman, A.H.; Banik, D.M.; Hlubocky, F.; et al. 2005. "Trusting God and Medicine: Spirituality in Advanced Cancer Patients Volunteering for Clinical Trials of Experimental Agents." *Psycho-Oncology* 14/2: 135–146.

Dawkins, Richard. 1976. *The Selfish Gene*, 1st edition. Oxford: Oxford University Press.

—. *The Selfish Gene*, 2nd edition. Oxford: Oxford University Press.

—. *The God Delusion*. Boston, New York: Houghton Mifflin Company.

De Waal, Frans B.M.; Lanting, Frans. 1998. *Bonobo: The Forgotton Ape*. Berkeley: University of California Press.

Deacon, Terrence W. 1997. *The Symbolic Species: The Co-evolution of Language and the Brain*. New York: Norton.

Dembski, William A.; Ruse, Michael. 2004. *Debating Design: From Darwin to DNA*. Cambridge and New York: Cambridge University Press.

Dennett, Daniel C. 2006. *Breaking the Spell: Religion as a Natural Phenomenon*. New York: Viking.

Derrida, Jacques. 1982. "Différance." Translated by Alan Bass. In *Margins of Philosophy*, pp. 3–27. Chicago: University of Chicago Press.

Dewey, John. 1938. *Logic: The Theory of Inquiry*. New York: Henry Holt and Company.

Doidge, Norman. 2007. *The Brain the Changes Itself: Stories of Personal Triumph from the Frontiers of Brain Science*. New York: Viking Adult.

Dreger, Alice Domurat. 1998. *Hermaphrodites and the Medical Invention of Sex*. Cambridge: Harvard University Press.

Durkheim, Émile. 1915. *The Elementary Forms of the Religious Life: A Study in Religious Sociology*. Translated by Joseph Ward Swain. London: G. Allen & Unwin; New York: Macmillan.

Eagleton, Terry. 1991. *Ideology: An Introduction*. London; New York: Verso.

Eisler, Riane. 1995. *Sacred Pleasure: Sex, Myth, and the Politics of the Body*. New York: HarperCollins.

Eliade, Mircea. 1959. *The Sacred and the Profane: The Nature of Religion*. Translated from the French by Willard R. Trask. New York: Harcourt Brace.

Ellison, C.G.; Gay, D.A.; Glass, T.A. 1989. "Does Religious Commitment Contribute to Individual Life Satisfaction?" *Social Forces* 68: 100–123.

Emmons, Robert A; McNamara, Patrick. 2006. "Sacred Emotions and Affective Neuroscience; Gratitude, Costly Signaling, and the Brain," pp. 11–30 in McNamara 2006.

Epstein, M. 1995. *Thoughts without a Thinker*. New York: Basic Books.

—. 2005. *Open to Desire, Embracing a Lust for Life*. New York: Gotham Books.

Fausto-Sterling, Anne. 2000. *Sexing the Body: Gender Politics and the Construction of Sexuality*. New York: Basic Books.

Fincher, Corey L.; Thornhill, Randy. 2008. "Assortative Sociality, Limited Dispersal, Infectious Disease and the Genesis of the Global Pattern of

Religion Diversity." *Proceedings of the Royal Society B: Biological Sciences* doi:10.1098/rspb.2008.0688.

Fisher, Helen. E. 1992. *The Anatomy of Love: A Natural History of Mating, Marriage, and Why We Stray*. New York: Ballantine Books.

—. 2004. *Why We Love: The Nature and Chemistry of Romantic Love*. New York: Henry Holt and Co.

Fisher, Ronald A. 1930. *The Genetical Theory of Natural Selection*. Oxford: Clarendon Press.

Forman, Robert K.C. 1999. *Mysticism, Mind, Consciousness*. Albany, NY: State University of New York Press.

Fowler, J.W. 1981. *Stages of Faith: The Psychology of Human Development and the Quest for Meaning*. San Francisco: HarperSanFrancisco.

Fraser, Colin; Gaskell, George, eds. 1990. *The Social Psychological Study of Widespread Beliefs*. Oxford and New York: Oxford University Press.

Freeden, Michael. 2003. *Ideology: A Very Short Introduction*. Oxford: Oxford University Press.

Freeman, Scott. 2002. *Biological Science*. Upper-Saddle River, NJ: Prentice Hall.

Fromm, E.; Suzuki, D.T. 1986. *Psychoanalysis & Zen Buddhism*. London: Unwin Paperbacks.

Galanter, M. 2006. "Spirituality and Addiction: A Research and Clinical Perspective." *American Journal on Addictions* 15: 286–292.

Gazzaniga, Michael S. 2008. *Human: The Science Behind What Makes Us Unique*. New York: Ecco.

Gillings, V.; Joseph, S. 1996. "Religiosity and Social Desirability: Impression Management and Self-deceptive Positivity." *Personality & Individual Differences* 21/6: 1047–1050.

Gilovich, Thomas. 1991. *How We Know What Isn't So: The Fallibility of Human Reason in Everyday Life*. New York: The Free Press.

Girard, René. 1972. *La Violence et le Sacré*. Paris: Grasset. English translation: *Violence and the Sacred*. Translated by Patrick Gregory. Baltimore: Johns Hopkins University Press, 1977.

Glick, Thomas F.; Artigas, Mariano; Martínez, Rafael A. 2006. *Negotiating Darwin: The Vatican Confronts Evolution 1877–1902*. Baltimore: Johns Hopkins University Press.

Gollwitzer, P.M. 1993. "Goal Achievement: The Role of Intentions." *European Review of Social Psychology* 4: 141–185.

—. 1999. "Implementation Intentions: Strong Effects of Simple Plans." *American Psychologist* 54: 493–503.

Gollwitzer, P.M.; Moskowitz, G.B. 1996. "Goal Effects on Action and Cognition." In E.T. Higgins and A.W. Kruglanski (eds.), *Social Psychology: Handbook of Basic Principles*, pp. 361–399. New York: Guilford Press.

Gollwitzer, P.M.; Schaal, B. 1998. "Metacognition in Action: The Importance of Implementation Intentions." *Personality and Social Psychology Review* 2: 124–136.

Gosling, David L. 2007. *Science and the Indian Tradition: When Einstein Met Tagore*. New York: Routledge.

Gould, Stephen J. 1991. "Exaptation: A Crucial Tool for Evolutionary Psychology." *Journal of Social Issues* 47: 43–65.

Gould, Stephen J.; Lewontin, Richard C. 1979. "The Spandrels of San Marco and the Panglossian Paradigm: A Critique of the Adaptationist Programme." *Proceedings of the Royal Society of London B* 205: 581–598.

Gould, Stephen J.; Vrba, E. 1982. "Exaptation—A Missing Term in the Science of Form." *Paleobiology* 8/1: 4–15.

Grafen, Alan. 1990. "Biological Signals as Handicaps." *Journal of Theoretical Biology* 144: 517–546.

Greenberg, Jay R.; Mitchell, Stephen A. 1983. *Object Relations in Psychoanalytic Theory*. Cambridge, MA: Harvard University Press.

Greene, Joshua D.; Haidt, Jonathan. 2002. "How (and Where) does Moral Judgment Work?" *TRENDS in Cognitive Sciences* 6/12 (December): 517–523.

Greene, Joshua D. 2003. "From Neural 'Is' to Moral 'Ought': What are the Moral Implications of Neuroscientific Moral Psychology?" *Nature Reviews—Neuroscience* 4 (October): 847–850.

Gudorf, Christine E. 2001. "The Erosion of Sexual Dimorphism: Challenges to Religion and Religious Ethics." *Journal of the American Academy of Religion* 69/4: 863–891.

Guth, Alan H. 1997. *The Inflationary Universe: The Quest for New Theory of Cosmic Origins*. Reading, MA: Perseus Books.

Haidt, Jonathan. 2000. "The Emotional Dog and its Rational Tail: A Social Intuitionist Approach." *Psychological Review* 108: 814–834.

—. 2007. "The New Synthesis in Moral Psychology." *Science* 316: 998–1002.

Hamer, Dean H. 2004. *The God Gene: How Faith is Hardwired into Our Genes*. New York: Doubleday.

Harding, Stephan. 2006. *Animate Earth; Science, Intuition, and Gaia*. White River Junction, VT: Chelsea Green Publishing.

Hardwick, Charley D. 1996. *Events of Grace: Naturalism, Existentialism, and Theology*. New York; Cambridge: Cambridge University Press.

Harris, Sam. 2007. *Letter to a Christian Nation*. New York: Knopf.

Harrison, M.O.; Edwards, C.L.; Koenig, H.G.; Bosworth, H.B.; Decastro, L.; Wood, M. 2005. "Religiosity/Spirituality and Pain in Patients with Sickle Cell Disease." *Journal of Nervous & Mental Disease* 193/4: 250–257.

Harvey, Van. 1970. "The Alienated Theologian." *McCormick Quarterly* 23/4: 234–265.

Haught, John F. 2003. *Deeper than Darwin: The Prospect for Religion in the Age of Evolution*. Boulder: Westview Press.

Hausfater, Glenn; Hrdy, Sarah Blaffer; eds. 1984. *Infanticide: Comparative and Evolutionary Perspectives*. Chicago: Aldine Publishing Company.

Heatherton, Todd F.; Weinberger, Joel L., eds. 1994. *Can Personality Change?* Washington DC: American Psychological Association.

Hefner, Philip. 1993. *The Human Factor: Evolution, Culture, and Religion*. Minneapolis: Fortress Press.

Hill, T.D.; Angel, J.L.; Ellison, C.G.; Angel, R.J. 2005. "Religious Attendance and Mortality: An Eight-year Follow-up of Older Mexican Americans." *Journals of Gerontology, Series B—Psychological Sciences & Social Sciences* 60 (Suppl. 2): S102–S109.

Hines, Melissa. 2005. *Brain Gender*. New York: Oxford University Press.

Hitchens, Christopher. 2007. *God is Not Great: How Religion Poisons Everything*. New York: Twelve Books.

Hixson, K.A.; Gruchow, H.W.; Morgan, D.W. 1998. "The Relation Between Religiosity, Selected Health Behaviors, and Blood Pressure Among Adult Females." *Preventative Medicine* 27/4: 545–552.

Hogue, David. 2003. *Remembering the Future, Imagining the Past: Story, Ritual, and the Human Brain*. Pilgrim Press.

Hollywood, Amy. 2002. *Sensible Ecstasy: Mysticism, Sexual Difference, and the Demands of History*. Chicago: University of Chicago Press.

Hrdy, Sarah Blaffer. 1999a [1981]. *The Woman that Never Evolved*, Anniversary edition, with a new Preface and bibliographical updates. Cambridge, MA: Harvard University Press.

Hrdy, Sarah Blaffer. 1999b. *Mother Nature: Maternal Instincts and How They Shape the Human Species*. New York: Ballantine Books.

Husserl, Edmund. 1931. *Ideas: General Introduction to Pure Phenomenology*. Library of Philosophy, Gen. Ed. J.H. Muirhead. Translated by W.R. Boyce Gibson. London: George Allen & Unwin; New York: Macmillan.

Iacoboni, Marco. 2008. *Mirroring People: The New Science of How We Connect with Others*. New York: Farrar, Strauss and Giroux.

Idler, E.L. 1987. "Religious Involvement and the Health of the Elderly: Some Hypotheses and an Initial Test." *Social Forces* 66: 226–238.

Idler, E.L.; Kasl, S.V. 1992. "Religion, Disability, Depression, and the Timing of Death." *Journal of Gerontology* 52B: S306–S316.

James, William. 1902. *The Varieties of Religious Experience: A Study in Human Nature, being the Gifford Lectures on Natural Religion Delivered at Edinburgh in 1901–1902*. New York; London: Longmans, Green.

Janov, Arthur. 2000. *The Biology of Love*. Amherst: Prometheus Books.

John Paul II, Pope. 1996. "Message to the Pontifical Academy of Sciences on Evolution." (October 22).

Jung, Patricia Beattie; Coray, Joseph Andrew, eds. 2001. *Sexual Diversity and Catholicism: Toward the Development of Moral Theology*. Collegeville, MN: Michael Glazier Books.

Kant, Immanuel. 1993. *Critique of Practical Reason*, 3rd edition. Edited and translated with notes and an introduction by Lewis White Beck. Upper Saddle River, NJ: Prentice Hall.

Katz, Steven T., ed. 1978. *Mysticism and Philosophical Analysis*. New York and Oxford: Oxford University Press.

Kaufman, Gordon D. 1993. *In Face of Mystery: A Constructive Theology*. Cambridge, MA: Harvard University Press.

—. 2004. *In the Beginning ... Creativity*. Minneapolis: Fortress Press.

—. 2006. *Jesus and Creativity*. Minneapolis: Fortress Press.

Kelly, E.W., Jr. 1995. *Spirituality and Religion in Counseling and Psychotherapy*. Alexandria, VA: American Counseling Association.

Kelsey, M.T. 1982. *Christo-Psychology*. New York: Crossroad.

Kennair, Leif Edward Ottesen. 2002. "Evolutionary Psychology: An Emerging Integrative Perspective within the Science and Practice of Psychology." *The Human Nature Review* 2 (January 15): 17–61.

Kevles, Daniel J. 1995 [1985]. *In the Name of Eugenics: Genetics and the Uses of Human Heredity*, 2nd ed. with a New Preface. Cambridge, MA: Harvard University Press.

King, M.; Speck, P.; Thomas, A. 1999. "The Effect of Spiritual Beliefs on Outcome from Illness." *Social Science & Medicine* 48/9: 1291–1299.

Kinney, A.Y.; Bloor, L.E.; Dudley, W.N.; Millikan, R.C.; Marshall, E.; Martin, C.; et al. 2003. "Roles of Religious Involvement and Social Support in the Risk of Colon Cancer among Blacks and Whites." *American Journal of Epidemiology* 158/11: 1097–1107.

Kirkpatrick, Lee A. 2004. *Attachment, Evolution, and the Psychology of Religion*. New York: Guilford.

—. 2006. "Religion is not an Adaptation," pp. 159–179 in McNamara 2006.

Kirkpatrick, Mark. 1986. "The Handicap Mechanism of Sexual Selection Does not Work." *American Naturalist* 127: 222–40.

Koenig, H.G. 2000. "Religion and Medicine I." *International Journal of Psychiatry in Medicine* 30/4: 385–398.

—. 2001a. *Handbook of Religion and Health*. New York and Oxford: Oxford University Press.

—. 2001b. "Religion and Medicine II." *International Journal of Psychiatry in Medicine* 31/1: 97–109.

—. 2001c. "Religion and Medicine III." *International Journal of Psychiatry in Medicine* 31/2: 119–216.

—. 2001d. "Religion and Medicine IV." *International Journal of Psychiatry in Medicine* 31/3: 321–336.

—. 2001e. *The Healing Power of Faith: How Belief and Prayer can Help You Triumph over Disease*. New York, NY: Simon & Schuster.

—. 2002. *The Link between Religion and Health: Psychoneuroimmunology and the Faith Factor*. New York and Oxford: Oxford University Press.

Koenig, H.G.; George, L.K.; Hays, J.C.; Larson, D.B.; Cohen, H.J.; Blazer, D.G. 1998. "The Relationship Between Religious Activities and Blood Pressure in Older Adults." *International Journal of Psychiatry in Medicine* 28/2: 189–213.

Koenig, H.G.; Hays, J.C.; Larson, D.B.; George L.K.; Cohen, H.J.; McCullough, M.E.; et al. 1999. "Does Religious Attendance Prolong Survival? A Six Year Follow-up Study of 3,968 Older Adults." *Journal of Gerontology: Medical Sciences* 54A/7: M370–M376.

Koenig, Laura B.; Bouchard, Thomas J., Jr. 2006. "Genetic and Environmental Influences on the Traditional Moral Values Triad—Authoritarianism, Conservatism, and Religiousness—as Assessed by Quantitative Behavior Genetic Methods," pp. 31–60 in McNamara 2006.

Koenig, Laura B.; McGue, M.; Krueger, R.F.; Bouchard, Thomas J., Jr. 2005. "Genetic and Environmental Influences on Religiousness: Findings from Retrospective and Current Religiousness Ratings." *Journal of Personality* 73: 471–488.

Kristeller, Jean. 2007. "Mindfulness Meditation." In P. Lehrer, R.L. Woolfolk, and W.E. Sime (eds.), *Principles and Practice of Stress Management*, 3rd edition. New York: Guilford Press.

Krueger, Joel W. 2008. *William James and Kitaro Nishida on "Pure Experience," Consciousness, and Moral Psychology*. Dissertation, Purdue University.

Kune, G.A.; Kune, S.; Watson, L.F. 1993. "Perceived Religiousness is Protective for Colorectal Cancer: Data from the Melbourne Colorectal Cancer Study." *Journal of the Royal Society of Medicine* 86: 645–647.

Lakoff, George; Johnson, Mark. 1980. *Metaphors We Live By*. Chicago: University of Chicago Press.

Lakoff, George; Johnson, Mark. 1999. *Philosophy in the Flesh: The Embodied Mind and Its Challenge to Western Thought*. New York: Basic Books.

Landis, Dan. 2000. "Cross-Cultural Aspects of Passionate Love." *Journal of Cross-Cultural Psychology* 31/6: 752–777.

Larson, Edward J. 1997. *Summer for the Gods: The Scopes Trial and America's Continuing Debate over Science and Religion*. New York: Basic Books.

Larson, Edward J.; Witham, Larry. 1997. "Scientists are Still Keeping the Faith." *Nature* 386: 435–436.

Larson, Edward J.; Witham, Larry. 1998. "Leading Scientists Still Reject God." *Nature* 394: 313.

LeDoux, Joseph. 2002. *Synaptic Self: How Our Brains Become Who We Are*. New YorkL Viking Adult.

Levin, J.S.; Taylor, R.J.; Chatters, L.M. 1995. "A Multidimensional Measure of Religious Involvement for African Americans." *Sociology Quarterly* 36: 157–173.

Levin, J.S.; Vanderpool, H.Y. 1989. "Is Religion Therapeutically Significant for Hypertension?" *Social Science & Medicine* 29/1: 69–78.

Livingstone, David N. 1984. *Darwin's Forgotten Defenders: The Encounter Between Evangelical Theology and Evolutionary Thought*. Vancouver: Regent College Publishing.

Livingstone, David N.; Hart, D.G.; Noll, Mark A., eds. 1999. *Evangelicals and Science in Historical Perspective*. Oxford and New York: Oxford University Press.

Loughlin, Gerard, ed. 2007. *Queer Theology: Rethinking the Western Body*. Wiley-Blackwell.

Lovelock, James E. 1965. "A Physical Basis for Life Detection Experiments." *Nature* 207(7): 568–570.

—. 2000. *Gaia: A New Look at Life on Earth*. New York and Oxford: Oxford University Press.

Lutz, Antoine; Greischar, Lawrence L.; Rawlings, Nancy B.; Ricard, Matthieu; Davidson, Richard J. (2004). "Long-term Meditators Self-induce High-amplitude Gamma Synchrony During Mental Practice." *Proceedings of the National Academy of Sciences* 101/46: 16369–1673.

Lyell, Charles. 1830–1833. *Principles of Geology*, 3 vols. London: John Murray.

Margulis, Lynn. 1981. *Symbiosis in Cell Evolution: Life and its Environment on the Early Earth*. New York: W.H. Freeman & Company.

—. 1998. *Symbiotic Planet: A New Look at Evolution*. London: Weidenfeld and Nicholson.

Marion, Jean-Luc. 1991. *God without Being*. Chicago: University of Chicago Press.

—. 2006. *The Erotic Phenomenon*. Chicago: University of Chicago Press.

Masters, K.S.; Hill, R.D.; Kircher, J.C.; Lensegrav-Benson T.L.; Fallon, J.A. 2004. "Religious Orientation, Aging, and Blood Pressure Reactivity to Interpersonal and Cognitive Stressors." *Annals of Behavioral Medicine* 28/3: 171–178.

Maynard Smith, John. 1976. "Sexual Selection and the Handicap Principle." *Journal of Theoretical Biology* 57: 239–242.

Maynard Smith, John; Harper, David. 2003. *Animal Signals*. Oxford: Oxford University Press.

McClenon, James. 2001. *Wondrous Healing: Shamanism, Human Evolution, and the Origin of Religion*. DeKalb: Northern Illinois University Press.

—. 2006. "The Ritual Healing Theory: Therapeutic Suggestion and the Origin of Religion," pp. 135–158, in McNamara 2006.

McDargh, J. 1983. *Psychoanalytic Object Relations Theory and the Study of Religion: On Faith and the Imaging of God*. Lanham, MD: University Press of America.

McNamara, Patrick. 2002. "The Frontal Lobes, Social Intelligence, and Religious Worship." In *Ideas for Creative Research in Neurobiology*, pp. 50–59. Philadelphia: The John Templeton Foundation.

—. 2006. *Where God and Science Meet: How Brain and Evolutionary Studies Alter Our Understanding of Religion*, vol. 1: *Evolution, Genes, and the Religious Brain*. Westport, CT: Praeger Publishers.

Meckel, D.J.; Moore, R.L., eds. 1992. *Self and Liberation: The Jung/Buddhism Dialogue*. New York: Paulist Press.

Milbank, John. 2006. *Theology and Social Theory: Beyond Secular Reason*, 2nd edition. Oxford; Malden, MA: Wiley-Blackwell.

Miller, Geoffrey. 2001. *The Mating Mind: How Sexual Choice Shaped the Evolution of Human Nature*. New York: Anchor Books.

Molino, A. 1999. *The Couch and the Tree*. Constable.

Moore, James R. 1979. *The Post-Darwinian Controversies: A Study of the Protestant Struggle to Come to Terms with Darwin in Great Britain and America, 1870–1900*. Cambridge and New York: Cambridge University Press.

Murphy, P.E.; Ciarrocchi, J.W.; Piedmont, R.L.; Cheston, S.; Peyrot, M.; Fitchett, G. 2000. "The Relation of Religious Beliefs and Practices, Depression, and Hopelessness in Persons with Clinical Depression." *Journal of Consulting & Clinical Psychology* 68/6: 1102–1106.

Musick, M.A.; Traphagan, J.W.; Koenig, H.G.; Larson, D.B. 2000. "Spirituality in Physical Health and Aging." *Journal of Adult Development* 7/2: 73–86.

Neville, Robert Cummings. 1968. *God the Creator: On the Transcendence and Presence of God*. Chicago: University of Chicago Press.

—. 1981. *Reconstruction of Thinking. Axiology of Thinking*, vol. 1. Albany: State University of New York.

—. 1989. *Recovery of the Measure: Interpretation and Nature. Axiology of Thinking*, vol. 2. Albany: State University of New York.

—. 1995. *Normative Cultures. Axiology of Thinking*, vol. 3. Albany: State University of New York.

—. 1996. *The Truth of Broken Symbols*. Albany: State University of New York.

—. 2001a. *The Human Condition: A Volume in the Comparative Religious Ideas Project*. Albany: State University of New York.

—. 2001b. *Ultimate Realities: A Volume in the Comparative Religious Ideas Project*. Albany: State University of New York.

—. 2001c. *Religious Truth: A Volume in the Comparative Religious Ideas Project*. Albany: State University of New York.

—. 2006. *On the Scope and Truth of Theology*. Albany: State University of New York.

Newberg, Andrew; d'Aquili, Eugene; Rause, Vince. 2001. *Why God Won't Go Away: Brain Science & the Biology of Belief*. New York: Ballantine Books.

Newlin, K.; Melkus, G.D.; Chyun, D.; Jefferson, V. 2003. "The Relationship of Spirituality and Health Outcomes in Black Women with Type 2 Diabetes." *Ethnicity & Disease* 13/1: 61–68.

Niebuhr, Reinhold. 1941. *The Nature and Destiny of Man: A Christian Interpretation*. New York: Charles Scribner's Sons.

Nielson, Kai. 2001. *Naturalism and Religion*. Amherst: Prometheus Books.

Nietzsche, Friedrich. 1907. *Beyond Good and Evil: A Prelude to a Philosophy of the Future*. Authorized tr. by Helen Zimmern. Edinburgh, London: T.N. Foulis.

—. 1954. *Thus Spake Zarathustra*. Translated by Walter Kaufmann. New York: Viking Penguin.

—. 1974. *The Gay Science: With a Prelude in Rhymes and an Appendix of Songs*. Translated by Walter Kaufmann. New York: Vintage Books.

Norcross, John C.; Beutler, Larry E.; Levant, Ronald F.; eds. 2005. *Evidence-Based Practices in Mental Health: Debate and Dialogue on the Fundamental Questions*. Washington DC: American Psychological Association.

Numan, Michael; Insel, Thomas R. 2003. *The Neurobiology of Parental Behavior*. Hormones, Brain, and Behavior series. New York: Springer.

Numbers, Ronald L. 2006. *The Creationists: From Scientific Creationism to Intelligent Design*, expanded edition. Cambridge, MA: Harvard University Press.

Oman, D.; Kurata, J. H.; Strawbridge, W.J.; Cohen, R. D. 2002. "Religious Attendance and Cause of Death over 31 Years." *International Journal of Psychiatry in Medicine* 32/1, 69–89.

Orbell, S.; Sheeran, P. 2000 "Motivational and Volitional Processes in Action Initiation: A Field Study of the Role of Implementation Intentions." *Journal of Applied Social Psychology* 30: 780–797.

Orbell, S.; Hodgkins, S.; Sheeran, P. 1997. "Implementation Intentions and the Theory of Planned Behavior." *Personality and Social Psychology Bulletin* 23: 945–954.

Otto, Rudolf. 1923. *The Idea of the Holy: An Inquiry into the Non-Rational Factor in the Idea of the Divine and Its Relation to the Rational*. Translated from the ninth German edition by John W. Harvey. London and New York: Oxford University Press.

Peacocke, Arthur. 1993. *Theology for a Scientific Age: Being and Becoming— Natural, Divine, and Human*, expanded edition. Minneapolis: Fortress Press.

Peirce, Charles S. 1940. *The Philosophy of Peirce: Selected Writings*. Edited with an introduction by Philip P. Wiener. New York: Routledge and Kegan Paul.

—. 1958. *Selected Writings: Values in a Universe of Chance*. Edited with an introduction by Philip P. Wiener. New York: Dover Publications.

Persinger, Michael A. 1987. *Neuropsychological Bases of God Beliefs*. New York: Praeger Press.

Piatelli-Palmarini, Massimo. 1996. *Inevitable Illusions: How Mistakes of Reason Rule Our Minds*. John Wiley and Sons.

Pinker, Steven. 1994. *The Language Instinct*. New York: W. Morrow and Co.

—. 2006. "The Evolutionary Psychology of Religion," pp. 1–9 in McNamara 2006. This is a reprint of an October 29, 2004 speech on receipt of an "Emperor's New Clothes Award" from the Freedom From Religion Foundation, in Madison, WI.

Plous, Scott. 1993. *The Psychology of Judgment and Decision Making*. New York: McGraw-Hill.

Porter, Jean. 2000. *Natural and Divine Law: Reclaiming the Tradition for Christian Ethics*. Saint Paul University Series in Ethics. Grand Rapids: Wm. B. Eerdmans Publishing Company.

Post, Stephen G.; Underwood, Lynn G.; Schloss, Jeffrey P.; Hurlbut, William B. 2002. *Altruism and Altruistic Love: Science, Philosophy, and Religion in Dialogue*. New York and Oxford: Oxford University Press.

Prestwich, A.; Lawton, R.; Conner, M. 2003. "The Use of Implementation Intentions and the Decision Balance Sheet in Promoting Exercise Behavior." *Psychology and Health* 18: 707–721.

Proudfoot, Wayne 1985. *Religious Experience*. Berkeley: University of California Press.

Pyysiäinen, Ilkka. 2001. *How Religion Works: Toward a New Cognitive Science of Religion*. Leiden, Netherlands: Brill.

—. 2006. "Amazing Grace: Religion and the Evolution of the Human Mind," pp. 209–225 in McNamara 2006.

Ramachandran, V.S. 2004. *A Brief Tour of Human Consciousness: From Imposter Poodles to Purple Numbers*. Canada: Pi Press.

Ramachandran, V.S.; Blakeslee, Sandra. 1998. *Phantoms in the Brain: Probing the Mysteries of the Human Mind*. New York: Praeger.

Rao, K. Ramakrishna; Paranjpe, Anand C. 2008. "Yoga Psychology: Theory and Application." In K. Ramakrishna Rao and Anand C. Paranjpe (eds.), *Handbook of Indian Psychology*, pp. 186–216. New Delhi, India: Cambridge University Press India and Foundation Books.

Revonsuo, A. 2006. *Inner Presence: Consciousness as a Biological Phenomenon*. Cambridge, MA: The MIT Press.

Richardson, W. Mark; Russell, Robert John; Clayton, Philip; Wegter-McNelly, Kirk. 2002. *Science and the Spiritual Quest: New Essays by Leading Scientists*. London & New York: Routledge.

Ricoeur, Paul. 1977. "Toward a Hermeneutic of the Idea of Revelation." Translated by David Pellauer. *Harvard Theological Review* 70/1–2.

Ridley, Matt. 1993. *The Red Queen: Sex and the Evolution of Human Nature*. London: Viking.

Rinpoche, L.; Napper, E. 1986. *Mind in Tibetan Buddhism*. Ithaca, NY: Snow Lion Publications.

Rizzolatti, Giacomo. 2008. *Mirrors in the Brain: How Our Minds Share Actions, Emotions, and Experience*. New York: Oxford University Press.

Roberts, Jon H. 1988. *Darwinism and the Divine in America: Protestant Intellectuals and Organic Evolution, 1859–1900*. Notre Dame: University of Notre Dame Press.

Roth, Anthony; Fonagy, Peter. 2004. *What Works for Whom? A Critical Review of Psychotherapy Research*, 2nd edition. New York: Guildford Press.

Roughgarden, Joan. 2002. *Evolution's Rainbow: Diversity, Gender, and Sexuality in Nature and People*. Berkeley: University of California Press.

Ruf, Henry. 1989. *Religion, Ontotheology, and Deconstruction*. New York: Paragon House.

Russell, Robert John. 1998. "Special Providence and Genetic Mutation: A New Defense of Theistic Evolution." In Robert John Russell, William R. Stoeger, SJ, Francisco J. Ayala, eds., *Evolutionary and Molecular Biology: Scientific Perspectives on Divine Action*, pp. 191–224. Berkeley: Center for Theology and the Natural Sciences; Vatican City: Vatican Observatory.

Safran, J.D., ed. 2003. *Psychoanalysis and Buddhism: An Unfolding Dialogue*. Boston, MA: Wisdom.

Saiving, Valerie. 1960. *The Human Situation: A Feminine View*. Reprinted in Carol P. Christ and Judith Plaskow, eds. 1979. *Womanspirit Rising*, pp. 25–42. New York: Harper & Row.

Saliba, John A. 1976. "Homo Religiosus." In *Mircea Eliade: An Anthropological Evaluation*. Leiden: E.J. Brill.

Sandner, Donald. 1996. *The Sacred Heritage: The Influence of Shamanism on Analytical Psychology*. New York: Routledge.

Sax, Leonard. 2002. "How Common is Intersex? A Response to Anne Fausto-Sterling." *Journal of Sex Research* 39(3): 174–178.

Schlauch, Chris R. 1995. *Faithful Companioning: How Pastoral Counseling Heals*. Minneapolis: Fortress Press.

Schleiermacher, Friedrich D. E. 1928. *The Christian Faith*. Edinburgh: T&T Clark.

Schwartz, Jeffrey M.; Begley, Sharon. 2002. *The Mind and the Brain: Neuroplasticity and the Power of Mental Force*. New York: Harper.

Sheeran, P. 2002. "Intention–behavior Relations: A Conceptual and Empirical Review." *European Review of Social Psychology* 12: 1–36.

Sheeran, P.; Orbell, S. 1999. "Implementation Intentions and Repeated Behaviour: Augmenting the Predictive Validity of the Theory of Planned Behavior." *European Journal of Social Psychology* 29: 329–369.

—. 2000. "Using Implementation Intentions to Increase Attendance for Cervical Cancer Screening." *Health* Psychology 19: 283–289.

Sheeran, P.; Silverman, M. 2003. "Evaluation of Three Interventions to Promote Workplace Health and Safety: Evidence for the Utility of Implementation Intentions." *Social Science and Medicine* 56: 2153–2163.

Sheeran, P.; Webb, T.L.; Gollwitzer, P.M. 2005. "The Interplay between Goal Intentions and Implementation Intentions." *Personality and Social Psychology Bulletin* 31: 87–98.

Singer, J.L.; Bonanno, G.A. 1990. "Personality and Private Experience: Individual Variations in Consciousness and in Attention to Subjective Phenmoena," pp. 419–444 in L. Pervin, ed., *Handbook of Personality*. New York: Guildford Press.

Slingerland, Edward. 2008. *What Science Offers the Humanities: Integrating Body and Culture*. Cambridge and New York: Cambridge University Press.

Sober, Eliot; Wilson, David Sloane. 1999. *Unto Others: The Evolution and Psychology of Unselfish Behavior*. Cambridge, MA: Harvard University Press.

Sosis, Richard. 2003. "Why Aren't We All Hutterites? Costly Signaling Theory and Religion." *Human Nature* 14: 19–127.

Sosis, Richard. 2004. "The Adaptive Value of Religious Ritual." *American Scientist* 92: 166–172.

Sosis, Richard. 2005. "Does Religion Promote Trust? The Role of Signaling, Reputation, and Punishment." *Interdisciplinary Journal of Research on Religion* 1: 1–30.

—. 2006. "Religious Behaviors, Badges, and Bans: Signaling Theory and the Evolution of Religion," pp. 61–86 in McNamara 2006.

Sosis, Richard; Alcorta, C. 2003. "Signaling, Solidarity and the Sacred: The Evolution of Religious Behavior." *Evolutionary Anthropology* 12: 264–274.

Sosis, Richard; Bressler, E. 2003. "Cooperation and Commune Longevity: A Test of the Costly Signaling Theory of Religion." *Cross-cultural Research* 37: 211–239.

Sosis, Richard; Ruffle, B. 2003. "Religious Ritual and Cooperation: Testing for a Relationship on Israeli Religious and Secular Kibbutzim." *Current Anthropology* 44: 713–722.

Sosis, Richard; Ruffle, B. 2004. "Ideology, Religion, and the Evolution of Cooperation: Fields Tests on Israeli Kibbutzim." *Research in Economic Anthropology* 23: 89–117.

Sperber, Dan. 1996. *Explaining Culture: A Naturalistic Approach.* Oxford; Cambridge, MA: Blackwell.

Steffen, P.R.; Hinderliter, A.L.; Blumenthal, J.A.; Sherwood, A. 2001. "Religious Coping, Ethnicity, and Ambulatory Blood Pressure." *Psychosomatic Medicine* 63/4: 523–530.

Steinhardt, Paul J.; Turok, Neil. 2007. *Endless Universe: Beyond the Big Bang.* New York: Doubleday.

Sternberg, Robert J. 1998. *Love is a Story: A New Theory of Relationships.* New York and Oxford; Oxford University Press.

Strassman, Rick J. 2001. *DMT: The Spirit Molecule: A Doctor's Revolutionary Research into the Biology of Near-Death and Mystical Experiences.* Rochester, VT: Park Street Press.

Strawbridge, W.J.; Cohen, R.D.; Shema, S.J.; Kaplan, G.A. 1997. "Frequent Attendance at Religious Services and Mortality Over 28 Years." *American Journal of Public Health* 87: 957–961.

Strawbridge, W.J.; Shema, S.J.; Cohen, R.D.; Kaplan, G.A. 2001. "Religious Attendance Increases Survival by Improving and Maintaining Good Health Behaviors, Mental Health, and Social Relationships." *Annals of Behavioral Medicine* 23/1: 68–74.

Susskind, Leonard. 2005. *The Cosmic Landscape: String Theory and the Illusion of Intelligent Design.* Little, Brown and Company.

Swinburne, Richard 1979. *The Existence of God.* Oxford: Clarendon Press.

Takahashi, Mariko; Arita, Hiroyuki; Hiraiwa-Hasegawa, Mariko; Hasegawa, Toshikazu. 2008. "Peahens do not Prefer Peacocks with More Elaborate Trains." *Animal Behaviour* 75 (April): 1209–1219.

Tillich, Paul. 1951. *Systematic Theology*, vol. 1. Chicago: University of Chicago Press.

—. 1957. *Systematic Theology*, vol. 2. Chicago: University of Chicago Press.

—. 1963. *Systematic Theology*, vol. 3. Chicago: University of Chicago Press.

Tracy, David. 1981. *The Analogical Imagination: Christian Theology and the Culture of Pluralism.* New York: Crossroad.

Travis, Frederick; Pearson, Craig. 2000. "Pure Consciousness: Distinct Phenmomenological and Physiological Correlates of 'Consciousness Itself'." *International Journal of Neuroscience* 100/1–4 (Jan–Feb): 77–89.

Trivers, Robert L. 1985. *Social Evolution.* Menlo Park, CA: Benjamin Cummings.

Turner, Victor W. 1969. *The Ritual Process; Structure and Anti-Structure*. New York: Walter De Gruyter.

United Nations. 1948. Universal Declaration of Human Rights.

—. 1979. Convention on the Elimination of All Forms of Discrimination against Women.

—. 1981. Declaration on the Elimination of All Forms of Intolerance and Discrimination Based on Religion or Belief.

—. 1990. Convention on the Rights of the Child.

Van der Leeuw, Gerardus. 1986. *Religion in Essence and Manifestation*. Translated by J.E. Turner. Princeton: Princeton University Press.

Van Huyssteen, J. Wentzel. 2006. *Alone in the World? Human Uniqueness in Science and Theology*. Grand Rapids: William B. Eerdmans Publishing Company.

Verplanken, B.; Faes, S. 1999. "Good Intentions, Bad Habits, and Effects of Forming Implementation Intentions on Healthy Eating." *European Journal of Social Psychology* 29: 591–604.

Vilenkin, Alexander. 2006. *Many Worlds in One: The Search for Other Universes*. New York: Hill and Wang.

Vyner, Henry M. 2007. "The Dialectal Phenomena and Processes of the Mind." *Imagination, Cognition and Personality* 27/2: 163–196.

Wallace, B. Alan. 2007. *Contemplative Science: Where Buddhism and Neuroscience Converge*. New York: Columbia University Press.

Walsh, Anthony. 1991. *The Science of Love: Understanding Love and its Effects on Mind and Body*. Buffalo, NY: Prometheus Books.

Wampold, Bruce E. 2008. *The Great Psychotherapy Debate: Models, Methods, and Findings*, 2nd edition. Mahwah, NJ: Lawrence Erlbaum Associates.

Ward, Keith. 1998. *Religion and Human Nature*. Oxford: Oxford University Press.

Weber, Max. 2002 [1904–05]. *The Protestant Ethic and the Spirit of Capitalism*. English translation by Pater Baehr and Gordon C. Wells, 1930. New York: Penguin Books.

—. 1951. *The Religion of China*. New York: Macmillan.

Wellings, N.; McCormick, E.W. 2005. *Nothing To Lose: Psychotherapy, Buddhism and Living Life*. New York: Continuum.

Westphal, Merold. 2001. *Overcoming Onto-Theology: Toward a Postmodern Christian Faith*. New York: Fordham University Press.

Whitehead, Alfred North. 1978. *Process and Reality: An Essay in Cosmology*, corrected edition. Edited by David Ray Griffin and Donald W. Sherburne. New York: The Free Press.

Whitehead, E.E.; Whitehead, J.D. 1992. *Christian Life Patterns: The Psychological Challenges and Religious Invitations of Adult Life*. New York: Crossroad.

Whitehead, Neil E.; Whitehead, Briar. 1999. *My Genes Made Me Do It: A Scientific Look at Sexual Orientation*. Lafayette, LA: Huntington House Publishers.

Wierzbicki, Michael; Pekarik, Gene. 1993. "A Meta-Analysis of Psychotherapy Dropout." *Professional Psychology: Research and Practice* 24/2: 190–195.

Wildman, Wesley J. 1999. "The Use and Abuse of Biotechnology: A Modified Natural-Law Approach." *American Journal of Theology and Philosophy* 20/2: 165–79.

—. 2006a. "Comparative Natural Theology." *American Journal of Theology and Philosophy* 27/2&3 (May/September): 173–90.

—. 2006b. "Ground-of-Being Theologies." In Philip Clayton (ed.), *The Oxford Handbook of Religion and Science*, pp. 612–632. Oxford: Oxford University Press.

—. 2007a. "Behind, Between, and Beyond Anthropomorphic Models of Ultimate Reality." *Philosophia* 35/3–4: 407–425.

—. 2007b. "Incongruous Goodness, Perilous Beauty, Disconcerting Truth: Ultimate Reality and Suffering In Nature." In Nancey Murphy, Robert J. Russell, and William R. Stoeger (eds.), *Physics and Cosmology: Scientific Perspectives on the Problem of Natural Evil*, pp. 267–294. Vatican City State: Vatican Observatory and Berkeley: Center for Theology and the Natural Sciences.

—. 2008a. "From Law and Chance in Nature to Ultimate Reality." In Fraser Watts (ed.), *Creation, Law, and Probability*, pp. 155–179. Aldershot, UK: Ashgate Publishing.

—. 2008b. "The Philosophical Import of Contemporary Physical Cosmology." *Theology and Science* 6/2 (May): 197–212.

—. 2009. *Religious Philosophy as Multidisciplinary Comparative Inquiry: Envisioning a Future for the Philosophy of Religion*. Albany: State University of New York Press. (Forthcoming).

—. 2010. *Religious and Spiritual Experiences: A Multidisciplinary Comparative Inquiry*. (Forthcoming).

Wildman, Wesley J.; Brothers, Leslie A. 1999. "A Neuropsychological-Semiotic Model of Religious Experiences." In Robert J. Russell, Nancey Murphy, Theo C. Meyering, and Michael A. Arbib (eds.), *Neuroscience and the Person: Scientific Perspectives on Divine Action*, pp. 347–416. Vatican City State, Vatican Observatory, Berkeley, CA: Center for Theology and the Natural Sciences.

Wildman, Wesley J.; McNamara, Patrick. 2008. "Challenges Facing the Neurological Study of Religious Belief, Behavior and Experience." *Method and Theory in the Study of Religion* 20/3: 212–242.

Wilson, David Sloan. 2002. *Darwin's Cathedral: Evolution, Religion, and the Nature of Society*. Chicago: University of Chicago Press.

Wrathall, Mark A. 2003. *Religion After Metaphysics*. New York; Cambridge; Cambridge University Press.

Young-Eisendrat, Polly. 2004. *Subject to Change: Analytical Psychology, Psychoanalysis, and Subjectivity*. New York: Routledge.

Zahavi, Amotz. 1975. "Mate Selection: A Selection for a Handicap." *Journal of Theoretical Biology* 53: 205–214.

—. 1977a. "The Cost of Honesty (Further Remarks on the Handicap Principle)." *Journal of Theoretical Biology* 67: 603–605.

—. 1977b. "Reliability in Communication Systems and the Evolution of Altruism." In B. Stonehouse and C.M. Perrins (eds.), *Evolutionary Ecology*, pp. 253–259. London: Macmillan.

Zahavi, Amotz; Zahavi, Avishag. 1997. *The Handicap Principle: A Missing Piece of Darwin's Puzzle*. New York, Oxford University Press.

Zimmer, Carl. 2004. "Faith Boosting Genes" (review of Dean Hamer, *The God Gene*). *Scientific American* 291/4 (October): 110–112.

Name Index

Subject Index

Note: Some entries contain references to the Name Index.